PENGUIN (P) CLASSICS

PENGUIN ENGLISH POETS
GENERAL EDITOR: CHRISTOPHER RICKS

WYATT: THE COMPLETE POEMS

THOMAS WYATT was born around 1503 at Allington Castle in Kent. His father was Privy Councillor to both Henry VII and VIII. The young Wyatt appeared as a minor functionary at the court of Henry VIII and in the same year, 1516, entered St John's College, Cambridge. Thereafter, he spent most of his adult life in service at the court. His first appointments abroad were to France and Italy, where he may have been in contact with the leading writers of the time, after which he translated Plutarch's *Quiet of Mind* for Catherine of Aragon from the Latin version of Budé; it was published the following year. From 1528 to 1530 Wyatt was High Marshal of Calais. Between 1537 and 1540, he was Ambassador to the court of Emperor Charles V and travelled to France, Spain and The Netherlands. After the disgrace and execution of his friend and patron, Thomas Cromwell, Wyatt was arrested for treason in 1541, but released and pardoned two months later. Taken back into royal favour in 1542, he died of a fever while on a diplomatic errand for Henry VIII. The bulk of his poems began to be published five years later.

R. A. REBHOLZ, a native of St Louis, Missouri, earned a BA degree from St Louis University and, as a Rhodes Scholar at Worcester College, Oxford, a BA in the Honours School of English Language and Literature, and a D. Phil. Rebholz joined the faculty of Stanford University in California in 1961 and is a professor there. His special field is Renaissance literature, with emphases on the development of the short poem and Shakespeare. His publications include *The Life of Fulke Greville, First Lord Brooke*, a contemporary of Shakespeare, and articles on the poems of Greville, Wyatt and Shakespeare.

Sir Thomas Wyatt

The Complete Poems

EDITED BY R. A. REBHOLZ

PENGUIN BOOKS

PENGUIN BOOKS

Published by the Penguin Group
Penguin Books Ltd, 27 Wrights Lane, London W8 5TZ, England
Penguin Books USA Inc., 375 Hudson Street, New York, New York 10014, USA
Penguin Books Australia Ltd, Ringwood, Victoria, Australia
Penguin Books Canada Ltd, 10 Alcorn Avenue, Toronto, Ontario, Canada M4V 3B2
Penguin Books (NZ) Ltd, 182–190 Wairau Road, Auckland 10, New Zealand

Penguin Books Ltd, Registered Offices: Harmondsworth, Middlesex, England

First published 1978
Reprinted with revised Further Reading 1997
11

Introduction and notes copyright © R. A. Rebholz, 1978, 1997
All rights reserved

Printed in England by Clays Ltd, St Ives plc
Set in Monotype Ehrhardt

www.greenpenguin.co.uk

Penguin Books is committed to a sustainable future
for our business, our readers and our planet.
The book in your hands is made from paper
certified by the Forest Stewardship Council.

Mixed Sources
Product group from well-managed
forests and other controlled sources
www.fsc.org Cert no. SA-COC-1592
© 1996 Forest Stewardship Council

Contents

Poems Attributed to Sir Thomas Wyatt After the Sixteenth Century

Abbreviations are given on pages 59 and 335.

Acknowledgements

No brief statement can adequately acknowledge the many kinds of help that I have received from many people and institutions in the course of preparing this edition. I am indebted to the National Endowment for the Humanities and to Stanford University for summer grants that freed me to work on these poems. For permission to consult and use manuscripts I am indebted to the Bodleian Library, the British Museum, the Cambridge University Library, the library of Corpus Christi College, Cambridge, and the Library of Trinity College, Dublin. The members of the staff of the British Museum, the Henry E. Huntington Library, and the Stanford University Library were unfailingly patient and generous.

I wish particularly to thank Kenneth Budge for his help with the note on Wyatt's language and many other facets of this edition, Emily Olmstead for translating Aretino's difficult Italian, Joy Weston, Marsha Shankman, Josephine Guttadauro, and John Bishop for preparing and proof-reading the typescript, and the members of a seminar on textual criticism at Stanford University for their help with CXLIX, both the text and the commentary.

Preface

In this edition I have printed all the poems attributed to Sir Thomas Wyatt in the three most important modern editions of his poems – those by George Nott (1815–16), A. F. Foxwell (1913), and Kenneth Muir and Patricia Thomson (1969). But the reader should not assume that all the poems in this book were written by Wyatt. The problem of determining which poems Wyatt wrote is as yet unsolved and is likely to be solved only by a brilliant linguist who knows how to use a computer with great skill. Not possessing those attributes, I have had to rely on simpler evidence and procedures.

The external evidence for Wyatt's having written a poem can be arranged in a hierarchy of authority. No one doubts that Wyatt wrote the poems in his own handwriting in Egerton Manuscript 2711 in the British Museum; in the case of the Penitential Psalms, the nature of some of his revisions proves that he was composing the poems in the manuscript. It is almost as certain that he wrote the poems in that manuscript which, while in the handwriting of a scribe, have revisions in Wyatt's hand. (I say 'almost' because it is conceivable that he was 'improving' poems of another writer, just as his poems were 'improved' within a few years of his death.) Next, in the margin by some of his poems in the Egerton MS, there is written 'Tho.' or 'Tho', presumably an attribution to Wyatt by a person sufficiently intimate with him to call him by his Christian name. In a different hand, 'Wyat' appears in the margin by some poems; that attribution, though less intimate in its reference, still has considerable authority.

The first poems attributed to Wyatt in print were his Penitential Psalms, printed in 1549; but this edition merely confirms the fact of his authorship already inferred from his having composed the poems in the Egerton MS. When we come to the first edition in which other poems were attributed to Wyatt – Richard Tottel's *Songs and Sonnets*, usually called Tottel's *Miscellany* – we encounter an editor or editors apparently conscientious about the matter of authorship: one of the poems attributed to Wyatt in the first edition of 5 June 1557 was moved to a section entitled 'Uncertain Authors' in the second edition of 31 July 1557. Tottel's attribution of poems to Wyatt probably possesses, therefore, as much authority as the attribution of poems to 'Wyat' in Egerton. Attributions of poems to Wyatt in sources other than Egerton and Tottel carry much less authority. Finally, and least authoritative, is the location of a poem, in a manuscript other than Egerton, amidst poems for which we have the previously mentioned evidence for Wyatt's authorship. Such 'sections' of poems probably by Wyatt occur in several sixteenth-century manuscript anthologies of poems. While appearance in a group of this kind ordinarily amounts to an attribution of a poem to Wyatt, it does not, in my view, have that character if the poem in question is in the midst of poems attributed to Wyatt in the Egerton MS but is not there or else-where attributed to him: presence in a manuscript containing so many poems attributed to Wyatt but absence of attribution of the poem to him anywhere combine, in my view, to suggest that he probably did not write the poem (CLXXVIII is an instance).

When we move from external to internal evidence for Wyatt's authorship, we must rely on our sense of his attitudes and style, inferred from poems for which there is the kind of external evidence of his authorship described above. This procedure, while legitimate in theory, has in practice usually led modern editors and critics to ascribe to Wyatt every poem that they like from the period. Along with the tendency to ascribe to him most poems in a manuscript that contains some poems attri-buted to him, this desire to credit Wyatt with good poems has been responsible for swelling the body of works supposedly by Wyatt to its present, rather enormous bulk.

In this edition I have divided the poems into two sections: those in Wyatt's hand, with revisions in his hand, or attributed

to him in the sixteenth century, and those attributed to him
after the sixteenth century. While we do not know with pre-
cision the dates in which the manuscripts containing 'sections'
of Wyatt's poems were compiled, his poems were certainly
written in them before 1600. In effect, then, I am distinguishing
between poems for which there is external evidence of authorship
in the form of Tudor attributions and poems ascribed to Wyatt
by modern editors and critics on grounds of attitude, style, or
presence in a manuscript that contains poems attributed to
him. The different degrees of reliability of the external evidence
render impossible any absolute certainty that all the poems in
the first section are in fact by Wyatt; and it is indeed possible
that some or many of the poems in the second section are his:
readers acquainted with Wyatt and the criticism of his poems
may well think that CCXI and CCXVI are by him. The
second item in the note on each poem presents the external
evidence for his authorship, if any; I do not bother to call
attention to the absence of such evidence unless the attribution
seems particularly far-fetched.

Dating the poems is as problematic as establishing authorship.
Only a few of the poems can be dated with anything approaching
precision and certainty. XXIV was composed after 1537, the
date of its source. LV was probably composed in October 1532,
when Wyatt accompanied Henry VIII and Anne Boleyn to
France. In XXVIII there is a line (subsequently emended to
veil the reference) which appears to refer to Anne and is in the
past tense; the poem was therefore probably composed after
her execution in May 1536. CXCVII, which alludes to the
execution of Anne's alleged lovers, was also composed after
May 1536. XLVI, LX, and LXXVI, which contain refer-
ences to Spain, were probably written while Wyatt was ambas-
sador in Spain from the summer of 1537 to the summer of 1539.
CXLIX, CL., and CLI, the three Epistolary Satires, were com-
posed after 1532–3 when Luigi Alamanni's works, on which
CXLIX and the *terza rima* of all three poems depend, were
published. The Penitential Psalms (CLII) were composed some-
time between the publication of George Joye's *David's Psalter* in
1534 and Wyatt's death in 1542. CLIV was possibly written in

October 1539 on the occasion of the completion of the new clock at St James's Palace. Attempts to date other poems or to establish the chronology of their composition have been based on the supposition that Wyatt became interested in foreign genres, like the rondeau and sonnet, when he visited the countries of their origin (see the Table of Dates, page 19, for those visits), and on the assumption that the order of the poems in the Egerton MS corresponds to the order of their composition. Certainly the latter assumption is unwarranted, except probably for the poems in Wyatt's own hand, and the Psalms should probably be excluded from that exception because they occupy a portion of the manuscript set off from the rest. The notes give the evidence, if there is any beyond mere speculation, for the dating of the poems.

Determining the text of the poems is, perhaps, even more difficult than determining who wrote them and when. I have made a fresh attempt to establish the words of the poems from the manuscripts and the pertinent early printed editions. I have worked with the originals of the Egerton and Devonshire MSS, Ruth Hughey's edition of the Arundel Harington MS, microfilm copies of the other relevant manuscripts, the original of the *Certain Psalms* of 1549, Hyder Rollins's edition of Tottel's *Miscellany*, and Russell Fraser's edition of fragments of some other printed anthologies of the century. But while my text is a new one, I am, like every editor, deeply indebted to my predecessors, especially for the help they have given in reading the manuscripts, and to H. A. Mason who, in his monograph *Editing Wyatt*, has challenged and corrected the readings by earlier editors and thereby, I hope, kept me alert.

When a poem is complete in Egerton, I have, with the exception of LXXV and CXLVII, based my text on Egerton. I have introduced readings from other witnesses or made conjectural emendations only to turn what I perceive as nonsense into sense and, when the rhythm of the poem seems to me absolutely clear, to make a deviant line conform provided I can explain the original in terms of common scribal errors. In this respect my text is less conservative than that of Muir and Thomson, who virtually transcribe Egerton, but conservative measured by the standards of Mason, who grants Egerton no special authority and argues for printing the 'best' reading whatever its source, with frequent conjectural emendations to improve rhythm and rhyme. For me, Egerton's authority rests on the assumption that Wyatt, because he composed and corrected some poems in the manuscript, gave a tacit approval to the texts of other poems by him there. I also do not find Wyatt's standards in rhythm and rhyme so clear-cut as Mason suggests (see A Note on Wyatt's Metres, page 44).

When Egerton does not have a version of the poem, I have used as copy-text the source that seems to me, taking the whole poem into account, to offer the best text, which I assume to be the text closest to the author's intention. I have found the most important sources to possess, in general, the following order of excellence: the Arundel Harington MS, Devonshire MS, Blage MS, and Tottel. Arundel Harington is later than and usually based on Egerton as corrected by Wyatt; it modernizes the language of Egerton and at times smooths Egerton's rhythms. Devonshire and Blage both seem to offer a similar and probably an earlier version of poems than that in Egerton and to smooth the rhythm of its version; Blage tends, I think, to 'sophisticate' the earlier version more than Devonshire. Tottel apparently had access to versions related to Egerton and Arundel Harington, but usually before Wyatt's corrections were incorporated; Tottel modernizes the language of the poems and tries to make their rhythms approximate iambic pentameter as closely as possible. Only rarely have there been sufficient witnesses with close enough 'family connections' to enable me to form a 'family tree' or stemma that describes their relationship and give my introduction of variants into the copy-text some authority. Otherwise I have departed from my copy-text only when I thought a manifest superiority of sense or rhythm seemed likely to be pointing to the author's intention. The first item in the note on each poem lists the witnesses to the text, and the first witness mentioned is the one I have chosen as copy-text. The notes also give my departures from copy-text and variant readings which are both significantly different from those of the copy-text and may point to a different stage of the poem's composition. Earlier readings of poems that Wyatt composed in Egerton, such as the psalms (CLII), offer especially illuminating insights into his methods and priorities as an artist.

I have modernized the punctuation and spelling of the text (and the textual variants) except in a few instances where an old spelling is recognizable and preserves the appearance of a rhyme. A modernized text of the poems of Wyatt or his contemporaries has obvious limitations. Wyatt rarely punctuated his poems; when he did so he usually marked breaths in reading rather than major breaks in syntax, though the two often, of course, coincide. (See A Note on Wyatt's Punctuation, p. 56.) Some readers believe he intentionally used little or no punctuation in order to create ambivalent meanings. Certainly punctuation according to any modern system, even the system of light syntactical punctuation I have employed, sometimes involves choosing between two possible meanings and 'fixing' the poem in one of them. In fact I think the problem occurs rarely, and in the notes I have called attention to the major instances.

Modernizing spelling has the serious disadvantage of often so changing the appearance of rhyme-words that the rhyme disappears for a modern reader because the pronunciation of words has changed from the early sixteenth century to the present and spelling has followed it. (See A Note on Wyatt's Language, page 33, for a discussion of Wyatt's rhymes and for a list of the most common instances in which spelling has affected rhyme-words.) Also, modern spelling may suppress a syllable which might optionally be pronounced or unpronounced by Wyatt and his contemporaries: Wyatt's plurals in 'es', for example, are sometimes pronounced as two syllables and sometimes as one ('thinges' in CLII, ll. 16 and 375, is an instance). With respect to the problem of rhymes, a consonantal assonance survives in most cases at the end of rhyme-words otherwise disguised by modern spelling, so that the formal quality of Wyatt's verse is to some extent preserved. I have also indicated in the notes the instances in which modernization has probably led to a reduction of syllables.

At first the undesirable consequences of modernizing the text gave me pause. But as I worked through the poems, I became convinced that the sacrifices were eminently worthwhile because they make the poems genuinely available to modern readers when texts preserving old accidentals are frequently unintelligible. I think the advantages of modernizing will be evident if the reader compares the following versions of CLII, ll. 142–9:

> How ofte have I calde vpp with diligence
> This slowthful flesshe longe afore the daye
> For to confesse his faulte and negligence
> That to the done for ought that I coold say
> Hath still returnd to shrowde it self from colde
> Whearbye it sufferth nowe for suche delaye
> By nightlye playntes in stede of pleasures olde
> I wasshe my bed with teares continuall

> How oft have I called up with diligence
> This slothful flesh long afore the day,
> For to confess his fault and negligence,
> That to the down, for aught that I could say,
> Hath still returned to shroud itself from cold,
> Whereby it suffer'th now for such delay.
> By nightly plaints instead of pleasures old
> I wash my bed with tears continual.

I have arranged the poems in each section of this edition by genres, with each genre defined in the notes before the first poem in it. Within each genre I have grouped the poems with known sources in foreign languages before those without known sources. Further, within the latter groups I have arranged the poems in the order of the probable reliability of their copy-texts described above, so that, for example, poems with the Egerton MS as copy-text precede poems with the Arundel Harington MS as copy-text. I hope that these somewhat complicated subdivisions will enable readers interested in translation and imitation to find the relevant poems grouped together at the start of each generic section and those interested in textual issues to know the likely proximity of the words in the poem to the poet's own.

If a difficult word is not defined in the notes, the reader should consult the glossary.

Because my manuscript was already at the press when I read Richard Harrier's *The Canon of Sir Thomas Wyatt's Poetry*, I could not take into account his arguments in my preface. Harrier assumes that, because Wyatt composed and revised some poems in the Egerton MS, 'all the poems in *E* likely to have been entered before Wyatt's death in 1542 are in fact his' (7). I still find this assumption unconvincing because of the presence of clear attributions in some cases and their absence in others. Harrier regards a signature beneath a poem as Wyatt's initial approval of the text and a marginal 'Tho' or 'Tho.' as Wyatt's own later approval of a revised text (11). But, as he points out in his comments on 'From these high hills', the faded character of the signature beneath the text suggests that it was added sometime after Wyatt wrote the poem in the manuscript (204). And, in the case of 'Venemous thorns', for example, the marginal 'Tho' cannot be Wyatt's later approval of a revised text because the poem is in Wyatt's hand and without revisions. Moreover, a comparison of the hand responsible for the additions of 'Tho' in the margin with the 'Th' in Wyatt's book hand on, for example, folios 87 and 90, leaves me unconvinced that 'Tho' is Wyatt's signature. More probably it is an attribution by someone familiar with Wyatt. This hypothesis returns us to the further probability that the person familiar with Wyatt's work left some poems unattributed because he did not know or believe them to be Wyatt's.

My disagreement with Harrier about the standing of the Egerton MS in establishing the canon does not detract from my esteem for the importance of his arguments and the value of his transcript of Egerton. Consideration of both has convinced me of one certain and one probable error in my attributions. LXXXIX lacks an explicit attribution in the Egerton and Blage manuscripts. I should therefore not have placed it in the first section of poems attributed to Wyatt in the sixteenth century but in the second section, with the ballades. In Harrier's comments on CCLXVI, he argues (202) that Wyatt has written in his own hand the words 'their felicity' in l.4. I think, after re-examining the manuscript, that he is probably right. If he is, this filling of a gap, while not technically a revision of a scribal copy, comes so close to revision that the poem, according to my criteria of attribution, belongs in the first section of poems, preferably before the Penitential Psalms.

Harrier and I disagree about the existence of two sections in the Devonshire MS. I see a group of ten poems by Wyatt on folios 30ᵛ to 39ᵛ; Harrier (46–49) has doubts and therefore does not think XCI, XCII, and CXIX attributed to Wyatt in the manuscript. He argues (50–51), mainly on stylistic grounds, for the probability of a group of nine poems by Wyatt on folios 49ʳ to 50ᵛ: he therefore thinks CLXVI, CLXVII, CLXXXI, CLXXXII, CCXVI, CCXLIV, and CCLIV probably attributed to Wyatt in the manuscript.

Finally, Harrier attributes four poems to Wyatt not in this edition. He thinks (70) 'Cursed be he that first began', a poem on folio 82 of the Blage MS, is possibly by Wyatt because it has a tone like that of CXLIX; the poem is printed in the edition of Muir and Thomson on pp. 394–5. I do not think that the poem – an attack, in four-beat terza rima, on women who sell their favours to men – resembles CXLIX in style or subject. Harrier argues (22) that Wyatt probably wrote 'Vengeance must fall on thee' and 'Spring of all my woe' because he thinks they are members of a Wyatt section on folios now missing from the Arundel Harington MS and printed in *Nugae Antiquae* in 1769 and later. The poems are printed in Hughey's edition of the manuscript (I, 380–1). I am not certain that the poems in *Nugae Antiquae* constitute a group taken from the manuscript; Harrier's supporting evidence – that the poems are linked with CLXIII and CLXXIII in the Hill MS – is weakened by the fact that they are there separated from those poems by two blank pages and a missing leaf. Lastly, he thinks (21) that 'But, Lord, how strange is this', a fragment in the Arundel Harington MS, may be part of a Wyatt group and therefore probably by Wyatt; the poem is printed in Hughey's edition (I, 178–9). The absence of the two preceding leaves from the manuscript and the lines' similarity in style and content to Surrey's biblical paraphrases, noted by both Hughey and Harrier, make uncertain the existence of an attribution.

Table of Dates

c. 1503   Born at Allington Castle, near Maidstone, in
           Kent, a castle bought by his father in 1492.
           Father, Henry, born c. 1460, probably in
           Yorkshire. Suffered torture and imprisonment in
           reign of Richard III because of his loyalty to
           Henry Tudor. In 1504 made Privy Councillor to
           Henry VII. At the death of Henry VII in 1509
           retained as Privy Councillor by the new king,
           Henry VIII, and is one of the Council appointed
           to manage affairs during the youth of Henry.
           Created Knight of the Bath on 23 June 1509, the
           day before the coronation of Henry VIII. In
           August 1513 made Knight Banneret for services at
           the Battle of Spurs against the French. c. 1516
           made Knight Marshal. 1520, present at the
           'Field of Cloth of Gold', a meeting of Henry VIII
           and Francis I, the king of France, in the Val d'Or,
           between Guisnes and Ardres (the meeting,
           celebrated by two weeks of lavish spectacle and
           entertainment, is intended to symbolize the
           friendship of England and France, a friendship
           that gives way, again, to war in 1523). Made
           Master of the King's Jewels in 1521 and
           Treasurer of the Royal Chamber in 1524. In
           November 1527 entertains Henry VIII and
           Cardinal Wolsey at Allington on the latter's
           return from a diplomatic mission in France.
           c. 1502 marries Anne Skinner, daughter of John
           Skinner of Reigate in Surrey. Anne bears him
           three children: Thomas, Margaret, and Henry.

1516	Thomas first appears at court of Henry VIII as ewerer extraordinary. Enters St John's College, Cambridge (no evidence of the length of his study there).
c. 1520	Marries Elizabeth Brooke, daughter of Thomas, Lord Cobham.
c. 1521	Son Thomas born.
1524	Becomes Clerk of the King's Jewels.
1524–5	*Christmas* Participates in a tournament at Greenwich before the king with a group of courtiers including Sir George Cobham, his brother-in-law, Sir Francis Bryan and John Poyntz (to whom he addressed CLI and CXLIX respectively), and Henry Norris (mourned in CXCVII). The king himself participated in the tilting on one of the days of the tournament.
by 1525	Made an 'esquire of the royal body'.
c. 1525	Probably becomes interested in Anne Boleyn.
c. 1525 (probably)	Separates from his wife, whom he charges with adultery.
1526	*March–May* Accompanies Sir Thomas Cheyney on a diplomatic mission to the French court. Helps negotiate England's relationship to what becomes the Holy League of Cognac (22 May 1526) in which France, Florence, Venice, Milan, and Pope Clement VII combine against the emperor, Charles V. England, though assuming the role of 'protector' of the alliance, declines full membership, partly because France is her traditional enemy and a continuing threat to English trade routes to Bordeaux, Spain, and the Mediterranean, and partly because war against Charles V endangers cloth trade with his subjects in the Low Countries and Spain. In so far as English foreign policy is governed by discernible principles throughout this period, it has two ends:

to prevent a coalition of the French, under
Francis I, with Charles V, which will be hostile to
England; and, whenever possible, to gain French
land.

During his stay in France, Wyatt possibly makes
the acquaintance of writers like Guillaume Budé
(1468–1540), Mellin de Saint-Gelais (1487–1558),
and Clément Marot (1492–1549), whose works
become important to him.

1527   *7 January–May* At his own request, accompanies
Sir John Russell (1486?–1555) on a diplomatic
mission to the papal court in Rome. The League
of Cognac having proved ineffectual in stopping
the emperor's victories in Italy, Pope Clement
VII is on the verge of agreeing to an armistice
with him. Russell and Wyatt reach Rome early in
February with money from Henry VIII. Russell
urges the pope to ask aid from Venice before
succumbing to Charles V. The pope agrees to let
Russell and Wyatt appeal to Venice, and they
leave for Venice on 12 February. Russell, having
been injured in a fall, sends Wyatt on alone.
Wyatt, with the aid of Giovanni Casale, the
English ambassador, gets the Venetians to agree,
after much delay, to send money and troops to the
pope. Casale and Wyatt then carry the same
appeal to Ferrara in early March, but there they
are turned down. The pope, even before hearing
that the Venetians will send aid, makes an
armistice of eight months with the emperor, an
armistice that will not prevent the sack of Rome
on 6 May 1527 by the Imperialist forces. Wyatt,
desiring to visit some of Italy's major cities, is
taken prisoner by the Imperialists after leaving
Ferrara for Bologna. Casale and Ferrara secure
his release. He then returns to Rome in April by
way of Florence. He and Russell leave Rome for

England a few days before the sack of the city, having failed in their mission to thwart the emperor's conquests in Italy.

In his visit to Italian cities, Wyatt possibly makes the acquaintance of writers like Pietro Bembo (1470–1547), Lodovico Ariosto (1474–1533), and Niccolò Machiavelli (1469–June 1527).

May On his return from Italy, probably learns of the king's serious interest in Anne Boleyn.

c. 1527   Asked by Queen Katherine to translate Petrarch's *De remediis utriusque fortunae* (Of the remedies of ill fortune). Finding Petrarch's amplitude too great for a graceful rendering in English, translates instead Plutarch's *Quiet of Mind* from Budé's Latin version and offers it to the queen as a more concise form of the kind of moral treatise she is seeking.

c. 1528   Translation of Plutarch's *Quiet of Mind* published by Richard Pynson.

1529   *September* Given a licence to import 1000 casks of Gascoigne wine or Toulouse woad (a blue dye-stuff).

1528–30   Serves as High Marshal of Calais. Service in Calais may be a form of exile from court, imposed by the king because of Wyatt's interest in Anne Boleyn.

1532   *February* Made Commissioner of the Peace in Essex.

by 1532   Friendly with Thomas Cromwell.

1532   *1 September* Anne Boleyn becomes Marchioness (technically Marquis) of Pembroke. Now confident that the king will marry her, she consents to become his mistress.

October Among the courtiers who accompany King Henry and Anne to Calais for meeting with the French king. (See L V.)

1533   *28 January* Anne Boleyn, already pregnant, secretly marries the king.

1 June Serves, at the coronation of Anne Boleyn, in the place of his father as chief ewerer.

7 September Anne Boleyn gives birth to a daughter, Elizabeth, who will become queen in 1558.

1534   *May* Committed briefly to the Fleet after a brawl with the Sergeants of London in which one Sergeant is killed.

June Granted for life the conduct and command of all men able for war in various hundreds and parishes of Kent, with the licence to have twenty men in his livery.

1535   *February* Made High Steward of the Abbey of West Malling in Kent.

18 March Knighted.

July Leases from the crown the estate of Aryngden Park in Yorkshire.

c. 1536   Becomes attached to Elizabeth Darrell, the woman who remains his mistress until the end of his life.

1536   *7 January* Former Queen Katherine dies.

February Queen Anne, having suffered a miscarriage on 29 January 1536, completely loses Henry's favour.

March The king indicates to Jane Seymour he intends to marry her.

24 April Cromwell creates a commission to investigate Queen Anne's behaviour. Mark Smeaton, a court musician, confesses to adultery with the queen. Sir William Brereton, Sir Henry Norris, and Sir Francis Weston are also arrested on the charge of adultery with the queen. Her brother, Thomas Boleyn, Viscount Rochford, is arrested on the charge of incest with her.

5 May Arrested and imprisoned in the Tower.

There is no evidence of the reason for his arrest, although his contemporaries generally assume that it is because he is suspected of being one of Anne's lovers or has information about her crimes. Charles Brandon, Duke of Suffolk, may have encouraged the king to arrest him, for Wyatt, in 1541, imputes his imprisonment to Suffolk's 'undeserved evil will'.

17 May Smeaton, Brereton, Norris, Weston, and Rochford are executed on Tower Hill.

19 May Queen Anne Boleyn is executed, probably within sight of Wyatt's cell.

30 May Henry VIII marries Jane Seymour.

by 14 June Freed from the Tower and sent to Allington 'to address himself better'.

31 July Sir Henry Wyatt entertains Henry VIII at Allington.

September Made Steward of Conisborough Castle in Yorkshire.

October Required to supply from Kent 150 men to be used against the rebels in Lincolnshire and 200 men to attend upon the king's person.

10 November Sir Henry Wyatt dies.

1536-7   Sheriff of Kent.

1536 (late) or 1537 (early) His son Thomas marries Jane Hawte, daughter of Sir William Hawte, of Bourne, in Kent.

1537-9 ? A version of CLX published in *The Court of Venus*.

1537   *29 January* The king announces his intention to recall Stephen Gardiner and Sir John Wallop and to make Wyatt ambassador to the court of the emperor, Charles V.

1 February Given the livery of the lands inherited from his father.

March His brother-in-law asks Thomas Cromwell, Wyatt's patron and friend, to get Wyatt to make some provision for Wyatt's wife before leaving for the continent.

12 March Wyatt receives his instructions as ambassador to the emperor's court. His objectives during the next two years in Spain are two: (1) to help deter Charles V from an alliance with Francis I against England (an alliance sought by Pope Paul III); (2) once an approach to that alliance is made in the truce of Nice of June 1538, to discern the intentions of Charles with respect to a possible attack on England (an attack made more likely by the pope's excommunication of Henry and declaration, in December 1538, that Henry no longer is king, by a pact of mutual consultation between Charles V and Francis I in January 1539, and by the pope's appointment of Reginald Pole, grandson of George, Duke of Clarence, as his agent in inspiring and coordinating that attack).

April Leaves England and travels to Valladolid in Spain by way of Paris, Lyons, Avignon, Barcelona, and Zaragoza. In Lyons he may have acquired Luigi Alamanni's *Opere Toscane* (1532–3) (see head-note to Epistolary Satires, pp. 662–4).

15 April Having stopped in Paris to confer with Stephen Gardiner, the Bishop of Winchester, who is English ambassador in Paris, writes to his son, encouraging him to live an honest and godly life and to try, along with his wife, to make a loving marriage – unlike the unhappy marriage of his parents.

after 15 April Writes to his son recommending Seneca and Epictetus as useful sources of moral philosophy.

22 June Has his first audience with the emperor.
16 October Is at Barbastro, near Monzòn (see XLVI).
24 October Queen Jane Seymour dies shortly after

giving birth to a son who will become King
Edward VI.

November Along with Sir John Dudley, informs
the emperor of the birth of Edward on
12 October 1537.

1538   *April* Dr Edmund Bonner, the Archdeacon of
Leicester, later Bishop of London, and Dr Simon
Heynes, the Dean of Exeter, are sent on a special
mission to France and Spain, mainly to assist
Wyatt in his embassy.

c. 24 May–13 July At the suggestion of the
emperor, returns to England with the emperor's
proposals that Princess Mary marry Don Lodovic
of Portugal, that Milan be settled on Don
Lodovic, and that Henry VIII marry the
Duchess of Milan. The emperor promises that no
treaty will be concluded during his absence if he
returns within 25 days, an impossibly short time.
Charles V and Francis I conclude a ten-year
peace in the Truce of Nice on 20 June 1538.

late July Complains bitterly to the emperor's
chancellor, Cardinal Grandvela, that Henry VIII
has been excluded from the treaty.

2 September, 15 October Edmund Bonner, in two
letters to Cromwell, accuses Wyatt of misconduct
as ambassador. Of Bonner's eleven particular
accusations, three are central: 1) Wyatt said that,
unless the king agreed to Charles V's marriage
proposals, Henry would be 'cast out at the cart's
tail', and deserved to be so, as a result of the truce
which Pope Paul III is arranging at Nice between
Charles V and Francis I; 2) Wyatt did not
complain to Charles V with sufficient vehemence
about the Truce of Nice and Henry's omission
from its terms; 3) Wyatt instructed John Mason
to establish contact with Cardinal Reginald Pole,
the pope's agent for organizing an attack on

England by the major continental powers. The latter charge is investigated immediately by Cromwell and other representatives of the Privy Council: Mason is interrogated, Elizabeth Darrell is questioned about Wyatt's conversations with her in June, and Wyatt is told he is under suspicion. But by early 1539 both Wyatt and Mason are apparently exonerated of this charge by the Privy Council and the king. Bonner's other, more personal charges – for example, that Wyatt wasted his ambassador's allowance on whores, begrudged his imprisonment in 1536, and showed no respect for Bonner, Heynes, or their mission – are presented to support Bonner's general conclusion that Wyatt is a dissolute and vain man whose pride had been hurt by his imprisonment of 1536 and who values his standing with Charles V more than his service to Henry VIII.

1539   Purchases house of the White Friars at Aylesford in Kent.

January Charles V and Francis I agree, in the Treaty of Toledo, that neither will make a new alliance without the other's consent.

18 March Wyatt writes to Cromwell that once he has returned to England he will inform him and the king of an important plot that can be carried out in Italy, probably the assassination of Cardinal Pole.

c. 3 June Leaves Toledo for England. Probably proceeds along the Tagus River and sails from Lisbon. (See LX.)

June–November Probably living at Allington Castle.

November Sent as ambassador to the emperor in place of Richard Tate. The emperor is now visiting Francis I and passing through France to the Low Countries. Wyatt's objective is to discern if the emperor's actions portend an invasion of England by Charles V and Francis I.

28 November–1 December Arrives in Paris, proceeds to Orleans where he meets Edmund Bonner, ambassador to France and now bishop-elect of London, and then hurries to Blois to have audience with Francis I on 1 December.

1539–40   *11 December–May* Having had his first audience with the emperor on 11 December, at Châtellerault, follows the emperor's court for the next five months to Paris, Brussels, and Ghent, sending regular accounts of his views of the emperor's intentions to Henry and Cromwell. In the event, Charles proves as frightened of a Protestant alliance against him – the point of Cromwell's arrangement of Henry's marriage to Anne of Cleves in January 1540 – as Henry is of a Catholic alliance against England; and Charles V and Francis I are too mistrustful of each other to agree on a war against England. By July 1540 the threat of invasion passes.

1540   *May* Returns to England and presumably to Allington Castle. In residence at the Castle are Elizabeth Darrell; Wyatt's son and daughter-in-law; and Lady Poynings, wife of Sir Thomas Poynings, who is a friend of Wyatt's.

10 June Because Cromwell's insistence on a Protestant alliance no longer seems necessary, because his own religious sympathies appear too Lutheran in the face of a conservative reaction at court and in the country, and because Henry finds Anne of Cleves too ugly to bear, Henry has Cromwell arrested.

12 July Marriage between Henry VIII and Anne of Cleves is annulled.

28 July Witnesses Cromwell's execution. When Cromwell calls out to him for prayers, Wyatt's tears prevent his answering (see XXIX). On the same day Henry VIII marries Catherine Howard.

1541   *17 January* Having been summoned to Hampton Court, is arrested and taken, bound and handcuffed, to the Tower. John Mason has already been arrested earlier in January after interrogation of him, Bonner, and Heynes. Both Wyatt and Mason are arrested for treason on the basis of the accusations made by Bonner in 1538, revived now that Cromwell's death makes the former ambassadors vulnerable. The major charges against Wyatt are that he 'had intelligence' with the traitor, Cardinal Pole, and that he had said 'the king should be cast out of a cart's arse' and deserved to be so. Bonner's other accusations are now presented to support the image of a traitor who was seeking revenge for his imprisonment of 1536 by consorting with the Catholic enemy and working to undermine the interests of the king he was pretending to serve.
20 January The Privy Council instructs Sir Richard Southwell to confiscate and send to London the plate, household goods, weapons, and horses at Allington Castle, dismiss Wyatt's servants, eject Lady Poynings and Jane Wyatt, née Hawte (Wyatt's daughter-in-law), and question Elizabeth Darrell, who is pregnant, probably with Francis Darrell, alias Wyatt, the illegitimate son of Elizabeth and Wyatt. If she refuses to disclose her intentions to stay or move, Southwell is to detain her.
February–March Ordered by the Privy Council to give an account of his behaviour as ambassador from April to July 1538, especially of any treasonous words, deeds, or communications. Writes 'A Declaration . . . of his Innocence'.

Later in the same period, confronted with the detailed 'indictment and evidence' drawn from Bonner's accusations, he writes his 'Defence to the Judges'. The 'Defence' begins with a short appeal to the judges to instruct the jury impartially in the law; it continues as a statement to the jury. To the main charge of having intelligence with Pole, Wyatt answers that he, with the consent of Bonner and Heynes, had suggested to Mason that he make contact with Pole to gather information that could be used against the Cardinal's devices. He explains the 'cart's arse' as his heated statement of a fear about the consequences of the Truce of Nice for the king's interests. While answering the other charges in turn and arguing that Bonner's malice motivated them, he counters the general suggestion of his being a traitor with a reminder of his subsequent service as ambassador, approved by the king and council. Though the 'Defence' has the form of a speech, there is no record of Wyatt's actually being tried.

26 March The Privy Council writes to Lord William Howard that Wyatt has confessed all the things objected against him, protested they proceeded from anger and vanity and not malice, and yielded himself to the king's mercy; and that the king, out of his own mercy and at the request of Queen Catherine Howard, has pardoned him. The Spanish ambassador thinks the pardon conditional on Wyatt's giving up Elizabeth Darrell and resuming conjugal relations with his wife on penalty of death and confiscation of property. While these conditions may not be official, it is possible that they are enforced.

April Made captain of 300 light cavalry to protect Calais until new fortifications are ready.

12 June Makes his will, bequeathing Elizabeth

Darrell lands in Dorset and Somerset, with
remainder to Francis Darrell, alias Wyatt.

1542   *January* Perhaps becomes Member of Parliament
for Kent, but there is no documentary evidence.
13 February Queen Catherine Howard is executed
for fornication and adultery. Wyatt is given
several offices which belonged to her alleged
paramour, Thomas Culpeper.
March Exchanges with the king estates and
property in over thirty places in Kent for estates
and property in Kent, Dorset, and Somerset.
Made High Steward of the royal manor of
Maidstone in Kent.
August Rumoured that Wyatt will be captain of a
galley and vice-admiral of a fleet preparing for a
possible war with France.
3 October Dispatched by the king to ride in haste
to Falmouth, welcome the emperor's envoy,
Montmorency de Corrierez, and escort him to
London. Overheated from hard riding, he is
seized with a fever and stops for rest at
Sherborne in Dorset, the home of Sir John
Horsey.
11 October Dies at Sherborne, where he is buried,
probably in the Horsey tomb.

1547–9 ? Some poems published in *A Book of Ballets*.

1549   *Certain Psalms* published.

1557   Many poems published in Tottel's *Miscellany*.

1561–4 ? Some poems published in *The Court of Venus*.

A Note on Wyatt's Language

Wyatt, born and raised in Kent and educated at Cambridge, spent much of his adult life in the court, which was based mainly in London. According to Helge Kökeritz, Wyatt retained some of the traits of his native Kentish dialect but mainly adopted 'the characteristics of educated or courtly London speech'; since there are no certain vestiges of his father's Yorkshire dialect, the influence of the north must have been 'neutralized by his mother's southern idiom and by his own daily contact with Kentish-speaking members of the household'.* Furthermore, the dialects of Kent and courtly London, like most British dialects, were undergoing enormous and rapid changes during Wyatt's lifetime. Therefore Wyatt had available to him a variety of forms of words, syntactic patterns, and pronunciations that he apparently expected his predominantly courtly audience to accept and that were a useful resource to him as he disposed his material in a medium demanding control of rhythms and the use of rhyme. His having, in effect, two dialects, his writing in a period of linguistic instability, and the utility of both factors help to explain what might otherwise seem an eccentric arbitrariness in the facets of his language described below.

While the language in the various manuscripts may be mainly Wyatt's or that of poets with the same basic dialects, scribes and editors certainly took liberties with the forms of words, the syntax, and the spelling of their originals. I have therefore based most of the discussion below on the poems in Wyatt's hand or

* 'Dialectal Traits in Sir Thomas Wyatt's Poetry', *Franciplegius: Medieval and Linguistic Studies in Honour of F. P. Magoun, Jr*, edited by J. B. Bessinger, Jr, and R. P. Creed (1965), pp. 294–303. Kökeritz's article is especially useful on pronunciation.

with revisions in his hand in the Egerton MS. When I use examples from other poems, I point out that fact. Since the sophisticating scribes and editors tended to make the language more like that in the later sixteenth century with which we are more familiar, a description of what is certainly Wyatt's language will cover most of the problems that he might set a modern reader. This discussion focuses on what I perceive to be the major and recurring problems; other archaic or unfamiliar forms, especially of individual words, are explained in the notes.

Pronouns and articles

Wyatt distinguishes regularly between 'thou' and 'thee', confining the former to the nominative, the latter to the oblique cases (XLV, 5, 6). He generally makes the same distinction between 'ye' and 'you', though once he uses 'you' in the nominative (CLII, 291; this exception is matched in his letters by one use of 'you' in the nominative and one use of 'ye' in an oblique case).* This distinction is not so regularly made in poems not in Wyatt's hand: in XXX, 10, 11, for example, 'you' and 'ye' are both used in the nominative. In all the poems, 'ye' and 'you' can be either singular or plural (see CLII, 289, 290 for their plural use), 'thou' and 'thee' only singular.

I suspect that Wyatt's choice between 'thou/thee' and 'ye/you' is governed by a set of principles, but I am not certain I have discovered them. We should expect Wyatt to use 'thou/thee' as pronouns of condescension or familiar address, 'you/ye' as pronouns showing respect or the desire to maintain distance. In the Penitential Psalms (CLII), the speaker, without exception, addresses God as 'thou/thee' in keeping with his desire to be intimate with God. When he turns to the reader, he uses 'ye/you' (CLII, 289–90), creating a tone appropriate for addressing men who are just. But in the love poems it is more difficult to discern the criteria, if any, governing his choice. The speaker uses 'ye' or a related form to address a disdainful and hence cruel woman whose pity he is begging (CVI, 9, 14), a woman whose beauty has caused him woe and who therefore presumably disdains him (LXI, 4), but also a beloved mistress

* K. Muir, *Life and Letters of Sir Thomas Wyatt* (1963), pp. 127, 129.

who may doubt his fidelity (CXVI, 4). Perhaps distance or the threat of it is implied in each case. He uses 'thou' or a related form to address his own spirit (LXXVI, 8–12), his own desire (LVIII, 2, 4, 5, 7), the reader of a riddle (XLVIII, 7), a child (in person of a mother, XLV, 4–6), but also a disdainful and hence cruel woman for whom he feels intense passion (CXVII, 11, 12, 13, 17, 18, 20). The desire to create a tone of intimacy might explain the first four instances; perhaps the very intensity of the passion expressed in CXVII accounts for the use of 'thou' in that poem, while the desire to create a cooler tone in an identical situation leads him to 'ye' in CVI. These are guesses in which I feel limited confidence. (In Wyatt's letters, which are outside the scope of this discussion, he consistently uses 'you/ye' to address the king and Thomas Cromwell – creating the appropriate tone of respect. But, apart from a formulaic 'I pray thee', he also consistently addresses his son as 'ye/you' when we should expect 'thou/thee' to express familiarity or condescension.) Certainly, in the poems not in Wyatt's hand, there seem to be no principles governing the choice of pronouns. In XVI, for example, the speaker's tongue is addressed as 'thee', his tears and sighs as 'ye/you'.

Wyatt at times uses the ordinary personal pronouns reflexively: for example, 'he hides him' (LXXVI, 18); 'my soul doth fret it to the bones' (CLII, 122). But he also uses the more familiar 'myself' (LXXVI, 83), 'thyself' (LVIII, 2), 'himself' (LXXVI, 45), and 'itself' (CLIV, 16).

Wyatt, of course, does not have the possessive 'its' and instead uses 'his', the common form well into the seventeenth century (for example, LXXVI, 4). He always uses the relative pronoun 'that' in the nominative case when the reference is to a person (CLII, 369–420); but he does use 'whom' as the relative pronoun in the accusative case (XLI, 5; CLII, 420). 'That' is his favourite relative pronoun when the reference is to things, but 'which' also occurs (CLIV, 14).

He ordinarily uses 'mine', 'thine', 'none', and 'an' before words beginning with a vowel or 'h' and in contexts where they have nominal rather than adjectival force: for example, 'thine eyes' cure' (CLII, 481); 'mine offence' (CLII, 257); 'mine heart' (LXXVI, 67), 'judging thy sight as none' (CLII, 448). But at times he uses 'my' before vowels and 'h': 'my offence' (CLII, 89), 'my heart' (CLII, 151); and the forms ending in vowels always occur before words beginning with consonants.

Similarly, before words beginning with a vowel or 'h', Wyatt usually contracts the definite article: for example, 'th'unhappy' (LXXVI, 5). Only once he does not contract: 'the heavens' (CLII, 410). He uses the contractions 't'one' and 't'other' (CLIV, 25); and at times, probably for metrical purposes, he uses 'the t'one' and 'the t'other' (CLIV, 19).

Verbs

The second person singular indicative in the present and past tenses usually ends in '(e)st': hence, 'how long . . ./Forbearest thou' (CLII, 112-13); 'Thou wrought'st the earth' (CLII, 620). There are also the expected forms with the auxiliary 'do': 'thou dost oppress' (CXVII, 12); 'thou . . . didst wash' (CLII, 256). More unusual are the contracted forms: 'thou loves' (CLII, 461); 'thou delights' (CLII, 498); 'thou seeks' (CLII, 680). The uninflected form is normal with the subject 'ye': 'ye can' (CVI, 14).

The third person singular indicative in the present tense usually ends in '(e)th': hence, 'The sun returneth' (XLII, 2); 'that shew'th her wealthy pride' (LX, 4). But there are also the forms with 'do' and '-s': 'the wind/ Doth rise again' (XLII, 7-8); 'it suffers' (CLII, 147). An anomalous uninflected form occurs once in Wyatt's hand: 'He dare importune' (CLII, 537).

Other persons and numbers in the indicative show no inflection in poems in Wyatt's hand, though the ending '(e)th' occasionally appears in the third person plural in poems in scribal hands: for example, 'I am of them that farthest cometh behind' (XI, 4).

In the subjunctive, used to express doubt, concession, or condition, the verb is uninflected: for example, 'Though my . . . love/ Have' (CVI, 3-4); 'If such record, alas, provoke th'inflamed mind' (LXXVI, 43).

Past participles ordinarily inflected occasionally appear

without '-ed' in forms that have a precedent in Chaucer or other early writers: for example, 'entrails infect with fervent sore' (CLII, 353); 'their fault was never execute' (CLII, 230); 'His bow your hand ... should have unfold' (LXI, 4). Closely related to this form is a past participial adjective, also with precedent in Chaucer: for example, 'corrupt by use' (CLII, 109). Past participles not in Wyatt's hand occasionally have the prefix 'y-', forms which Kökeritz identifies as archaic Kenticisms derived ultimately from Chaucer: for example, 'yfixed' (XII, 6); 'ystricken' (XXV, 9). Kökeritz identifies the unusual past participle 'brent' (LV, 1) as another Kenticism. In Wyatt's phrase 'where it was withstand' (CLII, 300), 'withstand' is the normal past participle of the strong verb 'stand, stood' well into the sixteenth century.

Wyatt uses several verbs impersonally: for example, 'Him seemeth' (CLII, 421); 'May chance thee' (LXXVI, 96). In poems in scribal hands there occur 'Methink' (CLV, 11), 'it liketh me' (LXXIII, 146), 'what needeth these words' (XL, 1), and 'Me lusteth' (XXXI, 14). The verb 'do' sometimes has causative force: for example, 'Made her own weapon do her finger bleed' (made her own weapon cause her finger to bleed) (XLI, 7); 'He shall do make my senses .../ Obey' (CLII, 174-5).

Though the poems in Wyatt's hand do not offer an instance, the verb 'to wit' (to know), with present tense 'wot' and past tense 'wist', is quite common throughout the poems. Wyatt has the negative form 'not' (know not) in his own hand (CLII, 426). But he also uses 'know not' (LXXVI, 25).

In addition to the forms of the verb 'to be' with which the modern reader is acquainted, Wyatt uses several older forms. In the second person singular indicative after the subject 'thou', 'art' occurs in the present tense, 'wast' and 'wert' in the past: 'Thou art my refuge' (CLII, 263); 'That thou wast erst' (CLII, 626); 'thou wert generate' (XLV, 6). In the third person singular indicative 'be' occurs rarely: 'The ... talk .../ Be far from me' (LXXVI, 73-5). Much more common are 'be' and 'been' in the third person plural indicative and as the auxiliary for the past participle: 'There be two points' (CLIV, 18); 'they been uncorrupt' (CLIV, 29); 'these been called the poles' (CLIV, 23); 'my days been passed away' (CLII, 551). Wyatt once uses 'arn' in the third person plural indicative (CLII, 692), a form that the *OED* identifies as northern or north midland and that may be an exception to Kökeritz's claim that Wyatt's father made no impact on his son's language.

In the subjunctive of the verb 'to be', the poems in Wyatt's hand have 'be' in the singular and 'been' in the plural: 'Though this be strange' (LVII, 5); 'if these been true' (XLIV, 6). In the poems not in Wyatt's hand, 'be' is sometimes used in the plural: 'if that ye have found it, ye that be here' (V, 2).

The forms of the verb 'to have' include 'thou hast' in the indicative present (CXVII, 13), 'hath' in the third person singular indicative (CLII, 222), and 'thou hadst' in the indicative past (CLII, 495).

Wyatt often uses 'doth' as an auxiliary in forming the third person plural indicative in the present tense, a form that Kökeritz identifies as southern: 'doth roar/ The shivered pieces' (XLIII, 4–5); 'the beams of love doth still increase their heat' (LXXVI, 71); 'these kings doth lack' (CLII, 18). Correspondingly, he also uses 'do' or 'have' as auxiliaries in forming the third person singular: 'to treat/ Do me provoke' (LXXVI, 61–2); 'She ... have done' (XLI, 1–2); 'it have ... off flowed' (XLVII, 4). Occasionally he forms the third person plural indicative present with a final '-s': 'plaints .../ That from his heart distils' (CLII, 58–9); 'thy arrows ... sticks deep' (CLII, 331–3).

Prepositions and conjunctions

Wyatt sometimes uses the preposition 'in' with its Latin force of 'into' and the preposition 'to' as meaning 'against': 'in such decay ... this Zion lower' (CLII, 589–90); 'that that do intend/ My foes to me' (CLII, 762–3). In addition to the ordinary purposive conjunctions, Wyatt frequently uses 'for to'; and in addition to 'because', he uses 'for because' and 'for that'.

Possessive case of nouns

Wyatt sometimes forms the possessive case of a noun without the apostrophe and 's': 'At other will' (LXXVI, 89); 'before King David sight' (CLII, 4); and possibly 'his subject hearts' (CLII, 1), though 'subject' might be construed as a past participle without '-ed'.

Negation

Though double negatives do not occur in the poems in Wyatt's hand, they are common in the other poems and do not, of course, yield a positive significance: 'My word nor I shall not be variable' (XXX, 13); 'Against the which ne vaileth no defence' (XXV, 2).

Pronunciation and rhymes

Wyatt's mixture of dialects, his writing at a time of rapid linguistic change, and certain licences assumed by poets of his time made available to him different ways of pronouncing the same word that he expected his audience, as in the case of the forms discussed above, to accept and that were useful to him when manipulating rhythms and finding rhymes. He had the 'licence', for example, of giving a word derived from the French a 'romance' pronunciation if he chose: he could and did at times, for example, stress the last syllable of 'succoúrs', as in LXXVI, 3, although in other contexts he could place an 'English' stress on the first syllable (XVI, 5; a poem not in Wyatt's hand). Likewise he could sound or not sound the final '-ed' of verbs and participles and the final '-es' of plural nouns: contrast 'It seemèd now that of his fault the horror' (CLII, 193) with a line in the same stanza, 'Eased, not yet healed, he feeleth his disease' (l. 200), where 'healed' is spelled 'held' in the MS and is almost certainly monosyllabic; and the pronunciation of 'hertes' in 'By hope whereof thou dost our hertès move' (CLII, 682) with 'In hertes returned, as thou thyself hast said' (CLII, 441), where the latter noun is almost certainly monosyllabic. He apparently did not, however, exercise the option of pronouncing or not pronouncing the final, formerly inflexional 'e' in nouns, adjectives, or verbs. Take, for example, CLII, 309–16, in the original spelling and with a probable scansion marked:

> This while | a beme | that | bryght sonne | forth sendes,
> That sonne | the wych | was neu|er clowd | cowd hide,
> Percyth | the cave | and on | the harpe | discendes,
> Whose glaunc|yng light | the cordes | did o|uerglyde,
> And such | luyster | apon | the harpe | extendes
> As lyght | off lampe | apon | the gold | clene tryde:
> The torne | wheroff | into | his Iyes | did sterte,
> Surprisd | with Joye | by pen|ance off | the herte.

While a reader is tempted to sound the final 'e' of 'beme' in l. 309, the ease with which all the other lines scan as iambic pentameters without the pronunciation of the final 'e' suggests that 'beme' should be pronounced as a monosyllable.

Because Wyatt's metres remain a subject of debate and because the decision to sound or not sound, accent or not accent a syllable depends on one's view of his metre in a particular poem, I have not in the text used the customary marks (ˇ) to indicate supposedly sounded or accented marks lest I prejudice the reader's view of the metre. But I have given my views of the pronunciation in the notes, and in A Note on Wyatt's Metres (page 44) I have presented the issues of the debate about Wyatt's metres and my position.

When we turn to rhymes, it is clear that Wyatt could and did use different pronunciations of the same word to make rhymes or near-rhymes that would have been impossible for a speaker or writer of only one dialect and in a period of more phonological stability. While there was no fixed spelling system such as we know today, philologists assume that there was a tendency for people of the same dialect to spell in roughly the same way because their spelling tended towards the phonetic. Working in terms of this assumption, we can see that Wyatt probably was using a London pronunciation of 'depart' in his rhyming of 'depart/apart' at LXXVI, 5–6, but a Kentish pronunciation in his rhyming of 'depert/desert' at CLII, 523–4, where the 'er' probably sounded something like the 'er' in modern 'there'. Similarly, though in the original MS spelled 'hert', the word rhymes with 'overthwart' and 'apart' at CLII, 461, 463, and 465, but rhymes with 'sterte' at CLII, 315–16.* One sometimes suspects that Wyatt is verging on 'eye rhymes' ('pelycane/betane/bygane' at CLII, 560, 562, and 564), but more probably here, as in most instances, he is rhyming vowels that are at least nearly of the same quality (see, for another example, CXLIX, 5, 7, 9, although the poem is not in Wyatt's hand).

As I said in the Preface, modernizing of spelling has frequently masked or nearly destroyed the evidence of a rhyme (apart from the consonantal assonance at the end of rhyme-words). I list below the most important instances of that blurring of rhymes with the modernized spelling followed by the original spelling and then the rhyme-words. The first word cited is the word to which the line-numbers are keyed; I do not repeat it when giving rhymes with it from several poems. I give the old spelling of the rhyme-words when it might cast light on the way the rhyme-words were pronounced or on the possibility that the poet is using 'eye rhymes'. These changes will not be mentioned in the notes.

advice (advise): wise CXXXI, 18
beast (best): best: gest CLI, 84
brands (bronds): fonds CCLXVI, 41
briers (breers): rivers: desire CL, 86
cast (kest): best: rest CXI, 21
cease (cesse, cese): distress CXIV, 7: redresse CXXXI, 10:
   presse CXI, 10
complisheth (complyseth): poiseth (paysith): praiseth CLII, 522
counterpoise (conterpese): appease (apese): disease (disese) CLII,
   70
creed (crede): dead (dede) CII, 42
deceit (decayte): wait (whaite): bait (baite) CLII, 180

* A comparable case presents itself with the modern 'clerk'. The Scot or northern Englishman has available to him his native pronunciation 'klerk' and also the southern form 'klārk'. For the southern Englishman the Scots form is scarcely acceptable.

depart (depert): desert CLII, 524
desert (desart): part CXXXVII, 10: part: smart CXLIX, 20:
    smart CLXXV, 11
device (devise): guise XXX, 1; LXXV, 1: vice (vise): rise
    CXLIX, 59: wise CXXXII, 59, 99
doom (dome): come: lome CLII, 707
dread (dred): dead (deed): lead (lede) CLII, 20: lead (lede)
    CXX, 22: deed (dede): speed (spede) LXXXIII, 29
fly (fle): see CXLIII, 34
fret (freat): heat CXXVI, 27
fret (frete): great (grete) LXXIII, 85
gloze (glose): lose CLXXIX, 7
good (gyd): tried CXCVII, 12
grant (graunt): avaunt CXV, 15
groins (groyns): bones: nonce (noyns) CLI, 18
haste (hast): forecast: fast CLII, 21
heart (hert, herte): revert XCVII, 13; CX, 17: desert (deserte)
    CLXXVIII, 7: desert: smart (smert) CXXXII, 108
heat (hette): sweat (swete) CCLXII, 48
increase (encresse): confess (confesse): cease (cesse) CLII, 385
increased (increst): best: breast (brest) CXC, 9
key (kay): alway: day CXXXV, 16: day CLII, 532
lack (lake): forsake: make CCXLIX, 17
least (lest): possessed (possest) CXXVI, 20: request CVI, 18:
    request: best CLII, 600
mad (madde): fade: bad CL, 85
moan (mone): none XCVII, 11; LXXXIII, 32; CXXVIII, 8,
    13, 48; CXXIX, 2
mock (moke): cloak (cloke): stroke CXLIX, 7
moon (mone): done CIX, 28
moveth (meveth): breaketh (breketh): entreateth I, 10
neck: break (breke) CXII, 14
neck (nekke): speak (speke) CXLI, 22
nice (nise): wise: prize (prise) CLI, 76
none: soon (sone): done CIX, 8
not (note): note XCVIII, 4, 8, 12, 16, 20
overthrown (overthrawn): drawn: gnawn LXXIII, 116
pace (pase): was (wase) CLIV, 47
pass (pase, passe): apace: grace CLII, 757: face (fase) CLII, 541
profit (profet): let LXXXIV, 21
proved (preved): moved (meved) CCXIII, 5
quartan (quartain): pain CCLII, 33

quit (quyte): right CXV, 8
reck (reke): break (breke) CXII, 18
reproof (repreffe): chief (chefe): grief (greef): relief (releffe)
  CCXVII, 20
release (reles): redress CCLIX, 24
repeat (repete): fet XCVII, 4
scarce (scase): case (cace): place: was CCXVIII, 8
service (servise): wise LXXIII, 113
shut (shitt): writ: quit IX, 5: submit: fit XCI, 39
smart (smert): shirt (shert): heart (hert) CCIV, 1
sole (sowle): school (scole) CLXXVIII, 15
space (spas): alas CXL, 5
speed (spede): stead (stede): fed LXXXVIII, 5
stand (stond): bond: land (lond) CLII, 607
swoon (swoune): done CIX, 33
taste (tast): fast: haste (hast): waste (wast) CXXXII, 100: last:
  fast CXXXII, 63
then (than): on (an): man: can CXXXII, 19: man: ban CLI, 61:
  began CCXXXVII, 15: man CCLX, 8: man: can: began
  CXXIX, 21: when (whan): man CLII, 451
threat (threte): fret (frete): treat (trete) CVII, 25
turn (torne): mourn (morne) CXXXIX, 22
two (tow): now CLIV, 39
vouchsafe (vouchsave, witsave): crave CVI, 9; CLXXVIII, 19
waste (wast): last: past CIX, 2: past CXXX, 20: fast CLXII, 8:
  fast: last CLI, 6: blast CCVI, 3
wert (wart): overthwart: part CLXXXIV, 11, 16
when (whan): began: can CCXVI, 6
womanhood (womanhede): lead (lede) CCLIV, 8
wrest (wrast): haste (hast) CCXLVIII, 19

A Note on Wyatt's Metres

Any discussion of metre in general and the vexed subject of Wyatt's metres in particular best starts with some definitions. I take it that all language has rhythm and that the rhythm of language is the movement of some element or elements of its sound – a movement which forms a pattern. In verse the rhythmic pattern is more susceptible to description or measurement than in prose, partly because the patterned elements are arranged more systematically, partly because in verse (from Latin *vertor*, 'to turn') one line 'turns the corner' into another line with a comparable pattern. (I leave aside here the subject of modern 'free verse', where the point is often, perhaps always, to arrange the crucial elements in ways that differ from line to line.)

Poets have arranged various elements of sound to create rhythm in verse: for example, syllables of different duration, the number of syllables in the line, or the number of speech stresses or accents in the line. In English verse since at least the second half of the sixteenth century and probably earlier, the most common pattern has been the alternation of relatively strong and relatively weak speech stresses or accents in lines containing about the same number of syllables. English verse is therefore usually called accentual-syllabic.

Metre, from the poet's perspective, might be described as the mental pattern or model of sound-elements which he imitates and varies in actual sounds to produce the poem's rhythm. Metre, from the reader's perspective, is the 'measure' of the rhythmic pattern – that is, the instrument for measuring or describing the pattern.

Modern linguists are developing very sophisticated systems for measuring the rhythms of verse. The system I use in this discussion is more traditional. It assumes that some English lines are definable in terms of the number of stresses in each line, that others are definable in terms of the number of 'feet' or rhythmic units, that feet consist of at least one syllable but usually of two or three in rising or falling patterns determined by accent, and that feet and lines are named in the traditional terms of prosody (for example, 'iambic pentameter' is a metre that describes a line consisting of five feet, each foot rising from an unaccented to an accented syllable). I distinguish between the elements in the metre or model (accented syllable, un-accented syllable) and the elements in the real line (stressed syllable, relatively unstressed syllable), so that, for example, a metrical accent may not be realized in a major or even secondary stress but is nonetheless apprehended as a virtual stress relative to the other syllable or syllables in the same foot.

When we turn to Wyatt, it seems safe to say that few readers disagree about the rhythm of his poems written in 'short' lines of two, three, or, most commonly, four feet. Indeed Wyatt is generally acknowledged as a master of the iambic tetrameter line.* Nor are his poems in 'poulter's measure' – a couplet consisting of a line of six feet and a line of seven feet – a matter of much metrical controversy (though their aesthetic value is debated and usually disparaged). Most disagreements focus on the rhythms Wyatt achieves and, presumably, intends to achieve in the poems that are the subject of this note: that is, poems in what I hereafter will call 'long lines' of 9 to 12 syllables. Readers do not, in other words, read those poems aloud in the same way.

The differences stem largely from disagreements about Wyatt's metres. Metre is theoretically – and, by good readers, actually – apprehended from a reading of the whole poem's rhythm. But metre soon becomes a model in the mind of the reader, a model which determines the way he reads the poem

---

* It is, of course, possible that scribes and early 'editors' have smoothed the poems in short lines. Of the poems in Wyatt's hand or with his revisions, only three contain lines that are clearly intended to be short. In CVI, the metre of the third and fourth lines of each stanza is not clear. CXVI is a fragment. In CXVII iambic trimeter lines occur only in the refrain.

and hence its rhythm, especially when he feels uncertain about the poem's rhythm as he proceeds. Wyatt makes no statement about his intended metres. And it is not always immediately clear, when we read his poems aloud, which elements of their sound he is arranging into a pattern. It is therefore not surprising that different readers of Wyatt will infer different metres from even the same poem, or parts of it, and then force, even torture, the rhythm to comply with their sense of the metre.

The readers of Wyatt who have written on his metres have taken at least three different positions on his long line. Some hold that he intends each line to contain four major speech-stresses or accents, usually but not always separated by a caesura into two groups of two stresses each, with the number of unstressed syllables and their position relative to the stressed syllables finally not mattering.* In this view Wyatt is writing in the tradition of stress or accentual verse dating back to Anglo-Saxon poetry. IX is a poem to which this metre seems appropriate:

> Caesar, when that the traitor of Egypt
> With th'honourable head did him present,
> Covering his gladness, did represent
> Plaint with his tears outward, as it is writ.
> And Hannibal eke, when fortune him shut
> Clean from his reign and from all his intent,
> Laughed to his folk whom sorrow did torment,
> His cruel despite for to disgorge and quit.
> So chanceth it oft that every passion
> 10 The mind hideth by colour contrary
> With feigned visage, now sad, now merry;
> Whereby if I laughed any time or season,

---

* Elias Schwartz, 'The Meter of Some Poems of Wyatt', *SP*, LX (1963), pp. 155–65.

It is for because I have n'other way
To cloak my care but under sport and play.

Others contend that Wyatt's long lines contain anywhere from four to six stresses; that at least four of them are major while the fifth or sixth may be major or secondary; that the lines are usually though not always divided into two by a caesura; and that the stressed syllables, while usually separated by relatively unstressed syllables, may be juxtaposed. I will refer to this metre hereafter as the 'flexible' metre. The proponents of this metre as Wyatt's norm notice that such a line may approximate to or be identical with an iambic pentameter line. They attribute the mixture of iambic pentameter lines with other types of lines to Wyatt's writing in a tradition of verse including Chaucer (possibly misread because his successors in the fifteenth and sixteenth centuries no longer sound some of his inflexional endings, like the final e), Lydgate, and other poets of the fifteenth century for whom this mixture is a conscious choice or the product of chance.* XXXII illustrates this view of Wyatt's metre:

There was never file || half so well filed
To file a file || for every smith's intent
As I was made a filing instrument
To frame other, || while I was beguiled.
But reason hath at my folly smiled
And pardoned me || since that I me repent
Of my lost years || and time misspent:
For youth did me lead || and falsehood guiled.
Yet this trust I have || of full great appearance:

* See, for example: C. S. Lewis, 'The Fifteenth Century Heroic Line', *Essays and Studies by Members of the English Association*, XXIV (1938), pp. 28–41; Alan Swallow, 'The Pentameter Lines in Skelton and Wyatt', *MP*, XLVIII (1950), pp. 1–11; D. W. Harding, 'The Rhythmical Intention in Wyatt's Poetry', *Scrutiny*, XIV (1946), pp. 90–102.

10   Since that deceit || is ay returnable,

Of very force || it is agreeable

That therewithal be done the recompense.

Then guile beguiled || plained should be never

And the reward little trust forever.

Thirdly, there are those readers who believe that Wyatt is always striving to write iambic pentameter lines and that, given several 'licences', he generally succeeds.* XLVII can be scanned as perfect iambic pentameter:

From these | high hills | as when | a spring | doth fall

It tril|leth down | with still | and sub|tle course,

Of this | and that | it gath|ers ay| and shall

Till it | have just | off flowed | the stream | and force,

Then at | the foot | it rag|eth o|ver all –

So far|eth love | when he | hath ta'en | a source:

His rein | is rage; | resis|tance vail | eth none;

The first | eschew | is re|medy | alone.

But clearly iambic pentameter is not a metre appropriate to IX. Applying it leads to the torturing of speech stresses:

Caesar, | when that | the trai | tor of | Egypt.

And in many other poems to which the metre has been applied, the third, fifth, and seventh syllables are so frequently stressed – that is, to use traditional terms, there are so many trochees in the second, third, and fourth feet of the lines – that one's sense of an iambic pattern is undermined. On the other hand, while it

---

* See, for example: A. K. Foxwell, *A Study of Sir Thomas Wyatt's Poems* (1911); F. M. Padelford, 'The Scansion of Wyatt's Early Sonnets', *SP*, xx (1923), pp. 137–52; R. D. Evans, 'Some Aspects of Wyatt's Metrical Technique', *JEGP*, LIII (1954), pp. 197–213.

would be possible to scan XLVII as patterned in four-stress lines, such a metre would disregard many obvious speech stresses and thereby fail to distinguish between the rhythm of this poem and that of IX. Moreover, there are too few poems to which the metre of four stresses certainly applies to make it useful as a general measure. My first tentative conclusion, then, is that neither the metre of four major stresses nor that of iambic pentameter, while each is applicable to some poems, adequately describes all of Wyatt's poems.

Of course it is possible to apply to IX, XLVII, and poems with similar rhythms the flexible metre of four to six speech stresses. And certainly those poems that mix lines of five major stresses with lines of four or six major stresses require a metre of this flexibility (for example, LXXX, XVI, and XLV). Perhaps we should rest with this metre as the most comprehensive and best available explanation of Wyatt's rhythms and end the discussion here.

But I do not find this conclusion entirely satisfactory. For one thing the metre attributes to chance whole poems and the many lines that scan, without strain, as iambic pentameter. Of the poems in Wyatt's hand or with revisions in his hand – and hence with the most authoritative texts – XLVII, LX, and LXI scan entirely as iambic pentameter. About 75 per cent of the 775 lines in the Penitential Psalms scan as iambic pentameter; if one allows the trochaic substitution common in the first foot, the percentage is about 82 per cent. Of the 306 lines in the Epistolary Satires (not in Wyatt's hand), about 64 per cent are iambic pentameter; if one allows the trochaic substitution in the first foot, the percentage is about 70. These statistics suggest that at times Wyatt writes the iambic pentameter line deliberately, and that when he writes the satires and psalms it is his favourite line.

Secondly, the flexible metre does not take into account the fact that Wyatt's long lines usually contain ten syllables, a pattern which he may derive from French verse, in which only the number of syllables in each line constitutes a poem's metre. In the Egerton MS, there are 921 'long lines' in Wyatt's hand or with revisions in his hand. 844 of these lines contain 10

syllables. Of the remainder, 25 contain 9 syllables, 47 contain
11 syllables, and 5 contain 12 syllables. These figures, while
approximate because different readers might pronounce some
of the words differently, remain weighty evidence that the
10-syllable line was, at least at times, part of Wyatt's metrical
norm.

Perhaps most important, the very comprehensiveness of the
flexible metre, which is its strength as an explanatory device, also
renders it incapable of making finer discriminations, like that
between the rhythms of IX and XLVII, which Wyatt may
intend.

For these reasons I should like to propose an additional
hypothesis which, if correct, offers a metre that explains most of
Wyatt's rhythms. I suggest that Wyatt frequently has as his
model a line of five feet or rhythmic units, not necessarily iambic,
with each unit containing a stress or virtual stress. My hypothesis
depends on the possibility of monosyllabic feet occurring any-
where in the line, on the possibility that a trochee, anapest, or
dactyl may occur anywhere in the line, and on the assumption
that Wyatt has a few licences of pronunciation available to him
(fewer certainly than those assumed by the proponents of
iambic pentameter as his norm): mainly the elision or pro-
nunciation of 'e' in 'eth', the option to sound or not sound 'es'
at the end of nouns and 'ed' at the end of verbs, and the option
to use either a 'romance' or an 'English' pronunciation of words
borrowed from the French (for example, pleasúre or pléasure).*
Let me offer a scansion of X that illustrates the metre I am
proposing; monosyllabic feet are in italics.

The long | *love* | that in | my thought | doth har|bour
And in | mine heart | doth keep | his re|sidence
Into | my face | presseth | with bold | pretence
And there|in camp|*eth,* | spreading | his ban|ner.

* Lines in Wyatt's hand do not suggest that he exercises the option of
pronouncing or not pronouncing the final, formerly inflexional 'e' in nouns,
adjectives, or verbs.

She that | me learn|*eth* | to love | and suf|fer

And will | that my | trust and | lust's neg|ligence

Be reined | by rea|son, shame, | and re|verence,

With his | hardi|*ness* | taketh | displeas|ure.

Wherewith|al un|to the heart's | forest | he fle|eth,

10   Leaving | his en|terprise | with pain | and cry,

And there | him hid|*eth* | and not | appear|eth.

What may | I do | *when* | my mas|ter fear|eth,

But in | the field | with him|to live | and die?

For good | is the life | *end*|ing faith|fully.

As an explanatory device this metre has three obvious weak-
nesses: there is no rule governing the location of monosyllabic
feet in the line; one frequently must read the entire line before
determining that a monosyllabic foot has occurred earlier in the
line; and the monosyllables constituting these feet have unequal
rhetorical force: for example, camp*eth*, learn*eth*, hardi*ness*, hid*eth*,
and *when*, as opposed to *love* and *end*ing. Its strengths, I think,
are several. It takes into account the juxtaposed stresses that
create what has been called the 'pausing rhythm' of Wyatt's verse
because of the pause such stresses frequently necessitate (as in
lines 1 and 14 of X). It underscores the probability that Wyatt
regards the line of ten syllables as his norm (only l. 9 exceeds
ten), but saw the potentiality, even within that line, for
feminine endings (that is, unstressed syllables, additional to the
five feet, as in lines 1, 4, 5, 8, 9, 11 and 12 in X). It also draws
attention to those feminine endings in a way that scansion in
terms of the four-stress line or the metre of four to six stresses
does not.* It does not wrench the likely pronunciation of words
in the fashion of those who try to impose an iambic pattern on
the five-foot line. Most important, it explains a large proportion

* In some instances my scansion also reminds the reader that Wyatt's
rhymes are often confined to identical feminine endings. Compare, for
example, the 'eth' rhymes in lines 9, 11, and 12 of X with those in I.

of Wyatt's poems. Using as a sample the poems with long lines in Wyatt's hand or with revisions in his hand – and hence with the most authoritative texts – I find that the metre describes all but two lines of these poems (CLII, 647, 649). The number of poems mixing lines with four, five, or six stresses – poems in which at least some readers sense metrical formlessness – is correspondingly reduced.

I should like to return briefly to the flexible metre to ask if Wyatt mixes lines of different numbers of stresses with complete arbitrariness. I suspect that, in at least some instances, the mixture is the result of an imperfection in Wyatt's art rather than his use of the flexible metre. Unfortunately, Wyatt's revisions of his poems in the Egerton MS do not offer examples of the flexible metre. But they do suggest his priorities in composition which may explain some of the poems in what seems flexible metre. Those priorities, as I perceive them, were: first, sense or meaning; second, rhyme, especially difficult in the *terza rima* of the psalms; third, the iambic pentameter line; and finally, the line of five feet. Wyatt, I think, regards precision, clarity, or concentration of meaning as of primary importance. In CLII, 198, for example, he alters his first version

Himself | accus|ing and know|ledging | his case
to

Himself | accus|ing, | beknow|ing his case,

because, instead of the redundancy of the phrases in the first version, he wants to establish the causal connection between self-knowledge and self-accusation. To achieve this precision and concentration, he sacrifices a tolerable iambic pentameter line, with an anapest in the third foot, to a line that maintains the five-foot metre but at the expense of 'roughness'. He sacrifices two versions of CLII, 26, both iambic pentameter if we allow the substitution in the third foot of the first version,

Whom he | doth love | more than | himself | or God
Whom more | than God | or else | himself | he lov'th,

to a non-iambic five-foot line,

> Whom more | than God | or | himself | he mind|eth,

for the sake of the rhymes 'mindeth'/ 'findeth'/ 'undermindeth'
that he foresees as easier to handle than rhymes with 'God' and
'lov'th'. His two versions of CLII, 237,

> I, | for that | I hid | it still | within
> I, for | because | I hid | it still | within,

suggest that he prefers an iambic pentameter line to a line in the
five-foot metre (see also CLII, 78, 500, 547, and 672). The very
existence of these priorities suggests that Wyatt's art is not
always adequate to his ideal objective. Perhaps a comparable
inadequacy is responsible for lines like XL, 7,

> She took | from me | an heart | and I | a glove | from her,

in a poem of otherwise five-foot lines; or XVII, 3 and 9,

> I fly | above | the wind | yet can | I not | arise
> Without | eyen | I see | and with|out tongue | I plain,

in a poem of otherwise five-foot lines.

In other cases, however, I think it possible that Wyatt mixes
different kinds of lines for reasons of art rather than because his
art is imperfect. The famous LXXX may provide an example:

> They flee | from me | that some|time did | me seek
> With na|ked foot | stalk|ing in | my cham|ber.
> I|have seen | them gen|tle, tame, | and meek
> That now | are wi|ld and | do not | remem|ber
> That some|time | they put | themself | in dan|ger
> To take | bread at | my hand; | and now | they range
> Busi|ly seek|ing with | a contin|ual change.

Thanked | be for|tune it hath | been oth|erwise

Twenty | times bet|ter, but once | in spe|cial,

10 In thin | array | after | a pleas|ant guise,

When her | loose gown | from her | shoulders | did fall

And she | me caught | in her arms | long | and small,

There|withal | sweet|ly did | me kiss

And soft|ly said, | 'Dear heart, | how like | you this?'

It was | no dream: | I lay | broad wak|ing.

But all | is turned | thorough | my gen|tleness

Into | a strange | fashion | of forsak|ing.

And I | have leave | to go | of her | goodness

And she | also | to use | newfang|leness.

20 But since | that I | so | kindly | am served

I would | fain know | what | she hath | deserved.

As my scansion indicates, I think the poem's metre is five feet to
the line. But lines 15 and 17 scan most naturally as four-stress
lines. I think it likely that these lines are deliberate variations to
reinforce the speaker's astonishment at the reality of his past
union and the strangeness of his present desertion.* .Though
neither a failure nor an achievement of art can finally be demon-
strated, I think the probabilities ought to be weighed for each
poem to which the flexible metre is appropriate.

I draw five tentative conclusions from this discussion of
Wyatt's poems with long lines. First, the metre of four stresses
to the line applies to very few poems. Second, there are too

* For an alternative but related scansion of this poem, see Y. Winters,
Forms of Discovery (1967), pp. 4–8. Winters preserves a five-foot line in
lines 15 and 17 by taking 'It' in line 15 as a monosyllabic foot and scanning
the last three feet of each line as trochees. With the exception of line 13,
which Winters scans as four iambs, he applies to this poem, though with a
scansion different from mine, a metre of five feet to the line.

many lines not in iambic pentameter to make it Wyatt's metrical norm. Third, if my hypothesis about the metre based on five feet is correct, the number of poems that are best described in terms of the flexible metre of four, five, or six stresses to the line is also relatively small. Fourth, the metre of five feet to the line explains most of the poems. Finally, in at least the satires and psalms, iambic pentameter is Wyatt's favourite version of that five-foot metre.

A Note On Wyatt's Punctuation

The punctuation of the poems that Wyatt writes out in the
Egerton MS is almost certainly his own: a professional scribe or
someone 'improving' the text would surely have been more
systematic. It is equally certain that the punctuation of the rest
of the poems in the manuscript is not Wyatt's: they are
punctuated either by the scribes or, in the case of the poems on
folios 4 to 11, by Nicholas Grimald.* From the poems in
Wyatt's hand I have tried to infer the principles of his punctua-
tion to guide my punctuating of all the poems.

The sporadic character of Wyatt's punctuation is its most
striking quality. Apparently he is at times in a punctuating vein,
at other times not. In the latter mood he can write out long
passages with no punctuation at all or passages with only the
most occasional punctuation. Some critics have argued that
Wyatt deliberately omits punctuation in order to increase
ambivalences of syntax and meaning.† That intention might
explain the lack of punctuation in some cases, like the following
line:

Assured I doubt I be not sure (LXXXV).

But most of the unpunctuated passages do not yield this kind of
ambivalence, and Wyatt does sometimes punctuate. It therefore

* R. Hughey, 'The Harington Manuscript at Arundel Castle and Related
Documents', *The Library*, xv (1935), pp. 415–16. K. Muir disregards
Hughey's argument when he implies that Wyatt might be 'responsible for
all or most of the two hundred punctuation marks in the first hundred lines
of the MS' (K. Muir and P. Thomson, *Collected Poems of Sir Thomas Wyatt*
(1969), p. xxvi).

† R. Southall, *The Courtly Maker* (1964), p. 75. Southall cites the lines
from LXXXV quoted in the text.

seems likely that the absence of punctuation is generally due to his whim or his carelessness.

When Wyatt does punctuate, he does so lightly, and primarily with the period and the virgule (/), which is his favourite mark. XLV, which Muir transcribes as an example,* is quite untypical in the amount of its punctuation and in its comma and colon: to my knowledge the colon occurs only once again and the comma never again in poems in Wyatt's hand. Along with the period and virgule, Wyatt ordinarily uses the question mark, exclamation mark, parentheses, and, very rarely, an apostrophe or ∧ to mark elision.

I do not think Wyatt's punctuation is random, but I remain uncertain about its governing principles. I offer the following as tentative hypotheses:

1. Wyatt rarely marks the end of a line. Writing largely end-stopped verse, he assumes, at the end of virtually every line, a pause that signals the completion of a syntactic unit and a rhythmic caesura.

2. When he does mark the end of the line, he is indicating a major syntactic break or the end of a stanza which coincides with a major syntactic break. He does not mark all such breaks. He ordinarily uses periods to mark the major syntactic breaks and the end of a stanza. He rarely uses virgules, which mark less important breaks than periods, at the ends of lines.

3. He is inclined to use punctuation within the line after enjambment unless the line has no significant pause. That internal punctuation indicates both a break in syntax and a caesura. He uses it frequently after 'of' and 'with' phrases, rarely after a 'by' phrase.

4. He uses other internal punctuation to mark primarily a rhythmic caesura: in the poulter's measure of CLIV, for example, he marks caesuras that do not coincide with syntactic breaks. The caesura, of course, frequently coincides with a syntactic break. In those instances, Wyatt tends to punctuate most often before the coordinating conjunction 'and' and the

* Muir and Thomson, op. cit., p. xxxv.

disjunctive conjunction 'nor' when they link clauses, verbs, and adjectives:

> My days like shadow decline / and I do dry (CLII, 578)

> Like one that hears not / nor hath to reply
> One word again   (CLII, 373-4)

> For I am weak / and clean without defence (CLII, 93)

and between parallel phrases, between words and phrases in apposition, and between members of a catalogue:

> Himself accusing / beknowing his case (CLII, 198)

> My bread of life / the word of truth I say (CLII, 555)

> Of people frail / palace / pomp / and riches / (CLII, 164).

He by no means always marks caesuras or the coincidence of caesuras and syntactic breaks. His most ordinary mark of internal punctuation is the virgule, which, in addition to marking a caesura, has a force like that of a comma, more rarely a semicolon, very rarely a period.

5. He very rarely punctuates between main and subordinate clauses.

6. He does not capitalize personifications.

7. He occasionally uses the virgule after a term of direct address: for example, o lord/ (CLII, 753, 762).

I experimented with punctuating the poems in accord with these principles and with the virgule in place of our lighter marks. Both experiments had the effect of confusing modern readers. I decided in favour of as light a syntactic punctuation as seemed consonant with making the poems intelligible. I also decided to use modern punctuation marks. I have introduced quotation marks for dialogue and soliloquy, capitalized personifications, and set off with commas words of direct address, salutations, exclamations, and expletives. At least the relative lightness of the punctuation is in keeping with the spirit of Wyatt's.

Further Reading

ABBREVIATIONS

EC	Essays in Criticism
ELH	A Journal of English Literary History
ELR	English Literary Renaissance
JEGP	Journal of English and Germanic Philology
HLQ	Huntington Library Quarterly
MP	Modern Philology
N & Q	Notes and Queries
RES	Review of English Studies
RN	Renaissance News
SEL	Studies in English Literature 1500–1900
SP	Studies in Philology
TLS	The Times Literary Supplement

EDITIONS

Certain Psalms . . . drawen into English metre by Sir Thomas Wyatt, 1549.

The Gorgeous Gallery of Gallant Inventions, 1578.

Nugae Antiquae . . . Selected from Authentic Remains by the Rev. Henry Harington (London), 1779.

G. Nott, ed., The Works of Henry Howard, Earl of Surrey, and of Sir Thomas Wyatt the Elder, 2 vols. (London), 1815–16, Vol. II only.

A. K. Foxwell, ed., The Poems of Sir Thomas Wiat, 2 vols. (London: University of London Press), 1913.

E. M. W. Tillyard, The Poetry of Sir Thomas Wyatt (London: The Scholartis Press), 1929.

R. A. Fraser, ed., The Court of Venus (Durham, N. C.: Duke University Press), 1955.

R. Hughey, ed., *The Arundel Harington Manuscript of Tudor Poetry*, 2 vols. (Columbus: The Ohio State University Press), 1960.

H. A. Mason, *Sir Thomas Wyatt: A Literary Portrait* (Bristol: Bristol Classical Press), 1986.

K. Muir, ed., *Sir Thomas Wyatt and his Circle, Unpublished Poems* (Liverpool: Liverpool University Press), 1961.

H. E. Rollins, ed., *Tottel's Miscellany (1557–1587)*, 2 vols. (Cambridge, Mass.: Harvard University Press), 2nd ed., 1965.

K. Muir and P. Thomson, *Collected Poems of Sir Thomas Wyatt* (Liverpool: Liverpool University Press), 1969.

J. Daalder, ed., *Sir Thomas Wyatt, Collected Poems* (London, Oxford, New York: Oxford University Press), 1975.

GENERAL REFERENCE

E. C. Hangen, *A Concordance to the Complete Poetical Works of Sir Thomas Wyatt* (Chicago: The University of Chicago Press), 1941.

E. C. Caldwell, 'Recent Studies in Sir Thomas Wyatt', *ELR*, 19 (1989), 226–46.

B. Fishman, 'Recent Studies in Wyatt and Surrey', *ELR*, 1 (1971), 178–91.

C. W. Jentoft, *Sir Thomas Wyatt and Henry Howard, Early of Surrey: A Reference Guide* (Boston: Hall), 1980.

M. C. O'Neel, 'A Wyatt Bibliography', *Bulletin of Bibliography*, 27 (1970), 76–9, 93–4.

W. G. Smith and J. E. Heseltine, *The Oxford Dictionary of English Proverbs* (Oxford: The Clarendon Press), 2nd ed., 1948.

M. P. Tilley, *A Dictionary of the Proverbs in England in the Sixteenth and Seventeenth Centuries* (Ann Arbor: University of Michigan Press), 1950.

SOURCES

A. The Penitential Psalms

[Anon.], *A paraphrasis upon all the Psalms of David, made by Joannis Campensis*, 1535.

P. Aretino, *I Sette Salmi de la Penitentia di David*, 1534.

P. Aretino, *Paraphrase upon the Seven Penitential Psalms of the Kingly Prophet translated out of Italian by I. H.* [John Hawkins], 1635.

[J. Campensis and U. Zwingli], *Enchiridon Psalmorum Eorundem ex veritate Hebraica versionem, ac Joannis Campensis e regione paraphrasim . . . complectens*, 1533.

Biblia Magna, 1525.

Biblia, The Bible faithfully and truly translated into English [by Miles Coverdale], 1535.

G. E. Duffield, ed., *The Work of William Tyndale* (Philadelphia: Fortress Press), 1965.

J. Fisher, *The English Works*, ed. J. E. B Mayor (London: N. Trübner & Co.), 1876.

G. Joye, *David's Psalter*, 1534.

H. A. Mason, 'Wyatt and the Psalms', Part I, *TLS* (27 February 1953), 144; Part II, *TLS* (6 March 1953), 160.

B. Other Poems

B. Bauer-Formiconi, ed., *Die Strambotti des Serafino dall'Aquila* (Munich: W. Fink), 1967.

K. A. Bleeth, 'Wyatt and Chaucer's "Lusty Leese"', *N & Q*, 18 (1971), 214.

G. Chaucer, *The Poetical Works of Chaucer*, ed. F. N. Robinson (Boston: Houghton Mifflin Co.), 2nd ed., 1957.

J. Daalder, 'Seneca and Wyatt's Second Satire', *Etudes Anglaises: Grande-Bretagne, Etats-Unis*, 38 (1985), 422–6.

A. M. Endicott, 'A Note on Wyatt and Serafino D'Aquilano', *RN*, 17 (1964), 301–3.

J. G. Fucilla, 'The Direct Source of Wyatt's Epigram: In Dowtfull Brest . . .', *RN*, 9 (1956), 187–8.

C. E. Nelson, 'A Note on Wyatt and Ovid', *Modern Language Review*, 58 (1963), 60–63.

F. Petrarca, *Rime e Trionfi*, ed. Ferdinando Neri, 2nd ed. (Turin), 1960.

F. Petrarca, *Sonnets and Songs*, trans. Anna Maria Armi (New York: Pantheon), 1946.

F. Petrarca, *Rime, English and Italian*, trans. and ed. Robert Durling (Cambridge, Mass.: Harvard University Press), 1976.

P. Thomson, 'Wyatt and the Petrarchan Commentators', *RES*, 10 (1959), 225–33.

P. Thomson, 'Wyatt and the School of Serafino', *Comparative Literature*, 13 (1961), 289–315.

P. Thomson, 'Wyatt's Boethian Ballade', *RES* 15 (1964), 262–7.

L. Thorndike, ed., Johannes de Sacrobosco's *Textus de Sphaera* (Chicago: University of Chicago Press), 1949.

PROBLEMS OF CANON AND TEXT

H. Baron, 'Mary Fitzroy's Transcript of Surrey's Poem'; 'Mary (Howard) Fitzroy's Hand in the Devonshire Manuscript', *RES*, 45 (1994), 314–15; 318–35.

J. Daalder, 'Editing Wyatt', *EC*, 23 (1973), 399–413.

J. Daalder, 'The Significance of the "Tho" Signs in Wyatt's Egerton Manuscript', *Studies in Bibliography*, 40 (1987), 86–100.

J. Daalder, 'Are Wyatt's Poems in Egerton MS 2711 in Chronological Order?', *English Studies: A Journal of English Language and Literature*, 69 (1988), 205–23.

A. K. Donald, ed., *The Poems of Alexander Scott*, Early English Text Society, Extra Series, 85 (London: Kegan Paul, Trench, Trübner & Co.), 1902.

R. C. Harrier, *The Canon of Sir Thomas Wyatt's Poetry* (Cambridge, Mass.: Harvard University Press), 1975.

R. Hughey, 'The Harington Manuscript at Arundel Castle', *The Library*, 15 (1935), 388–444.

H. A. Mason, *Editing Wyatt*, *The Cambridge Quarterly* (1972).

H. A. Mason, '*Ecce iterum Crispinus* – Progress in Wyatt Studies?', *The Cambridge Quarterly* 10 (1981–2), 219–35.

R. A. Rebholz, 'The Humanist's Wyatt', review of *Sir Thomas Wyatt: A Literary Portrait*, intro. and ed. H. A. Mason, *The Cambridge Quarterly*, 17 (1988), 187–96.

R. Southall, 'The Devonshire Manuscript Collection of Early Tudor Poetry, 1532–41', *RES*, 15 (1964), 142–50.

R. Southall, 'The Egerton Manuscript', 'The Devonshire Manuscript', *The Courtly Maker, An Essay on the Poetry of Wyatt and His Contemporaries* (Oxford: Basil Blackwell & Mott; New York: Barnes & Noble), 1964, pp. 160–73.

LANGUAGE AND METRE

R. D. Evans, 'Some Aspects of Wyatt's Metrical Technique', *JEGP*, 53 (1954), 197–213.

D. W. Harding, 'The Rhythmical Intention in Wyatt's Poetry', *Scrutiny*, 14 (1946), 90–102.

H. Kökeritz, 'Dialectal Traits in Sir Thomas Wyatt's Poetry', *Franciplegius: Medieval and Linguistic Studies in Honor of F. P. Magoun, Jr*, ed. J. B. Bessinger, Jr, and R. P. Creed (New York: New York University Press), 1965, 294–303.

C. S. Lewis, 'The Fifteenth Century Heroic Line', *Essays and Studies by Members of the English Association*, 24 (1938), 28–41.

R. R. Noguchi, 'Wyatt's Satires and the Iambic Pentameter Tradition', *SP*, 80 (1983), 126–41.

F. M. Padelford, 'The Scansion of Wyatt's Early Sonnets', *SP*, 20 (1923), 137–52.

E. Partridge, *Shakespeare's Bawdy* (London: Routledge & Kegan Paul; New York: E. P. Dutton & Co.), 1968.

E. Schwartz, 'The Meter of Some Poems of Wyatt', *SP*, 60 (1963), 155–65.

A. Swallow, 'The Pentameter Lines in Skelton and Wyatt', *MP*, 48 (1950), 1–11.

Y. Winters, *Forms of Discovery* (Chicago: A. Swallow), 1967, 4–8.

S. Woods, *Natural Emphasis: English Versification from Chaucer to Dryden* (San Marino: Huntington Library), 1984, 1–103.

G. T. Wright, 'Wyatt's Decasyllabic Line', *SP*, 82 (1985), 129–56.

BIOGRAPHY

S. M. Foley, *Sir Thomas Wyatt* (Boston: Twayne), 1990.

E. W. Ives, *Anne Boleyn* (Oxford: Blackwell), 1986.

H. A. Mason, *Sir Thomas Wyatt: A Literary Portrait* (Bristol: Bristol Classical Press), 1986.

K. Muir, *Life and Letters of Sir Thomas Wyatt* (Liverpool: Liverpool University Press), 1963.

J. Ridley, *Henry VIII* (New York: Viking), 1985.

R. M. Warnicke, *The Rise and Fall of Anne Boleyn: Family Politics at the Court of Henry VIII* (New York: Cambridge University Press), 1989.

CRITICAL STUDIES

S. Baldi, *La Poesia di Sir Thomas Wyatt, il Primo Petrarchista Inglese* (Firenze: Le Monnier), 1953.

S. Baldi, *Sir Thomas Wyatt*, trans. F. T. Prince (London, New York: Longmans, Green), 1961.

C. Bates, '"A Mild Admonisher": Sir Thomas Wyatt and Sixteenth-Century Satire', *HLQ*, 56 (1993), 243–58.

A. Berthoff, 'The Falconer's Dream of Trust: Wyatt's "They Fle from Me"', *Sewanee Review*, 71 (1963), 477–94.

C. Burrow, 'Horace at Home and Abroad: Wyatt and Sixteenth-Century Horatianism', pp. 27–49 in *Horace Made New: Horatian Influences on British Writing from the Renaissance to the Twentieth Century*, ed. C. Martindale and D. Hopkins (Cambridge: Cambridge University Press), 1993.

E. K. Chambers, *Sir Thomas Wyatt and Some Collected Studies* (London: Sidgwick and Jackson), 1933.

H. Cooper, 'Wyatt and Chaucer: A Reappraisal', *Leeds Studies in English*, 13 (1982), 104–23.

J. J. Crewe, 'Wyatt's Craft', pp. 23–47, in *Trials of Authorship: Anterior Forms and Poetic Reconstruction from Wyatt to Shakespeare* (Berkeley, Los Angeles, Oxford: University of California Press), 1990.

R. W. Dasenbrock, *Imitating the Italians: Wyatt, Spenser, Synge, Pound, Joyce* (Baltimore: Johns Hopkins Press), 1991, 1–31.

B. L. Estrin, 'Becoming the Other/The Other Becoming in Wyatt's Poetry', *ELH*, 51 (1984), 431–45.

B. L. Estrin, 'Wyatt's Unlikely Likenesses: Or, Has the Lady Read Petrarch?', pp. 219–32, in *Rethinking the Henrician Era, Essays on Early Tudor Texts and Contexts*, ed. Peter Herman (Urbana & Chicago: University of Illionis Press), 1994.

A. Fowler, 'Obscurity of Sentiment in the Poetry of Wyatt', *Conceitful Thought: The Interpretation of English Renaissance Poems* (Edinburgh: Edinburgh University Press), 1975, 1–20.

A. Fox, *Politics and Literature in the Reigns of Henry VII and Henry VIII* (Oxford, New York: Blackwell), 1989, chap. 14.

A. K. Foxwell, *A Study of Sir Thomas Wyatt's Poems* (London: University of London Press), 1911.

D. M. Friedman, 'The "Thing" in Wyatt's Mind', *EC*, 16 (1966), 375–81.

D. M. Friedman, 'The Mind in the Poem: Wyatt's "They Fle from Me"', *SEL*, 7 (1967), 1–13.

D. M. Friedman, 'Wyatt and the Ambiguities of Fancy', *JEGP*, 67 (1968), 32–48.

K. J. E. Graham, 'Wyatt's Antirhetorical Verse: Privilege and the Performance of Conviction', pp. 25–49, in *The Performance of Conviction: Plainness and Rhetoric in the Early English Renaissance* (Ithaca and London: Cornell University Press), 1994.

S. Greenblatt, *Renaissance Self-Fashioning: From More to Shakespeare* (Chicago: University of Chicago Press), 1980, 115–56, 276–83.

R. Greene, 'The Colonial Wyatt: Contexts and Openings', pp. 240–66 in *Rethinking the Henrician Era* (see Estrin above).

T. Greene, *The Light in Troy: Imitation and Discovery in Renaissance Poetry* (New Haven: Yale University Press), 1982, chap. 12.

A. Halasz, 'Wyatt's David', pp. 193–218 in *Rethinking the Henrician Era* (see Estrin above).

O. Hietsch, *Die Petrarcaübersetzungen Sir Thomas Wyatts* (Vienna: W. Braunmüller), 1960.

J. Z. Kamholtz, 'Thomas Wyatt's Poetry: The Politics of Love', *Criticism*, 20 (1978), 349–65.

J. Kerrigan, 'Wyatt's Selfish Style', *Essays and Studies*, 34 (1981), 1–18.

L. M. Klein, 'The Petrarchism of Sir Thomas Wyatt Reconsidered', pp. 134–47 in *The Work of Dissimilitude: Essays from the Sixth Citadel Conference on Medieval and Renaissance Literature* (Newark; London: University of Delaware Press; Associated University Press), 1992.

N. S. Leonard, 'The Speaker in Wyatt's Lyric Poetry', *HLQ*, 41 (1977–8), 1–18.

C. S. Lewis, *English Literature in the Sixteenth Century Excluding Drama* (Oxford: The Clarendon Press), 1954, 220–30.

H. A. Mason, *Humanism and Poetry in the Early Tudor Period* (London: Routledge and Kegan Paul), 1959.

H. A. Mason, 'Wyatt's Greatest Adventure?', *The Cambridge Quarterly*, 7 (1977), 151–71.

L. E. Nathan, 'Tradition and Newfangleness in Wyatt's "They fle From Me"', *ELH*, 32 (1965), 1–16.

S. Panja, 'Ranging and Returning: The Mood-Voice Dichotomy in Wyatt', *ELR*, 18 (1988), 347–68.

D. P. Peterson, *The English Lyric from Wyatt to Donne* (Princeton: Princeton University Press), 1967, chap. 3.

R. A. Rebholz, 'Love's Newfangleness: A Comparison of Greville and Wyatt', *Studies in the Literary Imagination*, 11 (1987), 17–30.

D. M. Rosen, 'Time, Identity, and Context in Wyatt's Verse', *SEL*, 21 (1981), 5–20.

D. M. Ross, *Self-Revelation and Self-Protection in Wyatt's Lyric Poetry* (New York & London: Garland Publishing, Inc.), 1988.

W. A. Sessions, 'Surrey's Wyatt: Autumn 1542 and the New Poet', pp. 168–92 in *Rethinking the Henrician Era* (see Estrin above).

R. Southall, *The Courtly Maker, An Essay on the Poetry of Wyatt and His Contemporaries* (New York: Barnes & Noble), 1964.

R. Southall, *Literature and the Rise of Capitalism: Critical Essays Mainly on the Sixteenth and Seventeenth Centuries* (London: Lawrence & Wishart), 1973, chap. 2.

R. Southall, '"Love, Fortune and My Mind": The Stoicism of Wyatt', *EC*, 39 (1989), 18–28.

A. C. Spearing, *Medieval to Renaissance in English Poetry* (Cambridge: Cambridge University Press), 1985, chap. 7.

P. Thomson, *Sir Thomas Wyatt and His Background* (London: Routledge and Kegan Paul; Stanford, Cal.: Stanford University Press), 1964.

P. Thomson, ed., *Wyatt: The Critical Heritage* (London and Boston: Routledge & Kegan Paul), 1974.

W. Trimpi, *Ben Jonson's Poems* (Stanford, Cal.: Stanford University Press), 1962.

R. G. Twombly, 'Thomas Wyatt's Paraphrase of the Penitential Psalms of David', *Texas Studies in Literature and Language*, 12 (1970), 345–80.

G. Waller, *English Poetry of the Sixteenth Century* (London: Longman), 1986, 1–118.

M. Waller, 'The Empire's New Clothes: Refashioning the Renaissance', pp. 160–83 in *Seeking the Woman in Late Medieval and Renaissance Writings: Essays in Feminist Contextual Criticism*, ed. S. Fisher and j. Halley (Knoxville: University of Tennessee), 1989.

C. F. Williamson, 'Wyatt's Use of Repetitions and Refrains', *ELR*, 12 (1982), 291–300.

P. Zagorin, 'Sir Thomas Wyatt and the Court of Henry VIII: The Courtier's Ambivalence', *Journal of Medieval and Renaissance Studies*, 23 (Winter 1993), 113–41.

MUSIC AND THE POEMS

O. Gombosi, 'Blame not Wyatt', *RN*, 8 (1955), 12–14.

R. L. Greene, 'Wyatt's "I am as I am" in Carol-form', *RES*, 15 (1964), 175–80.

J. Hall, *The Court of Virtue (1565)*, ed. R. A. Fraser (London: Routledge and Kegan Paul; New Brunswick, N. J.: Rutgers University Press), 1961.

J. H. Long, 'Blame Not Wyatt's Lute', *RN*, 7 (1954), 127–30.

W. Maynard, 'The Lyrics of Wyatt: Poems or Songs?' *RES*, 16 (1965), 1–13, 245–57.

W. Maynard, 'To Smith of Camden', *RES*, 18 (1967), 162–3.

I. L. Mumford, 'Musical Settings to the Poems of Sir Thomas Wyatt', *Music and Letters*, 37 (1956), 315–22.

I. L. Mumford, 'Sir Thomas Wyatt's Songs: a Trio of Problems in Manuscript Sources', *Music and Letters*, 39 (1958), 262–4.

I. L. Mumford, 'Sir Thomas Wyatt's Verse and Italian Musical Sources', *English Miscellany*, 14 (1963), 9–26.

I. L. Mumford, 'Petrarchism and Italian Music at the Court of Henry VIII', *Italian Studies*, 26 (1971), 49–67.

J. Stevens, *Music and Poetry in the Early Tudor Court* (London: Methuen), 1961.

Poems in the Hand of Sir Thomas Wyatt, Poems with Revisions in His Hand, and Poems Attributed to Him in the Sixteenth Century

Rondeaux

I

Behold, Love, thy power how she despiseth,
My great pain how little she regardeth.
The holy oath whereof she taketh no cure
Broken she hath, and yet she bideth sure
Right at her ease and little she dreadeth.
Weaponed thou art and she unarmed sitteth.
To thee disdainful her life she leadeth,
To me spiteful without cause or measure.
    Behold, Love.
10 I am in hold. If pity thee moveth,
Go bend thy bow that stony hearts breaketh
And with some stroke revenge the displeasure
Of thee and him that sorrow doth endure
    And, as his lord, thee lowly entreateth.
        Behold, Love.

II

If it be so that I forsake thee
As banished from thy company,
Yet my heart, my mind, and mine affection
Shall still remain in thy perfection,
And right as thou list so order me.
But some would say in their opinion
Revulsed is thy good intention.
Then may I well blame thy cruelty
    If it be so.

10 But myself I say on this fashion:
   I have her heart in my possession,
   And of itself there cannot, perdie,
   By no means love an heartless body;
   And on my faith good is the reason
      If it be so.

III

Go, burning sighs, unto the frozen heart.
Go break the ice which pity's painful dart
Might never pierce; and if mortal prayer
In heaven may be heard, at last I desire
That death or mercy be end of my smart.
Take with thee pain whereof I have my part
And eke the flame from which I cannot start,
And leave me then in rest, I you require.
   Go, burning sighs.
10 I must go work, I see, by craft and art
For truth and faith in her is laid apart.
Alas, I cannot therefore assail her
With pitiful plaint and scalding fire
That out of my breast doth strainably start.
   Go, burning sighs.

IV

What vaileth truth or by it to take pain,
To strive by steadfastness for to attain
To be just and true and flee from doubleness,
Sithens all alike, where ruleth craftiness,
Rewarded is both false and plain?
Soonest he speedeth that most can feign;
True meaning heart is had in disdain.
Against deceit and doubleness
   What vaileth truth?

10 Deceived is he by crafty train
    That meaneth no guile and doth remain
    Within the trap without redress
    But for to love, lo, such a mistress
    Whose cruelty nothing can refrain.
      What vaileth truth?

V

    Help me to seek for I lost it there;
    And if that ye have found it, ye that be here,
    And seek to convey it secretly,
    Handle it soft and treat it tenderly
    Or else it will plain and then appair.
    But rather restore it mannerly
    Since that I do ask it thus honestly,
    For to lose it it sitteth me too near.
      Help me to seek.
10 Alas, and is there no remedy
    But have I thus lost it wilfully?
    Iwis it was a thing all too dear
    To be bestowed and wist not where:
    It was mine heart! I pray you heartily
      Help me to seek.

VI

    Thou hast no faith of him that hath none.
    But thou must love him needs by reason
    For, as sayeth a proverb notable,
    Each thing seeketh his semblable,
    And thou hast thine of thy condition.
    Yet is it not the thing I pass on,
    Nor hot nor cold is mine affection;
    For since thine heart is so mutable,
      Thou hast no faith.

10   I thought thee true without exception.
  But I perceive I lacked discretion
  To fashion faith to words mutable:
  Thy thought is too light and variable.
  To change so oft without occasion,
    Thou hast no faith.

VII

Ye old mule that think yourself so fair,
Leave off with craft your beauty to repair,
For it is true without any fable
No man setteth more by riding in your saddle.
Too much travail so do your train appair,
    Ye old mule.
With false savours though you deceive the air,
Whoso taste you shall well perceive your lair
Savoureth somewhat of a kappur's stable,
10   Ye old mule.
Ye must now serve to market and to fair,
All for the burden, for panniers a pair;
For since grey hairs been powdered in your sable,
The thing ye seek for you must yourself enable
To purchase it by payment and by prayer,
    Ye old mule.

VIII

What no, perdie, ye may be sure!
Think not to make me to your lure
With words and cheer so contraring,
Sweet and sour counterweighing.
Too much it were still to endure.
Truth is tried where craft is in ure.
But though ye have had my heart's cure,
Trow ye I dote without ending?
    What no, perdie!

10   Though that with pain I do procure
     For to forget that once was pure
     Within my heart, shall still that thing
     Unstable, unsure, and wavering
     Be in my mind without recure?
         What no, perdie!

Sonnets

IX

Caesar, when that the traitor of Egypt
With th'honourable head did him present,
Covering his gladness, did represent
Plaint with his tears outward, as it is writ.
And Hannibal eke, when fortune him shut
Clean from his reign and from all his intent,
Laughed to his folk whom sorrow did torment,
His cruel despite for to disgorge and quit.
So chanceth it oft that every passion
10   The mind hideth by colour contrary
With feigned visage, now sad, now merry;
Whereby if I laughed any time or season,
It is for because I have n'other way
To cloak my care but under sport and play.

X

The long love that in my thought doth harbour
And in mine heart doth keep his residence
Into my face presseth with bold pretence
And therein campeth, spreading his banner.
She that me learneth to love and suffer
And will that my trust and lust's negligence
Be reined by reason, shame, and reverence,
With his hardiness taketh displeasure.
Wherewithal unto the heart's forest he fleeth,
10   Leaving his enterprise with pain and cry,

And there him hideth and not appeareth.
What may I do when my master feareth,
But in the field with him to live and die?
For good is the life ending faithfully.

XI

Whoso list to hunt, I know where is an hind,
But as for me, helas, I may no more.
The vain travail hath wearied me so sore,
I am of them that farthest cometh behind.
Yet may I by no means my wearied mind
Draw from the deer, but as she fleeth afore
Fainting I follow. I leave off therefore
Sithens in a net I seek to hold the wind.
Who list her hunt, I put him out of doubt,
10   As well as I may spend his time in vain.
And graven with diamonds in letters plain
There is written her fair neck round about:
'*Noli me tangere* for Caesar's I am,
And wild for to hold though I seem tame.'

XII

Was I never yet of your love grieved
Nor never shall while that my life doth last.
But of hating myself that date is past,
And tears continual sore have me wearied.
I will not yet in my grave be buried
Nor on my tomb your name yfixed fast
As cruel cause that did the spirit soon haste
From th'unhappy bones by great sighs stirred.
Then if an heart of amorous faith and will
10   May content you without doing grief,
Please it you so to this to do relief.

If otherwise ye seek for to fulfil
Your disdain, ye err and shall not as ye ween,
And ye yourself the cause thereof hath been.

XIII

If amorous faith in heart unfeigned,
A sweet languor, a great lovely desire,
If honest will kindled in gentle fire,
If long error in a blind maze chained,
If in my visage each thought depainted,
Or else in my sparkling voice lower or higher
Which now fear, now shame, woefully doth tire,
If a pale colour which love hath stained,
If to have another than myself more dear,
10 If wailing or sighing continually,
With sorrowful anger feeding busily,
If burning afar off and freezing near
Are cause that by love myself I destroy,
Yours is the fault and mine the great annoy.

XIV

My heart I gave thee, not to do it pain;
But to preserve, it was to thee taken.
I served thee, not to be forsaken,
But that I should be rewarded again.
I was content thy servant to remain
But not to be paid under this fashion.
Now since in thee is none other reason,
Displease thee not if that I do refrain,
Unsatiate of my woe and thy desire,
10 Assured by craft to excuse thy fault.
But since it please thee to feign a default,
Farewell, I say, parting from the fire:
For he that believeth bearing in hand,
Plougheth in water and soweth in the sand.

XV

Some fowls there be that have so perfect sight
Again the sun their eyes for to defend,
And some because the light doth them offend
Do never 'pear but in the dark or night.
Other rejoice that see the fire bright
And ween to play in it, as they do pretend,
And find the contrary of it that they intend.
Alas, of that sort I may be by right,
For to withstand her look I am not able
10 And yet can I not hide me in no dark place,
Remembrance so followeth me of that face.
So that with teary eyen, swollen and unstable,
My destiny to behold her doth me lead,
Yet do I know I run into the gleed.

XVI

Because I have thee still kept from lies and blame
And to my power always have I thee honoured,
Unkind tongue, right ill hast thou me rendered
For such desert to do me wreak and shame.
In need of succour most when that I am
To ask reward, then standest thou like one afeard,
Alway most cold; and if thou speak toward,
It is as in dream, unperfect and lame.
And ye salt tears, again my will each night
10 That are with me when fain I would be alone,
Then are ye gone when I should make my moan.
And you so ready sighs to make me shright,
Then are ye slack when that ye should outstart,
And only my look declareth my heart.

XVII

I find no peace and all my war is done.
I fear and hope, I burn and freeze like ice.
I fly above the wind yet can I not arise.
And naught I have and all the world I seize on.
That looseth nor locketh, holdeth me in prison
And holdeth me not, yet can I scape no wise;
Nor letteth me live nor die at my device
And yet of death it giveth me occasion.
Without eyen I see and without tongue I plain.
10 I desire to perish and yet I ask health.
I love another and thus I hate myself.
I feed me in sorrow and laugh in all my pain.
Likewise displeaseth me both death and life,
And my delight is causer of this strife.

XVIII

Though I myself be bridled of my mind,
Returning me backward by force express,
If thou seek honour to keep thy promise,
Who may thee hold, my heart, but thou thyself unbind?
Sigh then no more since no way man may find
Thy virtue to let though that frowardness
Of fortune me holdeth; and yet as I may guess,
Though other be present, thou art not all behind.
Suffice it then that thou be ready there
10 At all hours, still under the defence
Of time, truth, and love to save thee from offence,
Crying, 'I burn in a lovely desire
With my dear master's that may not follow,
Whereby his absence turneth him to sorrow.'

XIX

My galley charged with forgetfulness
Thorough sharp seas in winter nights doth pass
'Tween rock and rock; and eke mine enemy, alas,
That is my lord, steereth with cruelness;
And every oar a thought in readiness
As though that death were light in such a case.
An endless wind doth tear the sail apace
Of forced sighs and trusty fearfulness.
A rain of tears, a cloud of dark disdain
10 Hath done the wearied cords great hindrance,
Wreathed with error and eke with ignorance.
The stars be hid that led me to this pain.
Drowned is reason that should me comfort
And I remain despairing of the port.

XX

Avising the bright beams of these fair eyes,
Where he is that mine oft moisteth and washeth,
The wearied mind straight from the heart departeth
For to rest in his worldly paradise
And find the sweet bitter under this guise.
What webs he hath wrought well he perceiveth,
Whereby with himself on Love he plaineth
That spurreth with fire and bridleth with ice.
Thus is it in such extremity brought:
10 In frozen thought now, and now it standeth in flame,
'Twixt misery and wealth, 'twixt earnest and game,
But few glad and many a diverse thought,
With sore repentance of his hardiness.
Of such a root cometh fruit fruitless.

XXI

Ever mine hap is slack and slow in coming,
Desire increasing, mine hope uncertain,
That leave it or wait it doth me like pain
And tiger-like swift it is in parting.
Alas, the snow shall be black and scalding,
The sea waterless, fish in the mountain,
The Thames shall return back into his fountain,
And where he rose the sun shall take lodging
Ere that I in this find peace or quietness
10 In that Love or my lady rightwisely
Leave to conspire again me wrongfully.
And if that I have after such bitterness
Anything sweet, my mouth is out of taste,
That all my trust and travail is but waste.

XXII

Love and Fortune and my mind, rememb'rer
Of that that is now with that that hath been,
Do torment me so that I very often
Envy them beyond all measure.
Love slayeth mine heart. Fortune is depriver
Of all my comfort. The foolish mind then
Burneth and plaineth as one that seldom
Liveth in rest, still in displeasure.
My pleasant days, they fleet away and pass,
10 But daily yet the ill doth change into the worse,
And more than the half is run of my course.
Alas, not of steel but of brickle glass
I see that from mine hand falleth my trust,
And all my thoughts are dashed into dust.

XXIII

How oft have I, my dear and cruel foe,
With those your eyes for to get peace and truce
Proffered you mine heart! But you do not use
Among so high things to cast your mind so low.
If any other look for it, as ye trow,
Their vain weak hope doth greatly them abuse.
And thus I disdain that that ye refuse:
It was once mine, it can no more be so.
If I then it chase, nor it in you can find
10 In this exile no manner of comfort,
Nor live alone, nor, where he is called, resort,
He may wander from his natural kind.
So shall it be great hurt unto us twain
And yours the loss and mine the deadly pain.

XXIV

Like to these unmeasurable mountains
Is my painful life, the burden of ire:
For of great height be they and high is my desire,
And I of tears and they be full of fountains.
Under craggy rocks they have full barren plains;
Hard thoughts in me my woeful mind doth tire.
Small fruit and many leaves their tops do attire;
Small effect with great trust in me remains.
The boist'rous winds oft their high boughs do blast;
10 Hot sighs from me continually be shed.
Cattle in them and in me love is fed.
Immovable am I and they are full steadfast.
Of the restless birds they have the tune and note,
And I always plaints that pass thorough my throat.

XXV

The lively sparks that issue from those eyes
Against the which ne vaileth no defence
Have pressed mine heart and done it none offence
With quaking pleasure more than once or twice.
Was never man could anything devise
The sunbeams to turn with so great vehemence
To daze man's sight, as by their bright presence
Dazed am I, much like unto the guise
Of one ystricken with dint of lightning,
10 Blinded with the stroke, erring here and there.
So call I for help, I not when ne where,
The pain of my fall patiently bearing.
For after the blaze, as is no wonder,
Of deadly 'Nay' hear I the fearful thunder.

XXVI

Such vain thought as wonted to mislead me
In desert hope by well assured moan
Maketh me from company to live alone
In following her whom reason bid me flee.
She fleeth as fast by gentle cruelty
And after her mine heart would fain be gone,
But armed sighs my way do stop anon,
'Twixt hope and dread locking my liberty.
Yet as I guess, under disdainful brow
10 One beam of pity is in her cloudy look,
Which comforteth the mind that erst for fear shook.
And therewithal bolded, I seek the way how
To utter the smart that I suffer within,
But such it is I not how to begin.

XXVII

Unstable dream, according to the place,
Be steadfast once or else at least be true.
By tasted sweetness make me not to rue
The sudden loss of thy false feigned grace.
By good respect in such a dangerous case
Thou brought'st not her into this tossing mew
But madest my sprite live my care to renew,
My body in tempest her succour to embrace.
The body dead, the sprite had his desire;
10 Painless was th'one, th'other in delight.
Why then, alas, did it not keep it right,
Returning to leap into the fire,
And where it was at wish it could not remain?
Such mocks of dreams they turn to deadly pain.

XXVIII

If waker care, if sudden pale colour,
If many sighs, with little speech to plain,
Now joy, now woe, if they my cheer distain,
For hope of small, if much to fear therefore,
To haste, to slack my pace less or more
Be sign of love, then do I love again.
If thou ask whom, sure since I did refrain
Brunet that set my wealth in such a roar,
Th'unfeigned cheer of Phyllis hath the place
10 That Brunet had. She hath and ever shall.
She from myself now hath me in her grace.
She hath in hand my wit, my will, and all.
My heart alone well worthy she doth stay
Without whose help scant do I live a day.

XXIX

The pillar perished is whereto I leant,
The strongest stay of mine unquiet mind;
The like of it no man again can find –
From east to west still seeking though he went –
To mine unhap, for hap away hath rent
Of all my joy the very bark and rind,
And I, alas, by chance am thus assigned
Dearly to mourn till death do it relent.
But since that thus it is by destiny,
10 What can I more but have a woeful heart,
My pen in plaint, my voice in woeful cry,
My mind in woe, my body full of smart,
And I myself myself always to hate
Till dreadful death do cease my doleful state?

XXX

Each man me telleth I change most my device,
And on my faith me think it good reason
To change purpose like after the season.
For in every case to keep still one guise
Is meet for them that would be taken wise;
And I am not of such manner condition
But treated after a diverse fashion,
And thereupon my diverseness doth rise.
But you that blame this diverseness most,
10 Change you no more, but still after one rate
Treat yè me well and keep ye in the same state;
And while with me doth dwell this wearied ghost,
My word nor I shall not be variable
But always one, your own both firm and stable.

XXXI

Farewell, Love, and all thy laws forever.
Thy baited hooks shall tangle me no more.
Senec and Plato call me from thy lore
To perfect wealth my wit for to endeavour.
In blind error when I did persevere,
Thy sharp repulse that pricketh ay so sore
Hath taught me to set in trifles no store
And scape forth since liberty is lever.
Therefore farewell. Go trouble younger hearts
10 And in me claim no more authority.
With idle youth go use thy property
And thereon spend thy many brittle darts:
For hitherto though I have lost all my time,
Me lusteth no longer rotten boughs to climb.

XXXII

There was never file half so well filed
To file a file for every smith's intent
As I was made a filing instrument
To frame other, while I was beguiled.
But reason hath at my folly smiled
And pardoned me since that I me repent
Of my lost years and time misspent:
For youth did me lead and falsehood guiled.
Yet this trust I have of full great appearance:
10 Since that deceit is ay returnable,
Of very force it is agreeable
That therewithal be done the recompense.
Then guile beguiled plained should be never
And the reward little trust forever.

XXXIII

You that in love find luck and abundance
And live in lust and joyful jollity,
Arise for shame, do away your sluggardy,
Arise, I say, do May some observance!
Let me in bed lie dreaming in mischance,
Let me remember the haps most unhappy
That me betide in May most commonly,
As one whom love list little to avance.
Sephame said true that my nativity
10 Mischanced was with the ruler of the May.
He guessed, I prove of that the verity:
In May my wealth and eke my life, I say,
Have stood so oft in such perplexity.
Rejoice! Let me dream of your felicity.

XXXIV

The flaming sighs that boil within my breast
Sometime break forth and they can well declare
The heart's unrest and how that it doth fare,
The pain thereof, the grief, and all the rest.
The watered eyes from whence the tears do fall
Do feel some force or else they would be dry.
The wasted flesh of colour dead can try
And something tell what sweetness is in gall.
And he that list to see and to discern
10 How care can force within a wearied mind,
Come he to me: I am that place assigned.
But for all this no force, it doth no harm.
The wound, alas, hap in some other place
From whence no tool away the scar can rase.

But you that of such like have had your part
Can best be judge. Wherefore, my friend so dear,

I thought it good my state should now appear
To you and that there is no great desert.
And whereas you, in weighty matters great,
20 Of fortune saw the shadow that you know,
For trifling things I now am stricken so
That, though I feel my heart doth wound and beat,
I sit alone, save on the second day
My fever comes with whom I spend the time
In burning heat while that she list assign.
And who hath health and liberty alway,
Let him thank God and let him not provoke
To have the like of this my painful stroke.

XXXV

To rail or jest ye know I use it not,
Though that such cause sometime in folks I find.
And though to change ye list to set your mind,
Love it who list, in faith I like it not.
And if ye were to me as ye are not
I would be loath to see you so unkind.
But since your faith must needs be so by kind,
Though I hate it, I pray you leave it not.
Things of great weight I never thought to crave;
10 This is but small, of right deny it not:
Your feigning ways as yet forget them not
But like reward let other lovers have,
That is to say, for service true and fast,
Too long delays and changing at the last.

XXXVI

My love took scorn my service to retain
Wherein me thought she used cruelty
Since with goodwill I lost my liberty
To follow her which causeth all my pain.

Might never care cause me for to refrain,
But only this which is extremity,
Giving me naught, alas, not to agree
That, as I was, her man I might remain.
But since that thus ye list to order me
10   That would have been your servant true and fast,
Displease thee not my doting days be past
And with my loss to live I must agree.
For as there is a certain time to rage
So is there time such madness to assuage.

XXXVII

Such is the course that nature's kind hath wrought
That snakes have time to cast away their stings.
A'inst chained prisoners what need defence be sought?
The fierce lion will hurt no yielden things.
Why should such spite be nursed then in thy thought
Sith all these powers are prest under thy wings?
And eke thou seest and reason thee hath taught
What mischief malice many ways it brings.
Consider eke that spite availeth naught.
10   Therefore this song thy fault to thee it sings.
Displease thee not for saying thus my thought
Nor hate thou him from whom no hate forth springs,
For furies, that in hell be execrable,
For that they hate are made most miserable.

XXXVIII

Alas, madam, for stealing of a kiss
Have I so much your mind there offended?
Have I then done so grievously amiss
That by no means it may be amended?
Then revenge you, and the next way is this:
Another kiss shall have my life ended.
For to my mouth the first my heart did suck;
The next shall clean out of my breast it pluck.

XXXIX

The wandering gadling in the summer tide
That finds the adder with his retchless foot
Starts not dismayed so suddenly aside
As jealous Despite did, though there were no boot,
When that he saw me sitting by her side
That of my health is very crop and root.
It pleased me then to have so fair a grace
To sting that heart that would have my place.

XL

What needeth these threnning words and wasted wind?
All this cannot make me restore my prey.
To rob your good, iwis, is not my mind,
Nor causeless your fair hand did I display.

Let Love be judge or else whom next we meet
That may both hear what you and I can say:
'She took from me an heart and I a glove from her.
Let us see now if th'one be worth th'other.'

XLI

She sat and sewed that hath done me the wrong
Whereof I plain and have done many a day,
And whilst she heard my plaint in piteous song
Wished my heart the sampler as it lay.
The blind master whom I have served so long,
Grudging to hear that he did hear her say,
Made her own weapon do her finger bleed
To feel if pricking were so good indeed.

XLII

He is not dead that sometime hath a fall.
The sun returneth that was under the cloud.
And when Fortune hath spit out all her gall
I trust good luck to me shall be allowed.
For I have seen a ship into haven fall
After the storm hath broke both mast and shroud.
And eke the willow that stoopeth with the wind
Doth rise again and greater wood doth bind.

XLIII

The furious gun in his raging ire,
When that the ball is rammed in too sore
And that the flame cannot part from the fire,
Cracketh in sunder, and in the air doth roar
The shivered pieces. Right so doth my desire
Whose flame increaseth from more to more;
Which to let out I dare not look nor speak,
So inward force my heart doth all to-break.

XLIV

Venomous thorns that are so sharp and keen
Sometime bear flowers fair and fresh of hue.
Poison oft-time is put in medicine
And causeth health in man for to renew.
Fire that purgeth all thing that is unclean
May heal and hurt. And if these been true,
I trust sometime my harm may be my health
Since every woe is joined with some wealth.

XLV

In doubtful breast whilst motherly pity
With furious famine standeth at debate,
Saith th'Hebrew mother, 'O child unhappy,
Return thy blood where thou hadst milk of late.
Yield me those limbs that I made unto thee
And enter there where thou wert generate.
For of one body against all nature
To another must I make sepulture.'

XLVI

Of Carthage he, that worthy warrior,
Could overcome but could not use his chance.
And I likewise, of all my long endeavour,
The sharp conquest though fortune did advance,
Could not it use. The hold that is given over
I unpossessed. So hangeth in balance
Of war my peace, reward of all my pain.
At Monzòn thus I restless rest in Spain.

XLVII

From these high hills as when a spring doth fall
It trilleth down with still and subtle course,
Of this and that it gathers ay and shall
Till it have just off flowed the stream and force,
Then at the foot it rageth over all –
So fareth love when he hath ta'en a source:
His rein is rage; resistance vaileth none;
The first eschew is remedy alone.

XLVIII

Vulcan begat me. Minerva me taught.
Nature my mother. Craft nourished me year by year.
Three bodies are my food. My strength is in naught.
Slaughter, wrath, waste, and noise are my children dear.
Guess, friend, what I am and how I am wrought:
Monster of sea or of land or of elsewhere?
Know me and use me and I may thee defend
And, if I be thine enemy, I may thy life end.

XLIX

Stand whoso list upon the slipper top
Of court's estates, and let me here rejoice
And use me quiet without let or stop,
Unknown in court that hath such brackish joys.
In hidden place so let my days forth pass
That, when my years be done withouten noise,
I may die aged after the common trace.
For him death grip'th right hard by the crop
That is much known of other, and of himself, alas,
10 Doth die unknown, dazed, with dreadful face.

L

All in thy sight my life doth whole depend.
Thou hidest thyself and I must die therefore.
But since thou mayst so easily save thy friend,
Why dost thou stick to heal that thou madest sore?
Why do I die since thou mayst me defend?
For if I die, then mayst thou live no more,
Since t'one by t'other doth live and feed the heart,
I with thy sight, thou also with my smart.

LI

For shamefast harm of great and hateful need,
In deep despair as did a wretch go
With ready cord out of his life to speed,
His stumbling foot did find an hoard, lo,
Of gold, I say, where he prepared this deed,
And in exchange he left the cord tho.
He that had hid the gold and found it not,
Of that he found he shaped his neck a knot.

LII

Right true it is and said full yore ago,
'Take heed of him that by thy back thee claweth,'
For none is worse than is a friendly foe.
Though they seem good, all thing that thee delighteth,
Yet know it well that in thy bosom creepeth:
For many a man such fire oft kindleth
That with the blaze his beard singeth.

LIII

Who hath heard of such cruelty before,
That, when my plaint remembered her my woe
That caused it, she, cruel more and more,
Wished each stitch as she did sit and sew
Had pricked mine heart for to increase my sore!
And, as I think, she thought it had been so,
For as she thought, 'This is his heart indeed,'
She pricked hard and made herself to bleed.

LIV

What word is that that changeth not
Though it be turned and made in twain?
It is mine answer, God it wot,
And eke the causer of my pain.
It love rewardeth with disdain,
Yet is it loved. What would ye more?
It is my health eke and my sore.

LV

Sometime I fled the fire that me brent
By sea, by land, by water, and by wind,
And now I follow the coals that be quent
From Dover to Calais, against my mind.
Lo, how desire is both sprung and spent!
And he may see that whilom was so blind,
And all his labour now he laugh to scorn,
Meshed in the briers that erst was all to-torn.

LVI

Th'en'my of life, decayer of all kind,
That with his cold withers away the green,
This other night me in my bed did find
And offered me to rid my fever clean,
And I did grant, so did despair me blind.
He drew his bow with arrow sharp and keen
And strake the place where love had hit before
And drave the first dart deeper more and more.

LVII

Nature that gave the bee so feat a grace
To find honey of so wondrous fashion
Hath taught the spider out of the same place
To fetch poison, by strange alteration.
Though this be strange, it is a stranger case
With one kiss, by secret operation,
Both these at once in those your lips to find,
In change whereof I leave my heart behind.

LVIII

Desire, alas, my master and my foe,
So sore altered, thyself how mayst thou see?
Sometime I sought that drives me to and fro;
Sometime thou ledst that leadeth thee and me.
What reason is to rule thy subjects so
By forced law and mutability?
For where by thee I doubted to have blame,
Even now by hate again I doubt the same.

LIX

I lead a life unpleasant, nothing glad.
Cry and complaint afar voids joyfulness.
Sore chargeth me unrest that naught shall fade.
Pain and despite hath altered pleasantness.
Ago long, since that she hath truly made
Disdain for truth, set light is steadfastness.
I have cause good to sing this song.
Plain or rejoice who feeleth weal or wrong.

LX

Tagus, farewell, that westward with thy streams
Turns up the grains of gold already tried,
With spur and sail for I go seek the Thames,
Gainward the sun that shew'th her wealthy pride
And, to the town which Brutus sought by dreams,
Like bended moon doth lend her lusty side.
My king, my country, alone for whom I live,
Of mighty love the wings for this me give.

LXI

Of purpose Love chose first for to be blind,
For he with sight of that that I behold
Vanquished had been against all godly kind.
His bow your hand and truss should have unfold
And he with me to serve had been assigned.
But for he blind and reckless would him hold
And still by chance his deadly strokes bestow,
With such as see I serve and suffer woe.

LXII

Sighs are my food, drink are my tears;
Clinking of fetters such music would crave.
Stink and close air away my life wears.
Innocency is all the hope I have.
Rain, wind, or weather I judge by mine ears.
Malice assaulted that righteousness should save.
Sure I am, Brian, this wound shall heal again
But yet, alas, the scar shall still remain.

LXIII

A lady gave me a gift she had not
And I received her gift which I took not.
She gave it willingly, yet she would not;
And I received it, albeit I could not.
If she gave it me, I force not.
If she take again, she cares not.
Construe what is this and tell not,
For I am fast sworn I may not.

LXIV

Driven by desire, I did this deed,
To danger myself without cause why,
To trust the untrue, not like to speed,
To speak and promise faithfully.
But now the proof doth verify
That whoso trusteth ere he know
Doth hurt himself and please his foe.

LXV

The fruit of all the service that I serve
Despair doth reap, such hapless hap have I.
But though he have no power to make me swerve,
Yet by the fire for cold I feel I die,
In paradise for hunger still I sterve,
And in the flood for thirst to death I dry.
So Tantalus am I and in worse pain,
Amidst my help that helpless doth remain.

LXVI

Accused though I be without desert,
None can it prove, yet ye believe it true.
Nor never yet, since that ye had my heart,
Entended I to be false or untrue.
Sooner I would of death sustain the smart
Than break one thing of that I promised you.
Accept therefore my service in good part.
None is alive that ill tongues can eschew.
Hold them as false and let not us depart
10 Our friendship old in hope of any new.
Put not thy trust in such as use to feign
Except thou mind to put thy friends to pain.

LXVII

A face that should content me wondrous well
Should not be fair but comely to behold,
With gladsome look all grief for to expel,
With sober cheer so would I that it should
Speak, without words, such words that none can tell.
The tress also should be of crisped gold.
With wit, and these, might chance I might be tied
And knit again the knot that should not slide.

LXVIII

Lucks, my fair falcon, and your fellows all,
How well pleasant it were your liberty!
Ye not forsake me that fair might ye befall.
But they that sometime liked my company
Like lice away from dead bodies they crawl.
Lo, what a proof in light adversity!
But ye, my birds, I swear by all your bells,
Ye be my friends and so be but few else.

LXIX

Within my breast I never thought it gain
Of gentle minds the freedom for to lose.
Nor in my heart sank never such disdain
To be a forger, faults for to disclose.
Nor I cannot endure the truth to gloze,
To set a gloss upon an earnest pain.
Nor am I not in number one of those
That list to blow retreat to every train.

LXX

Throughout the world, if it were sought,
Fair words enough a man shall find.
They be good cheap; they cost right naught;
Their substance is but only wind.
But well to say and so to mean –
That sweet accord is seldom seen.

LXXI

In court to serve, decked with fresh array,
Of sugared meats feeling the sweet repast,
The life in banquets and sundry kinds of play
Amid the press of lordly looks to waste,
Hath with it joined oft-times such bitter taste
That whoso joys such kind of life to hold,
In prison joys, fettered with chains of gold.

LXXII

Speak thou and speed where will or power aught help'th.
Where power doth want, will must be won by wealth.
For need will speed where will works not his kind,
And gain, thy foes thy friends shall cause thee find.
For suit and gold, what do not they obtain?
Of good and bad the tryers are these twain.

Canzoni

LXXIII

Mine old dear en'my, my froward master,
Afore that Queen I caused to be accited
Which holdeth the divine part of nature,
That like as gold in fire he might be tried.
Charged with dolour, there I me presented
With horrible fear, as one that greatly dreadeth
A wrongful death and justice alway seeketh.

And thus I said: 'Once my left foot, Madam,
When I was young I set within his reign;
10 Whereby other than fierily burning flame
I never felt, but many a grievous pain.
Torment I suffered, anger and disdain,
That mine oppressed patience was past
And I mine own life hated at the last.

'Thus hitherto have I my time passed
In pain and smart. What ways profitable,
How many pleasant days have me escaped
In serving this false liar so deceivable?
What wit have words so prest and forcible
20 That may contain my great mishappiness
And just complaints of his ungentleness?

'O small honey, much aloes and gall
In bitterness have my blind life tasted.
His false sweetness, that turneth as a ball,
With the amorous dance have made me traced,
And where I had my thought and mind araced

From all earthly frailness and vain pleasure,
He took me from rest and set me in error.

'He hath made me regard God much less than I ought'
30   And to myself to take right little heed.
And for a woman have I set at naught
All other thoughts, in this only to speed.
And he was only counsellor of this deed,
Always whetting my youthly desire
On the cruel whetstone, tempered with fire.

'But, alas, where now had I ever wit
Or else any other gift given me of nature
That sooner shall change my wearied sprite
Than the obstinate will that is my ruler?
40   So robbeth my liberty with displeasure
This wicked traitor, whom I thus accuse,
That bitter life have turned me in pleasant use.

'He hath chased me thorough diverse regions,
Thorough desert woods and sharp high mountains,
Thorough froward people and strait pressions,
Thorough rocky seas, over hills and plains,
With weary travail and laborous pains,
Always in trouble and in tediousness,
In all error and dangerous distress.

50   'But nother he nor she, my t'other foe,
For all my flight did ever me forsake,
That, though timely death hath been too slow
That as yet it hath me not overtake,
The heavenly goodness of pity do it slake
And not this, his cruel extreme tyranny,
That feedeth him with my care and misery.

'Since I was his, hour rested I never
Nor look for to do, and eke the wakey nights,
The banished sleep may no wise recover.
60   By deceit and by force over my sprites
He is ruler; and since, there never bell strikes

Where I am that I hear not, my plaints to renew.
And he himself, he knoweth that that I say is true.

'For never worms have an old stock eaten
As he my heart where he is alway resident;
And doth the same with death daily threaten.
Thence come the tears and the bitter torment,
The sighs, the words, and eke the languishment
That annoy both me and peradventure other.
70 Judge thou that knowest th'one and th'other.'

Mine adversary with grievous reproof
Thus he began: 'Hear, Lady, th'other part,
That the plain truth from which he draweth aloof,
This unkind man, shall show ere that I part.
In young age I took him from that art
That selleth words and maketh a clattering knight,
And of my wealth I gave him the delight.

'Now shameth he not on me for to complain
That held him evermore in pleasant game
80 From his desire that might have been his pain.
Yet only thereby I brought him to some frame
Which as wretchedness he doth greatly blame.
And toward honour I quickened his wit
Where else as a dastard he might have sit.

'He knoweth that Atrides that made Troy fret,
And Hannibal to Rome so troublous,
Whom Homer honoured, Achilles that great,
And the African, Scipion the famous,
And many other by much virtue glorious,
90 Whose fame and honour did bring them above,
I did let fall in base dishonest love.

'And unto him, though he no deals worthy were,
I chose right the best of many a million,
That under the moon was never her peer
Of wisdom, womanhood, and discretion.
And of my grace I gave her such a fashion,

And eke such a way I taught her for to teach
That never base thought his heart might have reach.

'Evermore thus to content his mistress,
100 That was his only frame of honesty,
I steered him still toward gentleness
And caused him to regard fidelity;
Patience I taught him in adversity.
Such virtues he learned in my great school,
Whereof he repenteth, the ignorant fool.

'These were the deceits and the bitter gall
That I have used, the torment and the anger,
Sweeter than for to enjoy any other in all.
Of right good seed ill fruit I gather
110 And so hath he that th'unkind doth further.
I nourish a serpent under my wing
And of his nature now ginneth he to sting.

'And for to tell at last my great service:
From thousand dishonesties I have him drawn,
That by my means in no manner of wise
Never vile pleasure him hath overthrown,
Where in his deed shame hath him always gnawn,
Doubting report that should come to her ear.
Whom now he accuseth he wonted to fear.

120 'Whatsoever he hath of any honest custom,
Of her and me, that holdeth he every whit.
But lo, there was never nightly phantom
So far in error as he is from his wit
To plain on us: he striveth with the bit
Which may rule him and do him pleasure and pain
And in one hour make all his grief remain.

'But one thing there is above all other:
I gave him wings wherewith he might fly
To honour and fame and, if he would, farther
130 By mortal things above the starry sky.

Considering the pleasure that an eye
Might give in earth by reason of his love,
What should that be that lasteth still above?

'And he the same himself hath said ere this.
But now forgotten is both that and I
That gave her him, his only wealth and bliss.'
And at this word, with deadly shright and cry,
'Thou gave her me,' quod I, 'but by and by
Thou took her straight from me. That woe worth thee!'
140 'Not I,' quod he, 'but price that is well worthy.'

At last both, each for himself concluded,
I trembling, but he with small reverence:
'Lo, thus as we have now each other accused,
Dear Lady, we wait only thy sentence.'
She, smiling after this said audience,
'It liketh me,' quod she, 'to have heard your question,
But longer time doth ask resolution.'

LXXIV

Patience, though I have not
The thing that I require!
I must of force, God wot,
Forbear my most desire
For no ways can I find
To sail against the wind.

Patience, do what they will
To work me woe or spite!
I shall content me still
10 To think both day and night,
To think and hold my peace
Since there is no redress.

Patience, withouten blame,
For I offended naught!
I know they know the same

Though they have changed their thought.
Was ever thought so moved
To hate that it hath loved?

Patience of all my harm
20 For Fortune is my foe!
Patience must be the charm
To heal me of my woe.
Patience without offence
Is a painful patience.

LXXV

[Lover:] Patience for my device,
    Impatience for your part.
    Of contraries the guise
    Must needs be overthwart.
    Patience, for I am true;
    The contrary for you.

[Lady:] Patience, a good cause why!
    Yours hath no cause at all.
    Trust me, that stands awry
10   Perchance may sometime fall.
    'Patience' then say, and sup
    A taste of Patience' cup.

[Lover:] Patience! No force for that,
    Yet brush your gown again.
    Patience! Spurn not thereat
    Lest folks perceive your pain.
    Patience at my pleasure
    When yours hath no measure.

[Lady:] The t'other was for me;
20   This patience is for you:
    Change when ye list, let see,
    For I have ta'en a new.
    Patience with a good will
    Is easy to fulfil.

LXXVI

In Spain

So feeble is the thread that doth the burden stay
Of my poor life, in heavy plight, that falleth in decay,
That but it have elsewhere some aid or some succours,
The running spindle of my fate anon shall end his course.
Since th'unhappy hour that did me to depart
From my sweet weal, one only hope hath stayed my life
    apart,
Which doth persuade such words unto my sorry mind:
'Maintain thyself, O woeful sprite, some better luck to
    find.
For though thou be deprived from thy desired sight,
10 Who can thee tell if thy return be for thy most delight
Or who can tell thy loss if thou once mayst recover?
Some pleasant hour thy woe may rape and thee defend
    and cover.'
That is the trust that yet hath my life sustained,
And now, alas, I see'it faint and I by trust am trained.

The time doth fleet and I perceive th'hours how they
    bend
So fast that I have scant the space to mark my coming end.
Westward the sun from out th'east scant doth shew his
    light,
When in the west he hides him straight within the dark
    of night
And comes as fast where he began his path awry:
20 From east to west, from west to th'east, so doth his
    journey lie.
The life so short, so frail, that mortal men live here,
So great a weight, so heavy charge, the body that we
    bear
That, when I think upon the distance and the space
That doth so far divide me from my dear desired face,

I know not how t'attain the wings that I require
To lift my weight that it might fly to follow my desire.
Thus of that hope that doth my life something sustain,
Alas, I fear, and partly feel, full little doth remain.

Each place doth bring me grief where I do not behold
30 Those lively eyes which of my thoughts were wont the
keys to hold.
Those thoughts were pleasant sweet whilst I enjoyed that
grace.
My pleasure past, my present pain that I might well
embrace!
But for because my want should more my woe increase,
In watch, in sleep, both day and night my will doth
never cease
That thing to wish, whereof, since I did lose the sight,
I never saw the thing that might my faithful heart
delight.
Th'uneasy life I lead doth teach me for to mete
The floods, the seas, the land and hills that doth them
entremete
'Tween me and those shining lights that wonted to
clear
40 My dark pangs of cloudy thoughts as bright as Phoebus'
sphere.
It teacheth me also what was my pleasant state,
The more to feel by such record how that my wealth
doth bate.

If such record, alas, provoke th'inflamed mind
Which sprang that day that I did leave the best of me
behind,
If love forget himself, by length of absence let,
Who doth me guide, O woeful wretch, unto this baited
net
Where doth increase my care? Much better were for me,
As dumb as stone, all thing forgot, still absent for to be.
Alas, the clear crystal, the bright transparent glass,

50 Doth not bewray the colour hid which underneath it
   has,
   As doth th'accumbered sprite thoughtful throes discover
   Of fierce delight, of fervent love, that in our hearts we
   cover.
   Out by these eyes it shew'th that ever more delight
   In plaint and tears to seek redress, and that both day
   and night.

   These new kinds of pleasures wherein most men rejoice,
   To me they do redouble still of stormy sighs the voice,
   For I am one of them whom plaint doth well content:
   It sits me well mine absent wealth, me seems me, to
   lament,
   And with my tears for to'assay to charge mine eyes twain
60 Like as mine heart above the brink is fraughted full of
   pain.
   And for because thereto of those fair eyes to treat
   Do me provoke, I shall return, my plaint thus to repeat;
   For there is nothing else that touches me so within
   Where they rule all, and I alone naught but the case or
   skin.
   Wherefore I do return to them as well or spring
   From whom descends my mortal woe above all other
   thing.
   So shall mine eyes in pain accompany mine heart
   That were the guides that did it lead of love to feel the
   smart.

   The crisped gold that doth surmount Apollo's pride;
70 The lively streams of pleasant stars that under it doth
   glide,
   Wherein the beams of love doth still increase their heat
   Which yet so far touch me so near in cold to make me
   sweat;
   The wise and pleasant talk, so rare or else alone,
   That did me give the courteous gift that such had never
   none –

Be far from me, alas. And every other thing
I might forbear with better will than that that did me
  bring,
With pleasant word and cheer, redress of lingered pain,
And wonted oft in kindled will to virtue me to train.
Thus am I driven to hear and hearken after news;
80 My comfort scant, my large desire in doubtful trust
  renews.

And yet, with more delight to moan my woeful case,
I must complain those hands, those arms that firmly do
  embrace
Me from myself and rule the stern of my poor life,
The sweet disdains, the pleasant wraths, and eke the
  lovely strife
That wonted well to tune, in temper just and meet,
The rage that oft did make me err by furor undiscreet –
All this is hid me fro with sharp and cragged hills.
At other will my long abode my deep despair fulfils.
But if my hope sometime rise up by some redress,
90 It stumbleth straight for feeble faint, my fear hath such
  excess.
Such is the sort of hope, the less for more desire,
Whereby I fear and yet I trust to see that I require:
The resting place of love where virtue lives and grows,
Where I desire my weary life also may take repose.

My song, thou shalt attain to find that pleasant place
Where she doth live by whom I live. May chance thee
  have this grace:
When she hath read and seen the dread wherein I sterve,
Between her breasts she shall thee put; there shall she
  thee reserve.
Then tell her that I come; she shall me shortly see;
100 If that for weight the body fail, this soul shall to her
  flee.

LXXVII

Perdie, I said it not
Nor never thought to do.
As well as I, ye wot
I have no power thereto.
And if I did, the lot
That first did me enchain
Do never slack the knot
But straiter to my pain.

And if I did, each thing
10 That may do harm or woe
Continually may wring
My heart whereso I go.
Report may always ring
Of shame of me for ay
If in my heart did spring
The word that ye do say.

If I said so, each star
That is in heaven above
May frown on me to mar
20 The hope I have in love.
And if I did, such war
As they brought out of Troy
Bring all my life afar
From all this lust and joy.

And if I did so say,
The beauty that me bound
Increase from day to day
More cruel to my wound.
With all the moan that may,
30 To plaint may turn my song.
My life may soon decay,
Without redress, by wrong.

If I be clear fro thought
Why do ye then complain?
Then is this thing but sought
To turn me to more pain.
Then that that ye have wrought
Ye must it now redress.
Of right therefore ye ought
40 Such rigour to repress.

And as I have deserved
So grant me now my hire.
Ye know I never swerved;
Ye never found me liar.
For Rachel have I served,
For Leah cared I never;
And her I have reserved
Within my heart for ever.

LXXVIII

Since Love will needs that I shall love,
Of very force I must agree
And since no chance may it remove
In wealth and in adversity,
I shall alway myself apply
To serve and suffer patiently.

Though for goodwill I find but hate
And cruelty my life to waste
And though that still a wretched state
10 Should pine my days unto the last,
Yet I profess it willingly
To serve and suffer patiently.

For since my heart is bound to serve
And I not ruler of mine own,
Whatso befall till that I sterve,

By proof full well it shall be known
That I shall still myself apply
To serve and suffer patiently.

Yea, though my grief find no redress
20   But still increase before mine eyes,
Though my reward be cruelness
With all the harm hap can devise,
Yet I profess it willingly
To serve and suffer patiently.

Yea, though Fortune her pleasant face
Should show, to set me up aloft,
And straight my wealth for to deface
Should writhe away as she doth oft,
Yet would I still myself apply
30   To serve and suffer patiently.

There is no grief, no smart, no woe
That yet I feel, or after shall,
That from this mind may make me go.
And whatsoever me befall,
I do profess it willingly
To serve and suffer patiently.

Ballades

LXXIX

Resound my voice, ye woods, that hear me plain,
Both hills and vales causing reflection.
And rivers eke record ye of my pain,
Which have ye oft forced by compassion
As judges to hear mine exclamation;
Among whom pity I find doth remain.
Where I it seek, alas, there is disdain.

Oft ye rivers, to hear my woeful sound,
Have stopped your course; and, plainly to express,
10 Many a tear by moisture of the ground
The earth hath wept to hear my heaviness,
Which causeless to suffer without redress
The hugy oaks have roared in the wind:
Each thing me thought complaining in their kind.

Why then, helas, doth not she on me rue?
Or is her heart so hard that no pity
May in it sink, my joy for to renew?
O stony heart, how hath this joined thee,
So cruel that art, cloaked with beauty?
20 No grace to me from thee there may proceed;
But, as rewarded, death for to be my meed.

LXXX

They flee from me that sometime did me seek
With naked foot stalking in my chamber.
I have seen them gentle, tame, and meek

That now are wild and do not remember
That sometime they put themself in danger
To take bread at my hand; and now they range
Busily seeking with a continual change.

Thanked be fortune it hath been otherwise
Twenty times better, but once in special,
10 In thin array after a pleasant guise,
When her loose gown from her shoulders did fall
And she me caught in her arms long and small,
Therewithal sweetly did me kiss
And softly said, 'Dear heart, how like you this?'

It was no dream: I lay broad waking.
But all is turned thorough my gentleness
Into a strange fashion of forsaking.
And I have leave to go of her goodness
And she also to use newfangleness.
20 But since that I so kindly am served
I would fain know what she hath deserved.

LXXXI

The restful place, reviver of my smart,
The labour's salve, increasing my sorrow,
The body's ease and troubler of my heart,
Quieter of mind and my unquiet foe,
Forgetter of pain, remembering my woe,
The place of sleep wherein I do but wake,
Besprent with tears, my bed, I thee forsake.

The frost, the snow, may not redress my heat
Nor yet no heat abate my fervent cold.
10 I know nothing to ease my pains meet:
Each cure causeth increase by twenty fold,
Reviving cares upon my sorrows old.
Such overthwart affects – they do me make,
Besprent with tears, my bed for to forsake.

Yet helpeth it not. I find no better ease
In bed or out. This most causeth my pain:
Where most I seek how best that I may please,
My lost labour, alas, is all in vain
Yet that I gave I cannot call again.
20 No place from me my grief can take,
Wherefore with tears, my bed, I thee forsake.

LXXXII

For want of will in woe I plain
Under colour of soberness,
Renewing with my suit my pain,
My wanhope with your steadfastness.
Awake therefore of gentleness.
Regard at length, I you require,
The swelting pains of my desire.

Betimes who giveth willingly,
Redoubled thanks ay doth deserve.
10 And I that sue unfeignedly,
In fruitless hope, alas, do sterve.
How great my cause is for to swerve
And yet how steadfast is my suit,
Lo, here ye see. Where is the fruit?

As hound that hath his keeper lost
Seek I your presence to obtain
In which my heart delighteth most
And shall delight though I be slain.
You may release my band of pain.
20 Loose then the care that makes me cry
For want of help, or else I die.

I die, though not incontinent,
By process, yet consumingly
As waste of fire which doth relent,
If you as wilful will deny.

Wherefore cease of such cruelty
And take me wholly in your grace
Which lacketh will to change his place.

LXXXIII

LOVER: It burneth yet, alas, my heart's desire.
LADY: What is the thing that hath inflamed thy heart?
LOVER: A certain point, as fervent as the fire.
LADY: The heat shall cease if that thou wilt convert.
LOVER: I cannot stop the fervent raging ire.
LADY: What may I do if thyself cause thy smart?
LOVER: Hear my request and rue my weeping cheer.
LADY: With right good will. Say on. Lo, I thee hear.

LOVER: That thing would I that maketh two content.
10 LADY: Thou seekest, perchance, of me that I may not.
LOVER: Would God thou wouldst, as thou mayst well, assent.
LADY: That I may not. Thy grief is mine, God wot.
LOVER: But I it feel, whatso thy words have meant.
LADY: Suspect me not. My words be not forgot.
LOVER: Then say, alas, shall I have help or no?
LADY: I see no time to answer. Yea. But no.

LOVER: Say yea, dear heart, and stand no more in doubt.
LADY: I may not grant a thing that is so dear.
LOVER: Lo, with delays thou drives me still about.
20 LADY: Thou wouldest my death. It plainly doth appear.
LOVER: First may my heart his blood and life bleed out.
LADY: Then for my sake, alas, thy will forbear.
LOVER: From day to day thus wastes my life away.
LADY: Yet, for the best, suffer some small delay.

LOVER: Now, good, say yea. Do once so good a deed.
LADY: If I said yea, what should thereof ensue?
LOVER: An heart in pain, of succour so should speed.

'Twixt yea and nay my doubt shall still renew.
My sweet, say yea and do away this dread.
30 LADY: Thou wilt needs so. Be it so. But then be true.
LOVER: Naught would I else, nor other treasure none.

Thus hearts be won by love, request, and moan.

LXXXIV

If thou wilt mighty be, flee from the rage
Of cruel will and see thou keep thee free
From the foul yoke of sensual bondage.
For though thy empire stretch to Indian sea
And for thy fear trembleth the farthest Thule,
If thy desire have over thee the power,
Subject then art thou and no governor.

If to be noble and high thy mind be moved,
Consider well thy ground and thy beginning;
10 For he that hath each star in heaven fixed
And gives the moon her horns and her eclipsing,
Alike hath made thee noble in his working,
So that wretched no way thou may be
Except foul lust and vice do conquer thee.

All were it so thou had a flood of gold,
Unto thy thirst yet should it not suffice
And though with Indian stones, a thousand fold
More precious than can thyself devise,
Ycharged were thy back, thy covetise
20 And busy biting yet should never let
Thy wretched life, ne do thy death profit.

LXXXV

It may be good, like it who list.
But I do doubt. Who can me blame?
For oft assured yet have I missed

And now again I fear the same.
The windy words, the eyes' quaint game
Of sudden change maketh me aghast.
For dread to fall I stand not fast.

Alas, I tread an endless maze
That seek to accord two contraries;
10 And hope still, and nothing haze,
Imprisoned in liberties;
As one unheard and still that cries;
Always thirsty yet naught I taste.
For dread to fall I stand not fast.

Assured I doubt I be not sure.
And should I trust to such surety
That oft hath put the proof in ure
And never hath found it trusty?
Nay, sir, in faith it were great folly.
20 And yet my life thus I do waste:
For dread to fall I stand not fast.

LXXXVI

In faith I not well what to say,
Thy chances been so wondrous,
Thou Fortune, with thy diverse play
That causeth joy full dolourous
And eke the same right joyous.
Yet though thy chain hath me enwrapped,
Spite of thy hap, hap hath well happed.

Though thou me set for a wonder
And seekest thy change to do me pain,
10 Men's minds yet may thou not order,
And honesty, an it remain,
Shall shine for all thy cloudy rain.
In vain thou seekest to have me trapped.
Spite of thy hap, hap hath well happed.

In hindering thou diddest further
And made a gap where was a stile.
Cruel wills been oft put under.
Weening to lour thou diddest smile.
Lord! how thyself thou diddest beguile
20 That in thy cares wouldest me have lapped!
But spite of thy hap, hap hath well happed.

LXXXVII

Such hap as I am happed in
Had never man of truth, I ween.
At me Fortune list to begin
To shew that never hath been been –
A new kind of unhappiness.
Nor I cannot the thing I mean
   Myself express.

Myself express my deadly pain,
That can I well if that might serve.
10 But why I have not help again,
That know I not unless I sterve
For hunger still amidst my food –
So granted is that I deserve
   To do me good.

To do me good what may prevail?
For I deserve and not desire
And still of cold I me bewail
And raked am in burning fire.
For though I have – such is my lot –
20 In hand to help that I require,
   It helpeth not.

It helpeth not but to increase
That that by proof can be no more:
That is the heat that cannot cease,
And that I have, to crave so sore.

What wonder is this greedy lust:
To ask and have, and yet therefore
   Refrain I must.

Refrain I must, what is the cause?
30 Sure, as they say, 'So hawks be taught.'
But in my case layeth no such clause
For with such craft I am not caught.
Wherefore I say, and good cause why,
With hapless hand no man hath raught
   Such hap as I.

LXXXVIII

My hope, alas, hath me abused
And vain rejoicing hath me fed.
Lust and joy have me refused
And careful plaint is in their stead.
Too much advancing slacked my speed,
Mirth hath caused my heaviness,
And I remain all comfortless.

Whereto did I assure my thought
Without displeasure steadfastly?
10 In Fortune's forge my joy was wrought
And is revolted readily.
I am mistaken wonderly:
For I thought naught but faithfulness
Yet I remain all comfortless.

In gladsome cheer I did delight
Till that delight did cause my smart
And all was wrong where I thought right:
For right it was that my true heart
Should not from truth be set apart
20 Since truth did cause my hardiness;
Yet I remain all comfortless.

Sometime delight did tune my song
And led my heart full pleasantly;
And to myself I said among,
'My hap is coming hastily.'
But it hath happed contrary:
Assurance caused my distress
And I remain all comfortless.

Then if my note now do vary
30 And leave his wonted pleasantness,
The heavy burden that I carry
Hath altered all my joyfulness.
No pleasure hath still steadfastness,
But haste hath hurt my happiness
And I remain all comfortless.

LXXXIX

Though this thy port and I thy servant true
And thou thyself dost cast thy beams from high
From thy chief house, promising to renew
Both joy and eke delight, behold yet how that I,
Banished from my bliss, carefully do cry,
'Help now, Cytherea my lady dear,
My fearful trust *en voguant la galère*.'

Alas, the doubt that dreadful absence giveth!
Without thine aid assurance is there none.
10 The firm faith that in the water fleeteth
Succour thou therefore; in thee it is alone.
Stay that with faith that faithfully doth moan
And thou also givest me both hope and fear.
Remember thou me *en voguant la galère*.

By seas and hills elonged from thy sight,
Thy wonted grace reducing to my mind,
In stead of sleep thus I occupy the night.

A thousand thoughts and many doubts I find
And still I trust thou canst not be unkind,
20 Or else despair my comfort, and my cheer
Would flee forthwith *en voguant la galère*.

Yet, on my faith, full little doth remain
Of any hope whereby I may myself uphold,
For since that only words do me retain
I may well think thy affection is but cold.
But since my will is nothing as I would
But in thy hands it resteth whole and clear,
Forget me not *en voguant la galère*.

XC

Like as the bird in the cage enclosed,
The door unsparred and the hawk without,
'Twixt death and prison piteously oppressed,
Whether for to choose standeth in doubt –
Certes, so do I, which do seek to bring about
Which should be best by determination,
By loss of life liberty, or life by prison.

O, mischief by mischief to be redressed!
Where pain is the best there lieth little pleasure:
10 By short death out of danger yet to be delivered,
Rather than with painful life, thraldom, and dolour,
For small pleasure much pain to suffer.
Sooner therefore to choose, methinketh it wisdom,
By loss of life liberty than life by prison.

By length of life yet should I suffer,
Awaiting time and Fortune's chance.
Many things happen within an hour:
That which me oppressed may me advance.
In time is trust which by death's grievance
20 Is utterly lost. Then were it not reason
By death to choose liberty, and not life by prison?

But death were deliverance and life length of pain:
Of two ills, let see, now choose the best.
This bird to deliver, you that hear her plain,
Your advice, you lovers, which shall be best:
In cage in thraldom, or by hawk to be oppressed?
And which for to choose make plain conclusion:
By loss of life liberty, or life by prison.

XCI

The knot which first my heart did strain
When that your servant I became
Doth bind me still for to remain
Always your own, as now I am;
And if ye find that I do feign,
With just judgement myself I damn
   To have disdain.

If other thought in me do grow
But still to love you steadfastly,
10 If that the proof do not well show
That I am yours assuredly,
Let every wealth turn me to woe
And you to be continually
   My chiefest foe.

If other love or new request
Do seize my heart but only this,
Or if within my wearied breast
Be hid one thought that mean amiss,
I do desire that mine unrest
20 May still increase and I to miss
   That I love best.

If in my love there be one spot
Of false deceit or doubleness
Or if I mind to slip this knot

By want of faith or steadfastness,
Let all my service be forgot
And, when I would have chief redress,
   Esteem me not.

But if that I consume in pain
30 With burning sighs and fervent love
And daily seek none other gain
But with my deed these words to prove,
Methink of right I should obtain
That ye would mind for to remove
   Your great disdain.

And for the end of this my song,
Unto your hands I do submit
My deadly grief and pains so strong
Which in my heart be firmly shut.
40 And when ye list, redress my wrong
Since well ye know this painful fit
   Hath last too long.

XCII

That time that mirth did steer my ship
Which now is fraught with heaviness,
And Fortune bit not then the lip
But was defence of my distress,
Then in my book wrote my mistress,
'I am yours, you may well be sure,
And shall be while my life doth dure.'

But she herself which then wrote that
Is now mine extreme enemy.
10 Above all men she doth me hate,
Rejoicing of my misery.
But though that for her sake I die,
I shall be hers, she may be sure,
As long as my life doth endure.

It is not time that can wear out
With me that once is firmly set.
While Nature keeps her course about,
My love from her no man can let.
Though never so sore they me threat,
20   Yet am I hers, she may be sure,
And shall be while that life doth dure.

And once I trust to see that day,
Renewer of my joy and wealth,
That she to me these words shall say,
'In faith, welcome to me myself,
Welcome, my joy, welcome, my health,
For I am thine, thou mayst be sure,
And shall be while that life doth dure.'

Ho me, alas, what words were these?
30   In covenant I might find them so!
I reck not what smart or disease,
Torment or trouble, pain or woe
I suffered so that I might know
That she were mine, I might be sure,
And should be while that life doth dure.

XCIII

It was my choice, it was no chance
That brought my heart in other's hold,
Whereby it hath had sufferance
Longer, perdie, than reason would.
Since I it bound where it was free,
Methinks, iwis, of right it should
    Accepted be.

Accepted be without refuse
Unless that Fortune hath the power
10   All right of love for to abuse;

For, as they say, one happy hour
May more prevail than right or might.
If Fortune then list for to lour
   What vaileth right?

What vaileth right if this be true?
Then trust to chance and go by guess.
Then who so loveth may well go sue
Uncertain hope for his redress.
Yet some would say assuredly
20 Thou mayst appeal for thy release
   To fantasy.

To fantasy pertains to choose.
All this I know for fantasy
First into love did me induce.
But yet I know as steadfastly
That if love have no faster knot
So nice a choice slips suddenly.
   It lasteth not.

It lasteth not that stands by change.
30 Fancy doth change, Fortune is frail.
Both these to please, the way is strange.
Therefore, methinks, best to prevail,
There is no way that is so just
As truth to lead though t'other fail,
   And thereto trust.

XCIV

Blame not my lute for he must sound
Of this or that as liketh me.
For lack of wit the lute is bound
To give such tunes as pleaseth me.
Though my songs be somewhat strange
And speaks such words as touch thy change
   Blame not my lute.

My lute, alas, doth not offend
Though that perforce he must agree
10 To sound such tunes as I intend
To sing to them that heareth me.
Then though my songs be somewhat plain
And toucheth some that use to feign
   Blame not my lute.

My lute and strings may not deny
But as I strike they must obey.
Break not them then so wrongfully
But wreak thyself some wiser way.
And though the songs which I indite
20 Do quit thy change with rightful spite
   Blame not my lute.

Spite asketh spite and changing change
And falsed faith must needs be known.
The faults so great, the case so strange
Of right it must abroad be blown.
Then since that by thine own desert
My songs do tell how true thou art
   Blame not my lute.

Blame but thyself that hast misdone
30 And well deserved to have blame.
Change thou thy way so evil begun
And then my lute shall sound that same.
But if till then my fingers play
By thy desert their wonted way
   Blame not my lute.

Farewell, unknown, for though thou break
My strings in spite with great disdain
Yet have I found out for thy sake
Strings for to string my lute again.
40 And if perchance this foolish rhyme
Do make thee blush at any time
   Blame not my lute.

XCV

The joy so short, alas, the pain so near,
The way so long, the departure so smart!
The first sight, alas, I bought too dear
That so suddenly now from hence must part.
The body gone, yet remain shall the heart
With her, which for me salt tears did rain,
And shall not change till that we meet again.

Though time doth pass, yet shall not my love.
Though I be far, always my heart is near.
10 Though other change, yet will not I remove.
Though other care not, yet love I will and fear.
Though other hate, yet will I love my dear.
Though other will of lightness say adieu,
Yet will I be found steadfast and true.

When other laugh, alas, then do I weep.
When other sing, then do I wail and cry.
When other run, perforced I am to creep.
When other dance, in sorrow I do lie.
When other joy, for pain well near I die.
20 Thus brought from wealth, alas, to endless pain,
That undeserved, causeless to remain.

Songs (1)

XCVI

Madam, withouten many words
Once I am sure ye will or no.
And if ye will then leave your bourds
And use your wit and shew it so

And with a beck ye shall me call.
And if of one that burneth alway
Ye have any pity at all
Answer him fair with yea or nay.

If it be yea I shall be fain.
10 If it be nay friends as before.
Ye shall another man obtain
And I mine own and yours no more.

XCVII

Where shall I have at mine own will
Tears to complain? Where shall I fet
Such sighs that I may sigh my fill
And then again my plaints repeat?

For though my plaint shall have none end
My tears cannot suffice my woe.
To moan my harm have I no friend
For Fortune's friend is Mishap's foe.

 Comfort, God wot, else have I none
10 But in the wind to waste my words.
 Nought moveth you my deadly moan
 But all you turn it into bourds.

 I speak not now to move your heart
 That you should rue upon my pain.
 The sentence given may not revert.
 I know such labour were but vain.

 But since that I for you, my dear,
 Have lost that thing that was my best,
 A right small loss it must appear
20 To leese these words and all the rest.

 But though they sparkle in the wind
 Yet shall they show your falsed faith
 Which is returned unto his kind,
 For 'like to like' the proverb saith.

 Fortune and you did me advance.
 Methought I swam and could not drown –
 Happiest of all – but my mischance
 Did lift me up to throw me down.

 And you with your own cruelness
30 Did set your foot upon my neck,
 Me and my welfare to oppress,
 Without offence your heart to wreck.

 Where are your pleasant words, alas,
 Where your faith, your steadfastness?
 There is no more but all doth pass
 And I am left all comfortless.

 But for because it doth you grieve
 And also me my wretched life,
 Have here my truth: shall naught relieve
40 But death alone my weary strife.

Therefore, farewell, my life, my death,
My gain, my loss, my salve, my sore.
Farewell also, with you, my breath
For I am gone for evermore.

XCVIII

Like as the swan towards her death
Doth strain her voice with doleful note,
Right so sing I with waste of breath,
'I die! I die! and you regard it not.'

I shall enforce my fainting breath
That all that hears this deadly note
Shall know that you doth cause my death.
'I die! I die! and you regard it not.'

Your unkindness hath sworn my death
10 And changed hath my pleasant note
To painful sighs that stops my breath.
'I die! I die! and you regard it not.'

Consumeth my life, faileth my breath.
Your fault is forger of this note,
Melting in tears a cruel death.
'I die! I die! and you regard it not.'

My faith with me after my death
Buried shall be, and to this note
I do bequeath my weary breath
20 To cry 'I died and you regarded not.'

XCIX

Heaven and earth and all that hear me plain
Do well perceive what care doth cause me cry,
Save you alone to whom I cry in vain,
'Mercy, madam, alas, I die, I die!'

If that you sleep I humbly you require
Forbear a while and let your rigour slake –
Since that by you I burn thus in this fire –
To hear my plaint, 'Dear heart, awake, awake!'

Since that so oft ye have made me to wake
10 In plaint and tears and in right piteous case,
Displease you not if force do now me make
To break your sleep, crying 'Alas, alas!'

It is the last trouble that ye shall have
Of me, madam, to hear my last complaint.
Pity at least your poor unhappy slave
For in despair, alas, I faint, I faint!

It is not now but long and long ago
I have you served as to my power and might
As faithfully as any man might do,
20 Claiming of you nothing of right, of right,

Save of your grace only to stay my life
That fleeth as fast as cloud afore the wind;
For since that first I entered in this strife
An inward death hath fret my mind, my mind.

If I had suffered this to you unware
Mine were the fault and you nothing to blame.
But since you know my woe and all my care,
Why do I die, alas? For shame, for shame!

I know right well my face, my look, my tears,
30 Mine eyes, my words, and eke my dreary cheer
Have cried my death full oft unto your ears.
Hard of belief it doth appear, appear.

A better proof I see that you would have
How I am dead. Therefore when ye hear tell,
Believe it not although ye see my grave.
Cruel, unkind! I say, 'Farewell, farewell!'

C

Process of time worketh such wonder
That water which is of kind so soft
Doth pierce the marble stone asunder
By little drops falling from aloft.

And yet an heart that seems so tender
Receiveth no drop of the stilling tears
That alway still cause me to render
The vain plaint that sounds not in her ears.

So cruel, alas, is naught alive,
10 So fierce, so froward, so out of frame,
But some way, some time may so contrive
By means the wild to temper and tame.

And I that always have sought and seek
Each place, each time, for some lucky day,
This fierce tiger, less I find her meek
And more denied the longer I pray.

The lion in his raging furor
Forbears that sueth meekness, for his boot;
And thou, alas, in extreme dolour
20 The heart so low thou treads under foot.

Each fierce thing, lo, how thou dost exceed
And hides it under so humble a face.
And yet the humble to help at need –
Naught helpeth time, humbleness, nor place.

CI

To seek each where where man doth live –
The sea, the land, the rock, the clive,
France, Spain, and Ind, and everywhere –
Is none a greater gift to give,
Less set by oft, and is so lief and dear,
Dare I well say, than that I give to year.

I cannot give brooches nor rings –
These goldsmiths' work and goodly things –
Perrie nor pearl, orient and clear.
10 But for all that is, no man brings
Liefer jewel unto his lady dear,
Dare I well say, than that I give to year.

Nor I seek not to fetch it far;
Worse is it not though it be nar.
And as it is it doth appear,
Uncounterfeit, mistrust to bar,
Left whole and pure withouten peer,
Dare I well say, the gift I give to year.

To thee therefore the same retain.
20 The like of thee to have again
France would I give if mine it were.
Is none alive in whom doth reign
Lesser disdain. Freely therefore, lo, here
Dare I well give, I say, my heart to year.

CII

[Argument:] Most wretched heart, most miserable,
Since the comfort is from thee fled,
Since all the truth is turned to fable,
Most wretched heart, why art thou not
dead?

[Reply:] No, no, I live and must do still
Whereof I thank God and no moe,
For I myself have at my will
And he is wretched that weens him so.

[Argument:] But yet thou hast both had and lost
10 The hope so long that hath thee fed,
And all thy travail and thy cost.
Most wretched heart, why art thou not
dead?

[Reply:]   Some other hope must feed me new.
                  If I have lost, I say 'What though?'
                  Despair shall not through it ensue
                  For he is wretched that weens him so.

[Argument:]   The sun, the moon doth frown on thee.
                  Thou hast darkness in daylight's stead.
                  As good in grave as so to be.
20   Most wretched heart, why art thou not
                     dead?

[Reply:]   Some pleasant star may show me light.
                  But though the heaven would work me
                     woe,
                  Who hath himself shall stand upright
                  And he is wretched that weens him so.

[Argument:]   Hath he himself that is not sure?
                  His trust is like as he hath sped.
                  Against the stream thou mayst not dure.
                  Most wretched heart, why art thou not
                     dead?

[Reply:]   The last is worst. Who fears not that,
30   He hath himself whereso he go.
                  And he that knoweth what is what
                  Saith he is wretched that weens him so.

[Argument:]   Seest thou not how they whet their teeth
                  Which to touch thee sometime did dread?
                  They find comfort for thy mischief.
                  Most wretched heart, why art thou not
                     dead?

[Reply:]   What though that curs do fall by kind
                  On him that hath the overthrow?
                  All that cannot oppress my mind
40   For he is wretched that weens him so.

[Argument:] Yet can it not be then denied.
It is as certain as thy creed.
Thy great unhap thou canst not hide.
Unhappy then, why art thou not dead?

[Reply:] Unhappy, but no wretch therefore,
For hap doth come again and go;
For which I keep myself in store
Since unhap cannot kill me so.

CIII

What means this when I lie alone?
I toss, I turn, I sigh, I groan.
My bed me seems as hard as stone.
    What means this?

I sigh, I plain continually.
The clothes that on my bed do lie
Always methink they lie awry.
    What means this?

In slumbers oft for fear I quake.
10 For heat and cold I burn and shake.
For lack of sleep my head doth ache.
    What means this?

A mornings then when I do rise
I turn unto my wonted guise,
All day after muse and devise.
    What means this?

And if perchance by me there pass
She unto whom I sue for grace,
The cold blood forsaketh my face.
20   What means this?

But if I sit near her by
With loud voice my heart doth cry
And yet my mouth is dumb and dry.
    What means this?

To ask for help no heart I have.
My tongue doth fail what I should crave.
Yet inwardly I rage and rave.
    What means this?

Thus have I passed many a year
30 And many a day, though naught appear
But most of that that most I fear.
    What means this?

CIV

When first mine eyes did view and mark
Thy fair beauty to behold
And when mine ears listened to hark
The pleasant words that thou me told,
I would as then I had been free
From ears to hear and eyes to see.

And when my lips gan first to move,
Whereby my heart to thee was known,
And when my tongue did talk of love
10 To thee that hast true love down thrown,
I would my lips and tongue also
Had then been dumb, no deal to go.

And when my hands have handled aught
That thee hath kept in memory
And when my feet have gone and sought
To find and get thy company,
I would each hand a foot had been
And I each foot a hand had seen.

And when in mind I did consent
20 To follow this my fancy's will
And when my heart did first relent
To taste such bait my life to spill,
I would my heart had been as thine
Or else thy heart had been as mine.

CV

Farewell, the reign of cruelty!
Though that with pain my liberty
Dear have I bought, yet shall surety
Conduct my thought of joys needy.

Of force I must forsake pleasure –
A good cause, just, since I endure
Thereby my woe which be ye sure
Shall therewith go, me to recure.

I fare as one escaped that fleeth:
10 Glad he is gone yet still feareth,
Spied, to be caught, and so dreadeth
That he for naught his pain leeseth.

In joyful pain rejoice, mine heart,
Thus to sustain of each a part.
Let not this song from thee astart,
Welcome among my pleasant smart.

CVI

Though I cannot your cruelty constrain
For my goodwill to favour me again,
Though my true and faithful love
Have no power your heart to move,
   Yet rue upon my pain.

Though I your thrall must evermore remain
And for your sake my liberty restrain,
The greatest grace that I do crave
Is that ye would vouchsafe
10   To rue upon my pain.

Though I have not deserved to obtain
So high reward, but thus to serve in vain,

Though I shall have no redress,
Yet of right ye can no less
  But rue upon my pain.

But I see well that your high disdain
Will no wise grant that I shall more attain.
Yet ye must grant at the least
This my poor and small request:
20   Rejoice not at my pain.

CVII

To wish and want and not obtain,
To seek and sue ease of my pain,
Since all that ever I do is vain
  What may it avail me?

Although I strive both day and hour
Against the stream with all my power,
If fortune list yet for to lour
  What may it avail me?

If willingly I suffer woe,
10 If from the fire me list not go,
If then I burn to plain me so,
  What may it avail me?

And if the harm that I suffer
Be run too far out of measure,
To seek for help any further
  What may it avail me?

What though each heart that heareth me plain
Pityeth and plaineth for my pain,
If I no less in grief remain
20   What may it avail me?

Yea, though the want of my relief
Displease the causer of my grief,
Since I remain still in mischief
  What may it avail me?

Such cruel chance doth so me threat
Continually inward to fret.
Then of release for to treat
    What may it avail me?

Fortune is deaf unto my call.
30 My torment moveth her not at all.
And though she turn as doth a ball
    What may it avail me?

For in despair there is no rede.
To want of ear speech is no speed.
To linger still alive as dead
    What may it avail me?

CVIII

Once, as methought, Fortune me kissed
And bade me ask what I thought best
And I should have it as me list,
Therewith to set my heart in rest.

I asked naught but my dear heart
To have for evermore mine own.
Then at an end were all my smart.
Then should I need no more to moan.

Yet for all that, a stormy blast
10 Had overturned this goodly day
And Fortune seemed at the last
That to her promise she said nay.

But like as one out of despair
To sudden hope revived I:
Now Fortune sheweth herself so fair
That I content me wonderly.

My most desire my hand may reach.
My will is alway at my hand.
Me need not long for to beseech
20 Her that hath power me to command.

What earthly thing more can I crave?
What would I wish more at my will?
Nothing on earth more would I have
Save, that I have, to have it still.

For Fortune hath kept her promise
In granting me my most desire:
Of my sufferance I have redress
And I content me with my hire.

CIX

My lute, awake! Perform the last
Labour that thou and I shall waste,
And end that I have now begun;
For when this song is sung and past,
My lute, be still for I have done.

As to be heard where ear is none,
As lead to grave in marble stone,
My song may pierce her heart as soon.
Should we then sigh or sing or moan?
10 No, no, my lute, for I have done.

The rocks do not so cruelly
Repulse the waves continually
As she my suit and affection,
So that I am past remedy,
Whereby my lute and I have done.

Proud of the spoil that thou hast got
Of simple hearts thorough Love's shot
By whom, unkind, thou hast them won,
Think not he hath his bow forgot
20 Although my lute and I have done.

Vengeance shall fall on thy disdain
That makest but game on earnest pain.
Think not alone under the sun
Unquit to cause thy lovers plain
Although my lute and I have done.

May chance thee lie withered and old
The winter nights that are so cold,
Plaining in vain unto the moon.
Thy wishes then dare not be told.
30 Care then who list for I have done.

And then may chance thee to repent
The time that thou hast lost and spent
To cause thy lovers sigh and swoon.
Then shalt thou know beauty but lent
And wish and want as I have done.

Now cease, my lute. This is the last
Labour that thou and I shall waste
And ended is that we begun.
Now is this song both sung and past.
40 My lute, be still, for I have done.

CX

I have sought long with steadfastness
To have had some ease of my great smart
But naught availeth faithfulness
To grave within your stony heart.

But hap and hit or else hit not
As uncertain as is the wind:
Right so it fareth by the shot
Of Love, alas, that is so blind.

Therefore I played the fool in vain
10 With pity when I first began
Your cruel heart for to constrain,
Since love regardeth no doleful man.

But of your goodness all your mind
Is that I should complain in vain.
This is the favour that I find:
Ye list to hear how I can plain.

But though I plain to please your heart,
Trust me I trust to temper it so
Not for to care which do revert:
20 All shall be one in wealth or woe.

For fancy ruleth though right say nay,
Even as the good man kissed his cow:
None other reason can ye lay
But as who sayeth, 'I reck not how.'

CXI

In aeternum I was once determed
For to have loved, and my mind affirmed
That with my heart it should be confirmed
  In aeternum.

Forthwith I found the thing that I might like
And sought with love to warm her heart alike,
For as me thought I should not see the like
  In aeternum.

To trace this dance I put myself in press.
10 Vain hope did lead and bade I should not cease
To serve, to suffer, and still to hold my peace
  In aeternum.

With this first rule I furthered me apace
That, as methought, my troth had taken place
With full assurance to stand in her grace
  In aeternum.

It was not long ere I by proof had found
That feeble building is on feeble ground;
For in her heart this word did never sound:
20 *In aeternum.*

In aeternum then from my heart I cast
That I had first determined for the best.
Now in the place another thought doth rest
  In aeternum.

CXII

Comfort thyself, my woeful heart,
Or shortly on thyself thee wreak,
For length redoubleth deadly smart.
Why sighs thou, heart, and wilt not break?

To waste in sighs were piteous death.
Alas, I find thee faint and weak.
Enforce thyself to lose thy breath.
Why sighs thou then and wilt not break?

Thou knowest right well that no redress
10   Is thus to pine; and for to speak,
Perdie, it is remedyless.
Why sighs thou then and wilt not break?

It is too late for to refuse
The yoke when it is on thy neck.
To shake it off vaileth not to muse.
Why sighs thou then and wilt not break?

To sob and sigh it were but vain
Since there is none that doth it reck.
Alas, thou dost prolong thy pain.
20   Why sighs thou then and wilt not break?

Then in her sight, to move her heart,
Seek on thyself thyself to wreak
That she may know thou suffered'st smart.
Sigh there thy last and therewith break.

CXIII

To cause accord or to agree
Two contraries in one degree
And in one point, as seemeth me,
To all man's wit it cannot be.
    It is impossible.

Of heat and cold when I complain
And say that heat doth cause my pain
When cold doth shake my every vein,
And both at once, I say again
10   It is impossible.

That man that hath his heart away,
If life liveth there, as men do say,
That he heartless should last one day
Alive and not to turn to clay
    It is impossible.

'Twixt life and death, say what who saith,
There liveth no life that draweth breath,
They join so near. And eke i'faith
To seek for life by wish of death
20   It is impossible.

Yet love that all thing doth subdue,
Whose power there may no life eschew,
Hath wrought in me that I may rue
These miracles to be so true
    That are impossible.

CXIV

After great storms the calm returns
And pleasanter it is thereby.
Fortune likewise that often turns
Hath made me now the most happy.

Th'heaven that pitied my distress,
My just desire, and my cry
Hath made my languor to cease
And me also the most happy.

Whereto despaired ye, my friends?
10 My trust alway in him did lie
That knoweth what my thought intends,
Whereby I live the most happy.

Lo, what can take hope from that heart
That is assured steadfastly?
Hope therefore ye that live in smart,
Whereby I am the most happy.

And I that have felt of your pain
Shall pray to God continually
To make your hope your health retain
20 And me also the most happy.

CXV

[The man:] Th'answer that ye made to me, my dear,
When I did sue for my poor heart's redress,
Hath so appalled my countenance and my
cheer
That in this case I am all comfortless
Since I of blame no cause can well express.

I have no wrong where I can claim no
right.
Naught ta'en me fro where I nothing have
had.
Yet of my woe I cannot so be quit,
Namely, since that another may be glad
10 With that that thus in sorrow maketh me
sad.

[The lady:] Another? Why shall liberty be bound?
Free heart may not be bound but by desert.

[The man:] Nor none can claim, I say, by former grant
That knoweth not of any grant at all.
But by desert I dare well make avaunt:
Of faithful will there is nowhere that shall
Bear you more troth, more ready at your
call.

Now, good, then call again that friendly
    word
That slay'th your friend in saving of his
    pain,
20   And say, my dear, that it was said in bourd.
Late or too soon let that not rule the gain
Wherewith free will doth true desert retain.

CXVI

Prove whether I do change, my dear,
Or if that I do still remain
Like as I went, or far or near,
And if ye find ...

CXVII

What rage is this? What furor of what kind?
What pow'r, what plague doth weary thus my mind?
Within my bones to rankle is assigned
    What poison pleasant sweet?

Lo, see mine eyes swell with continual tears.
The body still away sleepless it wears.
My food nothing my fainting strength repairs
    Nor doth my limbs sustain.

In deep wide wound the deadly stroke doth turn,
10   To cured scar that never shall return.
Go to, triumph, rejoice thy goodly turn.
    Thy friend thou dost oppress.

Oppress thou dost, and hast of him no cure,
Nor yet my plaint no pity can procure.
Fierce tiger fell, hard rock without recure,
    Cruel rebel to love!

Once may thou love, never be loved again:
So love thou still and not thy love obtain.
So wrathful Love with spites of just disdain
20   May threat thy cruel heart.

CXVIII

Take heed betime lest ye be spied.
Your loving eyes ye cannot hide.
At last the truth will sure be tried.
    Therefore take heed!

For some there be of crafty kind,
Though you show no part of your mind,
Surely their eyes ye cannot blind.
    Therefore take heed!

For in like case theirselves hath been
10 And thought right sure none had them seen.
But it was not as they did ween.
    Therefore take heed!

Although they be of diverse schools
And well can use all crafty tools,
At length they prove themselves but fools.
    Therefore take heed!

If they might take you in that trap
They would soon leave it in your lap.
To love unspied is but a hap.
20   Therefore take heed!

CXIX

Alas, poor man, what hap have I
That must forbear that I love best?
I trow it be my destiny
Never to live in quiet rest.

No wonder is though I complain,
Not without cause ye may be sure.
I seek for that I cannot attain,
Which is my mortal displeasure.

Alas, poor heart, as in this case
10 With pensive plaints thou art oppressed,
Unwise thou were to desire place
Whereas another is possessed.

Do what I can to ease thy smart
Thou wilt not let to love her still.
Hers and not mine I see thou art.
Let her do by thee as she will.

A careful carcass full of pain
Now hast thou left to mourn for thee:
The heart once gone, the body is slain.
20 That ever I saw her, woe is me.

Mine eye, alas, was cause of this,
Which her to see had never his fill.
To me that sight full bitter is
In recompense of my goodwill.

She that I serve all other above
Hath paid my hire as ye may see.
I was unhappy, and that I prove,
To love above my poor degree.

CXX

So unwarely was never no man caught
With steadfast look upon a goodly face
As I of late; for suddenly methought
My heart was torn out of his place.

Thorough mine eye the stroke from hers did slide.
Directly down unto my heart it ran
In help whereof the blood thereto did glide
And left my face both pale and wan.

Then was I like a man for woe amazed
10 Or like the bird that flyeth into the fire;
For while that I upon her beauty gazed
The more I burnt in my desire.

Anon the blood stert in my face again,
Inflamed with heat that it had at my heart,
And brought therewith throughout in every vein
A quaking heat with pleasant smart.

Then was I like the straw when that the flame
Is driven therein by force and rage of wind.
I cannot tell, alas, what I shall blame
20 Nor what to seek nor what to find.

But well I wot the grief holds me so sore
In heat and cold, betwixt hope and dread,
That but her help to health doth me restore,
This restless life I may not lead.

CXXI

Since you will needs that I shall sing,
Take it in worth such as I have:
Plenty of plaint, moan, and mourning,
In deep despair and deadly pain,
Bootless for boot, crying to crave,
    To crave in vain.

Such hammers work within my head
That sound naught else unto my ears
But fast at board and wake abed;
10 Such tune the temper to my song
To wail my wrong, that I want tears
    To wail my wrong.

Death and despair afore my face,
My days decay, my grief doth grow;
The cause thereof is in this place,

Whom cruelty doth still constrain
For to rejoice though it be woe
   To hear me plain.

    A broken lute, untuned strings
20 With such a song may well bear part,
That neither pleaseth him that sings
Nor them that hear, but her alone
That with her heart would strain my heart
   To hear it groan.

If it grieve you to hear this same
That you do feel but in my voice,
Consider then what pleasant game
I do sustain in every part
To cause me sing or to rejoice
30   Within my heart.

CXXII

Live thou gladly if so thou may.
Pine not thou in looking for me
Since that despair hath shut the way
Thou to see me or I to see thee.

Make thou a virtue of a constraint.
Deem no fault where none is worthy.
Min is too much. What needs thy plaint?
God, he knoweth who is for me.

Cast upon the Lord thy cure.
10 Pray unto him thy cause to judge.
Believe, and he shall send recure.
Vain is all trust of man's refuge.

CXXIII

V. Innocentia
Veritas Viat Fides
Circumdederunt me inimici mei

Who list his wealth and ease retain,
Himself let him unknown contain.
Press not too fast in at that gate
Where the return stands by disdain,
For sure, *circa Regna tonat.*

The high mountains are blasted oft
When the low valley is mild and soft.
Fortune with Health stands at debate.
The fall is grievous from aloft.
10 And sure, *circa Regna tonat.*

These bloody days have broken my heart.
My lust, my youth did them depart,
And blind desire of estate.
Who hastes to climb seeks to revert.
Of truth, *circa Regna tonat.*

The bell tower showed me such sight
That in my head sticks day and night.
There did I learn out of a grate,
For all favour, glory, or might,
20 That yet *circa Regna tonat.*

By proof, I say, there did I learn:
Wit helpeth not defence too yerne,
Of innocency to plead or prate.
Bear low, therefore, give God the stern,
For sure, *circa Regna tonat.*

CXXIV

Disdain me not without desert
Ne leave me not so suddenly.
Sith well ye wot that in my heart
I mean it not but honestly,
   Refuse me not.

Refuse me not without cause why
Ne think me not to be unjust.
Sith that by lot of fantasy
The careful knot needs knit I must,
10   Mistrust me not.

Mistrust me not though some there be
That fain would spot my steadfastness.
Believe them not sith well ye see
The proof is not as they express.
   Forsake me not.

Forsake me not till I deserve
Ne hate me not till I offend.
Destroy me not till that I swerve.
Sith ye well wot what I intend
20   Disdain me not.

Disdain me not that am your own.
Refuse me not that am so true.
Mistrust me not till all be known.
Forsake me not now for no new.
   Thus leave me not.

CXXV

Sufficed not, madam, that you did tear
My woeful heart, but thus also to rent
The weeping paper that to you I sent
Whereof each letter was written with a tear?

Could not my present pains, alas, suffice
Your greedy heart, and that my heart doth feel
Torments that prick more sharper than the steel,
But new and new must to my lot arise?

Use then my death. So shall your cruelty,
10 Spite of your spite, rid me from all my smart
And I no more such torments of the heart
Feel as I do. This shalt thou gain thereby.

CXXVI

I see that chance hath chosen me
Thus secretly to live in pain
And to another given the fee,
Of all my loss to have the gain.
By chance assigned, thus do I serve,
And other have that I deserve.

Unto myself sometime alone
I do lament my woeful case.
But what availeth me to moan
10 Since truth and pity hath no place
In them to whom I sue and serve,
And other have that I deserve?

To seek by mean to change this mind,
Alas, I prove it will not be;
For in my heart I cannot find
Once to refrain, but still agree,
As bound by force, alway to serve,
And other have that I deserve.

Such is the fortune that I have
20 To love them most that love me least
And to my pain to seek and crave
The thing that other have possessed.
So thus in vain alway I serve,
And other have that I deserve.

And till I may appease the heat –
If that my hap will hap so well –
To wail my woe my heart shall fret
Whose pensive pain my tongue can tell.
Yet thus unhappy must I serve,
30 And other have that I deserve.

Songs (2)

CXXVII

If fancy would favour
As I deserve and shall,
My love, my paramour,
Should love me best of all.

But if I cannot attain
The grace that I desire
Then may I well complain
My service and my hire.

Fancy doth know how
10 To further my true heart
If fancy might avow
With faith for to take part.

But fancy is so frail
And flitting still so fast
That faith may not prevail
To help me first nor last.

For fancy at his lust
Doth rule all but by guess.
Whereto should I then trust
20 In truth or steadfastness?

Yet gladly would I please
The fancy of her heart
That may me only ease
And cure my careful smart.

Therefore, my lady dear,
Set once your fantasy
To make some hope appear
Of steadfast remedy.

For if he be my friend
30 And undertake my woe
My grief is at an end –
If he continue so.

Else fancy doth not right,
As I deserve and shall
To have you day and night
To love me best of all.

CXXVIII

At most mischief
I suffer grief,
For of relief
Since I have none
My lute and I
Continually
Shall us apply
To sigh and moan.

Naught may prevail
10 To weep or wail.
Pity doth fail
In you, alas.
Mourning or moan,
Complaint or none,
It is all one
As in this case.

For cruelty
Most that can be
Hath sovereignty
20 Within your heart,

Which maketh bare
All my welfare.
Naught do ye care
How sore I smart.

No tiger's heart
Is so pervert
Without desert
To wreak his ire.
And you me kill
30 For my good will!
Lo, how I spill
For my desire!

There is no love
That can ye move
And I can prove
None other way.
Therefore I must
Restrain my lust,
Banish my trust
40 And wealth away.

Thus in mischief
I suffer grief,
For of relief
Since I have none
My lute and I
Continually
Shall us apply
To sigh and moan.

CXXIX

Marvel no more although
The songs I sing do moan,
For other life than woe
I never proved none.
And in my heart also

Is graven with letters deep
A thousand sighs and moe,
A flood of tears to weep.

How may a man in smart
10   Find matter to rejoice?
How may a mourning heart
Set forth a pleasant voice?
Play who that can the part;
Needs must in me appear
How fortune overthwart
Doth cause my mourning cheer.

Perdie, there is no man,
If he never saw sight,
That perfectly tell can
20   The nature of the light.
Alas, how should I then,
That never tasted but sour,
But do as I began –
Continually to lour?

But yet perchance some chance
May chance to change my tune.
And when such chance doth chance
Then shall I thank Fortune –
And if I have such chance
30   Perchance ere it be long –
For such a pleasant chance
To sing some pleasant song.

CXXX

If chance assigned
Were to my mind
By very kind
Of destiny,
Yet would I crave
Naught else to have
But only life and liberty.

Then were I sure
I might endure
10 The displeasure
Of cruelty;
Where now I plain,
Alas, in vain,
Lacking my life for liberty.

For without th'one
Th'other is gone
And there can none
It remedy.
If th'one be past
20 Th'other doth waste
And all for lack of liberty.

And so I drive
As yet alive
Although I strive
With misery,
Drawing my breath,
Looking for death
And loss of life for liberty.

But thou that still
30 Mayst at thy will
Turn all this ill
Adversity,
For the repair
Of my welfare
Grant me but life and liberty.

And if not so
Then let all go
To wretched woe
And let me die.
40 For th'one or th'other,
There is none other –
My death, or life with liberty.

CXXXI

Since ye delight to know
That my torment and woe
 Should still increase
 Without release,
I shall enforce me so
That life and all shall go
For to content your cruelness.

And so this grievous train
That I too long sustain
10   Shall sometime cease
 And have redress
And you also remain
Full pleased with my pain
For to content your cruelness.

Unless that be too light
And that ye would ye might
 See the distress
 And heaviness
Of one yslain outright,
20   Therewith to please your sight
And to content your cruelness.

Then in your cruel mood
Would God forthwith ye would
 With force express
 My heart oppress
To do your heart such good
To see me bathe in blood
For to content your cruelness!

Then could ye ask no more.
30   Then should ye ease my sore
 And the excess
 Of mine excess.

And you should evermore
Defamed be therefore
For to repent your cruelness.

CXXXII

Lo, what it is to love!
Learn ye, that list to prove,
    At me, I say,
    No ways that may
The grounded grief remove.
    My life alway
    That doth decay –
Lo, what it is to love!

Flee alway from the snare.
10   Learn by me to beware
    Of such a train
    Which doubles pain.
And endless woe and care
    That doth retain,
    Which to refrain
Flee alway from the snare.

To love and to be wise!
To rage with good advice!
    Now thus, now then,
20   Now off, now on,
Uncertain as the dice!
    There is no man
    At once that can
To love and to be wise.

Such are the diverse throes,
Such pains that no man knows
    That hath not proved
    And once have loved.

Such are the raging woes
30   Sooner reproved
    Than well removed.
Such are the diverse throes.

Love is a fervent fire
Kindled by hot desire;
    For short pleasure
    Long displeasure.
Repentance is the hire,
    A poor treasure
    Without measure.
40 Love is a fervent fire.

Lo, what it is to love!

The Answer

Leave thus to slander love,
Though ill with such it prove
    Which often use
    Love to misuse
And loving to reprove.
    Such cannot choose
    For their refuse
But thus to slander love.

50 Flee not so much the snare.
Love seldom causeth care,
    But by deserts
    And crafty parts
Some leese their own welfare.
    Be true of hearts
    And for no smarts
Flee not so much the snare.

To love and not be wise
Is but a mad device.
60   Such love doth last
    As sure and fast
As chances on the dice.

> A bitter taste
> Comes at the last
> To love and not be wise.

> Such be the pleasant days,
> Such be the honest ways,
>   There is no man
>   That fully can
> 70 Know them but that he says
>   Loving to ban
>   Were folly then.
> Such be the pleasant days.

> Love is a pleasant fire
> Kindled by true desire.
>   And though the pain
>   Cause men to plain,
> Sped well is oft the hire.
>   Then though some feign
> 80 And leese the gain
> Love is a pleasant fire.

> *The Answer to This*

> Who most doth slander love
> The deed must alway prove.
>   Truth shall excuse
>   That you accuse
> For slander and reprove.
>   Not by refuse
>   But by abuse
> You most do slander love.

> 90 Ye grant it is a snare
> And would us not beware.
>   Lest that your train
>   Should be too plain
> Ye colour all the care.
>   Lo, how you feign
>   Pleasure for pain
> And grant it is a snare!

To love and to be wise –
It were a strange device!
100   But from that taste
    Ye vow the fast.
On syns though run your dice,
    Ambs-ace may haste
    Your pain to waste.
To love and to be wise!

Of all such pleasant days,
Of all such pleasant plays
    Without desert
    You have your part,
110 And all the world so says,
    Save that poor heart
    That for more smart
Feeleth not such pleasant days.

Such fire and such heat
Did never make ye sweat,
    For without pain
    You best obtain
To good speed and to great.
    Who so doth plain,
120   You best do feign
Such fire and such heat.

Who now doth slander love?

CXXXIII

The Ballad of Will

I will and yet I may not,
The more it is my pain.
What thing I will, I shall not.
Wherefore my will is vain.

Will willing is in vain,
This may I right well see.
Although my will would fain,
My will it may not be.

Because I will and may not,
10 My will is not my own.
For lack of will I cannot,
The cause whereof I moan.

Foy! that I will and cannot
Yet still I do sustain!
Between 'I will' and 'shall not'
My love cannot obtain.

Thus wishers wants their will
And they that will do crave.
But they that will not will
20 Their will the soonest have.

Since that I will and shall not,
My will I will refrain.
Thus, for to will and will not,
Will willing is but vain.

CXXXIV

And wilt thou leave me thus?
Say nay, say nay, for shame,
To save thee from the blame
Of all my grief and grame.
And wilt thou leave me thus?
    Say nay, say nay.

And wilt thou leave me thus
That hath loved thee so long
In wealth and woe among?
10 And is thy heart so strong
As for to leave me thus?
    Say nay, say nay.

And wilt thou leave me thus
That hath given thee my heart
Never for to depart,
Nother for pain nor smart?
And wilt thou leave me thus?
   Say nay, say nay.

And wilt thou leave me thus
20 And have no more pity
Of him that loveth thee?
Helas, thy cruelty!
And wilt thou leave me thus?
   Say nay, say nay!

CXXXV

Me list no more to sing
Of love nor of such thing,
How sore that it me wring;
For what I sung or spake
Men did my songs mistake.

My songs were too diffuse.
They made folk to muse.
Therefore, me to excuse,
They shall be sung more plain,
10 Neither of joy nor pain.

What vaileth then to sip
At fruit over the lip
. . . .
For fruit withouten taste
Doth naught but rot and waste.

What vaileth under key
To keep treasure alway
That never shall see day?
If it be not used
20 It is but abused.

What vaileth the flower
To stand still and wither?
If no man it savour
It serves only for sight
And fadeth towards night.

Therefore fear not t'assay
To gather, ye that may,
The flower that this day
Is fresher than the next.
30 Mark well, I say, this text.

Let not the fruit be lost
That is desired most;
Delight shall quit the cost.
If it be ta'en in time
Small labour is to climb.

And as for such treasure
That maketh thee the richer
And no deal the poorer
When it is given or lent,
40 Methinks it were well spent.

If this be under mist
And not well plainly wist,
Understand me who list
For I reck not a bean;
I wot what I do mean.

CXXXVI

Your looks so often cast,
Your eyes so friendly rolled,
Your sight fixed so fast,
Always one to behold –
Though hide it fain ye would,
It plainly doth declare
Who hath your heart in hold
And where good will ye bear.

Fain would ye find a cloak
10   Your burning fire to hide;
Yet both the flame and smoke
Breaks out on every side.
Ye cannot love so guide
That it no issue win.
Abroad needs must it glide
That burns so hot within.

For cause yourself do wink,
Ye judge all other blind,
And secret it you think
20   Which every man doth find.
In waste oft spend ye wind
Yourself in love to quit,
For agues of that kind
Will show who hath the fit.

Your sighs you fet from far,
And all to wry your woe.
Yet are you ne'er the nar:
Men are not blinded so.
Deeply oft swear ye no,
30   But all those oaths are vain,
So well your eye doth show
Who puts your heart to pain.

Think not therefore to hide
That still itself betrays,
Nor seek means to provide
To dark the sunny days.
Forget those wonted ways.
Leave off such frowning cheer.
There will be found no stays
40   To stop a thing so clear.

CXXXVII

Pass forth, my wonted cries,
Those cruel ears to pierce,
Which in most hateful wise
Doth still my plaints reverse.
Do you, my tears, also
So wet her barren heart
That pity there may grow
And cruelty depart.

For though hard rocks among
10 She seems to have been bred,
And with tigers full long
Been nourished and fed,
Yet shall that nature change
If pity once win place,
Whom as unknown and strange
She now away doth chase.

And as the water soft
Without forcing of strength
Where that it falleth oft
20 Hard stones doth pierce at length,
So in her stony heart
My plaints at length shall grave,
And, rigour set apart,
Cause her grant that I crave.

Wherefore, my plaints, present
Still so to her my suit
As it, through her assent,
May bring to me some fruit.
And as she shall me prove,
30 So bid her me regard
And render love for love,
Which is a just reward.

CXXXVIII

Mistrustful minds be moved
To have me in suspect.
The truth it shall be proved
Which time shall once detect.

Though falsehood go about
Of crime me to accuse,
At length I do not doubt
But truth shall me excuse.

Such sauce as they have served
10 To me without desert,
Even as they have deserved
Thereof God send them part.

Songs (3)

CXXXIX

    'Ah, Robin,
    Jolly Robin,
  Tell me how thy leman doth
And thou shall know of mine.'

'My lady is unkind, perdie!'
  'Alack, why is she so?'
'She loveth another better than me
  And yet she will say no.'

Réponse

  I find no such doubleness.
10   I find women true.
  My lady loveth me doubtless
    And will change for no new.

Le plaintif

Thou art happy while that doth last
  But I say as I find:
That women's love is but a blast
  And turneth like the wind.

Réponse

If that be true yet, as thou say'st,
  That women turn their heart,
Then speak better of them thou mayst
20   In hope to have thy part.

Le plaintif

Such folks shall take no harm by love
    That can abide their turn.
But I, alas, can no way prove
    In love but lack and mourn.

Réponse

But if thou wilt avoid thy harm
    Learn this lesson of me:
At others' fires thyself to warm
    And let them warm with thee.

CXL

O goodly hand
Wherein doth stand
My heart distressed in pain!
    Fair hand, alas,
    In little space
My life that doth restrain!

O fingers slight,
Departed right,
So long, so small, so round,
10   Goodly begone
    And yet alone
Most cruel in my wound.

With lilies white
And roses bright
Doth strive thy colour fair.
    Nature did lend
    Each finger's end
A pearl for to repair.

Consent at last,
20   Since that thou hast
My heart in thy demesne,
   For service true
   On me to rue
And reach me love again.

   And if not so
   Then with more woe
Enforce thyself to strain
   This simple heart,
   That suffereth smart,
30   And rid it out of pain.

CXLI

There was never nothing more me pained
   Nor nothing more me moved
As when my sweet heart her complained
   That ever she me loved,
     Alas the while!

With piteous look she said and sight:
   'Alas what aileth me
To love and set my wealth so light
   On him that loveth not me?
10   Alas the while!

'Was I not well void of all pain
   When that nothing me grieved?
And now with sorrows I must complain
   And cannot be relieved.
     Alas the while!

'My restful nights and joyful days
   Since I began to love
Be take from me. All thing decays
   Yet can I not remove.
20   Alas the while!'

She wept and wrung her hands withal.
  The tears fell in my neck.
She turned her face and let it fall,
  Scarcely therewith could speak,
    Alas the while!

Her pains tormented me so sore
  That comfort had I none
But cursed my fortune more and more
  To see her sob and groan,
30   Alas the while!

CXLII

What death is worse than this?
  When my delight,
My weal, my joy, my bliss
  Is from my sight
  Both day and night,
My life, alas, I miss.

For though I seem alive
  My heart is hence.
Thus, bootless for to strive
10 Out of presence
  Of my defence,
Toward my death I drive.

Heartless, alas, what man
  May long endure?
Alas, how live I then?
  Since no recure
  May me assure,
My life I may well ban.

Thus doth my torment go
20 In deadly dread.
Alas, who might live so,
  Alive as dead,
  Alive to lead
A deadly life in woe?

CXLIII

All heavy minds
Do seek to ease their charge,
And that that most them binds
 To let at large.

Then why should I
Hold pain within my heart
And may my tune apply
 To ease my smart?

My faithful lute
10 Alone shall hear me plain,
For else all other suit
 Is clean in vain.

For where I sue
Redress of all my grief,
Lo, they do most eschew
 My heart's relief.

Alas, my dear,
Have I deserved so
That no help may appear
20 Of all my woe?

Whom speak I to,
Unkind and deaf of ear?
Alas, lo, I do go
 And wot not where.

Where is my thought?
Where wanders my desire?
Where may the thing be sought
 That I require?

Light in the wind
30 Doth fly all my delight,
Where truth and faithful mind
 Are put to flight.

Who shall me give
Feathered wings for to fly,
The thing that doth me grieve
  That I may see?

Who would go seek
The cause whereby to plain?
Who would his foe beseek
40 For ease of pain?

My chance doth so
My woeful case procure
To offer to my foe
  My heart to cure.

What hope I then
To have any redress?
Of whom, or where, or when
  Who can express?

No, since despair
50 Hath set me in this case,
In vain oft in the air
  To say 'Alas!'

I seek nothing
But thus for to discharge
My heart of sore sighing,
  To plain at large

And with my lute
Sometime to ease my pain;
For else all other suit
60 Is clean in vain.

CXLIV

If in the world there be more woe
  Than I have in my heart,
Whereso it is, it doth come fro
And in my breast there doth it grow
  For to increase my smart.
 Alas, I am receipt of every care
And of my life each sorrow claims his part.
  Who list to live in quietness
  By me let him beware,
10 For I by high disdain
  Am mad without redress,
And unkindness, alas, hath slain
My poor true heart all comfortless.

CXLV

  Is it possible
  That so high debate,
So sharp, so sore, and of such rate,
Should end so soon and was begun so late?
  Is it possible?

  Is it possible
  So cruel intent,
So hasty heat and so soon spent,
From love to hate and thence for to relent?
10 Is it possible?

  Is it possible
  That any may find
Within one heart so diverse mind
  To change or turn as weather and wind?
  Is it possible?

Is it possible
To spy it in an eye
That turns as oft as chance on die?
The truth whereof can any try?
20   Is it possible?

It is possible
For to turn so oft,
To bring that lowest that was most aloft
And to fall highest yet to light soft.
    It is possible.

All is possible
Whoso list believe.
Trust therefore first and after preve,
As men wed ladies by licence and leave,
30   All is possible.

CXLVI

If with complaint the pain might be expressed
That inwardly doth cause me sigh and groan,
    Your hard heart and your cruel breast
      Should sigh and plain for my unrest;
        And though it were of stone
Yet should remorse cause it relent and moan.

But since it is so far out of measure
That with my words I can it not contain,
    My only trust, my heart's treasure,
10   Alas, why do I still endure
        This restless smart and pain
Since if ye list ye may my woe restrain?

CXLVII

Ye know my heart, my lady dear,
That since the time I was your thrall
I have been yours both whole and clear
Though my reward hath been but small.
So am I yet and more than all.
And ye know well how I have served
As, if ye prove, it shall appear:
   How well, how long,
   How faithfully,
10   And suffered wrong
   How patiently.
Then since that I have never swerved
Let not my pains be undeserved.

Ye know also, though ye say nay,
That you alone are my desire
And you alone it is that may
Assuage my fervent flaming fire.
Succour me then, I you require.
Ye know it were a just request,
20 Since ye do cause my heat, I say,
   If that I burn
   That ye will warm
   And not to turn
   All to my harm,
Sending such flame from frozen breast
Against all right for my unrest.

And I know well how frowardly
Ye have mista'en my true intent
And hitherto how wrongfully
30 I have found cause for to repent.
But if your heart doth not relent,
Since I do know that this ye know,
Ye shall slay me all wilfully;

For me and mine
And all I have
Ye may assign
To spill or save.
Why are you then so cruel foe
Unto your own that loves you so?

CXLVIII

If ever man might him avaunt
    Of Fortune's friendly cheer
It was myself, I must it grant,
    For I have bought it dear.
And dearly have I held also
    The glory of her name
In yielding her such tribute, lo,
    As did set forth her fame.

Sometime I stood so in her grace
10   That, as I would require,
Each joy I thought did me embrace
    That furthered my desire.
And all those pleasures, lo, had I
    That fancy might support
And nothing she did me deny
    That was to my comfort.

I had (what would you more, perdie?)
    Each grace that I did crave.
Thus Fortune's will was unto me
20   All thing that I would have.
But all too rathe, alas the while,
    She built on such a ground.
In little space too great a guile
    In her now have I found.

For she hath turned so her wheel
   That I, unhappy man,
May wail the time that I did feel
   Wherewith she fed me then.
For broken now are her behests
30   And pleasant looks she gave;
And therefore now all my requests
   From peril cannot save.

Yet would I well it might appear
   To her, my chief regard,
Though my deserts have been too dear
   To merit such reward.
Sith Fortune's will is now so bent
   To plague me thus, poor man,
I must myself therewith content
40   And bear it as I can.

Epistolary Satires

CXLIX

Mine own John Poyntz, since ye delight to know
      The cause why that homeward I me draw
      (And flee the press of courts whereso they go
Rather than to live thrall under the awe
      Of lordly looks) wrapped within my cloak,
      To will and lust learning to set a law,
It is not because I scorn or mock
      The power of them to whom Fortune hath lent
      Charge over us, of right to strike the stroke;
10 But true it is that I have always meant
      Less to esteem them than the common sort,
      Of outward things that judge in their intent
Without regard what doth inward resort.
      I grant sometime that of glory the fire
      Doth touch my heart; me list not to report
Blame by honour and honour to desire.
      But how may I this honour now attain
      That cannot dye the colour black a liar?
My Poyntz, I cannot frame my tune to feign,
20   To cloak the truth for praise, without desert,
      Of them that list all vice for to retain.
I cannot honour them that sets their part
      With Venus and Bacchus all their life long,
      Nor hold my peace of them although I smart.
I cannot crouch nor kneel to do such wrong
      To worship them like God on earth alone
      That are like wolves these silly lambs among.

I cannot with my words complain and moan
    And suffer naught, nor smart without complaint,
30   Nor turn the word that from my mouth is gone.
I cannot speak and look like a saint,
    Use wiles for wit and make deceit a pleasure
    And call craft counsel, for profit still to paint.
I cannot wrest the law to fill the coffer,
    With innocent blood to feed myself fat,
    And do most hurt where most help I offer.
I am not he that can allow the state
    Of him Caesar and damn Cato to die,
    That with his death did 'scape out of the gate
40 From Caesar's hands, if Livy doth not lie,
    And would not live where liberty was lost,
    So did his heart the common wealth apply.
I am not he such eloquence to boast
    To make the crow singing as the swan,
    Nor call 'the lion' of coward beasts the most
That cannot take a mouse as the cat can;
    And he that dieth for hunger of the gold,
    Call him Alexander, and say that Pan
Passeth Apollo in music many fold;
50   Praise Sir Thopas for a noble tale
    And scorn the story that the knight told;
Praise him for counsel that is drunk of ale;
    Grin when he laugheth that beareth all the sway,
    Frown when he frowneth and groan when he is
      pale,
On other's lust to hang both night and day.
    None of these points would ever frame in me.
    My wit is naught. I cannot learn the way.
And much the less of things that greater be,
    That asken help of colours of device
60   To join the mean with each extremity:
With the nearest virtue to cloak alway the vice
    And, as to purpose likewise it shall fall,
    To press the virtue that it may not rise.

As drunkenness good fellowship to call;
  The friendly foe with his double face
  Say he is gentle and courteous therewithal;
And say that Favel hath a goodly grace
  In eloquence; and cruelty to name
  Zeal of justice and change in time and place;
70 And he that suffereth offence without blame
  Call him pitiful, and him true and plain
  That raileth reckless to every man's shame;
Say he is rude that cannot lie and feign,
  The lecher a lover, and tyranny
  To be the right of a prince's reign.
I cannot, I! No, no, it will not be!
  This is the cause that I could never yet
  Hang on their sleeves that weigh, as thou mayst
    see,
A chip of chance more than a pound of wit.
80 This maketh me at home to hunt and to hawk
  And in foul weather at my book to sit;
In frost and snow then with my bow to stalk.
  No man doth mark whereso I ride or go;
  In lusty leas in liberty I walk.
And of these news I feel nor weal nor woe,
  Save that a clog doth hang yet at my heel.
  No force for that, for it is ordered so
That I may leap both hedge and dike full well.
  I am not now in France to judge the wine,
90 With savoury sauce the delicates to feel;
Nor yet in Spain where one must him incline,
  Rather than to be, outwardly to seem.
  I meddle not with wits that be so fine.
Nor Flander's cheer letteth not my sight to deem
  Of black and white nor taketh my wit away
  With beastliness they, beasts, do so esteem.
Nor I am not where Christ is given in prey
  For money, poison, and treason at Rome –
  A common practice used night and day.

100   But here I am in Kent and Christendom
             Among the Muses where I read and rhyme,
             Where if thou list, my Poyntz, for to come,
       Thou shalt be judge how I do spend my time.

CL

       My mother's maids when they did sew and spin,
             They sang sometime a song of the field mouse
             That, for because her livelood was but thin,
       Would needs go seek her townish sister's house.
             She thought herself endured too much pain.
             The stormy blasts her cave so sore did souse
       That when the furrows swimmed with the rain
             She must lie cold and wet in sorry plight.
             And worse than that, bare meat there did remain
10   To comfort her when she her house had dight –
             Sometime a barley corn, sometime a bean
             For which she laboured hard both day and
                   night
       In harvest time whilst she might go and glean;
             And when her store was 'stroyed with the flood,
             Then wellaway, for she undone was clean.
       Then was she fain to take instead of food
             Sleep, if she might, her hunger to beguile.
             'My sister,' quod she, 'hath a living good
       And hence from me she dwelleth not a mile.
20   In cold and storm she lieth warm and dry
             In bed of down. The dirt doth not defile
       Her tender foot. She laboureth not as I.
             Richly she feedeth and at the rich man's cost,
             And for her meat she needs not crave nor cry.
       By sea, by land, of the delicates the most
             Her cater seeks and spareth for no peril.
             She feedeth on boiled bacon meat and roast

And hath thereof neither charge nor travail.
>   And when she list, the liquor of the grape
30   Doth glad her heart till that her belly swell.'
And at this journey she maketh but a jape.
>   So forth she goeth, trusting of all this wealth
>   With her sister her part so for to shape
That, if she might keep herself in health,
>   To live a lady while her life doth last.
>   And to the door now is she come by stealth
And with her foot anon she scrapeth full fast.
>   Th'other for fear durst not well scarce appear,
>   Of every noise so was the wretch aghast.
40   At last she asked softly who was there.
>   And in her language as well as she could
>   'Peep,' quod the other, 'sister, I am here.'
'Peace,' quod the town mouse, 'why speakest thou so
>   loud?'
>   And by the hand she took her fair and well.
>   'Welcome,' quod she, 'my sister, by the Rood.'
She feasted her, that joy it was to tell
>   The fare they had. They drank the wine so clear
>   And, as to purpose now and then it fell,
She cheered her with 'How sister, what cheer!'
50   Amidst this joy befell a sorry chance
>   That, wellaway, the stranger bought full dear
The fare she had. For as she looked askance,
>   Under a stool she spied two steaming eyes
>   In a round head with sharp ears. In France
Was never mouse so feared, for though th'unwise
>   Had not yseen such a beast before,
>   Yet had nature taught her after her guise
To know her foe and dread him evermore.
>   The towny mouse fled; she knew whither to go.
60   Th'other had no shift, but wondrous sore
Feared of her life. At home she wished her tho!
>   And to the door, alas, as she did skip,
>   Th'heaven it would, lo, and eke her chance was
>   so,

At the threshold her silly foot did trip,
>And ere she might recover it again
>The traitor cat had caught her by the hip
And made her there against her will remain,
>That had forgotten her poor surety and rest
>For seeming wealth wherein she thought to
>reign.
70 Alas, my Poyntz, how men do seek the best
>And find the worst by error as they stray!
>And no marvel, when sight is so oppressed,
And blind the guide, anon, out of the way
>Goeth guide and all in seeking quiet life.
>O wretched minds, there is no gold that may
Grant that ye seek, no war, no peace, no strife.
>No, no, although thy head were hooped with
>gold,
>Sergeant with mace, halberd, sword, nor knife
Cannot repulse the care that follow should.
80 Each kind of life hath with him his disease.
>Live in delight even as thy lust would
And thou shalt find, when lust doth most thee please,
>It irketh straight and by itself doth fade.
>A small thing it is that may thy mind appease.
None of ye all there is that is so mad
>To seek grapes upon brambles or briers,
>Nor none, I trow, that hath his wit so bad
To set his hay for conies over rivers;
>Ne ye set not a drag-net for a hare.
90 And yet the thing that most is your desire
Ye do mis-seek with more travail and care.
>Make plain thine heart that it be not knotted
>With hope or dread, and see thy will be bare
From all affects whom vice hath ever spotted.
>Thyself content with that is thee assigned
>And use it well that is to thee allotted.
Then seek no more out of thyself to find
>The thing that thou hast sought so long before,
>For thou shalt feel it sitting in thy mind.

100 Mad, if ye list to continue your sore!
        Let present pass and gape on time to come
        And deep yourself in travail more and more.
Henceforth, my Poyntz, this shall be all and sum.
        These wretched fools shall have naught else of me.
        But to the great God and to his high doom
None other pain pray I for them to be
        But, when the rage doth lead them from the right,
        That looking backward, Virtue they may see
Even as she is, so goodly fair and bright.
110   And whilst they clasp their lusts in arms across,
        Grant them, good Lord, as thou mayst of thy
           might,
To fret inward for losing such a loss.

CLI

'A spending hand that alway poureth out
        Had need to have a bringer-in as fast';
        And 'On the stone that still doth turn about
There groweth no moss' – these proverbs yet do last.
        Reason hath set them in so sure a place
        That length of years their force can never waste.
When I remember this and eke the case
        Wherein thou stands, I thought forthwith to write,
        Brian, to thee, who knows how great a grace
10 In writing is to counsel man the right.
        To thee, therefore, that trots still up and down
        And never rests, but running day and night
From realm to realm, from city, street, and town,
        Why dost thou wear thy body to the bones
        And mightst at home sleep in thy bed of down
And drink good ale so nappy for the nonce,
        Feed thyself fat and heap up pound by pound?
        Likest thou not this? 'No.' Why? 'For swine so
           groins

In sty and chaw the turds moulded on the ground,
20   And drivel on pearls, the head still in the manger.
        Then of the harp the ass do hear the sound.
So sacks of dirt be filled up in the cloister
        That serves for less than do these fatted swine.
        Though I seem lean and dry without moisture,
Yet will I serve my prince, my lord and thine,
        And let them live to feed the paunch that list,
        So I may feed to live, both me and mine.'
By God, well said, but what and if thou wist
        How to bring in as fast as thou dost spend?
30   'That would I learn.' And it shall not be missed
To tell thee how. Now hark what I intend.
        Thou know'st well, first, whoso can seek to
            please
        Shall purchase friends where truth shall but
            offend.
Flee therefore truth: it is both wealth and ease.
        For though that truth of every man hath praise,
        Full near that wind goeth truth in great misease.
Use virtue as it goeth now-a-days,
        In word alone to make thy language sweet,
        And of the deed yet do not as thou says.
40 Else be thou sure thou shalt be far unmeet
        To get thy bread, each thing is now so scant.
        Seek still thy profit upon thy bare feet.
Lend in no wise, for fear that thou do want,
        Unless it be as to a dog a cheese;
        By which return be sure to win a cant
Of half at least – it is not good to leese.
        Learn at Kitson, that in a long white coat
        From under the stall without lands or fees
Hath leapt into the shop; who knoweth by rote
50   This rule that I have told thee herebefore.
        Sometime also rich age beginneth to dote;
See thou when there thy gain may be the more.
        Stay him by the arm whereso he walk or go.
        Be near alway and, if he cough too sore,

When he hath spit, tread out and please him so.
    A diligent knave that picks his master's purse
    May please him so that he, withouten moe,
Executor is, and what is he the worse?
    But if so chance you get naught of the man,
60   The widow may for all thy charge deburse.
A rivelled skin, a stinking breath, what then?
    A toothless mouth shall do thy lips no harm.
    The gold is good, and though she curse or ban,
Yet where thee list thou mayst lie good and warm:
    Let the old mule bite upon the bridle
    Whilst there do lie a sweeter in thine arm.
In this also see you be not idle:
    Thy niece, thy cousin, thy sister, or thy daughter,
    If she be fair, if handsome be her middle,
70 If thy better hath her love besought her,
    Advance his cause and he shall help thy need.
    It is but love. Turn it to a laughter.
But ware, I say, so gold thee help and speed
    That in this case thou be not so unwise
    As Pandar was in such a like deed;
For he, the fool, of conscience was so nice
    That he no gain would have for all his pain.
    Be next thyself, for friendship bears no prize.
Laugh'st thou at me? Why? Do I speak in vain?
80   'No, not at thee, but at thy thrifty jest.
    Wouldest thou I should for any loss or gain
Change that for gold that I have ta'en for best –
    Next godly things, to have an honest name?
    Should I leave that? Then take me for a beast!'
Nay then, farewell, and if you care for shame,
    Content thee then with honest poverty,
    With free tongue, what thee mislikes, to blame,
And, for thy truth, sometime adversity.
    And therewithal this thing I shall thee give –
90   In this world now, little prosperity,
And coin to keep, as water in a sieve.

A Paraphrase of the Penitential Psalms

CLII

Love, to give law unto his subject hearts,
Stood in the eyes of Barsabe the bright,
And in a look anon himself converts
Cruelly pleasant before King David sight;
First dazed his eyes, and further forth he starts
With venomed breath, as softly as he might
Touched his senses, and overruns his bones
With creeping fire sparpled for the nonce.

And when he saw that kindled was the flame,
10 The moist poison in his heart he lanced
So that the soul did tremble with the same.
And in this branle as he stood and tranced,
Yielding unto the figure and the frame
That those fair eyes had in his presence glanced,
The form that Love had printed in his breast
He honour'th it as thing of things best.

So that forgot the wisdom and forecast
(Which woe to realms when that these kings doth lack)
Forgetting eke God's majesty as fast,
20 Yea, and his own, forthwith he doth to make
Urie to go into the field in haste –
Urie I say, that was his idol's make –
Under pretence of certain victory,
For en'mies' swords a ready prey to die.

Whereby he may enjoy her out of doubt
Whom more than God or himself he mindeth.
And after he had brought this thing about

And of that lust possessed himself he findeth
That hath and doth reverse and clean turn out
30 Kings from kingdoms and cities undermindeth,
He, blinded, thinks this train so blind and close
To blind all thing, that naught may it disclose.

But Nathan hath spied out this treachery
With rueful cheer and sets afore his face
The great offence, outrage, and injury
That he hath done to God as in this case –
By murder for to cloak adultery.
He shew'th him eke from heaven the threats, alas,
So sternly sore this prophet, this Nathan,
40 That all amazed this aged woeful man.

Like him that meets with horror and with fear,
The heat doth straight forsake the limbs cold,
The colour eke droopeth down from his cheer,
So doth he feel his fire manifold,
His heat, his lust, and pleasure all in fear
Consume and waste; and straight his crown of gold,
His purple pall, his sceptre he lets fall
And to the ground he throw'th himself withal.

The pompous pride of state and dignity
50 Forthwith rebates repentant humbleness.
Thinner vile cloth than clotheth poverty
Doth scantly hide and clad his nakedness,
His fair hoar beard of reverent gravity
With ruffled hair knowing his wickedness.
More like was he the selfsame repentance
Than stately prince of worldly governance.

His harp he taketh in hand to be his guide
Wherewith he offer'th his plaints, his soul to save,
That from his heart distils on every side,
60 Withdrawing him into a dark cave ·
Within the ground, wherein he might him hide,
Fleeing the light as in prison or grave,

In which as soon as David entered had,
The dark horror did make his fault adrad.

But he, without prolonging or delay,
Rof that that might his Lord, his God appease,
Fall'th on his knees, and with his harp, I say,
Afore his breast, fraughted with disease
Of stormy sighs, his cheer coloured like clay,
70   Dressed upright, seeking to counterpoise
His song with sighs, and touching of the strings
With tender heart, lo, thus to God he sings.

Psalm 6. *Domine ne in furore*

O Lord, since in my mouth thy mighty name
    Suffer'th itself 'my Lord' to name and call,
    Here hath my heart hope taken by the same
That the repentance which I have, and shall,
    May at thy hand seek mercy as the thing,
    Only comfort of wretched sinners all;
Whereby I dare with humble bemoaning,
80   By thy goodness, of thee this thing require.
    Chastise me not for my deserving
According to thy just conceived ire.
    O Lord, I dread, and that I did not dread
    I me repent, and evermore desire
Thee, thee to dread. I open here and spread
    My fault to thee; but thou for thy goodness
    Measure it not in largeness nor in bread;
Punish it not as asketh the greatness
    Of thy furor provoked by my offence.
90   Temper, O Lord, the harm of my excess
With mending will that I for recompense
    Prepare again; and rather pity me
    For I am weak and clean without defence.
More is the need I have of remedy
    For of the whole the leech taketh no cure.
    The sheep that stray'th the shepherd seeks to see;

I, Lord, am strayed. I, sick without recure,
    Feel all my limbs, that have rebelled, for fear
    Shake – in despair unless thou me assure.
100 My flesh is troubled. My heart doth fear the spear –
    That dread of death, of death that ever lasts,
    Threateth of right, and draweth near and near!
Much more my soul is troubled by the blasts
    Of these assaults (that come as thick as hail)
    Of worldly vanities, that temptation casts
Against the weak bulwark of the flesh frail,
    Wherein the soul in great perplexity
    Feeleth the senses with them that assail
Conspire, corrupt by use and vanity;
110   Whereby the wretch doth to the shade resort
    Of hope in thee in this extremity.
But thou, O Lord, how long after this sort
    Forbearest thou to see my misery?
    Suffer me yet, in hope of some comfort,
Fear and not feel that thou forgettest me.
    Return, O Lord, O Lord I thee beseech,
    Unto thine old wonted benignity.
Reduce, revive my soul; be thou the leech
    And reconcile the great hatred and strife
120   That it hath ta'en against the flesh, the wretch
That stirred hath thy wrath by filthy life.
    See how my soul doth fret it to the bones:
    Inward remorse so sharp'th it like a knife
That, but thou help the caitiff that bemoans
    His great offence, it turn'th anon to dust.
    Here hath thy mercy matter for the nonce,
For if thy righteous hand that is so just
    Suffer no sin or strike with damnation,
    Thy infinite mercy want needs it must
130 Subject matter for his operation.
    For that in death there is no memory
    Among the damned, nor yet no mention
Of thy great name, ground of all glory,
    Then if I die and go whereas I fear

To think thereon, how shall thy great mercy
Sound in my mouth unto the world's ear?
    For there is none that can thee laud and love
    For that thou nilt no love among them there.
Suffer my cries thy mercy for to move
140   That wonted is one hundred years' offence
    In moment of repentance to remove.
How oft have I called up with diligence
    This slothful flesh long afore the day,
    For to confess his fault and negligence,
That to the down, for aught that I could say,
    Hath still returned to shroud itself from cold,
    Whereby it suffer'th now for such delay.
By nightly plaints instead of pleasures old
    I wash my bed with tears continual
150   To dull my sight that it be never bold
To stir my heart again to such a fall.
    Thus dry I up among my foes in woe
    That with my fall do rise and grow withal
And me beset even now where I am, so
    With secret traps to trouble my penance.
    Some do present to my weeping eyes, lo,
The cheer, the manner, beauty, and countenance
    Of her whose look, alas, did make me blind.
    Some other offer to my remembrance
160   Those pleasant words now bitter to my mind.
    And some shew me the power of my armour,
    Triumph and conquest, and to my head assigned
Double diadem. Some shew the favour
    Of people frail, palace, pomp, and riches.
    To these mermaids and their baits of error
I stop mine ears with help of thy goodness.
    And, for I feel it com'th alone of thee
    That to my heart these foes have none access,
I dare them bid: 'Avoid, wretches, and flee!
170   The Lord hath heard the voice of my complaint.
    Your engines take no more effect in me.
The Lord hath heard, I say, and seen me faint

Under your hand and pity'th my distress.
He shall do make my senses by constraint
Obey the rule that reason shall express,
    Where the deceit of your glosing bait
    Made them usurp a power in all excess.'
Shamed be they all, that so lie in wait
    To compass me, by missing of their prey!
180 Shame and rebuke redound to such deceit!
Sudden confusion's stroke without delay
    Shall so deface their crafty suggestion
    That they to hurt my health no more assay,
Since I, O Lord, remain in thy protection.

* * *

Whoso hath seen the sick in his fever,
After truce taken with the heat or cold
And that the fit is passed of his fervour,
Draw fainting sighs, let him, I say, behold
Sorrowful David after his langour,
190 That with the tears that from his eyes down rolled
Paused his plaint and laid adown his harp,
Faithful record of all his sorrows sharp.

It seemed now that of his fault the horror
Did make afeard no more his hope of grace,
The threats whereof in horrible terror
Did hold his heart as in despair a space,
Till he had willed to seek for his succour,
Himself accusing, beknowing his case,
Thinking so best his Lord for to appease.
200 Eased, not yet healed, he feeleth his disease.

Seemeth horrible no more the dark cave
That erst did make his fault for to tremble.
A place devout or refuge for to save
The succourless it rather doth resemble.
For who had seen so kneel within the grave
The chief pastor of th'Hebrews' assemble
Would judge it made, by tears of penitence,
A sacred place worthy of reverence.

With vapoured eyes he looketh here and there.
210 And when he hath awhile himself bethought,
Gathering his sprites that were dismayed for fear,
His harp again into his hand he rought.
Tuning accord by judgement of his ear,
His heart's bottom for a sigh he sought,
And therewithal upon the hollow tree
With strained voice again thus crieth he.

Psalm 32. Beati quorum remiss[a]e sunt
O happy are they that have forgiveness got
Of their offence, not by their penitence,
As by merit, which recompenseth not
220 (Although that yet pardon hath none offence
Without the same), but by the goodness
Of him that hath perfect intelligence
Of heart contrite and cover'th the greatness
Of sin within a merciful discharge.
And happy are they that have the wilfulness
Of lust restrained, afore it went at large,
Provoked by the dread of God's furor;
Whereby they have not on their backs the charge
Of other's fault to suffer the dolour,
230 For that their fault was never execute
In open sight, example of error.
And happy is he to whom God doth impute
No more his fault, by knowledging his sin,
But cleansed now the Lord doth him repute,
As adder fresh new stripped from his skin,
Nor in his sprite is aught undiscovered.
I, for because I hid it still within,
Thinking by state in fault to be preferred,
Do find by hiding of my fault my harm –
240 As he that feels his health to be hindered
By secret wound, concealed from the charm
Of leech's cure, that else had had redress –
And feel my bones consume and wax unfarm
By daily rage roaring in excess.

Thy heavy hand on me was so increast
Both day and night and held my heart in press,
With pricking thoughts bereaving me my rest,
　　That withered is my lustiness away
　　As summer heats that hath the grain oppressed.
250 Wherefore I did another way assay
　　And sought forthwith to open in thy sight
　　My fault, my fear, my filthiness, I say,
And not to hide from thee my great unright.
　　'I shall,' quod I, 'against myself confess
　　Unto the Lord all my sinful plight.'
And thou forthwith didst wash the wickedness
　　Of mine offence; of truth right thus it is.
　　Wherefore they that have tasted thy goodness
At me shall take example as of this
260　And pray and seek in time for time of grace.
　　Then shall the storms and floods of harm him miss
And him to reach shall never have the space.
　　Thou art my refuge and only safeguard
　　From the troubles that compass me the place.
Such joy as he that scapes his en'my's ward
　　With loosed bonds hath in his liberty,
　　Such joy, my joy, thou hast to me prepared;
That as the seaman in his jeopardy
　　By sudden light perceived hath the port,
270　So by thy great merciful property
Within thy look thus read I my comfort:
　　'I shall thee teach and give understanding
　　And point to thee what way thou shalt resort
For thy address, to keep thee from wand'ring.
　　Mine eye shall take the charge to be thy guide.
　　I ask thereto of thee alone this thing:
Be not like horse or mule that man doth ride
　　That not alone doth not his master know
　　But, for the good thou dost him, must be tied
280　And bridled lest his guide he bite or throw.'
　　O diverse are the chastisings of sin:
　　In meat, in drink, in breath that man doth blow,

In sleep, in watch, in fretting still within
   That never suffer rest unto the mind
   Filled with offence, that new and new begin
With thousand fears the heart to strain and bind.
   But for all this he that in God doth trust
   With mercy shall himself defended find.
Joy and rejoice, I say, ye that be just,
290   In him that mak'th and holdeth you so still.
   In him your glory alway set you must,
All ye that be of upright heart and will.

This song ended, David did stint his voice;
And in that while, about he with his eye
Did seek the cave with which, withouten noise,
His silence seemed to argue and reply
Upon this peace, this peace that did rejoice
The soul with mercy, that mercy so did cry
And found mercy at mercy's plentiful hand,
300 Never denied but where it was withstand.

As the servant that, in his master's face
Finding pardon of his passed offence,
Considering his great goodness and his grace,
Glad tears distils as gladsome recompense,
Right so David, that seemed in that place
A marble image of singular reverence
Carved in the rock with eyes and hands on high,
Made as by craft to plain, to sob, to sigh.

This while a beam that bright sun forth sends –
310 That sun the which was never cloud could hide –
Pierceth the cave and on the harp descends,
Whose glancing light the chords did overglide
And such lustre upon the harp extends
As light of lamp upon the gold clean tried;
The turn whereof into his eyes did start,
Surprised with joy by penance of the heart.

He, then inflamed with far more hot affect
Of God than he was erst of Barsabe,
His left foot did on the earth erect,
320 And just thereby remain'th the t'other knee.
To his left side his weight he doth direct –
Sure hope of health – and harp again tak'th he.
His hand his tune, his mind sought his lay
Which to the Lord with sober voice did say.

Psalm 38. Domine ne in furore tuo arguas me

O Lord, as I thee have both prayed and pray,
 (Although in thee be no alteration
 But that we men like as ourselves we say,
Measuring thy justice by our mutation)
 Chastise me not, O Lord, in thy furor
330 Nor me correct in wrathful castigation.
For that thy arrows of fear, of terror,
 Of sword, of sickness, of famine and fire
 Sticks deep in me, I, lo, from mine error
Am plunged up, as horse out of the mire
 With stroke of spur. Such is thy hand on me
 That in my flesh for terror of thy ire
Is not one point of firm stability,
 Nor in my bones there is no steadfastness:
 Such is my dread of mutability
340 For that I know my frailful wickedness.
 For why? My sins above my head are bound
 Like heavy weight that doth my force oppress
Under the which I stoop and bow to ground
 As willow plant haled by violence;
 And of my flesh each not well cured wound
That festered is by folly and negligence
 By secret lust hath rankled under skin,
 Not duly cured by my penitence.
Perceiving thus the tyranny of sin
350 That with his weight hath humbled and depressed
 My pride by grudging of the worm within
That never dieth, I live withouten rest.

So are mine entrails, infect with fervent sore,
Feeding the harm that hath my wealth oppressed
That in my flesh is left no health therefore.
So wondrous great hath been my vexation
That it hath forced my heart to cry and roar.
O Lord, thou know'st the inward contemplation
Of my desire. Thou know'st my sighs and plaints.
360   Thou know'st the tears of my lamentation
Cannot express my heart's inward restraints.
My heart panteth. My force I feel it quail.
My sight, mine eyes, my look decays and faints.
And when mine en'mies did me most assail,
My friends most sure wherein I set most trust –
Mine own virtues – soonest then did fail
And stand apart. Reason and wit unjust,
As kin unkind, were farthest gone at need.
So had they place their venom out to thrust
370   That sought my death by naughty word and deed.
Their tongues reproach, their wits did fraud apply.
And I like deaf and dumb forth my way yede,
Like one that hears not nor hath to reply
One word again. Knowing that from thy hand
These things proceed, thou, Lord, shalt supply
My trust in thee wherein I stick and stand.
Yet have I had great cause to dread and fear
That thou wouldst give my foes the overhand
For in my fall they shewed such pleasant cheer.
380   And therewithal I alway in the lash
Abide the stroke and with me everywhere
I bear my fault that greatly doth abash
My doleful cheer; for I my fault confess
And my desert doth all my comfort dash.
In the mean while mine en'mies safe increase
And my provokers hereby do augment,
That without cause to hurt me do not cease.
In evil for good against me they be bent
And hinder shall my good pursuit of grace.
390   Lo now, my God, that seest my whole intent,

My Lord, I am, thou know'st well, in what case.
  Forsake me not. Be not far from me gone.
  Haste to my help, haste, Lord, and haste apace,
O Lord, the Lord of all my health alone.

*

Like as the pilgrim that in a long way
Fainting for heat, provoked by some wind
In some fresh shade lieth down at mids of day,
So doth of David the wearied voice and mind
Take breath of sighs when he had sung this lay
400 Under such shade as sorrow hath assigned;
And as the t'one still minds his voyage end,
So doth the t'other to mercy still pretend.

On sonour chords his fingers he extends
Without hearing or judgement of the sound.
Down from his eyes a storm of tears descends,
Without feeling, that trickle on the ground,
As he that bleeds in bain right so intends
Th'altered senses to that that they are bound.
But sigh and weep he can none other thing
410 And look up still unto the heaven's king.

But who had been without the cave's mouth
And heard the tears and sighs that he did strain,
He would have sworn there had out of the south
A lukewarm wind brought forth a smoky rain.
But that so close the cave was and uncouth
That none but God was record of his pain,
Else had the wind blown in all Israel's ears
The woeful plaint and of their king the tears.

Of which some part when he up supped had,
420 Like as he whom his own thought affrays,
He turns his look. Him seemeth that the shade
Of his offence again his force assays
By violence despair on him to lade.
Starting like him whom sudden fear dismays,

His voice he strains and from his heart outbrings
This song that I not whether he cries or sings.

Psalm 51. *Miserere mei Domine*

Rue on me, Lord, for thy goodness and grace,
    That of thy nature art so bountiful,
    For that goodness that in the world doth brace
430 Repugnant natures in quiet wonderful.
    And for thy mercies' number without end,
    In heaven and earth perceived so plentiful
That over all they do themselves extend,
    For those mercies much more than man can sin,
    Do way my sins that so thy grace offend.
Again wash me, but wash me well within,
    And from my sin that thus mak'th me afraid
    Make thou me clean as ay thy wont hath been.
For unto thee no number can be laid
440   For to prescribe remissions of offence
    In hearts returned, as thou thyself hath said.
And I beknow my fault, my negligence,
    And in my sight my sin is fixed fast,
    Thereof to have more perfect penitence.
To thee alone, to thee have I trespassed
    For none can measure my fault but thou alone.
    For in thy sight I have not been aghast
For to offend, judging thy sight as none
    So that my fault were hid from sight of man,
450   Thy majesty so from my mind was gone.
This know I and repent. Pardon thou then,
    Whereby thou shalt keep still thy word stable,
    Thy justice pure and clean; because that when
I pardoned am, then forthwith justly able,
    Just I am judged by justice of thy grace.
    For I myself, lo, thing most unstable,
Formed in offence, conceived in like case,
    Am naught but sin from my nativity.
    Be not this said for my excuse, alas,
460 But of thy help to show necessity.

For, lo, thou loves the truth of inward heart
Which yet doth live in my fidelity
Though I have fallen, by frailty overthwart;
For wilful malice led me not the way
So much as hath the flesh drawn me apart.
Wherefore, O Lord, as thou hast done alway,
Teach me the hidden wisdom of thy lore
Since that my faith doth not yet decay.
And as the Jews to heal the leper sore

470 With hyssop cleanse, cleanse me and I am clean.
Thou shalt me wash and more than snow therefore
I shall be white, how foul my fault hath been.
Thou of my health shalt gladsome tidings bring
When from above remission shall be seen
Descend on earth. Then shall for joy upspring
The bones that were afore consumed to dust.
Look not, O Lord, upon mine offending
But do away my deeds that are unjust.
Make a clean heart in the mids of my breast

480 With sprite upright voided from filthy lust.
From thine eyes' cure cast me not in unrest
Nor take from me thy sprite of holiness.
Render to me joy of thy help and rest;
My will confirm with sprite of steadfastness.
And by this shall these goodly things ensue:
Sinners I shall into thy ways address,
They shall return to thee and thy grace sue;
My tongue shall praise thy justification;
My mouth shall spread thy glorious praises true.

490 But of thyself, O God, this operation
It must proceed by purging me from blood,
Among the just that I may have relation.
And of thy lauds for to let out the flood
Thou must, O Lord, my lips first unloose.
For if thou hadst esteemed pleasant good
The outward deeds that outward men disclose
I would have offered unto thee sacrifice.
But thou delights not in no such gloze

Of outward deed as men dream and devise.
500   The sacrifice that the Lord liketh most
    Is sprite contrite; low heart in humble wise
Thou dost accept, O God, for pleasant host.
    Make Zion, Lord, according to thy will,
    Inward Zion, the Zion of the ghost.
Of heart's Jerusalem strength the walls still.
    Then shalt thou take for good these outward deeds
    As sacrifice thy pleasure to fulfil.
Of thee alone thus all our good proceeds.

*

Of deep secrets that David here did sing,
510 Of mercy, of faith, of frailty, of grace,
Of God's goodness, and of justifying,
The greatness did so astone himself a space,
As who might say: 'Who hath expressed this thing?
I, sinner, I! What have I said, alas?
That God's goodness would within my song entreat
Let me again consider and repeat.'

And so he doth, but not expressed by word.
But in his heart he turneth and poiseth
Each word that erst his lips might forth afford.
520 He points, he pauseth, he wonders, he praiseth
The mercy that hides of justice the sword,
The justice that so his promise complisheth
For his words' sake to worthiless desert
That gratis his graces to men doth depart.

Here hath he comfort when he doth measure
Measureless mercies to measureless fault,
To prodigal sinners infinite treasure,
Treasure termless that never shall default.
Yea, when that sin shall fail and may not dure,
530 Mercy shall reign, 'gain whom shall no assault
Of hell prevail, by whom, lo, at this day,
Of heaven gates remission is the key.

And when David hath pondered well and tried
And seeth himself not utterly deprived
From light of grace that dark of sin did hide,
He finds his hope so much therewith revived
He dare importune the Lord on every side
(For he know'th well to mercy is ascribed
Respectless labour), importune, cry, and call;
540   And thus begin'th his song therewithal.

Psalm 102. Domine exaudi orationem meam

Lord, hear my prayer and let my cry pass
  Unto thee, Lord, without impediment.
  Do not from me turn thy merciful face,
Unto myself leaving my government.
  In time of trouble and adversity
  Incline to me thine ear and thine intent.
And when I call, help my necessity,
  Readily grant th'effect of my desire.
  These bold demands do please thy majesty
550 And eke my case such haste doth well require.
  For like as smoke my days been passed away,
  My bones dried up as furnace with the fire.
My heart, my mind is withered up like hay
  Because I have forgot to take my bread,
  My bread of life, the word of truth, I say.
And for my plaintful sighs and my dread,
  My bones, my strength, my very force of mind
  Cleaved to the flesh and from thy sprite were fled
As desperate thy mercy for to find.
560 So made I me the solein pelican
  And like the owl that fleeth by proper kind
Light of the day and hath herself beta'en
  To ruin life out of all company.
  With waker care that with this woe began,
Like the sparrow was I solitary
  That sits alone under the house's eaves.
  This while my foes conspired continually
And did provoke the harm of my disease.

Wherefore like ashes my bread did me savour;
570   Of thy just word the taste might not me please.
Wherefore my drink I tempered with liquor
  Of weeping tears that from mine eyes do rain
  Because I know the wrath of thy furor,
Provoked by right, had of my pride disdain
  For thou didst lift me up to throw me down,
  To teach me how to know myself again;
Whereby I know that helpless I should drown.
  My days like shadow decline and I do dry
  And thee forever eternity doth crown;
580 World without end doth last thy memory.
  For this frailty that yoketh all mankind –
  Thou shalt awake and rue this misery,
Rue on Zion, Zion that, as I find,
  Is the people that live under thy law.
  For now is time, the time at hand assigned,
The time so long that doth thy servants draw
  In great desire to see that pleasant day,
  Day of redeeming Zion from sin's awe.
For they have ruth to see in such decay,
590   In dust and stones, this wretched Zion lower.
Then the gentiles shall dread thy name alway;
  All earthly kings thy glory shall honour
  Then when thy grace this Zion thus redeemeth,
  When thus thou hast declared thy mighty power.
The Lord his servants' wishes so esteemeth
  That he him turn'th unto the poors' request.
  To our descent this to be written seemeth,
Of all comforts, as consolation best;
  And they that then shall be regenerate
600 Shall praise the Lord therefore, both most and least.
For he hath looked from the height of his estate;
  The Lord from heaven in earth hath looked on us
  To hear the moan of them that are algate
In foul bondage, to loose and to discuss
  The sons of death out from their deadly bond,
  To give thereby occasion gracious

In this Zion his holy name to stand
    And in Jerusalem his lauds, lasting ay,
    When in one church the people of the land
610 And realms been gathered to serve, to laud, to pray
    The Lord above so just and merciful.
    But to this sembly running in the way,
My strength faileth to reach it at the full.
    He hath abridged my days; they may not dure
    To see that term, that term so wonderful,
Although I have with hearty will and cure
    Prayed to the Lord: 'Take me not, Lord, away
    In mids of my years, though thine ever sure
Remain eterne, whom time cannot decay.
620   Thou wrought'st the earth; thy hands th'heavens did
      make:
    They shall perish and thou shalt last alway.
And all things age shall wear and overtake
    Like cloth, and thou shalt change them like apparel,
    Turn and translate, and they in worth it take.
But thou thyself the self remainest well
    That thou wast erst, and shalt thy years extend.
    Then since to this there may nothing rebel
The greatest comfort that I can pretend
    Is that the children of thy servants dear,
630   That in thy word are got, shall without end
Before thy face be stablished all in fere.'

                *

When David had perceived in his breast
The sprite of God returned that was exiled,
Because he knew he hath alone expressed
These great things that greater sprite compiled,
As shawm or pipe lets out the sound impressed,
By music's art forged tofore and filed,
I say when David had perceived this
The sprite of comfort in him revived is.

640   For thereupon he maketh argument
     Of reconciling unto the Lord's grace,
     Although some time to prophesy have lent
     Both brute beasts and wicked hearts a place.
     But our David judgeth in his intent
     Himself by penance clean out of this case,
     Whereby he hath remission of offence,
     And ginneth to allow his pain and penitence.

     But when he weigh'th the fault and recompense,
     He damn'th his deed and findeth plain
650   Atween them two no whit equivalence;
     Whereby he takes all outward deed in vain
     To bear the name of rightful penitence,
     Which is alone the heart returned again
     And sore contrite that doth his fault bemoan,
     And outward deed the sign or fruit alone.

     With this he doth defend the sly assault
     Of vain allowance of his void desert,
     And all the glory of his forgiven fault
     To God alone he doth it whole convert.
660   His own merit he findeth in default.
     And whilst he pondered these things in his heart,
     His knee, his arm, his hand sustained his chin
     When he his song again thus did begin.

Psalm 130. De profundis clamavi

     From depth of sin and from a deep despair,
       From depth of death, from depth of heart's sorrow,
       From this deep cave of darkness' deep repair,
     Thee have I called, O Lord, to be my borrow.
       Thou in my voice, O Lord, perceive and hear
       My heart, my hope, my plaint, my overthrow,
670   My will to rise, and let by grant appear
       That to my voice thine ears do well intend.
       No place so far that to thee is not near;
       No depth so deep that thou ne mayst extend

Thine ear thereto. Hear then my woeful plaint.
For, Lord, if thou do observe what men offend
And put thy native mercy in restraint,
If just exaction demand recompense,
Who may endure, O Lord? Who shall not faint
At such account? Dread and not reverence
680   Should so reign large. But thou seeks rather love
For in thy hand is mercy's residence
By hope whereof thou dost our hearts move.
I in thee, Lord, have set my confidence;
My soul such trust doth evermore approve.
Thy holy word of eterne excellence,
Thy mercy's promise that is alway just,
Have been my stay, my pillar, and pretence.
My soul in God hath more desirous trust
Than hath the watchman looking for the day
690   By the relief to quench of sleep the thrust.
Let Israel trust unto the Lord alway
For grace and favour arn his property.
Plenteous ransom shall come with him, I say,
And shall redeem all our iniquity.

               ✱

This word 'redeem' that in his mouth did sound
Did put David, it seemeth unto me,
As in a trance to stare upon the ground
And with his thought the height of heaven to see,
Where he beholds the Word that should confound
700   The sword of death, by humble ear to be
In mortal maid, in mortal habit made,
Eternal life in mortal veil to shade.

He seeth that Word, when full ripe time should come,
Do way that veil by fervent affection,
Torn off with death (for death should have her doom),
And leapeth lighter from such corruption
Than glint of light that in the air doth lome.

Man redeemed, death hath her destruction,
That mortal veil hath immortality,
710 David assurance of his iniquity.

Whereby he frames this reason in his heart:
'That goodness which doth not forbear his son
From death for me and can thereby convert
My death to life, my sin to salvation,
Both can and will a smaller grace depart
To him that sueth by humble supplication.
And since I have his larger grace assayed,
To ask this thing why am I then afraid?

'He granteth most to them that most do crave
720 And he delights in suit without respect.
Alas, my son pursues me to the grave,
Suffered by God my sin for to correct.
But of my sin since I my pardon have,
My son's pursuit shall shortly be reject.
Then will I crave with sured confidence.'
And thus begins the suit of his pretence.

Psalm 143. Domine exaudi orationem meam

Hear my prayer, O Lord, hear my request.
Complish my boon, answer to my desire
Not by desert but for thine own behest
730 In whose firm truth thou promised mine empire
To stand stable. And after thy justice
Perform, O Lord, the thing that I require;
But not of law after the form and guise
To enter judgement with thy thrall bondslave
To plead his right, for in such manner wise
Before thy sight no man his right shall save.
For of myself, lo, this my righteousness,
By scourge and whip and pricking spurs I have
Scant risen up, such is my beastliness.
740 For that my en'my hath pursued my life
And in the dust hath foiled my lustiness,
For that in herns to flee his rage so rife

He hath me forced as dead to hide my head,
And for because within myself at strife
My heart and sprite with all my force were fled,
I had recourse to times that have been past
And did remember thy deeds in all my dread
And did peruse thy works that ever last;
Whereby I knew above those wonders all
750   Thy mercies were. Then lift I up in haste
My hands to thee. My soul to thee did call
Like barren soil for moisture of thy grace.
Haste to my help, O Lord, afore I fall,
For sure I feel my sprite doth faint apace.
Turn not thy face from me, that I be laid
In count of them that headling down do pass
Into the pit. Shew me betimes thine aid
For on thy grace I wholly do depend.
And in thy hand since all my health is staid
760 Do me to know what way thou wolt I bend
For unto thee I have raised up my mind.
Rid me, O Lord, from that that do intend
My foes to me, for I have me assigned
Alway within thy secret protection.
Teach me thy will that I by thee may find
The way to work the same in affection.
For thou, my God, thy blessed upright sprite
In land of truth shall be my direction.
Thou for thy name, Lord, shalt revive my sprite
770 Within the right that I receive by thee,
Whereby my life of danger shall be quit.
Thou hast fordone their great iniquity
That vexed my soul. Thou shalt also confound
My foes, O Lord, for thy benignity,
For thine am I, thy servant ay most bound.

CLIII

From thought to thought, from hill to hill love doth me
    lead.
Clean contrary from restful life these common paths I
    tread.

CLIV

Iopas's Song

When Dido feasted first the wand'ring Trojan knight
Whom Juno's wrath with storms did force in Libyc
    sands to light,
That mighty'Atlas did teach, the supper lasting long,
With crisped locks, on golden harp Iopas sang in his
    song.
'That same,' quod he, 'that we the world do call and
    name,
Of heaven and earth with all contents it is the very
    frame.
Or thus: of heavenly pow'rs, by more pow'r kept in one;
Repugnant kinds, in mids of whom the earth hath place
    alone,
Firm, round, of living things the mother, place, and
    nurse.
10 Without the which in equal weight this heaven doth
    hold his course,
And it is called by name the first moving heaven.
The firmament is next, containing other seven.

Of heavenly powers that same is planted full and thick
As shining lights which we call stars that therein cleave
   and stick.
With great swift sway the first and with his restless
   source
Carry'th itself and all those eight in even continual
   course.
And of this world so round within that rolling case
There be two points that never move but firmly keep
   their place:
The t'one we see alway; the t'other stands object
20 Against the same, dividing just the round by line direct
Which by'imagination drawn from t'one to t'other
Toucheth the centre of the earth; way there is no
   nother.
And these been called the poles, described by stars not
   bright,
Arctic the t'one northward we see, Antarctic t'other
   hight.
The line that we devise from t'one to t'other so
As axle is upon the which th'heavens about doth go;
Which of water nor earth, of air nor fire have kind;
Therefore the substance of those same were hard for
   man to find.
But they been uncorrupt, simple and pure, unmixed;
30 And so we say been all those stars that in those same
   been fixed;
And eke those erring seven in circles as they stray –
So called because against that first they have repugnant
   way
And smaller byways too, scant sensible to man –
Too busy work for my poor harp, let sing them he that
   can.
The widest, save the first, of all these nine above,
One hundred year doth ask of space for one degree to
   move;
Of which degrees we make, in the first moving heaven,

Three hundred and three score in parts justly divided
even.
And yet there is another between those heavens two
40   Whose moving is so sly, so slack, I name it not for now.
The seventh heaven, or the shell next to the starry sky,
All those degrees that gather'th up with aged pace so sly
And doth perform the same, as elders' count hath been,
In nine and twenty years complete and days almost
sixteen,
Doth carry in his bowt the star of Saturn old,
A threat'ner of all living things with drought and with
his cold.
The sixth whom this contains doth stalk with younger
pace
And in twelve year doth somewhat more than t'other's
voyage was.
And this in it doth bear the star of Jove benign,
50   'Tween Saturn's malice and us men friendly defending
sign.
The fifth bear'th bloody Mars that in three hundred
days
And twice elev'n with one full year hath finished all
those ways.
A year doth ask the fourth, and hours thereto six,
And in the same the day his eye, the Sun, therein he
sticks.
The third, that governed is by that that govern'th me
And love for love and for no love provokes as oft we see,
In like space doth perform that course that did the
t'other.
So doth the next to the same that second is in order,
But it doth bear the star that called is Mercury
60   That many'a crafty secret step doth tread as calcars try.
That sky, is last and first next us, those ways hath gone
In seven and twenty common days and eke the third of
one
And beareth with his sway the diverse Moon about,

Now bright, now brown, now bent, now full, and now
    her light is out.
Thus have they of their own two movings all those
    seven:
One wherein they be carried still each in his sev'ral
    heaven,
Another of himselves where their bodies been led
In byways and in lesser rounds, as I afore have said;
Save, of them all, the Sun doth stray least from the
    straight,
70 The starry sky hath but one course, that we have called
    the eight.
And all these movings eight are meant from west to
    th'east
Although they seem to climb aloft, I say, from east to
    west;
But that is but by force of the first moving sky
In twice twelve hours from east to th'east that carry'th
    them by and by.
But mark we well also these movings of these seven
Be not about that axletree of the first moving heaven;
For they have their two poles directly t'one to t'other . . .'

Poems Attributed to Sir Thomas Wyatt
After the Sixteenth Century

Rondeau

For to love her for her looks lovely
My heart was set in thought right firmly,
Trusting by truth to have had redress.
But she hath made another promise
And hath given me leave full honestly.
Yet do I not rejoice it greatly
For on my faith I loved so surely.
But reason will that I do cease
    For to love her.

10 Since that in love the pains been deadly,
Methink it best that readily
I do return to my first address,
For at this time too great is the press
And perils appear too abundantly
    For to love her.

CLVI

Diverse doth use, as I have heard and know,
When that to change their ladies do begin,
To mourn and wail and never for to lin,
Hoping thereby to pease their painful woe.
And some there be that when it chanceth so
That women change and hate where love hath been
They call them false and think with words to win
The hearts of them which otherwhere doth grow.
But as for me, though that by chance indeed
10   Change hath outworn the favour that I had,
I will not wail, lament, nor yet be sad
Nor call her false that falsely did me feed
But let it pass and think it is of kind
That often change doth please a woman's mind.

CLVII

I abide and abide and better abide,
And after the old proverb, the happy day.
And ever my lady to me doth say,
'Let me alone and I will provide.'
I abide and abide and tarry the tide
And, with abiding, speed well ye may.
Thus do I abide, I wot, alway,
Neither obtaining nor yet denied.
Aye me, this long abiding
10   Seemeth to me, as who saith,
A prolonging of a dying death

Or a refusing of a desired thing.
Much were it better for to be plain
Than to say 'Abide' and yet shall not obtain.

CLVIII

Against the rock I climb, both high and hard,
When at the foot the ford doth bray so loud
That, save the heart so faithfully had vowed,
Seeing from the foot in midway I was forward,
. . . .
No heart so hardy nor courage that could
Adventure to climb so high a shroud,
Hope bids me hope of pain the right reward.
Now past the vales of danger and despite,
10 Mounted the rock of love and perfect joy,
Bained in the ford, despair to wash away,
Hoping hereafter from dark to find the light,
Brought to the highest, am of the deepest aghast.
For dread to fall, my hand, now hold thee fast.

CLIX

By bolstered words I am borne in hand,
As who saith, bidden I should obey.
Ye may threat twice ere once ye may
Prevail by power to underband
That I should yield and not withstand.
Your words do well your wits bewray,
Weening to bear so great a sway
To ween my will when ye command.
The free ye think to force by fear
10 To seek obedience of the thrall.
Your threat'ning words, of power but small,
Is wasted wind to use them here;
For like acquaintance of like scathe
Is my 'no fears' of your 'no faith'.

CLX

Driving to desire, adread also to dare,
Between two stools my tail goeth to the ground.
Dread and desire the reason doth confound,
The tongue put to silence. The heart, in hope and fear,
Doth dread that it dare and hide that would appear.
Desirous and dreadful, at liberty I go bound.
For pressing to proffer methinks I hear the sound:
'Back off thy boldness. Thy courage passeth care.'
This dangerous doubt, whether to obey
10 My dread or my desire, so sore doth me trouble
That cause causeth for dread of my decay.
In thought all one; in deeds to show me double,
Fearful and faithful! Yet take me as I am,
Though double in deeds, a inward perfect man.

Epigrams

CLXI

Patience, for I have wrong
And dare not show wherein!
Patience shall be my song
Since truth can nothing win.
Patience then for this fit!
Hereafter comes not yet.

CLXII

Thou sleepest fast and I with woeful heart
Stand here alone, sighing, and cannot fly.
Thou sleepest fast when cruel love his dart
On me doth cast, alas, so painfully.
Thou sleepest fast and I, all full of smart,
To thee, my foe, in vain do call and cry.
And yet, methinks, thou that sleepest fast,
Thou dreamest still which way my life to waste.

CLXIII

Plain ye, mine eyes. Accompany my heart
For, by your fault, lo, here is death at hand.
Ye brought him first into this bitter band
And of his harm as yet ye felt no part.
But now ye shall. Lo, here begins your smart.
Wet shall ye be – ye shall it not withstand –

With weeping tears that shall make dim your sight;
And misty clouds shall hang still in your light.
Blame but yourselves that kindled have this brand
10 With such desire to strain that past your might.
But since by you the heart hath caught his harm,
His flamed heat shall sometime make ye warm.

CLXIV

What thing is that that I both have and lack,
With goodwill granted and yet it is denied,
Always forward and yet full fair put back,
Ever more doing and yet unoccupied,
Most slow in that that I have most applied,
Whereby I see I lose all that I win,
For that that was ready is new to begin?

CLXV

In wilful riches I have found poverty
And in great pleasure I lived in heaviness.
In too much freedom I lacked liberty.
Nothing but plenty caused my scarceness.
Thus was I both in joy and in distress.
And, in few words if I should be plain,
In a paradise I suffered all this pain.

CLXVI

My love is like unto th'eternal fire
And I as those which therein do remain
Whose grievous pains is but their great desire
To see the sight which they may not attain.
So in hell's heat myself I feel to be
That am restrained by great extremity

The sight of her which is so dear to me.
O puissant love and power of great avail
By whom hell may be felt or death assail!

CLXVII

Since so ye please to hear me plain
And that ye do rejoice my smart,
Me list no longer to remain
To such as be so overthwart.
But cursed be that cruel heart
Which hath procured a careless mind
For me and mine unfeigned smart
And forceth me such faults to find.
More than too much I am assured
10   Of thine intent whereto to trust.
A speedless proof I have endured
And now I leave it to them that lust.

CLXVIII

O miserable sorrow withouten cure!
If it please thee, lo, to have me thus suffer,
At least yet let her know what I endure
And this my last voice carry thou thither
Where lived my hope now dead forever;
For as ill grievous is my banishment
As was my pleasure when she was present.

CLXIX

The loss is small to lose such one
That shrinketh for a slender nay,
And wit they lack that would make moan
Though all such pique were wiped away.

CLXX

Hate whom ye list for I care not.
Love whom ye list and spare not.
Do what ye list and dread not.
Think what ye list and fear not.
For as for me I am not
But even as one that recketh not
Whether ye hate or hate not,
For in your love I dote not.
Wherefore I pray you forget not
10 But love whom ye list and spare not.

CLXXI

Dido am I, the founder first of Carthage,
That, as thou seest, mine own death do procure
To save my faith and for no new love's rage,
To flee Iarbas and keep my promise sure.
But see Fortune, that would in 'nother age
Mine honest will in perfect bliss assure;
For while I lived, she made my day short,
And now with lies my shame she doth report.

CLXXII

Venus, in sport, to please therewith her dear,
Did on the helm of mighty Mars the red.
His spear she took; his targe she might not steer.
She looked as though her foes should all be dead,
So wantonly she frowneth with her cheer.
Priapus gan smile and said, 'Do way for dread,
Do way, madam, these weapons great and grim.
I, I for you am weapon fit and trim.'

CLXXIII

I see my plaint with open ears
Is heard, alas, and laughing eyes.
I see that scorn beholds my tears
And all the harm hap can devise.
I see my life away so wears
That I myself myself despise.
And most of all wherewith I strive
Is that I see myself alive.

Canzoni

CLXXIV

At last withdraw your cruelty
  Or let me die at once.
It is too much extremity,
  Devised for the nonce,
  To hold me still alive
  In pains still for to strive.
  What may I more sustain,
  Alas, that die would fain
  And cannot die for pain?

10 For to the flame wherewith I burn
  My thought and my desire,
When into ashes it should turn
  My heart by fervent fire
  You send a stormy rain
  That doth it quench again
  And makes my eyes express
  The tears that do redress
  My life in wretchedness.

Then when these should have drowned
20 And overwhelmed my heart
The heat doth them confound,
  Renewing all my smart.
  Then doth the flame increase.
  My torment cannot cease.
  My pains doth then revive
  And I remain alive
  With death still for to strive.

But if that you will have my death
And that you would no nother,
30 Then shortly for to stop my breath
Withdraw the one or other,
For this your cruelness
Doth let itself, doubtless,
And that is reason why
No man alive nor I
Of double death can die.

CLXXV

Patience of all my smart
For Fortune is turned awry!
Patience must ease my heart
That mourns continually.
Patience to suffer wrong
Is a patience too long.

Patience to have a nay
Of that I most desire!
Patience to have alway
10 And ever burn like fire!
Patience without desert
Is grounder of my smart.

Who can with merry heart
Set forth some pleasant song
That always feels but smart
And never hath but wrong?
Yet patience evermore
Must heal the wound and sore.

Patience to be content
20 With froward Fortune's train!
Patience to the intent
Somewhat to slake my pain!
I see no remedy
But suffer patiently.

To plain where is none ear
My chance is chanced so,
For it doth well appear
My friend is turned my foe.
But since there is no defence
30 I must take patience.

CLXXVI

Will ye see what wonders love hath wrought?
    Then come and look at me.
There need nowhere else to be sought.
    In me ye may them see.

For unto that that men may see
    Most monstrous thing of kind,
Myself may best compared be;
    Love hath me so assigned.

There is a rock in the salt flood,
10   A rock of such nature
That draweth the iron from the wood
    And leaveth the ship unsure.

She is the rock, the ship am I –
    The rock my deadly foe
That draweth me there where I must die
    And robbeth my heart me fro.

A bird there flieth, and that but one;
    Of her this thing ensueth:
That when her days be spent and gone,
20   With fire she reneweth.

And I with her may well compare
    My love that is alone,
The flame whereof doth ay repair
    My life when it is gone.

CLXXVII

Lament my loss, my labour, and my pain,
All ye that hear my woeful plaint and cry.
If ever man might once your heart constrain
To pity words of right, it should be I
That since the time that youth in me did reign
My pleasant years to bondage did apply,
Which, as it was, I purpose to declare
Whereby my friends hereafter may be ware.

And if perchance some readers list to muse
10   What meaneth me so plainly for to write,
My good intent the fault of it shall scuse,
Which mean nothing but truly to indite
The craft and care, the grief and long abuse
Of lover's law and eke her puissant might
Which though that men oft-times by pains doth know,
Little they wot which ways the guiles doth grow.

Yet well ye know it will renew my smart
Thus to rehearse the pains that I have passed.
My hand doth shake, my pen scant doth his part,
20   My body quakes, my wits begin to waste.
'Twixt heat and cold in fear I feel my heart
Panting for pain; and thus, as all aghast
I do remain scant wotting what I write,
Pardon me, then, rudely though I indite.

And patiently, O reader, I thee pray,
Take in good part this work as it is meant
And grieve thee not with aught that I shall say

Since with goodwill this book abroad is sent
To tell men how in youth I did assay
30 What love did mean, and now I it repent,
That, noting me, my friends may well be ware
And keep them free from all such pain and care.

CLXXVIII

And if an eye may save or slay
And strike more deep than weapon long,
And if an eye by subtle play
May move one more than any tongue,
How can ye say that I do wrong
Thus to suspect without desert?
For the eye is traitor of the heart.

To frame all well, I am content
That it were done unwittingly.
10 But yet I say who will assent
To do but well, do nothing why
That men should deem the contrary,
For it is said by men expert
That the eye is traitor of the heart.

But yet, alas, that look all sole
That I do claim of right to have
Should not, methinks, go seek the school
To please all folk, for who can crave
Friendlier thing than heart vouchsafe
20 By look to give in friendly part?
For the eye is traitor of the heart.

And my suspect is without blame
For, as ye say, not only I
But other moe have deemed the same.
Then is it not of jealousy,
But subtle look of reckless eye
Did range too far to make me smart.
For the eye is traitor of the heart.

But I, your friend, shall take it thus,
30 Since you will so, as stroke of chance,
And leave further for to discuss
Whether the stroke did stick or glance.
But scuse who can, let him advance
Dissembled looks. But for my part
My eye must still betray my heart.

And of this grief ye shall be quit
In helping troth steadfast to go.
The time is long that he doth sit
Feeble and weak and suffereth woe.
40 Cherish him well, continue so.
Let him not fro your heart astart.
Then fear not the eye to show the heart.

CLXXIX

To wet your eye withouten tear
And in good health to feign disease
That thou thereby mine eye might blear,
Therewith your other friends to please –
And though ye think ye need not fear,
Yet so ye cannot me appease.
But as ye list, feign, flatter, or gloze.
Ye shall not win if I do lose.

Prate and paint and spare not;
10 Ye know I can me wreck.
And if so be ye care not,
Be sure I do not reck.
And though ye swear it were not,
I can both swear and speak:
By God and by this cross
If I have the mock
Ye shall have the loss.

CLXXX

To my mishap, alas, I find
That happy hap is dangerous;
And Fortune worketh but her kind
To make the joyful dolorous.
But all too late it comes in mind
To wail the want which made me blind,
    So often warned.

Amidst my mirth and pleasantness
Such chance is chanced suddenly
10 That in despair to have redress
I find my chiefest remedy.
No new kind of unhappiness
Should thus have left me comfortless,
    So often warned.

Who could have thought that my request
Should have brought forth such bitter fruit?
But now is happed that I feared least
And all this grief comes by my suit;
For where I thought me happiest
20 Even there I found my chiefest unrest,
    So often warned.

In better case was never none
And yet unwares thus am I trapped.
My chief desire doth cause me moan
And to my pain my wealth is happed.
Was never man but I alone
That had such hap to wail and groan,
    So often warned.

Thus am I taught for to beware
30 And not to trust such pleasant chance.
My happy hap has bred this care
And turned my mirth to great mischance.

There is no man that hap will spare
But, when she list, our health is bare.
　　Thus am I warned.

CLXXXI

Since love is such that, as ye wot,
Cannot always be wisely used,
I say, therefore, then blame me not
Though I therein have been abused.
For as with cause I am accused,
Guilty I grant, such was my lot
And though it cannot be excused
Yet let such folly be forgot.

For in my years of reckless youth
10　Methought the power of love so great
That to her laws I bound my truth
And to my will there was no let.
Me list no more so far to fet
Such fruit, lo, as of love ensueth.
The gain was small that was to get
And of the loss the less the ruth.

And few there is but first or last
A time in love once shall they have;
And glad I am my time is past,
20　Henceforth my freedom to withsave.
Now in my heart there shall I grave
The grounded grace that now I taste.
Thanked be Fortune that me gave
So fair a gift, so sure and fast.

Now such as have me seen ere this –
When youth in me set forth his kind
And folly framed my thoughts amiss,
The fault whereof now well I find –
Lo, since that so it is assigned

30   That unto each a time there is,
     Then blame the lot that led my mind
     Sometime to live in love's bliss.

     But from henceforth I do protest
     By proof of that that I have passed
     Shall never cease within my breast
     The power that love so late outcast.
     The knot thereof is knit full fast
     And I thereto so sure professed
     For evermore with me to last
40   The power wherein I am possessed.

CLXXXII

     Lo, how I seek and sue to have
     That no man hath and may be had.
     There is no more but sink or save
     And bring this doubt to good or bad.
     To live in sorrows always sad
     I like not so to linger forth.
     Hap evil or good, I shall be glad
     To take that comes as well in worth.

     Should I sustain this great distress,
10   Still wand'ring forth thus to and fro,
     In dreadful hope to hold my peace
     And feed myself with secret woe?
     Nay, nay, certain I will not so.
     But sure I shall myself apply
     To put in proof this doubt to know
     And rid this danger readily.

     I shall assay by secret suit
     To show the mind of mine intent
     And my deserts shall give such fruit
20   As with my heart my words be meant.
     So by the proof of this consent

Soon out of doubt I shall be sure,
For to rejoice or to repent,
In joy or pain for to endure.

CLXXXIII

Pain of all pain, the most grievous pain
Is to love heartily and cannot be loved again.

Love with unkindness is causer of heaviness,
Of inward sorrow and sighs painful.
Whereas I love is no redress
To no manner of pastime: the sprites so dull
With privy mournings and looks rueful,
The body all wearish, the colour pale and wan,
More like a ghost than like a living man

10 When Cupido hath inflamed the heart's desires
To love there as is disdain;
Of good or ill the mind oblivious,
Nothing regarding but love t'attain;
Always imagining by what mean or train
It may be at rest thus in a moment
Now here, now there, being never content.

Tossing and turning when the body would rest,
With dreams oppressed and visions fantastical,
Sleeping or waking, love is ever pressed,
20 Sometime to weep, sometime to cry and call,
Bewailing his fortune and life bestial,
Now in hope of recure and now in despair –
This is a sorry life to live alway in care!

Record of Terence in his comedies poetical:
In love is jealousy and injuries many one,
Anger and debate with mind sensual,
Now war, now peace, musing all alone,
Sometime all mort and cold as any stone.
This causeth unkindness of such as cannot skill
30 Of true love, assured with heart and good will.

Lucrece the Roman, for love of our lord
And because perforce she had commit adultery
With Tarquinus, as the story doth record,
Herself did slay with a knife most piteously
Among her nigh friends, because that she
So falsely was betrayed. Lo, this was the guerdon
Whereas true love hath no dominion.

To make rehearsal of old antiquity
What needeth it? We see by experience
40 Among lovers it chanceth daily
Displeasure and variance for none offence.
But if true love might give sentence
That unkindness and disdain should have no place
But true heart for true love, it were a great grace.

O Venus, lady, of love the goddess,
Help all true lovers to have love again;
Banish from thy presence disdain and unkindness;
Kindness and pity to thy service retain:
For true love, once fixed in the cordial vein,
50 Can never be revulsed by no manner of art,
Unto the soul from the body depart.

CLXXXIV

Spite hath no power to make me sad
Nor scornfulness to make me plain.
It doth suffice that once I had
And so to leave it is no pain.
Let them frown on that least doth gain;
Who did rejoice must needs be glad.
And though with words thou ween'st to reign
It doth suffice that once I had.

Since that in checks thus overthwart
10 And coyly looks thou dost delight,
It doth suffice that mine thou wert

Though change hath put thy faith to flight.
Alas, it is a peevish spite
To yield thyself and then to part.
But since thou sett'st thy faith so light
It doth suffice that mine thou wert.

And since thy love doth thus decline
And in thy heart such hate doth grow,
It doth suffice that thou wert mine
20 And with goodwill I quit it so.
Sometime my friend, farewell, my foe!
Since thou change I am not thine.
But for relief of all my woe
It doth suffice that thou wert mine.

Praying you all that hears this song
To judge no wight, nor none to blame,
It doth suffice she doth me wrong
And that herself doth know the same.
And though she change, it is no shame:
30 Their kind it is and hath been long.
Yet I protest she hath no name;
It doth suffice she doth me wrong.

CLXXXV

Greeting to you both in hearty wise
As, unknown, I send (and this my intent
As I do here) you to advertise
Lest that perchance your deeds you do repent.
The unknown man dreads not to be shent
But says as he thinks: so fares it by me
That neither fear nor hope in no degree.

The body and the soul to hold together
It is but right, and reason wills the same;
10 And friendly the one to love the other

It increaseth your bruit and also your fame.
But mark well my words, for I fear no blame:
Trust well yourselves but ware ye trust no moe,
For such as ye think your friend may fortune be your
    foe.

Beware hardily ere ye have any need
And to friends reconciled trust not greatly,
For they that once with hasty speed
Exiled themselves out of your company,
Though they turn again and speak sweetly,
20 Feigning themselves to be your friends fast,
Beware of them for they will deceive you at last.

Fair words makes fools fain
And bearing in hand causeth much woe.
For time trieth troth; therefore refrain
And from such as be ready to do –
None do I name but this I know,
That by this fault cause causeth much.
Therefore beware if ye do know any such.

'To wise folks few words' is an old saying;
30 Therefore at this time I will write no more.
But this short lesson take for a warning:
By such light friends set little store;
If ye do otherwise ye will repent it sore.
And thus of this letter making an end,
To the body and the soul I me commend.

Written lifeless at the manor place
Of him that hath no chaff nor nowhere doth dwell,
But wandering in the wild world, wanting that he has,
And neither hopes nor fears heaven nor hell
40 But liveth at adventure. Ye know him full well.
The twenty day of March he wrote it in his house
And hath him recommended to the cat and mouse.

CLXXXVI

When that I call unto my mind
The time of hope that once I had,
The great abuse that did me blind
Doth force me always to be sad.
Yet of my grief I feign me glad
But am assured I was too bold
To trust to such a slipper hold.

I thought it well, that I had wrought,
Willing forthwith so to ensue.
10 But he that seeks as I have sought
Shall find most trust oft-times untrue,
For least I recked that most I rue:
Of that I thought myself most sure
Is now the want of all my cure.

Amidst my wealth I did not reck,
But soon, alas, ere that I wist,
The time was come that, all too weak,
I had no power for to resist.
Now am I proof to them that list
20 To flee such woe and wrongful pain
As in my heart I do sustain.

For feigned faith is always free
And doth incline to be unjust,
That sure I think there can none be
Too much assured without mistrust.
But hap what may to them that must
Sustain such cruel destiny
With patience for remedy.

As I am one which by restraint
30 Abides the time of my return
In hope that fortune by my plaint
Will slake the fire wherewith I burn
Since no ways else may serve my turn,

Yet for the doubt of this distress
I ask but right for my redress.

CLXXXVII

To make an end of all this strife,
No longer time for to sustain,
But now with death to change the life
Of him that lives always in pain –
Despair such power hath in his hand
That helpeth most, I know certain,
   May not withstand.

May not withstand that is elect
By Fortune's most extremity!
10 But all in worth to be, except
Withouten law or liberty –
What vaileth then unto my thought?
If right can have no remedy
   There vaileth naught.

There vaileth naught, but all is vain.
The fault thereof may none amend
But only death, for to constrain
This spiteful hap to have an end.
So great disdain doth me provoke
20 That dread of death cannot defend
   This deadly stroke.

This deadly stroke, whereby shall cease
The harboured sighs within my heart!
And for the gift of this release
My hand in haste shall play his part
To do this cure against his kind –
For change of life from long desert
   To place assigned.

To place assigned for evermore!
30 Now by constraint I do agree

To loose the bond of my restore
Wherein is bound my liberty.
Death and despair doth undertake
From all mishap now hardily
   This end to make.

CLXXXVIII

Deem as ye list. Upon good cause
I may or think of this or not.
But what or why myself best knows
   Whereby I think and fear not.
But thereunto I may well think
The doubtful sentence of this clause:
I would it were not as I think;
   I would I thought it were not.

For if I thought it were not so,
10 Though it were so, it grieved me not;
Unto my thought it were as though
   I hearkened though I hear not.
At that I see I cannot wink
Nor from my thought so let it go.
I would it were not as I think;
   I would I thought it were not.

Lo, how my thought might make me free
Of that perchance it needeth not.
Perchance none doubt the dread I see;
20   I shrink at that I bear not.
But in my heart this word shall sink
Unto the proof may better be:
I would it were not as I think;
   I would I thought it were not.

If it be not, show no cause why
I should so think, then care I not;

For I shall so myself apply
　　To be that I appear not:
That is as one that shall not shrink
30　To be your own until I die
And, if it be not as I think,
　　Likewise to think it is not.

CLXXXIX

All ye that know of care and heaviness,
My woeful fate when ye have heard,
Then judge the truth in this my great distress,
If any woe may be thereto compared;
And mark my thought as I shall it express,
For cause itself doth neither mar nor make
But even as the patient doth it take.

I think whoso doth behold my pain
Sees the soul of Sorrow grounded in grief,
10　The root of Woe portrayed in pain,
The cloud of Care despaired of relief,
The loathed life through-darted with Disdain.
Sorrow is I, and I even the same,
In that all men do call me by that name.

When I do cast my careful look downright
Upon the ground as though that I would fall,
Therein methinks is graven with my sight
The picture of my sorrowful thoughts all.
Yea, and the worms that appear against the night,
20　As me seems, they think that Death doth much ill
To leave me thus to live against my will.

Where I do use to lie right secretly
Upon a bank over a river clear,
So oft I there bewail my destiny
That the water disdaineth it to hear
And at my weeping takes great envy,

Lest the tears that from mine eyes do rain
Should cause the fish therein to mourn and plain.

Alone when I do walk the woods wand'ring,
30 Utt'ring my care with painful sighs and groans,
The birds, which on the boughs sit singing,
To hear my cry then cease they all at once,
Having great grudge at me and my wailing
Because it was so grievous shrill and loud
That it stunned their song thorough all the wood.

CXC

Alas! my dear, the word thou spakest
Hath struck the stroke within my breast
Of cruel death, since thou forsakest
Me and my faithful meant behest.
Too long I shewed that word to hear
That doth renew my great unrest
    And mourning cheer,

And mourning cheer, which by despair
For want of hope is much increased
10 So that, now past both hope and fear,
Of my judgement I know the best
Is life awhile in painful woe;
And how soon death will pierce my breast
    I do not know.

I do not know when nor how soon
The stroke thou smast within my heart
Will bleed me to a deadly swoon.
But well I know, though thou revert,
Till it doth bleed and I stark dead,
20 I shall renew with daily smart
    This life I lead,

This life I lead and live too long
Against my will in tears to melt,
Since none there is may right my wrong.

But I must feel that I have felt
The stroke of death and cannot die,
Guarded within the strongest belt
  Of cruelty,

Of cruelty and cruel death
30 Forced to abide extremity,
And yet to live, though I want breath
To show further how cruelly
My hope is turned to mourning cheer,
And ye the cause thereof only,
  Alas, my dear.

CXCI

Being as none is, I do complain
Of my mishap, torment, and my woe,
Wishing for death with all my might and main
For life is to me as my chief deadly foe.
Alas, alas, of comfort I have no moe,
Left but only to sing this doleful song:
'Patience, perforce, content thyself with wrong.'

Ever I hope some favour to obtain,
Trusting that she will recompense at last,
10 As reason were, my passing deadly pain.
And still I persevered and they increased so fast
That hope me left and I, as all aghast,
Had no comfort, but learned to sing this song:
'Patience, perforce, content thyself with wrong.'

I burn and boil, without redress.
I sigh, I weep, and all in vain,
Now hot, now cold. Who can express
The thousand part of my great pain?
But if I might her favour attain
20 Then would I trust to change this song,
With 'pity' for 'patience' and 'conscience' for 'wrong'.

CXCII

Do way, do way, ye little wily prat!
Your slyly slinking cannot you excuse
Nor words dissembled cannot hide that
That will peer out, if often ye it use.
If ye think other, yourself ye do abuse.
For heartly love unspied long to last,
If ye assay, your wits sore ye waste.

If it be possible that from a fire great
The black smoke shall not issue out
10 Or for a cripple to halt and counterfeit
And be not spied, then quickly go about
Us to beguile; for truly without doubt
We know the craft, the looks, and the price.
Wherefore, trust me, it is hard to blear our eyes.

If that we to you of this do speak,
For goodwill, to make ye leave your folly,
Then will ye not stint till ye be wreak
And ready to swear and still will deny
That that is true; yet will ye never apply
20 To your own faults, but always ye excuse.
Leave, fie, for shame! Ye make men to think and muse.

Ye think to cloak that cloaked cannot be
And think to hide that open is in sight.
Alas, methinketh it is a great pity
Yourself to bring in such a plight
That should us cause to think ye light.
Leave off therefore. In faith ye are to blame.
Ye hurt yourself and loseth your good name.

CXCIII

Since that my language without eloquence
Is plain, unpainted, and not unknown,
Dispatch answer with ready utterance:
The question is 'yours?' or else 'mine own?'
To be upholden and still to fawn,
I know no cause of such obedience.
To have such corn as seed was sown,
That is the worst. Therefore give sentence.

But if your will be in this case
10 To uphold me still, what needeth that?
Sith 'yea' or 'nay' my question was,
So long delay it needeth not.
If I have 'yea' then have I that
That I have sought to bring to pass.
If I have 'nay' yet reck I not.
Where naught is got, there is no loss.

The 'yea' desired, the 'nay' not.
No grief so great, nor desire so sore
But that I may forbear to dote.
20 If 'yea,' forever. If 'nay', no more
To trouble ye thus. Speak on therefore.
If that ye will, say 'yea.' If not,
We shall be friends even as before,
And I mine own, that yours may not.

CXCIV

Had I wist that now I wot
For to have found that now I find,
I would have done that I did not.
But feigned faith did make me blind
And by great oaths fixed in my mind
His faith to be faithful to trust.
The deed now proved, I find unjust.

It is not the thing that I pass on.
Of his faith though I had assurance,
10   Of that no more I will trust on
Than of a thing that lieth in balance.
Truth laid apart falsed is. His maintenance,
Ever double, never will be true.
Rooted at the heart must needs continue.

CXCV

Horrible of hue, hideous to behold,
Careful of countenance, his hair all clustered,
With dead droppy blood that down his face rolled,
Pale, painful, and piteously pierced,
His heart in sunder sorrowfully shivered,
Methought a man, thus marvellously murdered,
This night to me came and carefully cried:

'O man misfortunate, more than any creature,
That painfully yet lives more pain to perceive,
10   What hardened hath thy heart this harm to suffer?
Thy doubtful hope, it do thee but deceive.
No good nor grace to glad thee shalt receive.
By pain from thy pain then pain to procure,
Moe bitter it were than death to endure.

'Follow me,' saith he, 'hold here my hand.
Too long is death in tears to groan.
The sea shall sooner quench the brand
Of the desire that hath thee thus undone
Or sooner send thee to a deadly swoon.
20   Hold in thy hand the haft here of this knife
And with the blade boldly bereave thy life.

'Come off,' quod he. 'I come,' quod I.
Then therewith as methought
My breast I pierced painfully.

My heart right soon I it raught.
But, lord, alas, it was for naught
For with that stroke I did awake.
My heart for sorrow yet feel I quake.

CXCVI

I know not where my heavy sighs to hide.
My sorrowful heart is so vexed with pain
I wander forth as one without a guide
That seeketh to find a thing parted in twain
And so forth run that scant can turn again.
Thus time I pass and waste full piteously
For death it is out of thy sight to be.

I scantly know from whom comes all my grief,
But that I waste as one doth in sickness
10 And cannot tell which way comes my mischief.
For all I taste to me is bitterness
And of my health I have no sickerness
Nor shall not have till that I do thee see.
It is my death out of thy sight to be.

I live in earth as one that would be dead
And cannot die. Alas, the more my pain!
Famished I am and yet always am fed.
Thus contrary all thing doth me constrain
To laugh, to mourn, to walk, to joy, to plain,
20 And shall do still – there is no remedy –
Until the time that in thy sight I be.

There nis sickness but health it doth desire,
Nor poverty but riches like to have,
Nor ship in storm but that steering it doth require
Harbour to find so that they may her save.
And I, alas, naught in this world do crave
Save that thou list on him to have mercy
Whose death it is out of thy sight to be.

CXCVII

In mourning wise since daily I increase,
Thus should I cloak the cause of all my grief:
So pensive mind with tongue to hold his peace.
My reason sayeth there can be no relief;
Wherefore, give ear, I humbly you require,
The affects to know that thus doth make me moan.
The cause is great of all my doleful cheer
For those that were and now be dead and gone.

What though to death desert be now their call
10 As by their faults it doth appear right plain.
Of force I must lament that such a fall
Should light on those so wealthily did reign,
Though some perchance will say, of cruel heart,
'A traitor's death why should we thus bemoan?'
But I, alas, set this offence apart,
Must needs bewail the death of some be gone.

As for them all I do not thus lament
But as of right my reason doth me bind.
But as the most doth all their deaths repent,
20 Even so do I by force of mourning mind.
Some say, 'Rochford, hadst thou been not so proud,
For thy great wit each man would thee bemoan.'
Since as it is so, many cry aloud,
'It is great loss that thou art dead and gone.'

Ah, Norris, Norris, my tears begin to run
To think what hap did thee so lead or guide,
Whereby thou hast both thee and thine undone,
That is bewailed in court of every side.
In place also where thou hast never been
30 Both man and child doth piteously thee moan.
They say, 'Alas, thou art far overseen
By thine offences to be thus dead and gone.'

Ah, Weston, Weston, that pleasant was and young,
In active things who might with thee compare?
All words accept that thou didst speak with tongue,
So well esteemed with each where thou didst fare.
And we that now in court doth lead our life,
Most part in mind doth thee lament and moan.
But that thy faults we daily hear so rife,
40 All we should weep that thou art dead and gone.

Brereton, farewell, as one that least I knew.
Great was thy love with diverse, as I hear,
But common voice doth not so sore thee rue
As other twain that doth before appear.
But yet no doubt but thy friends thee lament
And other hear their piteous cry and moan.
So doth each heart for thee likewise relent
That thou giv'st cause thus to be dead and gone.

Ah, Mark, what moan should I for thee make more
50 Since that thy death thou hast deserved best,
Save only that mine eye is forced sore
With piteous plaint to moan thee with the rest?
A time thou hadst above thy poor degree,
The fall whereof thy friends may well bemoan.
A rotten twig upon so high a tree
Hath slipped thy hold and thou art dead and gone.

And thus, farewell, each one in hearty wise.
The axe is home, your heads be in the street.
The trickling tears doth fall so from my eyes,
60 I scarce may write, my paper is so wet.
But what can help when death hath played his part
Though nature's course will thus lament and moan?
Leave sobs therefore, and every Christian heart
Pray for the souls of those be dead and gone.

CXCVIII

My sweet, alas, forget me not
That am your own full sure possessed;
And for my part, as well ye wot,
I cannot swerve from my behest.
Since that my life lieth in your lot,
At this my poor and just request
   Forget me not.

Yet wot how sure that I am tried,
My meaning clean, devoid of blot.
10 Yours is the proof: ye have me tried
And in me, sweet, ye found no spot.
If all my wealth and health is the good,
That of my life doth knit the knot,
   Forget me not.

For yours I am and will be still
Although daily ye see me not.
Seek for to save that ye may spill
Since of my life ye hold the shot.
Then grant me this for my goodwill,
20 Which is but right, as God it wot:
   Forget me not.

Consider how I am your thrall
To serve you both in cold and hot.
My fault's for thinking naught at all,
In prison strong though I should rot.
Then in your ears let pity fall
And, lest I perish in your lot,
   Forget me not.

CXCIX

She that should most, perceiveth least
The unfeigned sufferance of my great smart.
It is to her sport to have me oppressed.
But they of such life which be expert
Say that I burn uncertain in my heart.
But where judge ye? No more! Ye know not.
Ye are to blame to say I came too late.

Too late? Nay, too soon methink rather,
Thus to be entreated and have served faithfully.
10　Lo, thus am I rewarded among the other.
I, though unvised which was too busy,
For fear of too late I came too hastily.
But thither I came not; yet came I for all that.
But whithersoever I came, I came too late.

Who hath more cause to plain than I?
There as I am judged, too late I came;
And there as I came, I came too hastily.
Thus may I plain as I that am
Misjudged, misentreated more than any man.
20　Now judge, let see, of this debate,
Whether I came too hastily or too late.

CC

Sith it is so that I am thus refused
And by no means I can it remedy,
Methinks of right I ought to be excused,
Though to my heart I set it not too nigh.
For now I see, alas, though I should die
For want of truth and faithful steadfastness
Of him that hath my heart only,
It would not be but false new-fangledness.

I set my heart. I thought not to withdraw;
10 The proof thereof is known too well, alas.
But now I see that never erst I saw:
Where I thought gold, I found but brittle glass.
Now it is this ye know; something it was
Not so promised; the truth is so, doubtless.
Who is my foe who brings me in this case?
I can none blame but false new-fangledness.

Yet reason would that true love were regarded
Without feigning, where it is meant faithfully,
And not with unkindness is to be rewarded.
20 But thus it is, alas, such hap had I.
I can no more, but I shall me apply
My woeful heart to bring out of distress
And withdraw my mind, so full of folly,
Sith thus doth reign this false new-fangledness.

CCI

Though some do grudge to see me joy,
Forcing their spite to slake my health,
Their false mistrust shall never noy
So long as thou dost will my wealth.
For though they frown, full well I know
No power they have to forge my woe.
Then grudge who list, I shall not cease
To seek and sue for my redress.

Whilst life doth last and thou content,
10 What should I doubt, what should I dread
Their spite that daily do consent
To make my joy from me be led?
What should I bow to friend or foe
That would me so thy sight forgo?
What should I do but pass full light
The frail mistrust of all their spite?

If cause were given of any part
To cause mistrust in them to spring,
Naught should it grieve me then to smart.
20 But I, alas, know none such thing.
Then by mishap and cruel lot,
Though they would so, forsake me not;
Nor will me not, my foes to please,
To slake the suit of all my ease.

Thine own and thine forevermore
I am and must continue still.
No woe nor pains, no hurt nor sore
Can cause me flee from this my will –
Thy own to be, and not to start
30 As long as life is in my heart.
Then grant me this my life to save:
As I deserve, so let me have.

CCII

Though of the sort there be that feign
And cloak their craft to serve their turn,
Shall I, alas, that truly mean,
For their offence thus guiltless burn?
And if I buy their fault too dear,
That their untruth thus heat my fire,
   Then have I wrong.

Though frailty fail not to appear
In them that wail as well as I,
10 And though the false by like desire
Doth swear himself thine own to be –
If thou dost judge me one of these
That so can feign such common ways
   Then have I wrong.

Though chance hath power to change their love
That all by chance their will doth guide,

Such chance may not my heart remove
For I by choice myself have tried
And not by chance; wherefore I say,
If thou dost not my welfare stay,
    Then have I wrong.

Though steadfastness in them do lack
That do protest the contrary
And though performance none they make
Of that they promise diversely,
Yet since their faults are none of mine,
If thou refusest me for thine,
    Then have I wrong.

CCIII

Tangled I was in love's snare,
Oppressed with pain, torment with care,
Of grief right sure, of joy full bare,
Clean in despair by cruelty.
But ha, ha, ha, full well is me
For I am now at liberty.

The woeful days so full of pain,
The weary night all spent in vain,
The labour lost for so small gain,
10 To write them all it will not be.
But ha, ha, ha, full well is me
For I am now at liberty.

Everything that fair doth show
When proof is made it proveth not so.
But turneth mirth to bitter woe
Which in this case full well I see.
But ha, ha, ha, full well is me
For I am now at liberty.

Too great desire was my guide
20 And wanton will went by my side.
Hope ruled still and made me bide
Of love's craft th'extremity.
But ha, ha, ha, full well is me
For I am now at liberty.

With feigned words which were but wind
Too long delays I was assigned.

Her wily looks my wits did blind;
Thus as she would I did agree.
But ha, ha, ha, full well is me
30   For I am now at liberty.

Was never bird tangled in lime
That brake away in better time
Than I that rotten boughs did climb
And had no hurt, but scaped free.
Now ha, ha, ha, full well is me
For I am now at liberty.

CCIV

Alas, the grief and deadly woeful smart,
The careful chance shapen afore my shirt,
The sorrowful tears, the sighs hot as fire
That cruel love hath long soaked from mine heart!
And for reward of over great desire
Disdainful doubleness have I for my hire!

O lost service! O pain ill rewarded!
O pitiful heart with pain enlarded!
O faithful mind too suddenly assented,
10   Return, alas, sithens thou art not regarded.
Too great a proof of true faith presented
Causeth by right such faith to be repented.

O cruel causer of undeserved change,
By great desire unconstantly to range,
Is this your way for proof of steadfastness?
Perdie, you know – the thing was not so strange –
By former proof too much my faithfulness.
What needeth then such coloured doubleness?

I have wailed thus, weeping in nightly pain,
20   In sobs and sighs, alas, and all in vain,
In inward plaint and heart's woeful torment.
And yet, alas, lo, cruelty and disdain

Have set at naught a faithful true intent
And price hath privilege truth to prevent.

But though I sterve and to my death still mourn,
And piecemeal in pieces though I be torn,
And though I die, yielding my wearied ghost,
Shall never thing again make me return.
I quit th'enterprise of that that I have lost
30 To whomsoever lust for to proffer most.

CCV

. . . .
But sithens you it assay to kill
By cruelty and doubleness,
That that was yours you seek to spill
Against all right and gentleness;
And sithens you will, even so I will.

And then, helas, when no redress
Can be, too late ye shall repent
And say yourself with words express,
'Helas, an heart of true intent
10 Slain have I by unfaithfulness!'

CCVI

Like as the wind with raging blast
Doth cause each tree to bow and bend,
Even so do I spend my time in waste,
My life consuming unto an end.

As flame by force doth quench the fire
And running streams consume the rain,
Even so do I myself desire
To augment my grief and deadly pain.

Whereas I find that hot is hot
10   And cold is cold by course of kind,
So shall I knit an endless knot:
Such fruit in love, alas, I find.

When I first saw those crystal streams
Whose beauty doth cause my mortal wound,
I little thought within those beams
So sweet a venom for to have found.

I feel and see mine own decay,
As one that beareth flame in his breast
Forgets, for thought, to put away
20   The thing that breedeth mine unrest;

Like as the fly doth seek the flame
And afterward playeth in the fire,
Who findeth her woe and seeketh her game,
Whose grief doth grow of her own desire.

Like as the spider doth draw her line
With labour lost, so is my suit.
The gain is hers, the loss is mine:
Of ill-sown seed such is the fruit.

CCVII

Heart oppressed with desperate thought
Is forced ever to lament,
Which now in me so sore hath wrought
That needs to it I must consent;
Wherefore all joy I must refuse
And cruel will thereof accuse.

If cruel will had not been guide,
Despair in me had had no place;
For my true meaning she well espied
10   And for all that would give no grace.
Therefore all joy I must refuse
And cruel will thereof accuse.

She well might see and yet would not,
And may daily, if that she will,
How painful is my hapless lot
Joined with despair me for to spill;
Whereby all joy I must refuse
Since cruel will doth me so use.

CCVIII

My pen, take pain a little space
To follow that which doth me chase
And hath in hold my heart so sore.
But when thou hast this brought to pass,
My pen, I prithee, write no more.

Remember, oft thou hast me eased
And all my pains full well appeased.
But now I know, unknown before,
That where I trust I am deceived.
10 And yet, my pen, thou canst no more.

A time thou had'st, as other have,
To write which way my hope to crave.
That time is passed. Withdraw therefore.
Since we do lose that other save
As good leave off and write no more

And use to work another way,
Not as we would, but as we may,
For once my loss is past restore
And my desire is my decay.
20 My pen, yet write a little more:

To love in vain whoever shall,
Of worldly pain it passeth all
As in like case I find. Wherefore
To hold so fast and yet to fall?
Alas, my pen, now write no more.

Since thou hast taken pain this space
To follow that which doth me chase
And hath in hold my heart so sore,
Now hast thou brought my mind to pass.
30   My pen, I prithee, write no more.

CCIX

I love, loved, and so doth she
And yet in love we suffer still.
The cause is strange, as seemeth me,
To love so well and want our will.

O deadly yea! O grievous smart!
Worse than refuse, unhappy gain!
In love whoever played this part
To love so well and live in pain?

Was ever hearts so well agreed
10   Since love was love, as I do trow,
That in their love so ill did speed
To love so well and live in woe?

This mourn we both and hath done long
With woeful plaint and careful voice.
Alas, it is a grievous wrong
To love so well and not rejoice.

And here an end of all our moan!
With sighing oft my breath is scant
Since of mishap ours is alone
20   To love so well and yet to want.

But they that causer is of this,
Of all our cares God send them part
That they may know what grief it is
To love so well and live in smart.

CCX

Suffering in sorrow, in hope to attain,
Desiring in fear and dare not complain,
True of belief in whom is all my trust,
Do thou apply to ease me of my pain,
Else thus to serve and suffer still I must.

Hope is my hold. Yet in despair to speak
I drive from time to time and do not reck
How long to live thus after love's lust,
In study still of that I dare not break;
10 Wherefore to serve and suffer still I must.

Encrease of care I find both day and night.
I hate that was sometime all my delight.
The cause thereof ye know I have discussed
And yet to refrain it passeth my might;
Wherefore to serve and suffer still I must.

Love whoso list, at length he shall well say:
To love and live in fear it is no play.
Record that knoweth, and if this be not just,
That whereas love doth lead, there is no way
20 But serve and suffer ever still he must.

Then for to live with loss of liberty
At last perchance shall be his remedy,
And for his truth, requit with false mistrust.
Who would not rue to see how wrongfully
Thus for to serve and suffer still he must?

Ontruth by trust oft-times hath me betrayed,
Misusing my hope, still to be delayed.
Fortune, always I have ye found unjust;
And so with like reward now am I paid –
30 That is, to serve and suffer still I must,

Never to cease nor yet like to attain
As long as I in fear dare not complain.

True of belief hath always been my trust
And, till she knoweth the cause of all my pain,
Content to serve and suffer still I must.

CCXI

The heart and service to you proffered
With right goodwill full honestly,
Refuse it not since it is offered,
But take it to you gentlely.

And though it be a small present,
Yet, good, consider graciously
The thought, the mind, and the intent
Of him that loves you faithfully.

It were a thing of small effect
10 To work my woe thus cruelly,
For my goodwill to be abject.
Therefore accept it lovingly.

Pain or travail, to run or ride,
I undertake it pleasantly.
Bid ye me go and straight I glide
At your commandment humblely.

Pain or pleasure now may you plant,
Even which it please you steadfastly.
Do which you list, I shall not want
20 To be your servant secretly.

And since so much I do desire
To be your own assuredly,
For all my service and my hire
Reward your servant liberally.

CCXII

As power and wit will me assist,
My will shall will even as ye list.

For as ye list my will is bent
In every thing to be content,
To serve in love till life be spent
And to reward my love thus meant
   Even as ye list.

To feign or fable is not my mind
Nor to refuse such as I find,
10 But as a lamb of humble kind
Or bird in cage to be assigned
   Even as ye list.

When all the flock is come and gone
Mine eye and heart agree'th in one,
Hath chosen you only alone
To be my joy or else my moan
   Even as ye list.

Joy, if pity appear in place,
Moan, if disdain do show his face.
20 Yet crave I not as in this case
But as ye lead to follow the trace
   Even as ye list.

Some in words much love can feign
And some for words give words again.
Thus words for words in words remain.
And yet at last words do obtain
   Even as ye list.

To crave in words I will eschew
And love in deed I will ensue.
30 It is my mind both whole and true.
And for my truth I pray you rue
   Even as ye list.

Dear heart, I bid your heart farewell
With better heart than tongue can tell.
Yet take this tale as true as gospel.
Ye may my life save or expel
   Even as ye list.

CCXIII

Sometime I sigh, sometime I sing,
Sometime I laugh, sometime mourning.
As one in doubt this is my saying:
Have I displeased you in anything?

Alack, what aileth you to be grieved?
Right sorry am I that ye be moved.
I am your own if truth be proved
And by your displeasure as one mischieved.

When ye be merry, then am I glad.
10 When ye be sorry, then am I sad.
Such grace or fortune I would I had
You for to please however I were bestad.

When ye be merry why should I care?
Ye are my joy and my welfare.
I will you love, I will not spare
Into your presence as far as I dare.

All my poor heart and my love true
While life doth last I give it you;
And you to serve with service due
20 And never to change you for no new.

CCXIV

Thy promise was to love me best
And that thy heart with mine should rest,
And not to break this thy behest
Thy promise was, thy promise was.

Thy promise was not to acquit
My faithfulness with such despite,
But recompense it if thou might
Thy promise was, thy promise was.

Thy promise was, I tell thee plain,
10   My faith should not be spent in vain,
But to have more should be my gain
Thy promise was, thy promise was.

Thy promise was to have observed
My faith like as it hath deserved,
And not causeless thus to a' swerved
Thy promise was, thy promise was.

Thy promise was, I dare avow –
But it is changed, I wot well how.
Though then were then and now is now,
20   Thy promise was, thy promise was.

But since to change thou dost delight
And that thy faith hath ta'en his flight,
As thou deserv'st I shall thee quit
I promise thee, I promise thee.

CCXV

I see the change from that that was
And how thy faith hath ta'en his flight.
But I with patience let it pass
And with my pen this do I write
To show thee plain by proof of sight
    I see the change.

I see the change of wearied mind
And slipper hold hath quit my hire.
Lo, how by proof in thee I find
10   A burning faith in changing fire.
Farewell, my part. Proof is no liar.
    I see the change.

I see the change of chance in love.
Delight no longer may abide.
What should I seek further to prove?
No, no, my trust, for I have tried
The following of a false guide.
    I see the change.

I see the change, as in this case,
20 Has made me free from mine avow;
For now another has my place
And ere I wist, I wot ne'er how,
It happened thus as ye hear now.
    I see the change.

I see the change. Such is my chance
To serve in doubt and hope in vain.
But since my surety so doth glance,
Repentance now shall quit thy pain,
Never to trust the like again.
30   I see the change.

CCXVI

Forget not yet the tried intent
Of such a truth as I have meant,
My great travail so gladly spent.
    Forget not yet.

Forget not yet when first began
The weary life ye know since when,
The suit, the service none tell can.
    Forget not yet.

Forget not yet the great assays,
10 The cruel wrong, the scornful ways,
The painful patience in denays.
    Forget not yet.

Forget not yet, forget not this:
How long ago hath been and is
The mind that never meant amiss.
   Forget not yet.

Forget not then thine own approved
The which so long hath thee so loved
Whose steadfast faith yet never moved.
20   Forget not this.

CCXVII

Give place all ye that doth rejoice
And love's pangs hath clean forgot.
Let them draw near and hear my voice
Whom love doth force in pains to fret.
For all of plaint my song is set
Which long hath served and naught can get.

A faithful heart so truly meant
Rewarded is full slenderly.
A steadfast faith with good intent
10 Is recompensed craftily.
Such hap doth hap unhappily
To them that mean but honestly.

With humble suit I have assayed
To turn her cruel-hearted mind,
But for reward I am delayed
And to my wealth her eyes be blind.
Lo, thus by chance I am assigned
With steadfast love to serve the unkind.

What vaileth truth or steadfastness
20 Or still to serve without reproof?
What vaileth faith or gentleness
Where cruelty doth reign as chief?
Alas, there is no greater grief
Than for to love and lack relief.

Care doth constrain me to complain
Of love and her uncertainty
Which granteth naught but great disdain
For loss of all my liberty.
Alas, this is extremity
30 For love to find such cruelty!

For hearty love to find such hate,
Alas, it is a careful lot.
And for to void so foul a mate
There is no way but slip the knot.
The gain so cold, the pain so hot,
Praise it who list, I like it not.

CCXVIII

Grudge on who list, this is my lot;
No thing to want, if it were not.

My years be young even as ye see.
All things thereto doth well agree.
In faith, in face, in each degree
No thing doth want, as seemeth me,
    If it were not.

Some men doth say that friends be scarce
But I have found, as in this case,
10 A friend which giveth to no man place
But makes me happiest that ever was,
    If it were not.

Grudge on who list, this is my lot;
No thing to want, if it were not.

A heart I have besides all this
That hath my heart and I have his.
If he doth well it is my bliss
And when we meet no lack there is,
    If it were not.

20 If he can find that can me please,
    He thinks he does his own heart's ease;
    And likewise I could well appease
    The chiefest cause of his misease,
      If it were not.

    Grudge on who list, this is my lot;
    No thing to want, if it were not.

    A master eke God hath me sent
    To whom my will is wholly bent
    To serve and love, for that intent
30 That both we might be well content,
      If it were not.

    And here an end. It doth suffice
    To speak few words among the wise.
    Yet take this note before your eyes:
    My mirth should double once or twice
      If it were not.

    Grudge on who list, this is my lot;
    No thing to want if it were not.

CCXIX

    Ah, my heart, ah, what aileth thee
    To set so light my liberty,
    Making me bound when I was free?
    Ah, my heart, ah, what aileth thee?

    When thou were rid from all distress,
    Void of all pain and pensiveness,
    To choose again a new mistress,
    Ah, my heart, ah, what aileth thee?

    When thou were well, thou could not hold.
10 To turn again, that were too bold.
    Thus to renew my sorrows old,
    Ah, my heart, ah, what aileth thee?

Thou knowest full well that but of late
I was turned out of Love's gate.
And now to guide me to this mate,
Ah, my heart, ah, what aileth thee?

I hoped full well all had been done
But now my hope is ta'en and won.
To my torment to yield so soon,
20   Ah, my heart, ah, what aileth thee?

CCXX

Absence! Absenting causeth me to complain,
My sorrowful complaints abiding in distress;
And departing most privy increaseth my pain.
Thus live I uncomforted, wrapped all in heaviness.

In heaviness I am wrapped devoid of all solace.
Neither pastime nor pleasure can revive my dull wit.
My sprites be all taken and death doth me menace
With his fatal knife the thread for to kit,

For to kit the thread of this wretched life
10   And shortly bring me out of this case.
I see it availeth not, yet must I be pensive
Since fortune from me hath turned her face.

Her face she hath turned with countenance contrarious
And clean from her presence she hath exiled me,
In sorrow remaining as a man most dolorous,
Exempt from all pleasure, all worldly felicity.

All worldly felicity now am I private
And left in desert most solitarily,
Wandering all about as one without mate.
20   My death approacheth. Alas, what remedy?

What remedy, alas, to rejoice my woeful heart,
With sighs suspiring most ruefully?
Farewell, all pleasure. Welcome, pain and smart.
Now welcome, death. I am ready to die.

CCXXI

I am as I am and so will I be
But how that I am none knoweth truly.
Be it evil, be it well, be I bound, be I free,
I am as I am and so will I be.

I lead my life indifferently,
I mean no thing but honestly.
And though folks judge full diversely
I am as I am and so will I die.

I do not rejoice nor yet complain.
10 Both mirth and sadness I do refrain
And use the mean since folks will feign.
Yet I am as I am, be it pleasure or pain.

Diverse do judge as they do trow,
Some of pleasure and some of woe.
Yet for all that, nothing they know.
But I am as I am wheresoever I go.

But since that judgers do thus decay
Let every man his judgement say.
I will it take in sport and play
20 For I am as I am whosoever say nay.

Who judgeth well, well God him send.
Who judgeth evil, God them amend.
To judge the best therefore intend
For I am as I am and so will I end.

Yet some there be that take delight
To judge folks' thought for envy and spite.
But whether they judge me wrong or right
I am as I am and so do I write,

Praying you all that this do read
30 To trust it as you do your creed
And not to think I change my weed
For I am as I am however I speed.

But how that is I leave to you.
Judge as ye list, false or true.
Ye know no more than afore ye knew.
Yet I am as I am whatever ensue.

And from this mind I will not flee,
But to you all that misjudge me
I do protest, as ye may see,
40 That I am as I am and so will I be.

CCXXII

Alas, dear heart, what hap had I
If that I might your grace attain!
And since I love you faithfully,
Why should ye not love me again?

Methinks of right ye should me love,
For well ye know I do not feign,
Nor never shall ye other prove.
Therefore, sweetheart, love me again.

I dare well say, if that ye knew
10 How long that I have suffered pain,
Ye would not change me for no new
But even of right love me again.

For as your own, ye may be sure,
Ye have my heart still to remain.
It lieth in you me to recure.
Therefore, sweetheart, love me again.

In hope I live and have done long,
Trusting yet still for to obtain,
And sure, methinks, I have great wrong
20 If that I be not loved again.

CCXXIII

Alas, Fortune, what aileth thee
Thus evermore to torment me?
Although that I unworthy be
    Thou wilt not change.

Fainest when I would obtain,
Then thou hast me still in disdain.
Wilt thou thus still increase my pain
    And wilt not change?

Alas! doth this not thee suffice?
10 What proof yet canst thou more devise
Than still to torment me in this wise
    And yet not change?

What should I more to thee now say?
Some hope in me doth rest alway,
Yet, bound to thee, I do obey.
    When wilt thou change?

Seeing there is no remedy,
I will thee suffer patiently,
Sure in trust at last, perdie,
20   That thou wilt change.

CCXXIV

Complaining, alas, without redress,
Thus woefully do I my life lead,
My heart lamenting in heaviness,
Through whose meekness I am near dead.

Thus I endure always in pain,
Devoid of pity, as in this case,
Yet my poor heart cannot refrain;
Wherefore, alas, I die, alas.

     So unkind, alas, saw I never none,
10   So hard-hearted, so much without pity,
     As she to whom I make my moan;
     Wherefore, alas, I die, I die.

     Where I love best I am refused;
     Where I am loved I do not pass;
     Where I would fainest, I am disdained;
     Wherefore I die, alas, alas.

     Comfortless, complaining, thus I remain;
     Merciless, remaining without remedy;
     Cruelness increasing through false disdain;
20   Pitiless remaining, alas, I die, I die.

     But from henceforth I hold it best
     Them for to love that loveth me;
     And then my heart shall have some rest,
     Where now for pain I die, I die.

CCXXV

     Duress of pains and grievous smart
     Hath brought me low and wondrous weak
     That I cannot comfort my heart.
     Why sighest thou, heart, and will not break?

     Thy sighs, thy plaints are all in vain,
     The tears void that thine eyes do leak.
     This life is death, this joy is pain.
     Why sighest thou, heart, and will not break?

     Thou climbs to catch where is no hold.
10   Thou strives where strength is all too weak.
     Thy careful life cannot be told.
     Why sighest thou, heart, and will not break?

     The faithfuller thou dost endure,
     Less she regards to hear thee speak
     And saith pity will not thee cure.
     Why sighest thou, heart, and will not break?

As good thou wert asunder rive
As thus in thought thyself to break.
Better were death than thus alive
20 Ever to sigh and never break.

Wherefore, Pity, now show redress,
Or else come, Death, thy vengeance wreak.
And since thou finds no gentleness,
Heart, sigh no more, I pray thee, break.

CCXXVI

Desire to sorrow doth me constrain,
Daily increasing my smart and pain.
I see there is no remedy plain
    But patience.

Despair doth put himself in press
To cause my sorrows to increase.
I trust at last that it will cease
    By patience.

Good hope doth bid me be content
10 And not myself thus to torment,
Promising me my whole intent
    Through patience.

I will not strive against the tide
For well I see, who doth abide
That sufferance to heart's desire is guide
    By patience.

CCXXVII

Defamed guiltiness by silence unkept,
My name all slanderous, my fault detect;
Guilty, I grant that I have done amiss.
Shall I never do so again, forgive me this.

Betrayed by trust and so beguiled,
By promise unjust my name defiled;
Wherefore I grant that I have done amiss.
Will I never do so again, forgive me this.

Accept mine excuse for this offence
10 And spare not to refuse me your presence.
Unless ye perceive ye do refrain
From doing amiss, will I live again.

CCXXVIII

The answer

Even when you lust, ye may refrain
To pain yourself thus wilfully.
Neither new nor old I do retain.
It is naught but your fantasy.

Your proffered service is nothing sweet
Yet would you fain it properly.
I do not love but where it is meet.
I change nothing my fantasy.

Your meat and drink, though it be gone,
10 Ye took enough when it was by;
Or ye may call for more anon,
When it shall please your fantasy.

It was your feeble founded love,
That fancy founded foolishly,
That made me love, longer to prove
Such foolish feigned fantasy.

If that your fancy, as you say,
Doth cause you plain thus piteously,
Easily to turn, perdie, you may,
20 When it shall please your fantasy.

Your chain is long, though you be bound,
For ye leap far and diversely.
To small effect your words doth sound.
They come but of your fantasy.

As ye did knit, so did I knit,
Even slack for slack right wisely.
I doubt it much, your new-fangled wit,
Which proved is by your fantasy.

Thus to complain withouten grief,
30   Thereto ye lust yourself apply.
The smartless needeth no relief:
I am not ruled by fantasy.

CCXXIX

I am ready and ever will be
    To do you service with honesty.
    There is nothing that lacks in me
        But that I have not.

My poor heart always and my mind
    Fixed in yours you shall still find.
    To love you best reason doth bind
        Although I have not.

And for your sake I would be glad
10   To have much more than I have had,
    The lack whereof doth make me sad
        Because I have not.

For I do love ye faithfully
    And ye me again right secretly.
    Of let there is no cause why
        But that I have not.

If I-you once of that might sure,
    Our love should increase and endure.
    To study therefore it is my cure
20   How I might have.

Such are called friends nowadays
  Which do muse and study always
  Betwixt young lovers to put delays
    Because they have not.

But this resisteth all my trust, verily,
  That ye again will love me steadfastly.
  And let thy word pass, as it hath done, hardily
    Till that we have.

But for this time, sweetheart, adieu.
30   Continue faithful and I will be true
  And love thee still, whatsoever ensue,
    Although I have not.

CCXXX

If I might have at mine own will
Such flood of tears wherewith to drown,
Of fire so hot as Aetna hill
With fervent fire that I might burn,
Then should I end this careful pain
That force perforce I do sustain.

Or if the sighs of woeful heart
Could cause myself asunder break,
Then by that means I should depart
10 My mourning days, and so to wreak
My wearied life and careful pain
That force perforce I do sustain.

Or if my hand such hap might find
With sword or knife to ease my woe,
Then should I ease my painful mind.
But since my hap cannot hap so,
I must abide this careful pain
That force perforce I do sustain.

Or if I might have at my wish
20   The heaven to fall to short my life,
So by such chance I could not miss
But I should end my woeful strife
That doth increase this careful pain
That force perforce I do sustain.

Or if the earth at my request
Had power to open, as in my will,
I know right well my wearied breast
Should need no more to sigh his fill,
For then should end this careful pain
30   That force perforce I do sustain.

CCXXXI

Mourning my heart doth sore oppress
That force constraineth me to complain;
For whereas I should have redress,
Alas, I cannot be loved again.

I serve, I sue, all of one sort.
My trust, my travail is all in vain
As, in despair without comfort,
Alas, I cannot be loved again.

Perdie, it is but now of late.
10   Not long ago ye knew my pain.
Will your rigour never abate?
Alas, when shall I be loved again?

It is both death and deadly smart.
No sharper sorrow can none sustain
Than for to love with faithful heart,
Alas, and cannot be loved again.

CCXXXII

O, what undeserved cruelty
Hath Fortune showed unto me
When all my wealth, joy, and felicity
Are turned to me most contrary!

My joy is woe, my pleasure pain,
My ease is travail. What remedy?
My mirth is mourning, hope is in vain.
Thus all thing turneth clean contrary.

The place of sleep that should my rest restore
10 Is unto me an unquiet enemy
And most my woe reneweth evermore.
Thus all thing turneth to me contrary.

I burn for cold, I starve for heat.
That lust liketh, desire doth it deny.
I fast from joy, sorrow is my meat.
Thus every joy turneth to me contrary.

The place of my refuge is my exile.
In Disdain's prison desperate I lie,
There to abide the time and woeful while
20 Till my careful life may turn contrary.

CCXXXIII

Once in your grace I know I was,
Even as well as now is he.
Though Fortune so hath turned my case
That I am down and he full high,
    Yet once I was.

Once I was he that did you please
So well that nothing did I doubt;

And though that now ye think it ease
To take him in and throw me out,
10   Yet once I was.

Once I was he in times past
That as your own ye did retain;
And though ye have me now outcast,
Showing untruth in you to reign,
     Yet once I was.

Once I was he that knit the knot
The which ye swore not to unknit;
And though ye feign it now forgot
In using your new-fangled wit,
20   Yet once I was.

Once I was he to whom ye said,
'Welcome, my joy, my whole delight';
And though ye are now well apaid
Of me, your own, to claim ye quit,
     Yet once I was.

Once I was he to whom ye spake,
'Have here my heart. It is thine own';
And though these words ye now forsake,
Saying thereof my part is none,
30   Yet once I was.

Once I was he before rehearst
And now am he that needs must die;
And though I die, yet at the least
In your remembrance let it lie
     That once I was.

CCXXXIV

O, cruel heart, where is thy faith?
Where is become thy steadfast vow?
Thy sobbing sighs with fainting breath,
Thy bitter tears, where are they now?

Thy careful looks, thy piteous plaint,
Thy woeful words, thy wonted cheer?
Now may I see thou didst but paint
And all thy craft doth plain appear.

For now thy sighs are out of thought.
10 Thine oath thou dost nothing regard.
Thy tears hath quenched thy love so hot
And spite for love is my reward.

Yet love for love I had awhile
Though thine were false and mine were true.
Thy feigned tears did me beguile
And caused me trust thee, most untrue.

To trust why did I condescend,
And yield myself so earnestly
To her that did nothing intend
20 But thus to trap me craftily?

O, falsed faith, hast thou forgot
That once of late thou wert mine own?
But slackly tied may slip the knot:
No marvel then though thou art gone.

Mine own but late assuredly,
With faith and truth so justly bound.
And thus to change so suddenly!
Each thing upon thy shame shall sound.

Each thing shall sound upon thy shame
30 Since that thy faith is not to trust.
What more reproach is to thy name
Than of thy word to prove unjust?

And from thy words if thou wilt swerve
And swear thou didst them never say,
Thy tokens yet I do reserve
That shall declare the hour and day,

The hour and day, the time and where
That thou thyself didst them indite,
Wherein thou show'dst what dread and fear
40   Thou hadst once spied thy bills to write.

This proof I think may well suffice
To prove it true that here I speak.
No forged tales will I devise
But with thy hand I shall me wreak.

When time and place thereto I see,
No doubt there is but thou shalt know
That thou didst pain me wrongfully,
Without offence to forge my woe.

And thus, farewell, most cruel heart.
50   Farewell thy falsed faith also.
Farewell my sighs, farewell my smart,
Farewell my love and all my woe.

CCXXXV

Quondam was I in my lady's grace,
I think as well as now be you;
And when that you have trod the trace
Then shall you know my words be true,
    That *quondam* was I.

Quondam was I. She said for ever.
That 'ever' lasted but a short while.
Promise made not to dissever,
I thought she laughed – she did but smile.
10   Then *quondam* was I.

Quondam was I – he that full oft lay
In her arms with kisses many one.
It is enough that this I may say:
Though among the moe now I be gone
    Yet *quondam* was I.

Quondam was I. Yet she will you tell
That, since the hour she was first born,
She never loved none half so well
As you. But what although she had sworn?
20   Sure *quondam* was I.

CCXXXVI

Spite of their spite which they in vain
Do stick to force my fantasy,
I am professed, for loss or gain,
To be thine own assuredly.
Who list thereat by spite to spurn,
My fancy is too hard to turn.

Although that some of busy wit
Do babble still, yea, yea, what though?
I have no fear nor will not flit
10 As doth the water to and fro.
Spite then their spite that list to spurn.
My fancy is too hard to turn.

Who is afraid? Yea, let him fly,
For I full well shall bide the brunt.
May grease their lips that list to lie
Of busy brains, as is their wont,
And yet against the prick they spurn.
My fancy is too hard to turn.

For I am set and will not swerve,
20 Whose faithful speech removeth naught.
And well I may thy grace deserve:
I think it is not dearly bought
And if they both do spite and spurn.
My fancy is too hard to turn.

Who list thereat to list or lour,
I am not he that aught doth reach.
There is no pain that hath the power

Out of my breast this thought to seek.
Then though they spite thereat and spurn,
30   My fancy is too hard to turn.

CCXXXVII

Driven by desire to set affection
A great way, alas, above my degree,
Chosen I am, I think by election,
To covet that thing that will not be.

I serve in love, not like to speed.
I look, alas, a little too high.
Against my will I do indeed
Covet that thing that will not be.

My fancy, alas, doth me so blind
10   That I can see no remedy
But still to follow my foolish mind
And covet that thing that will not be.

I hoped well when I began.
And since the proof is contrary,
Why should I any longer then
Covet that thing that will not be

But rather to leave now at the last
Than still to follow fantasy,
Content with the pain that is past
20   And not covet that thing that will not be?

CCXXXVIII

Shall she never out of my mind,
Nor shall I never out of this pain?
Alas, here she doth me so bind
Except her help I am near slain.

I never told her of my mind,
What pain I suffer for her sake.
Alas, what means might I now find
That no displeasure with me she take?

If I speak fair she saith I flatter,
10 And if I do not I shall not speed.
If I to her do write a letter
Then will she say she cannot read.

Shall I despair yet for all this?
Nay, nay, my heart will not do so.
I would, once my sweetheart to kiss,
A thousand times suffer more woe.

I am abashed when I should speak.
Alas, I cannot my mind express.
It maketh my heart in pieces break
20 To see her loving gentleness.

CCXXXIX

To whom should I sue to ease my pain?
To my mistress? Nay, nay, certain!
For fear she should me then disdain
I dare not sue, I dare not sue.

When I should speak to my mistress
In hope therefore to get redress,
[My words cannot my pain express]
When I should speak, when I should speak.

What hap had I, that suffereth pain,
10 An if I might her grace attain
Or else she would hear me complain?
What hap had I, what hap had I?

I fly for fear to be espied
Or of evil will to be destroyed.
The place where I would fainest abide
I fly for fear, I fly for fear.

Though I were bold who should me blame?
Love caused me to do the same.
With honesty it were no shame
20   Though I were bold, though I were bold.

And here an end with full glad will
In purpose for to serve her still;
And for to part I think none ill.
And here an end, and here an end.

CCXL

Longer to trow ye
What may it avail me?
For right well know ye,
Ye swore it unto me
Still for to love me
Alone and no moe.
But ye have deceived me.
Who could have thought so?

Your fair words caught me
10 And made me your mickle
But time hath taught me
Their truth is too tickle.
Since faith is fickle
And flitted you fro,
Your ware is too brickle.
Who would have thought so?

Your great assurance
Full oft-times did glad me.
But the performance
20 Hath as well made me,
As reason bade me,
To let your love go.
With lies ye have lade me.
Who could have thought so?

Your faith and your oath
Fly abroad in the wind.
I would be right loathe

To stay that by kind
Could never yet find
30 In change to say 'whoa'.
This mean I by your mind.
Who could have thought so?

Since wax nor writing
Can certain assure ye,
Nor love nor liking
Can no ways allure ye
Once to procure ye
To staidness to grow,
I cannot endure ye.
40 I care not who know.

But trust well that I
Shall never mistrust ye.
I care not a fly,
Go love where it lust ye;
For needs change must ye
In weal and in woe.
In that most I trust ye.
Who could have thought so?

Farewell, unstable,
50 For here I forsake thee.
True love is not able
True lover to make thee.
Therefore I betake thee
To them that do know
The ways how to break thee
Where I could not so.

CCXLI

With serving still
This have I won:
For my good will
To be undone.

And for redress
Of all my pain
Disdainfulness
I have again.

And for reward
10 Of all my smart,
Lo, thus unheard,
I must depart.

Wherefore all ye
That after shall
By fortune be,
As I am, thrall,

Example take
What I have won:
Thus for her sake
To be undone.

CCXLII

Who would have ever thought
A heart that was so set
To have such wrong me wrought
Or to be counterfeit?
But who that trusteth most
Is like to pay the cost.

I must of force, God wot,
This painful life sustain.
And yet I can know not
10 The chief cause of my pain.
This is a strange disease
To serve and never please.

I must of force endure
This draught drawn awry,
For I am fast and sure

To have the mate thereby.
But note I will this text
To draw better the next.

CCXLIII

'How should I
Be so pleasant
In my semblant
As my fellows be?'

Not long ago
It chanced so
As I did walk alone
I heard a man
That now and then
10   Himself did thus bemoan.

'Alas,' he said,
'I am betrayed
And utterly undone.
Whom I did trust
And think so just
Another man hath won.

'My service due
And heart so true
On her I did bestow.
20   I never meant
For to repent
In wealth nor yet in woe.

'Love did assign
Her to be mine
And not to love none new.
But who can bind
Their fickle kind
That never will be true?

    'The western wind
30   Hath turned her mind
And blown it clean away.
    Thereby my wealth,
    My mirth, and health
Are driven to great decay.

    'Fortune did smile
    A right short while
And never said me nay,
    With pleasant plays
    And joyful days
40   My time to pass away.

    'Alas, alas,
    The time so was,
So never shall it be,
    Since she is gone
    And I alone
Am left as ye may see.

    'Where is the oath,
    Where is the troth
That she to me did give?
50   Such feigned words
    With silly bourds
Let no wise man believe.

    'For even as I
    Thus woefully
Unto myself complain,
    If ye then trust
    Needs learn ye must
To sing my song in vain.

    'How should I
60   Be so pleasant
    In my semblant
As my fellows be?'

CCXLIV

Full well it may be seen
To such as understand
How some there be that ween
They have their wealth at hand
Through love's abused band;
But little do they see
Th'abuse wherein they be.

Of love there is a kind
Which kindleth by abuse,
As in a feeble mind
Whom fancy may induce
By love's deceitful use
To follow the fond lust
And proof of a vain trust.

As I myself may say
By trial of the same
No wight can well bewray
The falsehood love can frame.
I say, 'twixt grief and grame,
There is no living man
That knows the craft love can.

For love so well can feign
To favour for the while
That such as seeks the gain
Are served with the guile;
And some can this concile
To give the simple leave
Themselves for to deceive.

What thing may more declare
Of love the crafty kind
Than see the wise, so ware,

In love to be so blind?
If so it be assigned
Let them enjoy the gain
That thinks it worth the pain.

CCXLV

What should I say
Since faith is dead
And truth away
From you is fled?
Should I be led
With doubleness?
Nay, nay, mistress!

I promised you.
You promised me
10   To be as true
As I would be.
But since I see
Your double heart,
Farewell, my part.

Thought for to take
It is not my mind,
But to forsake
[One so unkind].
And as I find
20   So will I trust.
Farewell, unjust.

Can ye say nay
But that you said
That I alway
Should be obeyed?
And thus betrayed
Ere that I wist!
Farewell, unkissed.

CCXLVI

Fortune doth frown.
What remedy?
I am down
By destiny.

CCXLVII

I have been a lover
Full long and many days
And oft-times a prover
Of the most painful ways.
But all that I have passed
As trifles to this last.

By proof I know the pain
Of them that sue and serve
And nothing can attain
10 Of that which they deserve.
But those pangs have I passed
As trifles to this last.

I have ere this been thrall
And durst it never show
But glad to suffer all
And so to cloak my woe.
Yet that pang have I passed
As trifles to this last.

By length of time ere now
20 I have attained grace;
And ere I wist well how,
Another had my place.
Yet that pang have I passed
As trifles to this last.

My love well near once won
And I full like to speed,
Evil tongues have then begun
With lies to let my meed.
Yet that pang have I passed
30 As trifles to this last.

Sometime I loved one
That liked well my suit,
But of my deadly moan
Fair words was all the fruit.
Yet that pang have I passed
As trifles to this last.

My steadfast faith and will
With fair words have I told;
Yet have I found them still
40 In their belief too cold.
But that pang have I passed
As trifles to this last.

In love when I have been
With them that loved me
Such danger have I seen
That we would not agree.
But that pang have I passed
As trifles to this last.

Absence oft-times ere this
50 Hath doubled my disease
In causing me to miss
That thing that might me please.
Yet that pang have I passed
As trifles to this last.

To promise love for love
And make too long delays
Hath made me for to prove
Of love the painful ways.
Yet that pang have I passed
60 As trifles to this last.

Full many torments more
In loving I have found,
Which oft hath pained sore
My heart when it was bound.
Yet all that have I passed
As trifles to this last.

Now guess all ye that list
And judge now as ye please.
For oft-times have ye missed
70 In judging my disease,
Be nothing then aghast
Though ye misjudge these last.

CCXLVIII

Madam, I you require
No longer time detract.
Let truth in you appear
And give me that I lack.

Ye wot as well as I
That promise ye did make,
When time I could espy
I should have that I lack.

Both time and place ye have
10 My fervent pains to slack.
Nothing, alas, I crave
But only that I lack.

Which thing methink is due,
Rememb'ring what ye spake;
For if your words be true
I must have that I lack.

The Answer
Your foolish, feigned haste
Full small effect shall take.

Your words in vain ye wrest.
20 Ye get not that ye lack.

I wot, as ye shall find,
The promise I did make.
No promise shall me bind.
Ye get not that ye lack.

Though time and place I have
To slide if truth were slack,
Though still ye cry and crave,
Ye get not that ye lack.

Because ye think it due,
30 I speak that that I spake.
And this word shall be true:
Ye get not that ye lack.

CCXLIX

Sith I myself displease thee,
My friends why should I blame
That from the fault advise me
That conquered my good name
And made my mind to mourn,
That laughed my love to scorn
And bound my heart alway
To think this pain a play,
That would and never may?

10 To lead my life at liberty
I like it wondrous well,
For proof hath taught his property
That alway pain is hell.
But sith so well I wot
These kinds of cold and hot,
Such fancies I forsake
That doth their freedom lack.
Me list no more to make.

Grudge one that feels the grief.
20 I laugh that feel the game
Of freedom from the life
Whereby wild beasts be tame –
As fast and wake abed
With heart and heavy head,
That have a hungry heart.
To make myself well-fed –
That may redress my smart.

Sith I have slipped the knot
That doth my heart enchain,
30 I like the lucky lot
Too well to knit again.
So newly come to wealth,
Shall I deceive myself?
Nay, set thy heart at rest,
For wealth, my new-found guest,
Shall harbour in my nest.

To make a wilful band
Where I may well refuse,
To be a bird in hand
40 And not my freedom use
To sing and sorrow not,
If willingly I do't,
. . . .
To slip into the cage
It were a wilful rage.

CCL

Love whom ye list and spare not;
Therewith I am content.
Hate whom ye list for I care not,
For I am indifferent.

Do what ye list and dread not
After your own fancy.
Think what you list and fear not
For all is one to me.

But as for me I am not
10 Wavering as the wind
But even as one that recketh not
Which way ye turn your mind.

For in your love I dote not,
[Though you think I am caught.]
Whether you hate or hate not
Is least charge of my thought.

Wherefore I pray you forget not
But that I am well content.
So love whom ye list and spare not
20 For I am indifferent.

CCLI

I might by no means surmise
My fantasy to resist,
But after the old guise
To love her I did list.
And though it must suffice
That again I shall have none,
Yet can I not devise
To get again mine own.

It is my heart that I have lost.
10 God send it me again.
I should it have whatever it cost
Or else I am but slain.

I study day and night
And loud I cry and call
To be delivered quite

From her that I am thrall.
And yet against all right
Of force I must still moan
For it doth pass my might
20 To get again mine own.

It is my heart that I have lost.
God send it me again.
I should it have whatever it cost
Or else I am but slain.

In torments I am torn
That no rest find I can,
None so unhappy born
Since that the world began.
I ask for but such corn
30 And such seed that was sown;
And though I that have sworn,
I cannot get mine own.

It is my heart that I have lost.
God send it me again.
I should it have whatever it cost
Or else I am but slain.

But seeing that I cannot
Attain my true desire
Nor by no means may not
40 Creep out of the fire,
[And know that you intend not]
To give aught of your own
By reason that you should not –
Let me to have mine own.

It is my heart that I have lost.
God send it me again.
I should it have whatever it cost
Or else I am but slain.

CCLII

Now must I learn to feign
And do as other do,
Seeing no truth doth reign
That I may trust unto.
I was both true and plain
To one and to no moe,
And unto me again,
Alas, she was not so.

Unknowingly fell my heart
10   Into my foe's cruel hand;
And ere I could astart
Out of that careful band,
All the wit I had
Could scarce the knot undo.
This careful life I led
For one that was not so.

The nights right long and heavy,
The days of my torment,
The sighs continually
20   That thorough my heart went,
My colour pale and wan
To her did plainly show
That I was her true man
And yet she thought not so.

Out of her sight no pleasure
But to my heart great pain
And tears out of measure
That out of mine eyes did rain!
Her absence was my death,
30   For to depart her fro.
And yet, alas, her faith
Was feigned and not so.

Not the fever quartan
Doth half a man so shake
As did the woe and pain
That daily did me take.
Not sleep could I nor rest
But tossing to and fro.
And whereas I loved best,
40   Alas, she did not so.

And seeing it is my chance
My love in vain to waste,
I am not in that dance
The first nor yet the last.
But wise he is for the nonce
That can his folly know,
To revoke his love at once
Seeing she will not so.

CCLIII

Farewell, all my welfare,
My shoe is trod awry.
Now may I cark and care
To sing lullay by by.
Alas, what shall I do thereto?
There is no shift to help me now.

Who made it such offence
To love for love again?
God wot that my pretence
10   Was but to ease his pain
For I had ruth to see his woe.
Alas, more fool, why did I so?

For he from me is gone
And makes thereat a game
And hath left me alone
To suffer sorrow and shame.
Alas, he is unkind, doubtless,
To leave me thus all comfortless.

It is a grievous smart
20   To suffer pains and sorrow.
But most grieved my heart
He laid his faith to borrow;
And falsed hath his faith and truth
And he forsworn by many an oath.

All ye lovers, perdie,
Hath cause to blame his deed
Which shall example be
To let you of your speed.
Let never seely woman again
30 Trust to such words as men can feign.

For I unto my cost
Am warning to you all
That they whom you trust most
Soonest deceive you shall.
But complaint cannot redress
Of my great grief the great excess.

CCLIV

Now must I learn to live at rest
 And wean me of my will
For I repent where I was pressed
 My fancy to fulfil.

I may no longer more endure
 My wonted life to lead
But I must learn to put in ure
 The change of womanhood.

I may not see my service long
10 Rewarded in such wise
Nor I may not sustain such wrong,
 That ye my love despise.

I may not sigh in sorrows deep
 Nor wail the want of love
Nor I may neither crouch nor creep
 Where it doth not behove.

But I of force must needs forsake
 My faith so fondly set
And from henceforth must undertake
20 Such folly to forget.

Now must I seek some other ways
    Myself for to withsave
And, as I trust, by mine assays
    Some remedy to have.

I ask none other remedy
    To recompense my wrong
But once to have the liberty
    That I have lacked so long.

CCLV

Longer to muse
On this refuse
I will not use,
But study to forget;
    Letting all go
    Since well I know
    To be my foe
Her heart is firmly set.

Since my intent
10   So truly meant
Cannot content
Her mind as I do see,
    To tell you plain
    It were in vain
    For so small gain
To lose my liberty.

For if he thrive
That will go strive
A ship to drive
20   Against the stream and wind,
    Undoubtedly
    Then thrive should I
    To love truly
A cruel hearted mind.

But sith that so
The world doth go
That every woe
By yielding doth increase,
    As I have told
30   I will be bold
    . . . .
Thereby my pains to cease;

Praying you all
That after shall
By fortune fall
Into this foolish trade,
    Have in your mind
    (As I do find)
    That oft by kind
40   All women's love do fade.

Wherefore, apace,
Come take my place
Some man that has
A lust to burn the feet.
    For since that she
    Refuseth me
    I must agree
And study to forget.

CCLVI

Now all of change
Must be my song
And from my bond now must I break
    Since she so strange
    Unto my wrong
Doth stop her ears to hear me speak.

Yet none doth know
So well as she
My grief which can have no restraint.
10 That fain would follow,
Now needs must flee
For fault of ear unto my plaint.

I am not he
By false assays
Nor feigned faith can bear in hand,
Though must I see
That such always
Are best for to be understand.

But I that truth
20 Hath always meant
Doth still proceed to serve in vain.
Desire pursueth
My time misspent
And doth not pass upon my pain.

O Fortune's might
That each compels!
And me the most it doth suffice
Now for my right
To ask naught else
30 But to withdraw this enterprise.

And for the gain
Of that good hour
Which of my woe shall be relief,
I shall refrain
By painful power
The thing that most hath been my grief.

I shall not miss
To exercise
The help thereof which doth me teach
40 That after this
In any wise
To keep the right within my reach.

And she unjust
Which feareth not
In this her fame to be defiled –
Yet once I trust
Shall be my lot
To quit the craft that me beguiled.

CCLVII

Alone musing,
Remembering
The woeful life that I do lead,
Then sore sighing,
I lie crying
As one for pain near dead.

The unkindness
Of my mistress
In great distress hath me brought.
10   Yet disdaineth she
To take pity
And setteth my heart right naught.

Who would have thought
She would have wrought
Such sorrow unto my heart,
Seeing that I
Endeavoured me
From her never to depart?

CCLVIII

Absence, alas,
Causeth me pass
From all solace
To great grievance.

Yet though that I
Absent must be,
I trust that she
Hath remembrance.

Where I her find
10 Loving and kind,
There my poor mind
Eased shall be.
And for my part,
My love and heart
Shall not revert
Though I should die.

Beauty, pleasure,
Riches, treasure,
Or to endure
20 In prison strong
Shall not me make
Her to forsake.
Though I should lack
Her never so long.

For once trust I,
Ere that I die,
For to espy
The happy hour,
At liberty
30 With her to be
That pities me
In this dolour.

CCLIX

'Comfort at hand! Pluck up thy heart.
    Look, lo, where it doth stand.
Since the redress of all thy smart
    Doth lie so good at hand
        Pluck up thy heart.

'Pluck up thy heart. Why droopest thou so?'
  So said I, methought,
And from the hill I looked low,
  And with mine eye I sought
10   Comfort at hand.

'Comfort at hand mine eye hath found,'
  Methought. 'Therefore be glad.
If she be there may heal thy wound,
  Why shouldest thou then be sad?
        Pluck up thy heart.

'Pluck up thy heart. A mourning man
  Doth get no good by woe.
Be glad alway, for whoso can
  Shall find whereso he go
20   Comfort at hand.

'Comfort at hand! Go seek and find.
  Look if there be redress.
If not, abide a better wind.
  In hope of some release
        Pluck up thy heart.'

CCLX

Disdain not, madam, on him to look
Whom sometime you have loved;
And though you forswear it on a book,
Error it may be proved.
Though now your love be gone and spent,
May hap you may it soon repent.

Since that hereafter comes not yet
Nor now is so good as then,
Yet throw him not down but let him sit
10 That so long hath been your man.
The time may come he may you ease,
Which now so sore doth you displease.

Once I was he that now I am not.
Yourself knows this full well.
My mind you know well enough by rote;
You need no fashion to spell.
Fair word to you I use
Though that you cruelly me refuse.

What though new broom sweep very clean,
20   Yet cast not the old away.
That serves not sometime is often seen
To serve well another day.
And store of household is well had
To keep the best and leave the bad.

CCLXI

I must go walk the woods so wild
    And wander here and there
    In dread and deadly fear,
For where I trust, I am beguiled
    And all for your love, my dear.

I am banished from my bliss
    By craft and false pretence,
    Faultless, without offence;
And of return no certain is
10   And all for your love, my dear.

Banished am I, remediless,
    To wilderness alone,
    Alone to sigh and moan
And of relief all comfortless
    And all for your love, my dear.

My house shall be the greenwood tree,
    A tuft of brakes my bed.
    And this my life I lead
As one that from his joy doth flee
20   And all for your love, my dear.

The running streams shall be my drink.
   Acorns shall be my food.
   Naught else shall do me good
But on your beauty for to think
   And all for your love, my dear.

And when the deer draw to the green,
   Makes me think on a roe:
   How I have seen ye go
Above the fairest, fairest beseen!
30   And all for your love, my dear.

But where I see in any coast
   Two turtles sit and play,
   Rejoicing all the day,
Alas, I think, this have I lost
   And all for your love, my dear.

No bird, no bush, no bough I see
   But bringeth to my mind
   Something whereby I find
My heart far wandered, far fro me,
40   And all for your love, my dear.

The tune of birds when I do hear,
   My heart doth bleed, alas,
   Remembering how I was
Wont for to hear your ways so clear
   And all for your love, my dear.

My thought doth please me for the while:
   While I see my desire
   Naught else I do require.
So with my thought I me beguile
50   And all for your love, my dear.

Yet I am further from my thought
   Than earth from heaven above.
   And yet for to remove
My pain, alas, availeth naught
   And all for your love, my dear.

And where I lie, secret, alone,
 I mark that face anon
 That stayeth my life, as one
That other comfort can get none
60 And all for your love, my dear.

The summer days that be so long
 I walk and wander wide,
 Alone, without a guide,
Always thinking how I have wrong
 And all for your love, my dear.

The winter nights that are so cold
 I lie amid the [storms],
 Unwrapped, in pricking thorns,
Remembering my sorrows old
70 And all for your love, my dear.

A woeful man such desert life
 Becometh best of all.
 But woe might them befall
That are the causers of this strife
 And all for your love, my dear.

CCLXII

Love hath again
Put me to pain
And yet all is but lost.
I serve in vain
And am certain
Of all misliked most.

Both heat and cold
Doth so me hold
And cumbers so my mind
10 That, when I should
Speak and be bold,
It draweth me still behind.

My wits be past,
My life doth waste,
My comfort is exiled.
And I in haste
Am like to taste
How love hath me beguiled.

Unless that right
20   May in her sight
Obtain pity and grace,
Why should a wight
Have beauty bright
If mercy have no place?

Yet I, alas,
Am in such case
That back I cannot go
But still forth trace
A patient pace
30   And suffer secret woe.

For with the wind
My fired mind
Doth still increase in flame.
And she unkind
That did me bind
Doth turn it all to game.

Yet can no pain
Make me refrain
Nor here nor there to range.
40   I shall retain
Hope to attain
A heart that is so strange.

But I require
The painful fire
That oft doth make me sweat
For all my hire
With like desire
To give her heart a heat.

Then shall she prove
50   How I her love
And what I have her offered,
    Which should her move
    For to remove
The pain that I have suffered.

    A better fee
    Than she gave me
She shall of me attain;
    For whereas she
    Showed cruelty
60   She shall my heart obtain.

CCLXIII

Might I as well within my song belay
The thing I would, as in my heart I may,
    Repentance should draw from those eyes
Salt tears, with cries, remorse, and grudge of heart,
Causeless because that I have suffered smart.

Or might I else unclose my painful breast
That it might be in sight – my great unrest –
    There should ye see the torments remain
As hell of pain to move your cruel heart,
10 Causeless because that I have suffered smart.

There is in hell not such a fervent fire
As secret heat of inward hot desire
    That will not let the flame appear
That I have here within my wasted heart,
Causeless because that I have suffered smart.

Yet you cause it and ye may cause my wealth.
Once cause it, then return unto my health,
    And of all men relieve that man
That nothing can but cry, 'Relieve this heart,
20 Causeless because that I have suffered smart.'

Redress ye ought that harm that ye have done.
It is no game that ye now have begun;
  But worthy blame ye shall remain
To do him pain that knoweth not thought of heart,
Causeless because that I have suffered smart.

CCLXIV

Fortune, what aileth thee
Thus for to banish me
Her company whom I love best?
  For to complain me
  Nothing availeth me.
Adieu, farewell, this night's rest.

Her demure countenance,
Her homely patience
Hath wounded me through Venus' dart,
10   That I cannot refrain me
    Neither yet abstain me
But needs must love her with all my heart.

Long have I loved her,
Oft have I prayed her.
Yet, alas, she through disdain
  Nothing regards me
  Nor yet rewards me
But lets me lie in mortal pain.

Yet shall I love her still
20   With all my heart and will
Wheresoever I ride or go.
  My heart, my service,
  Afore all ladies',
Is hers all only and no moe.

She hath my heart and ever shall
In this terrestrial.
What can she more of me require?
Her whom I love best,
God send her good rest
30 And me heartily my whole desire.

CCLXV

What would ye more of me, your slave, require
Than for to ask and have that ye desire?
Yet I remain without recure.
I you insure there is no faithful heart
That without cause causeless thus suffer'th smart.

You have the joy and I have all the pain.
Yours the pleasure and I in woe remain.
Alas, and why do ye me blame?
It is no game thus to destroy my heart
10 Nor without cause thus to cause it smart.

I have assayed in all that ever I might
You for to please, for that was my delight.
All could not serve. Ye list not see,
But cruelly hath undone my poor heart
And without cause doth cause it suffer smart.

Ye make a play at all my woe and grief
And yet, alas, among all my mischief,
Nothing at all that ye regard,
Nor will reward a faithful-meaning heart
20 But thus causeless to cause it suffer smart.

If that ye list my painful death to see
Ye need no more but use this cruelty;
For shorter death cannot be found
Than, without ground, by force of cruel heart
Causeless by cause to cause me suffer smart.

Adieu! Farewell! I feel my joy's distress.
Fled is my wealth; my torments doth increase.
Thus have I won for all my hire
To burn in fire swelting my woeful heart
30 That without cause causeless thus suffer'th smart.

Psalm 37

Psalm 37. Noli emulare in maligna

Although thou see th'outrageous climb aloft,
    Envy not thou his blind prosperity.
    The wealth of wretches, though it seemeth soft,
Move not thy heart by their felicity.
    They shall be found like grass turned into hay
    And as the herbs that wither suddenly.
Stablish thy trust in God, seek right alway,
    And on the earth thou shalt inhabit long.
    Feed and increase such hope from day to day.
And if with God thou time thy hearty song
    He shall thee give whatso thy heart can lust.
    Cast upon God thy will, that right thy wrong.
Give him the charge for he, upright and just,
    Hath cure of thee and of thy cares all.
    And he shall make thy truth to be discussed
Bright as the sun; and thy righteousness shall
    (The curseds' wealth though now do it deface)
    Shine like the daylight that we the noon call.
Patiently abide the Lord's assured grace.
    Bear with even mind the trouble that he sends.
    Dismay thee not, though thou see the purchase
Increase of some, for such like luck God sends
    To wicked folk . . .
    Restrain thy mind from wrath that ay offends.
Do way all rage, and see thou do eschew
    By their like deed such deeds for to commit;
    For wicked folk their overthrow shall rue.

10

20

Who patiently abide and do not flit,
    They shall possede the world from heir to heir.
30   The wicked shall of all his wealth be quit
So suddenly, and that without repair,
    That all his pomp and his staring array
    Shall from thine eye depart as blast of air.
The sober then the world shall wield, I say,
    And live in wealth and peace so plentiful.
    Him to destroy the wicked shall assay
And gnash his teeth eke with girning ireful.
    The Lord shall scorn the threat'nings of the wretch
    For he doth know the tide is nigh at full
40   When he shall sink and no hand shall him seech.
    They have unsheathed eke their bloody brands
    And bent their bow to prove if they might reach
To overthrow the . . .
    Bare of relief the harmless to devour.
    The sword shall pierce the heart of such that fonds.
Their bow shall break in their most endeavour.
    A little living gotten rightfully
    Passeth the riches and eke the high power
Of that that wretches have gathered wickedly.
50   Perish shall the wickeds' posterity
And God shall stablish the just assuredly.
The just men's days the Lord doth know and see;
    Their heritage shall last for evermore.
    And of their hope beguiled they shall not be
When dismal days shall wrap the t'other sore.
    They shall be full when other faint for food.
    Therewhilst shall fail these wicked men therefore.
To God's enemies such end shall be allowed
    As hath lamb's grease, wasting in the fire,
60   That is consumed into a smoky cloud.
Borrow'th th'unjust without will or desire
    To yield again; the just freely doth give
    Where he seeth need as mercy doth require.
Who will'th him well for right therefore shall live;
    Who banneth him shall be rooted away.

His steps shall God direct still and relieve,
And please him shall what life him lust assay.
　And though he fall under foot, lie shall not he;
　Catching his hand, for God shall straight him stay.

70 ....
....
　Nor yet his seed foodless seen for to be.
The just to all men merciful hath been,
　Busy to do well; therefore his seed, I say,
　Shall have abundance, alway fresh and green.
Flee ill, do good, that thou mayst last alway.
　For God doth love for evermore the right.
　Never his chosen doth he cast away.
Forever he them mindeth day and night;
80　And wicked seed alway shall waste to naught.
　The just shall wield the world as their own right
And long thereon shall dwell as they have wrought.
　With wisdom shall the wise man's mouth him able;
　His tongue shall speak alway even as it ought.
With God's learning he hath his heart stable;
　His foot therefore from sliding shall be sure.
　The wicked watcheth the just for to disable,
And for to slay him doth his busy cure.
　But God will not suffer him for to quail
90　By tyranny, nor yet by fault unpure
To be condemned in judgement without fail.
　Await therefore the coming of the Lord.
　Live with his laws, in patience to prevail,
And he shall raise thee of thine own accord
　Above the earth, in surety to behold
　The wickeds' death that thou may it record.
I have well seen the wicked sheen like gold,
　Lusty and green as laurel lasting ay;
　But even anon and scant his seat was cold.
100 When I have passed again the self same way
　Where he did reign, he was not to be found;
　Vanished he was for all his fresh array.
Let uprightness be still thy steadfast ground;

Follow the right: such one shall alway find
Himself in peace and plenty to abound.
All wicked folk, reversed, shall be untwined
And wretchedness shall be the wickeds' end.
Health to the just from God shall be assigned.
He shall them strength whom trouble should offend.
110   The Lord shall help, I say, and them deliver
From cursed hands, and health unto them send,
For that in him they set their trust forever.

Other Poems

CCLXVII

Th' Argument

Sometime the pride of my assured truth
Contemned all help of God and eke of man.
But when I saw man blindly how he go'th
In deeming hearts, which none but God there can,
And his dooms hid, whereby man's malice grow'th,
Mine Earl, this doubt my heart did humble then,
For error so might murder innocents.
Then sang I thus in God my confidence.

CCLXVIII

[Woman:] 'Double, diverse, sullen, and strange,
           But I have sped and scaped unspied.
           Thanked be fortune of friendly chance.
           The deed is done and I not denied,
           My troth mistaken and I untried.
           If double drabs were so defied,
           As worthy is their wandering wit.'

[Man:]   'Iwis with reason doth not sit
           To do and undo and scape unquit.
           For your no faith such fault were fit,
           Forborne for fear. Nay, love is it
           Whereby is bound the body so.'

[Woman:] 'Thanked be fortune of every chance.'

[Man:] 'Of my mishap I thank myself.
    Pain or pleasure, woe or wealth,
    Wounded by words, and lacks advance.'

CCLXIX

Hap happeth oft unlooked for
As men may see before their eyes;
For he that daily doth labour
And study'th all he can devise
To bring his purpose to effect,
Yet by mishap most commonly
From his intent he is abject,
And hap doth hap clean contrary;
So that the proof doth verify,
10 As I have written here before,
That hap haps oft unlooked for.

Some to mishap when they are born
Are prefate by their destiny.
To some, though all the world had sworn
Fortune will not be contrary;
This hap doth hap at his own lust.
Some men to wealth and some to woe;
Sometime the strong he throw'th i'the dust.
Sometime the lame he maketh go
20 And the stark blind to see also.
Sometime the whole he maketh sore.
All this haps oft unlooked for.

Some by good hap are brought aloft
And some by mishap are thrown down.
And some by hap are set full soft
That think never for to come down.
But I will rede them for to take heed,
Sith hap doth turn so suddenly,
Lest he by change do chance them lead
30 Into some trade clean contrary

And bring him low that was full high
And set him hard that sat full soft.
Unlooked for, all this haps oft.

CCLXX

An Epitaph of Sir Thomas Gravener, Knight
Under this stone there lieth at rest
A friendly man, a worthy knight,
Whose heart and mind was ever prest
To favour truth, to further right.

The poors' defence, his neighbours' aid,
Most kind always unto his kin,
That stint all strife that might be stayed,
Whose gentle grace great love did win.

A man that was full earnest set
10 To serve his prince at all assays;
No sickness could him from that let,
Which was the short'ning of his days.

His life was good, he died full well;
The body here, the soul in bliss.
With length of words why should I tell
Or further shew that well known is,
Since that the tears of more and less
Right well declare his worthiness?

Vivit post funera Virtus.

Notes

In addition to the abbreviations cited under *Further Reading*, the following abbreviations and printing conventions are used in the notes.

A	Arundel Harington Manuscript, ed. Hughey.
Ash	Ashmole MS 48 in the Bodleian Library.
Bannatyne	The Bannatyne MS, ed. A. K. Donald in *The Poems of Alexander Scott*, 1902.
B	Trinity College, Dublin MS D.2.7. parts 2 and 3 (Blage MS).
BM	British Museum Additional MS 18752.
Cam	Cambridge University MS ff.5.14.
CP	*Certain Psalms . . . by Sir Thomas Wyatt*, 1549.
CT	*Canterbury Tales.*
CV	R. A. Fraser, ed., *The Court of Venus*, 1955.
D	Devonshire MS Additional 17492 (British Museum).
Da	J. Daalder, ed., *Sir Thomas Wyatt, Collected Poems*, 1975.
Daalder	'Some Problems of Punctuation and Syntax in Egerton MS 2711 of Wyatt's Verse', *N & Q*, XVIII (1971), pp. 214–16.
Douce	Fragment of *The Court of Venus* [1537–9 ?] in the Douce Collection of the Bodleian Library, ed. R. A. Fraser, *CV*, 1955.
E	Egerton MS 2711 (British Museum).
ed.	Editor's emendation.
F	A. K. Foxwell, ed., *The Poems of Sir Thomas Wiat*, 1913.
Folger	Fragment of *The Court of Venus* [1561–4 ?] in the Folger Library, ed. R. A. Fraser, *CV*, 1955.
FR	Further Reading (pp. 59–67 above).
G	Nicholas Grimald.
GG	*The Gorgeous Gallery of Gallant Inventions*, 1578.
H	Hill MS Additional 36529 (British Museum).
H78	Harleian MS 78 (British Museum).
Harrier	*The Canon of Sir Thomas Wyatt's Poetry*, 1975.
Hughey	R. Hughey, ed., *The Arundel Harington Manuscript of Tudor Poetry*, 1960.
JF	*The English Works of John Fisher*, ed. J. E. B. Mayor, 1876.
L	K. Muir, *Life and Letters of Sir Thomas Wyatt*, 1963.
M	H. A. Mason, *Editing Wyatt*, 1972.

M & T	K. Muir and P. Thomson, *Collected Poems of Sir Thomas Wyatt*, 1969.
Mason	H. A. Mason, *Humanism and Poetry in the Early Tudor Period*, 1959.
Mason (TLS)	H. A. Mason, 'Wyatt and the Psalms', Part I, *TLS* (27 February 1953), p. 144; Part II, *TLS* (6 March 1953), p. 160.
Maxwell	J. C. Maxwell, review of *M & T*, *N & Q*, XVI (1969), pp. 465-7.
MS	Manuscript.
MSS	Manuscripts.
Muir	K. Muir, ed., *Sir Thomas Wyatt and his Circle, Unpublished Poems*, 1961.
N	G. Nott, ed., *The Works of Henry Howard, Earl of Surrey, and of Sir Thomas Wyatt the Elder*, 1815-16, Vol. II only.
NA	*Nugae Antiquae*, 1779.
O	A gloss depends on the assumption that the poet is translating his original or source as closely as possible.
ODEP	W. G. Smith and J. E. Heseltine, *The Oxford Dictionary of English Proverbs*, 1948.
OED	*The Oxford English Dictionary*.
Parker	Parker MS 168 (Corpus Christi College, Cambridge).
R	Royal MS 17A, xxii (British Museum).
Ramsden	Ramsden Documents in Huddersfield Corporation.
Raw	Rawlinson Poetical MS 172, fol. 3^v (Bodleian Library).
Rollins	H. E. Rollins, ed., *Tottel's Miscellany (1557-1587)*, 1965.
S	R. Southall, *The Courtly Maker*, 1964.
Simonds	W. E. Simonds, *Sir Thomas Wyatt and His Poems*, 1889.
Stark	Fragment of *A Book of Ballets* [1547-9?] in Stark Collection at University of Texas; ed. R. A. Fraser, *CV*, 1955.
Stevens	J. Stevens, *Music & Poetry in the Early Tudor Court*, 1961.
T	*Tottel's Miscellany*, ed. H. E. Rollins, 1965.
Thomson	P. Thomson, *Sir Thomas Wyatt and His Background*, 1964.
Tilley	M. P. Tilley, *A Dictionary of the Proverbs in England in the Sixteenth and Seventeenth Centuries*, 1950.
Tillyard	E. M. W. Tillyard, *The Poetry of Sir Thomas Wyatt*, 1929.
Troilus	*Troilus and Criseyde*.
W	Wyatt.
WT	G. E. Duffield, ed., *The Work of William Tyndale*, 1965.
(?)	A gloss about which I am uncertain.
]	The reading in the text, which is copy-text unless otherwise stated.
[ ]	In textual notes, obscure letter(s); in glosses, words without matching words in the text but, in my view, implied by the context.

In textual notes, earlier or alternate versions still discernible in the MSS are designated, for example, *E1, E2* or *D1, D2*. For poems in a scribal hand with revisions in Wyatt's hand, *W* designates Wyatt's revision. For poems in Wyatt's hand with revisions by him, the first reading cited, unless otherwise stated, is Wyatt's final version in the MS; variants described as being from *E* are his earlier versions still discernible in *E*.

Texts and translations of Latin authors are, unless otherwise stated, from the Loeb Classical Library editions.

All allusions to Chaucer are from the edition by F. N. Robinson cited under SOURCES in *FR* (page 61).

The notes refer readers to the appropriate pages in *M & T* for the texts of sources in foreign languages.

The citation of *M & T, N, F,* or the like in or at the end of a note means that I have derived the information in that note from that edition. All poem numbers cited in the notes are the numbers in this edition. Readers may find the poems and notes in other editions by using their indexes of first lines.

RONDEAUX

Poems I–VIII are rondeaux. The rondeau, from the French *rond,* is a 'round' form in the sense that the two refrains circle back to the opening words. Apart from the refrains, it has only two rhymes throughout.

1. *E, D, T.*

Attributed to 'Tho.' in margin of *E* and to Wyatt by *T.*

The ultimate source of the poem is *Rime* 121 by Petrarch (1304–74) (*M & T* 263). Wyatt may have done a very free imitation of Petrarch's madrigal and changed its form to a rondeau; or he may have imitated an unknown French rondeau based on Petrarch's poem (*M & T*).

As in III and IV, *T* changes the poem into a sonnet by expanding the refrain in l. 9 ('Behold Love, how proudly she triumpheth') and omitting the last refrain. He entitles the poem: 'Request to Cupid, for revenge of his unkind love.'

3 *The holy oath.* The lover presumably refers to the lady's oath to love him, 'holy' because he would have it so.

   taketh Possibly monosyllabic (tak'th).
4 *bideth sure:* remains secure.
6 *unarmed* Probably unarmèd.
8 *measure* Probably measúre.
10 *in hold:* grasped, as in wrestling, or confined.
13 *that:* who.
14 *And:* and who (referring back to 'him', the lover).
   entreateth] T; entreath *E, D.*

II. E.

Attributed to 'Wyat' in margin of *E*.

The source of the poem is a rondeau by Jean Marot (*c.* 1460–1532), *S'il est ainsi que ce corps t'abandonne* (*M & T* 281). Marot's lover leaves his heart with the lady as a pledge of his fidelity; he then instructs her to respond to any rumours of his infidelity with the argument that his heartless body cannot love anew. He does not mention the possibility of the lady's being unfaithful. Wyatt's lover, apparently responding to the lady's charge that he is forsaking her, implies that he is banished by a third party – neither of the lovers consenting – and that any 'forsaking' on his part is only a matter of physical separation. He then proceeds to discuss the rumours of the lady's more serious forsaking of him.

4 *remain in:* dwell in, continue to be devoted to.

7 *Revulsed*] revolted *G*. Probably revulsèd: torn away, pulled back. Compare CLXXXIII.

10 *on:* in.

10–15 Compare XLII, 7–15, and CXIII, 11–15.

12–13 *there cannot . . . love an heartless body:* a heartless body cannot love.

14–15 *good is the reason/If it be so:* the argument is sound if the propositions – especially that he has her heart – are true.

III. E, D, T.

Attributed to 'Wyat' in margin of *E*; in Wyatt section of *T*.

The ultimate source of the poem is Petrarch's *Rime* 153, a sonnet (*M & T* 282). Wyatt may have done a very free imitation of that poem, translating the first quatrain quite closely, departing radically from the rest, and changing the form to a rondeau; or he may have imitated an unknown French rondeau based on Petrarch's poem (*M & T*). Compare I for the problem of source.

As in I and IV, *T* changes the poem into a sonnet by expanding the refrain in l. 9 ('Go burning sighs fulfil that I desire') and omitting the last refrain. *T* entitles the poem: 'The lover sendeth sighs to moan his suit'.

2 *which pity's*] *G or W; T*; with pity *E*; with piteous *D*.

pity's painful dart. Wyatt adds 'painful dart' to Petrarch's 'pity'. Two meanings seem possible for the whole phrase: 1) the lady's pity which, if she felt it, would give her pain; 2) the lady's pity caused by a dart that carries the lover's pain.

4 *heaven:* 1) God's heaven; 2) the mind of the lady (?).

at last: in the end; finally. The spelling of the manuscript (lest) makes 'at least' another, but less plausible, reading.

7 *start:* recoil.

6–7 *Take with thee pain . . ./ And eke the flame . . . :* express the 'pain' of my unrequited love and the 'flame' of my passions (hence 'burning').

8 *leave me then in rest:* 1) if the lady is moved by the sighs, the lover will have the 'rest' which comes from his passion's requital; 2) the sighs will take away the lover's pain and flame and thereby leave him in rest (the lover slips into taking his figure of speech literally – as if the sighs that *express* the pain and flame of passion could *take them away*).

11 *faith:* fidelity.

10–13 Is the defective logic of these lines intentional? The lover, never having secured the lady's 'pity', accuses her of disloyalty. He further argues that, because he must work by craft, he cannot move her with sighs.

14 *strainably:* compulsively, violently.

start: burst.

15 *Go:* go away, cease.

iv. E, T.

Attributed to Wyatt by *T.*

As in I and III, *T* changes this rondeau into a sonnet by expanding the refrain in l. 9 ('What vaileth truth, or perfect steadfastness') and omitting the last refrain. He entitles the poem: 'Complaint for true love unrequited.'

The first four lines appear to have five stresses each, the remaining lines (apart from the refrain) four each.

1 *by it to take pain:* by means of truth or steadfastness to strive. The phrases at the start of l. 2 are probably in apposition to and explain the end of l. 1. Omitting the comma after 'take pain', at first tempting, would bring the phrases close to nonsense: 'by truth to take pain to strive by truth.' But the piling on of infinitives, including '(to) flee' (l. 3), may have been intended (without regard for exact sense) to convey the effect of exerting moral energy.

3 *true:* (?) disposed to speak truthfully and plainly.

doubleness: hypocrisy.

4–5 *all alike . . ./Rewarded is both false and plain:* false and plain are rewarded alike.

13 *But for:* except; 'to love', then, is the only 'redress' for remaining 'within the trap' of loving. Moving the period from after 'refrain' to after 'redress' would change the last three lines into a question: 'What is the profit of loyalty except continuing to love such a cruel mistress?'

mistress. Possibly mistréss.

v. E.

Attributed to 'Wyat' in margin of *E.*

To describe falling in love as the heart leaving the body was a commonplace of medieval love poetry (*F, M & T*).

2 *ye.* Probably singular and referring to the lady whose finding of the lover's heart indicates her awareness of his love.

3 *convey:* to steal and, possibly, to manage with craft. To steal the lover's heart probably means to accept his love, but here the acceptance would be secret and the management of the affair crafty.

5 *appair:* deteriorate, decay.

6 *restore it mannerly:* return the heart in a considerate way. The lover apparently asks that the lady reject his love so that he can detach himself from her and regain his self-possession.

8 *it sitteth me too near*: it rests too close to me; it affects me too much.

11 *wilfully*: willingly and perhaps with some perversity. The lover discovers that he actually chose to fall in love, but with someone he does not really know (l. 13).

VI. E, D.

Attributed to 'Tho.' in margin of *E*.

1 *Thou hast no faith of him that hath none*: you have no hope of fidelity from him (your new lover) who is incapable of fidelity.

2 *by reason*: in agreement with the dictates of reason (ironic and with a pun on 'reason', since the proverbial 'reason' which follows explains conduct which is in fact contrary to the moral dictates of 'reason').

4 *semblable*: likeness. XCVII, 24, gives the proverb as 'like to like'. See *Tilley* L286 and *ODEP* 368–9.

5 *thou hast thine of thy condition*: you have (in your lover) someone who is your likeness with respect to your (unfaithful) nature.

6 *Yet is it not the thing I pass on*: yet I do not judge your infidelity. The emphasis is on 'I' because the lover is claiming detachment.

7 *is*] *G, D*; *of E*.

8 *since thine heart is so mutable*: because your affections are so capable of change.

9 *Thou hast no faith*: 1) you elicit no fidelity from me; 2) you are incapable of fidelity.

11–12 *I lacked discretion/To fashion faith to words mutable*: I lacked good judgement when I chose to be faithful to you in response to those verbal commitments which you could change.

14–15 *To change so oft . . ./Thou hast no faith*: to change so often [shows that] you have no capacity for fidelity. If the comma were placed after l. 13 instead of l. 14, 'to change so oft' would justify the charge in l. 13 that the lady's 'thought is too light and variable'.

VII. E.

Attributed to 'Tho.' in margin of *E*.

The refrain after l. 5 is unique in Wyatt's rondeaux and may be a scribal error.

1 *mule*: a term applied to Anne Boleyn by some of her enemies, presumably because it suggested sexual licence (*N*). There is no evidence that the poem is about Anne.

4 *setteth more by*: has a high estimate of; thinks well of.

5 *do*: does.
   appair: damage.

8 *lair*: bed; place where animals lie down.

9 *kappur*: probably related to kipper, a colt, used in northern dialects for a wanton person; here in its meaning of 'colt', implying 'wanton' (*F*).

11 *to market and to fair :* for market and for fair.

12 *panniers a pair :* a pair of large baskets for carrying provisions, usually carried by beasts of burden.

13 *powdered :* sprinkled like powder.

14-15 *you must yourself enable/To purchase it :* you must enable yourself to pay for sex.

VIII. *E, D.*

Attributed to 'Tho' in margin of *E*; subscribed in *D* 'Finis. Quod Wyatt' ('Quod', meaning 'Said', introduces the name of the author).

2 *make me to :* bring me to.

lure : 1) apparatus used by falconers to recall their hawks; 2) cry of falconers to recall hawks.

3 *contraring :* contrarying; contradicting (an intransitive verbal form; modern English would use the adjective 'contradictory').

4 *counterweighing :* acting as a counterpoise to each other; balancing.

6 *tried*] trayed *D*. *E*'s 'tried' refers to the lover's 'truth' (loyalty) *tested* by the lady's craft; 'trayed' would refer to the lady's loyalty, the truthfulness of her words, and the consistency of her conduct – all *betrayed* by her craft. I think 'tried' fits the sense of l. 5 – the lover's loyalty has been tested beyond endurance – well enough to support adherence to *E*.

in ure : in use; customary, habitual.

7 *But.* We should expect 'and', since the lover's refusal to continue doting is the result of his loyalty's being tested beyond endurance and of the lady's betrayal of her 'truth'. The antithesis implied by 'but' suggests that the preceding l. 6 relates to the first five lines as climactic statement rather than being syntactically linked to ll. 7-8. This pattern has no precedent in Wyatt's other rondeaux, where a clear syntactic break occurs after l. 5.

11 *that :* that which.

SONNETS

The sonnets of Petrarch, who was Wyatt's primary model and inspiration in this form, ordinarily divide into a section of 8 lines and a section of 6 lines, with a syntactic and rhetorical break of some importance after the eighth line. The octave is rhymed in two quatrains, abba abba. The sestet is rhymed variously – cdcdcd and cdecde are common – but does not normally end in a couplet. Wyatt's sonnets often, but not so consistently as Petrarch's, have an important break after the eighth line. They usually follow Petrarch in the abba abba rhyme of the octave. But, in the great majority of cases, the sestet is rhymed cddcee, and, whatever the variant of that scheme, the sestet always ends in a couplet.

IX. *E, D, T, NA.*

Attributed to Wyatt by *T*.

The sonnet is a translation of Petrarch's *Rime* 102, probably made with some reference to the commentary on Petrarch by Vellutello da Lucca (*M & T* 264). There is another translation of this sonnet in *H*, fol. 45ᵛ.

T entitles the poem: 'Of others' feigned sorrow, and the lover's feigned mirth.' But the speaker's genuine 'care' need not be the result of love.

3 *represent:* to show, exhibit, with the suggestion of playing a part on a stage.

1-4 Ptolemy sent Julius Caesar the head of his enemy, Pompey, and Caesar wept (*Rollins*).

5 *shut*] *ed.*; shit *E.*

8 *despite:* anger.

    disgorge: vomit up.

5-8 ... *him shut* ... *and quit.*] ... did flit/From him and to Rome did her wheel relent,/Did laugh among them whom tears had besprent,/Her cruel despite inwardly to shit. *D.*

10 *colour:* appearance.

11 *feigned.* Possibly feignèd.

13 *n'other*] *G;* not her *E.*

x. *E, A, T.*

Attributed to Wyatt by *T*; in Wyatt section of *A.*

The sonnet is a translation of Petrarch's *Rime* 140 (*M & T* 265). *T* entitles the poem: 'The lover for shamefastness hideth his desire within his faithful heart.'

1 *long:* enduring.

    harbour: to lodge.

1-4 *The long love* ... /*Into my face presseth* ... *spreading his banner:* the speaker's love, personified as his feudal lord, shows itself in his face (takes up a position for battle) instead of remaining hidden.

5 *me learneth:* teaches me.

6 *will*] wills *A, T.* The *E* reading makes 'will' parallel to 'love' and 'suffer'; all are actions the lover is being taught. In *A* and *T*, the lady 'wills' the lover to restrain himself. The latter reading translates Petrarch accurately.

    trust: confidence; here the lover's confidence that the lady will approve his showing of his feelings. The lady regards that confidence as a presumption which violates moral standards ('reason'), a sense of social proprieties ('shame'), and the 'reverence' due her person.

    lust's] *G, A, T;* lust *E.* 'lust's negligence' equates the feeling the lover is showing with a sexual desire that results from some form of neglect – of the lady's feelings and position (which demand 'reverence'), of self-restraint (dictated by 'reason'), or of social proprieties (reinforced by 'shame').

7 *reined.* The spelling of *E* is 'rayned', which can mean 'rein' or 'reign'; a pun is probably intended.

9 *forest.* Added to Petrarch's 'heart'.

12-14 Petrarch has: 'What can I do who fear my lord, except stay with him until the final hour? For he makes a good end who dies loving well.' Wyatt's 'when my master feareth' may be a deliberate variation or a misconstruing of the Italian. His addition of 'in the field' creates an apparent contradiction because the speaker's master, Love, has already left 'the field' of battle (overt affection). Is the speaker hinting at a future return to 'the field'? Or is he, despite the phrase, resigning himself, like Petrarch, to an enduring, faithful, but secret love that will last until death?

XI. *E, A, B.*

Attributed to 'Wyat' in margin of *E*; in Wyatt section of *A*.

This sonnet is probably a free imitation of Petrarch's *Rime* 190. Some scholars argue that it imitates instead Giovanni Antonio Romanello's fifteenth-century imitation of Petrarch, *Una cerva gentil*, or at least derives l. 13 from that source. For a summary of this controversy and the bibliography, see *M & T* (266–7).

M & T, who think Petrarch's poem the model, give this excellent description of the differences between the two poems:

> W[yatt] adapts Petrarch's description of his symbolic vision of a white hind who then disappears from his view into an account of a love chase in which many are involved and from which he, convinced of its futility, withdraws. He abandons Petrarch's picturesque landscape . . . , his dreamlike atmosphere, pathos and symbolism, and develops the metaphor of the hunt, making it central to his meaning (267).

Many commentators on this poem think that Wyatt is referring to his relationship with Anne Boleyn at the time when Henry VIII claimed her for himself (1526–7). Others doubt the reference. For a bibliography of the controversy, see *M & T* (267) and *Hughey* (II, 130).

2 *helas:* alas.
3 *vain travail:* futile effort.
6 *deer*, with a pun on 'dear'.
7 *leave off:* stop.
8 *Sithens*] Since *B, later change in E.*

Sithens in a net I seek to hold the wind. Proverbial in English and Italian; see *Tilley* W416 and *ODEP* 85 (*M & T*).

1–8 Any punctuation of these lines removes the ambiguities of the unpunctuated original in *E*. My punctuation makes l. 4 the result of the 'travail' and weariness of l. 3. It also turns 'Yet . . . follow' into a reversal of the decision in l. 2 to quit, followed by a renewed decision in 'I leave off therefore . . .' If one placed a comma after 'move' (l. 2) and a colon after 'sore' (l. 3), ll. 4–8 would explain the 'vain travail' and weariness and repeat the decision in l. 2 to give up the chase.

11 *diamonds.* 'In Petrarch . . . symbols of chastity' (*M & T* 267).
13 *Noli me tangere:* do not touch me. Whatever Wyatt's immediate source, l. 13 derives ultimately from a Latin motto, *Noli me tangere quia Caesaris sum*, supposedly inscribed on the collars of Caesar's hinds. That motto in turn was probably derived from a conflation of John xx, 17 and

Matthew xxii, 21. In the first, the risen Jesus tells Mary Magdalen not to touch his body. In the second, Jesus tells the Pharisees to render to Caesar the things that are Caesar's. (*M & T*)

XII. *E, A, T.*

Attributed to 'Wyat' in margin of *E*; in Wyatt section of *A* and *T*.

This sonnet translates Petrarch's *Rime* 82 (*M & T* 277).

T entitles the poem: 'The lover waxeth wiser, and will not die for affection.' The theme of the octave might be more precisely stated: 'If I have sufficient respect for my own worth, as I now do, I shall not feel pain at your refusal to reciprocate my love.' But notice that the sestet is the lover's attempt to persuade the lady to return his love – an attempt that rests on imputing blame to the lady for not loving him: he attributes her refusal to a 'disdain' intended to cause him grief. Here, as in many other poems by Wyatt, the lover assumes that his love for the lady makes her morally bound to reciprocate. Her relieving his pain by being 'content' with his love – that is, presumably, returning it – is her only way to escape his *moral* censure; even if, as in this poem, he carries out his implicit threat to end his love for her, some blame will attach to her.

Are we meant to question the lover's assumption that love creates a duty to return love?

1   *grieved*] dreared *M*. *M* (89) argues that the rhyme scheme requires a word ending in 'red' or 'ried', like 'dreared' (saddened). But 'ed' may be a sufficient rhyming syllable.

1-2   *Was I never yet of your love grieved/Nor never shall* . . . :   I have never yet been grieved by my love for you and I never shall . . .

4   *And tears . . . have me wearied.*   'And', which implies a parallel with l. 3, may be justified if the lover is wearied to the point of stopping his tears as well as his self-hatred.

5-8   Petrarch says he would rather have a beautiful and blank tomb than have Laura's name written, to his loss [that is, as the cause of his death], on some piece of marble where his body would be separated from his spirit – a body and spirit that can still remain together. Wyatt emphasizes the resistance to dying for love.

6   *yfixed:*   (have) fixed.

7   *did the spirit soon haste:*   did hurry the spirit early.

8   *bones:*   bodily frame, body.

by great sighs stirred.   Wyatt's addition; 'stirred' probably modifies 'bones', though it could refer back to 'spirit'.

10   *without doing grief:*   without doing harm [to itself] (*O*).

11   *Please it you so to this to do relief:*   may it please you in this way [being contented with my heart and not grieving it] to give to this [heart of mine] relief.

12   *otherwise:*   [acting] in a different way.

12-13   *to fulfil/Your disdain:*   (?) to satisfy your appetite for disdain; *or* to make your disdain complete.

13–14 *ye . . . shall not as ye ween,/And ye yourself the cause thereof hath been:* you shall not accomplish what you expect [the lover's misery?], and you yourself [shall] have been the cause [implicitly, of the relationship's ending?]. The clear attribution of fault to the lady in l. 14 departs from Petrarch who, in his final line, says: 'For this I give many thanks to Love and myself.'

XIII. *E, A, T.*

Attributed to 'Wyat' in margin of *E*; in Wyatt sections of *A* and *T*.

The sonnet closely translates Petrarch's *Rime* 224 (*M & T* 278). *T* entitles the poem: 'Charging of his love as unpiteous and loving other.'

1   *in*] *A, T*; an *E.*
2   *languor:* distress, pining, sorrow.
    lovely: loving (*Da*).
4   *blind:* dim, dark, gloomy.
5   *depainted:* depicted, portrayed.
6   *sparkling:* scattering, dispersing. Petrarch's *voce interrotte* means broken tones (*M & T*).
    lower or higher. Wyatt's substitute for Petrarch's 'barely heard'.
7   *tire:* exhaust.
8   *which love hath stained:* (?) from which love has removed the lustre; *or* which love has stained [my face]. The point of the line in either case is that love has made his face pale.
10   *sighing*] *A, T*; sighting *E.* 'sighting' is an alternate form of 'sighing'.
11   *With . . . anger feeding:* feeding on anger (*O*).

XIV. *E, A, D* (2 versions), *T.*

Attributed to 'Wyat' in margin of *E*; in Wyatt sections of *A* and *T*.

The sources of the sonnet are two consecutive *strambotti* by Serafino d'Aquilano (1466–1500). Wyatt translates the first to form the octave; he imitates the second more freely to form the sestet (*M & T* 279–80).

T entitles the poem: 'The lover forsaketh his unkind love.'

4   *again:* in return.
5   *servant*] slave *D1*; 'slave' is closer to the Italian, which, in lines translated by ll. 5–6, speaks of the lover as a person willing to be bought by the lady as a virtual slave but not willing to be paid such [scanty] money. Wyatt, while weakening the monetary metaphor, establishes the context of courtly love in 'servant' – the lover who submits (or tries to submit) to the lady's wishes, usually for sexual restraint, provided she gives him at least her affection.
7   *none other reason.* The Italian has 'little pity'; the English, which is unclear, probably means 'no other consideration or regard'.
8   *Displease thee not:* let it not displease thee.
    refrain: keep myself [from loving].
9   *Unsatiate of my woe and thy desire:* not [yet] glutted with my woe and your desire [to cause me even more woe?]. I take 'unsatiate', like 'Assured' in l. 10, to refer to 'thee' in l. 8.

10 *Assured:* (?) bold; feeling confident that you will be able.

by] *A, D2, T*; be *E*.

11 *But*. A loose connective, like the Latin *ac*, not uncommon in English written by those with a knowledge of Latin.

feign a default: pretend that I have been guilty of a fault, of neglect of duty (the crafty excuse of l. 10).

12 *fire:* figuratively, the ardour of love.

13 *bearing in hand:* deceptive pretending.

14 *Plougheth in water and sow*] *A, D2*; *corner of leaf torn away in E*.

Plougheth ... soweth. Proverbial expression for futility in Italian and English; see *Tilley* S87, S184, and *ODEP* 508 (*M & T*).

in the sand] in sand *A, D1*.

XV. *E, A, T*.

Attributed to 'Wyat' in margin of *E*; in Wyatt sections of *A* and *T*.

This sonnet translates Petrarch's *Rime* 19 (*M & T* 284). *T* entitles the sonnet: 'How the lover perisheth in his delight, as the fly in the fire.'

1-2 *Some fowls ... defend.* Perhaps a proverbial reference to the eagle; see *Tilley* E3 (*Da*).

4 *'pear:* appear (*O*).

5 *Other:* other fowls.

6 *as they do pretend.* 'A gap-filling phrase ... , but perhaps justified as emphasizing the *desio folle* [foolish desire] of those who play with fire' (*M & T* 284).

5-6 Since 'fowls' can in this period refer to any winged creature, it is probably *T*'s 'fly' or a moth that plays in the fire. Petrarch refers more generally to 'animals' throughout his poem.

7 *the contrary of it that they intend:* pain instead of pleasure.

8 *by right:* rightly (in the sense that the speaker's place in the latter category of 'fowls' is consonant with the facts about him).

7-8 Wyatt follows Petrarch in the unusual break after l. 7. In both sonnets l. 8 is transitional, concluding the rhyme scheme of the octave and introducing the argument of the sestet (*F*).

11 *Remembrance ... face.* An addition to Petrarch.

12 *eyen*] *ed.*; yen *E*: eyes.

unstable. Translates Petrarch's 'weak' or 'sick'.

14 *the gleed:* live coal, the ember; the fire.

XVI. *E, A, T*.

Attributed to 'Wyat' in margin of *E*; in Wyatt sections of *A* and *T*.

This sonnet translates Petrarch's *Rime* 49 (*M & T* 285). *T* entitles the poem: 'Against his tongue that failed to utter his suits.'

3-4 *right ill hast thou me rendered/For such desert to do me wreak and shame:* very badly have you paid me for what I deserve when you cause me harm and shame.

6 *like one afeard.* An addition to Petrarch.

7 *toward*] a word *A*.

speak toward : (?) speak to the point (state my love) (*M & T*); *or* speak towards her (*Da*).

9–10 *tears, again my will each night/That are with me when fain I would be alone :* tears that are with me each night against my will when I would gladly be alone.

11 *when I should make my moan.* The Italian has 'when I am in the presence of my peace (the lady who could give me peace)'.

12 *you so ready sighs to make me shright :* you sighs, so ready [on other occasions] to make me cry out.

13 *slack :* lacking in energy, slow to act.

outstart : spring forth.

XVII. *E, D, H, T, NA.*

Attributed to 'Wyat' in margin of *E*; in Wyatt section of *T*.

The sonnet translates Petrarch's *Rime* 134 (*M & T* 286). *T* entitles the poem: 'Description of the contrarious passions in a lover.' Petrarch and Wyatt frequently explore the 'contraries of love', often, as here, by means of antitheses. See CXIII for a statement of the absurdity of the 'contraries' and yet their truth to the speaker's experience as a lover.

4 *seize on*] *ed.*; seson *E*. Petrarch has 'embrace'.

5 *That :* that which. Probably refers to 'love' ('it' in l. 8). Petrarch's *Tal* might refer to 'love' but more likely to his lady, Laura.

6 *scape :* escape.

no wise : in no way.

7 *Nor letteth :* nor does it let.

device : desire, inclination.

8 *me occasion*] none occasion *H*.

7–8 Petrarch has 'Love neither kills me nor frees me; he neither wishes me alive nor frees me from the pain [of life through dying?]'.

9 *eyen*] *ed.*; iyen *E*: eyes.

10 *health.* Petrarch has the more general 'help'.

11 *I love another and thus I hate myself.* Wyatt reverses the order of Petrarch's antitheses and adds the causal 'thus'.

13 *death and life*] *D, H, T*; life and death *E*.

14 *strife.* Petrarch has 'state'.

XVIII. *E, A.*

Attributed to 'Tho.' in margin of *E*; in Wyatt section of *A*.

This sonnet freely imitates Petrarch's *Rime* 98 (*M & T* 287).

N and *Hughey* comment on the obscurity of the poem. *Hughey* suggests, rightly I think, that the poem is addressed by the lover to his heart; but neither her paraphrase nor the comment of *M & T* makes clear that the poem is about the lover's continued love during his physical *absence* (l. 14) from his lady. The poem's meaning turns on the notion that the speaker's heart can remain with the lady and speak to her even if the speaker himself is absent.

1 *of:* (?) by; *or* in; *or* with respect to. Though it is not perfectly clear which meaning Wyatt intends, I think the third is most likely.

mind: (?) the intellectual powers, contrasted with 'heart'; *or* desire, synonymous with 'heart'. Again, Wyatt's intention is not perfectly clear. I think 'desire' is more probable.

of my mind. Though several meanings are possible, two are more likely than the others: 1) by or in my intellectual powers, perhaps because they perceive a duty which takes me from the lady; *or* 2) with respect to my desires (that is, my desires are bridled or frustrated). I think the latter is more probable.

2 *Returning me backward:* turning back [towards a place where the lady is *not* in residence].

by force: (?) as a result of my exertion of force on myself; *or* as a result of someone else's exertion of force on me. I think the latter more probable since it is a froward or perverse fortune (ll. 6–7) – that is, some *external* circumstance – that keeps him from the lady. *N* suggests that it is the King who exerts the force to keep Wyatt from Anne Boleyn.

express: (?) explicit, definite, unmistakable in purpose; *or*, as an adverb, speedily.

3 *If thou seek honour to keep thy promise:* if you resort to your fine sense of what is right in order [to gain the strength] to keep your promise [of love].

4 *but thou thyself unbind:* unless you release yourself [from your promise of love].

1–4 *Though I myself be bridled ... Who may thee hold, my heart ...* The meaning of the first quatrain depends on the distinction and contrast between 'I myself' and 'my heart'. Although some details of the quatrain are obscure, I think the following is a plausible paraphrase of the general tenor: 'Though I am kept from being where I desire – being made to go back to a place where my lady is not present because of an explicit command from someone in power – if you, my heart, draw strength from your sense of honour to keep your promise of love, what can keep you from being where you desire unless you break that promise of love?'

5–6 *no way man may find/Thy virtue to let:* man can find no way to obstruct ('let') the exercise of your strength in love ('virtue').

6 *frowardness:* perversity.

8 *Though other be present, thou art not all behind:* though others be in the presence of the lady [already], you are not altogether behind [in the race or competition for her love].

10–11 *still under the defence/Of time, truth, and love to save thee from offence:* always being defended by your patience ('time'), loyalty, and love, a defence which will save you from being hurt by the offensive act of another [possibly the lady herself], and keep you from [giving her] offence.

12–13 *I burn in a ... desire/With my ... master's that may not follow:* I (the heart) burn in a desire along with my master's desire, [but, unlike me] my master may not follow his desire [to be physically present with you].

14 *Whereby his absence turneth him to sorrow :* For this reason – [because his absence prevents him from following his desire] – his absence makes him sorrowful.

XIX. *E, A, T.*

Attributed to 'Wyat' in margin of *E*; in Wyatt sections of *A* and *T*.

This sonnet translates Petrarch's *Rime* 189 (*M & T* 289). *T* entitles the poem: 'The lover compareth his state to a ship in perilous storm tossed on the sea.'

1 *charged.* Probably chargèd.

charged with forgetfulness : 'oppressed by love so as to forget all else' (*Tillyard* 151).

3 *rock and rock.* Wyatt's substitute for Petrarch's Scylla and Charybdis.

enemy. Probably disyllabic (en'my).

3–4 *mine enemy . . . my lord :* Love.

4 *my lord, steereth with cruelness.* Petrarch has 'at the rudder sits the lord'.

5–6 *every oar . . . in such a case :* every oar is a thought in readiness [to act] as if death were unimportant in such a situation. Petrarch has 'At each oar a thought, ready and evil, which seems that it holds in scorn the tempest and the goal'.

7–8 *An endless wind . . . of forced sighs and trusty fearfulness.* Petrarch has 'an endless, wet wind of sighing, hope, and desire'.

9 *tears . . . disdain.* Presumably the tears are the male speaker's, the disdain the lady's.

10 *hindrance.* Probably trisyllabic.

11 *Wreathed.* Probably wreathèd.

10–11 *cords . . ./Wreathed with error and . . . ignorance :* the lines (of the sail) twisted with the [male speaker's] erroneous and ignorant judgement [of what is valuable?].

12 *The stars . . . that led me to this pain.* Petrarch has 'My two sweet accustomed signs'. Both Petrarch and Wyatt are probably referring to the lady's eyes as stars; but for Petrarch those stars are reliable guides, while for Wyatt they mislead the speaker into pain.

13 *Drowned.* Probably drownèd.

reason. Petrarch has 'reason and art'.

comfort] consort *N*. A scribe might misread 'consort' as 'comfort'; 'consort' better sustains the nautical metaphor. Either word probably has the stress on the second syllable.

should me comfort. Wyatt's addition.

xx. E, A, T.

Attributed to 'Wyat' in margin of E; in Wyatt sections of A and T.

This sonnet translates Petrarch's *Rime* 173 (*M & T* 290). *T* entitles the poem: 'Of duteous love.'

1 *Avising:* advising; looking at, gazing at; considering.

2 *Where he is that mine oft moisteth:* where resides Love, or Cupid, that often makes my eyes moist [with tears]. The notion that Cupid resides in the eyes of the lady – derived from Anacreon – is common but difficult. Probably Cupid personifies the ways in which the lady's eyes look at the man. Those looks, like arrows, inspire love but also, since they are the looks of a chaste lady, pain. Tears are the manifestation of both love and pain in the man.

3 *mind:* the faculty for knowing and loving the beloved, including here a strong element of *desire* – hence the mind's departure from the heart, the seat of desire. The rest of the poem is about the experience of the 'mind'. Petrarch has 'soul'.

4 *to rest in his worldly paradise:* to find ease by loving the lady and, he thinks, being loved by her.

5 *And find the sweet bitter under this guise:* and find that the sweet is also bitter in this kind of relationship. Petrarch has 'finding some of the sweetness and depth of love'. Wyatt's addition of 'bitter' undermines the expectation of 'rest' in l. 4 and prepares for the 'contraries' of feeling which the rest of the poem describes.

6 *What webs he hath wrought . . . he perceiveth:* the web-like traps which Love or Cupid has woven, the 'mind' perceives.

7 *whereby:* wherefore.

8 *bridleth:* Probably trisyllabic.

fire . . . ice: the fire of the mind's desire . . . the ice of the lady's coldness which chills the mind's desire.

9 *it:* the mind of l. 3.

Thus is it in such extremity brought. Petrarch has 'In these two extremes, contrary and mixed, he stands . . .' Wyatt does not convey Petrarch's sense of the soul, or mind, being torn between the extremes of l. 8.

10 *In frozen thought . . . in flame:* in the mind's fancy, anticipation, or desire frustrated and immobilized by the lady's coldness . . . in ardent desire encouraged by the lady's warmth.

11 'Twixt . . . 'twixt] A; twist . . . twist E.

'twixt earnest and game: the opportunity for the mind to be serious in its love as opposed to its having to play a game [of pretended levity] because the lady is playing a game with the speaker. Wyatt adds this antithesis to Petrarch, probably to diminish the moral stature of the lady.

12 *diverse:* 1) diverse – that is, different in character (from the 'glad' thoughts); 2) differing from what is right, good, or profitable.

13 *hardiness:* boldness in undertaking to love the lady.

14 *fruitless.* Possibly fruitléss.

Of such a root cometh fruit fruitless. Echoes the proverb 'An evil tree brings forth ill fruit'; see *Tilley* T486 and compare T494 and T497.

XXI. *E, A, T.*

Attributed to 'Wyat' in margin of *E*; in Wyatt sections of *A* and *T*.

This sonnet closely translates Petrarch's *Rime* 57 (*M & T* 291). *T* entitles the poem: 'How unpossible it is to find quiet in his love.'

3 *That leave it or wait it doth me like pain:* so that to relinquish [expectation of] good luck or to continue in expectation of good luck causes me the same pain. The phrase 'leave it or wait it' may echo the proverb 'Take it or leave it', though there are no sixteenth-century instances of that proverb recorded in *Tilley* T128 or *ODEP* 640.

4 *it:* good luck.

7 *Thames.* Wyatt anglicizes Petrarch's Euphrates and Tigris.

5–8 The 'impossibilities' figure is ancient (*M & T*).

9 *this:* this situation or relationship.

10 *In that*] Or that *A, T, M & T.* 'In that', which is the more difficult reading, makes sense as a conjunction introducing the conditions for his finding peace.

rightwisely. Possibly trisyllabic: in a righteous manner.

11 *Leave:* cease.

13 *out of taste:* without the capacity to taste (*O*).

14 *That all my . . . travail is but waste:* so that all my effort is only a waste. Petrarch has 'But I never encounter their favours' (that is, the favours of Love and the lady).

XXII. *E, A, T.*

Attributed to 'Wyat' in margin of *E*; in Wyatt sections of *A* and *T*.

This sonnet translates Petrarch's *Rime* 124 (*M & T* 292). *T* entitles the poem: 'Of Love, Fortune, and the lover's mind.'

1 *rememb'rer*] *ed.*; remembre *E*. The emendation was first suggested by Otto Hietsch, *Die Petrarcaübersetzungen Sir Thomas Wyatts* (1960), pp. 116–17. The word here has the sense of 'that which retains things in the mind', since it is the faculty for knowing the present as well as the past and contrasting the two.

2 *Of that that is now with that that hath been:* of a present along with but different from the past. We should say 'of a past different from the present'.

4 *them beyond all measure:* those who are beyond all limitation – that is, the dead. Petrarch has 'those who are on the other bank'; but *riva* can mean 'limit' as well as 'bank' – an alternative that may have led Wyatt to his version.

8 *Liveth in rest*] later correction in *E, A, T*; Liveth and rest *original E*.

12 *brickle:* brittle.

12–13 *not of steel but of . . . glass/I see that from mine hand falleth my trust.* Petrarch has 'not of diamond but of glass I see from my hand fall every hope'. Since 'diamond' and 'glass' refer to 'hope' in Petrarch, 'steel' and 'glass' probably refer to 'trust' in Wyatt. Wyatt may have seen a submerged allusion to mirrors in Petrarch's diamond and glass coupled with 'hope' – a possibly illusory view of the future. If so, Wyatt substituted 'steel' for 'diamond' because mirrors were still made of steel in the sixteenth century, and 'trust' is an illusory confidence in some future good.

14 *dashed into dust.* Petrarch has 'broken in two', which is more consistent with the metaphor of falling glass.

XXIII. *E, A, T.*

Attributed to 'Wyat' in margin of *E*; in Wyatt sections of *A* and *T*.

This sonnet translates Petrarch's *Rime* 21 (*M & T* 293–4). *T* entitles the poem: 'The lover prayeth his offered heart to be received.'

1 *cruel.* Probably disyllabic; Wyatt's addition.

2 *With . . . your eyes for to get peace:* to make peace with your eyes. The lady's eyes make war on the speaker in the sense that her looks, like the arrows of Cupid, inspire his desire (compare XVIII, 2) but also attack or reject the desire they inspire. The speaker offers her his heart – a commitment of his love and loyalty – to secure the peace of not being tempted and rebuffed.

5 *If any other look for it:* if any other (women) look for my heart (*O*). *as ye trow.* Wyatt's addition.

7 *that that:* that (heart) which.

8 *It was once mine, it can no more be so:* I once controlled my heart – [my capacity to commit my love and loyalty]. But I no longer care to do so [because my heart is committed to you or to no one].

9 *chase:* put to flight, chase away.

10 *comfort.* Probably comfórt.

9–10 *nor it in you can find/In this exile no manner of comfort:* and the heart cannot find, in its exile from me, any kind of comfort in you.

11 *nor, where he is called, resort:* nor resort to where he is called [by the other women].

12 *He may wander from his natural kind:* 1) he (the heart) may die; 2) he may cease to love you [which is his natural inclination].

13 *hurt.* Petrarch has 'fault'. Perhaps Wyatt misread Petrarch's *colpa* as *colpo.* 'It is uncharacteristic of him [Wyatt] to miss the opportunity of bringing in blame and guilt . . .' (*M & T* 294).

14 *yours the loss and mine the deadly pain:* yours the loss of my love, mine the deadly pain of 1) dying and 2) ceasing to love you. Petrarch has 'your fault is as great as my love for you'. *N* suggests that Wyatt is translating the last line of Petrarch's *Rime* 224, the source of XIII (*M & T* 278).

XXIV. *E, A, T.*

Attributed to 'Tho.' in margin of *E*; in Wyatt sections of *A* and *T*.

This sonnet translates an Italian sonnet printed in the 1531 edition of *Le Rime* of Jacopo Sannazaro (*c.* 1456–1530), but its authorship is uncertain (*M & T* 295). *T* entitles the poem: 'The lover's life compared to the Alps.'

2 *ire.* Presumably the lady's. The Italian has 'grief' or 'pain'.

5 *Under craggy rocks they have full barren plains.* The Italian has 'They have high faces of rocks'.

6 *tire:* seize and tear. A term from falconry which refers to the hawk's seizing and tearing flesh.

Hard thoughts ... my ... mind doth tire: my mind seizes and tears hard thoughts (*O*).

8 *great trust:* great expectation of large effect [such as the lady's love].

9 *boist'rous*] *ed.*; boyseus *E*; boyst'ous *A*.

12 *full:* very.

13 *the restless*] *M & T*; that restless *E*, *A*. Wyatt's addition.

14 *plaints that pass thorough my throat.* The Italian has 'the spirit or mind [which suffers from] excessive shortness of breath due to mental agony'.

XXV. *E, A, D, T.*

Attributed to 'Tho' in margin of *E*; in Wyatt sections of *A* and *T*.

This sonnet imitates very freely Petrarch's *Rime* 258 (*M & T* 305). *T* entitles the poem: 'The lover describeth his being stricken with sight of his love.'

2 *ne vaileth no defence:* there does not avail no defence (the double negative does not yield a positive).

3 *have pressed:* have exerted force against. This verb suggests that the metaphor of 'lightning' is already present in 'lively sparks' of l. 1.

1–4 *sparks ... no defence ... pressed ... none offence ... quaking pleasure:* even when looks from the lady's eyes give no offence and, indeed, give pleasure, they still, like lightning, are potentially threatening.

8 *Dazed.* Probably dazèd.

9 *ystricken:* struck, with the possible pun 'eye-struck'.

10 *erring:* wandering.

13 *For.* May introduce the reason for his 'patiently bearing' (l. 12) or, more generally, the reason why the lady's looks, formerly pleasurable at least in the main, have become painful. Or 'For' may be a loose connective indicating a later moment in time ('then'). I prefer the latter reading because it fits what appears to be the sequential character of the speaker's experience. First the lady's looks give him mainly pleasure, possibly because they hint at her favour. Then they daze and blind him, possibly because he has fallen more deeply in love or because her vehemence (l. 6) has begun to show. Then he falls in pain, probably because her looks are now hostile. Finally she slays him ('deadly') with her thunderous 'Nay' (l. 14) to his request for help (her love).

XXVI. *E, A, D, T.*

Attributed to 'Wyat' in margin of *E*; in Wyatt sections of *A* and *T*; revision in Wyatt's hand; subscribed 'TW' in *D*.

This sonnet translates Petrarch's *Rime* 169 (*M & T* 309–10). *T* entitles the poem: 'The wavering lover willeth, and dreadeth, to move his desire.'

2 *In desert hope*: into a barren or empty hope (Wyatt's addition).

by well assured moan. The meaning of Wyatt's addition is unclear to me. If 'by' means 'in addition to' or 'beside', the phrase might mean: 'and a cry of woe quite certain [to be voiced].'

3 *Maketh.* Possibly mak'th.

4 *bid*: bids.

7 *armed.* Probably armèd.

armed sighs. Probably the lady's (*O*). They are ambivalent in character: as sighs, they inspire the speaker's 'hope' (l. 8); but they are sharp, like a weapon, in quality, and therefore inspire his 'dread' (l. 8). The phrase echoes the oxymoron 'gentle cruelty' (l. 5).

8 *locking*] *T*; lacking *E, A.*

'Twixt hope and dread locking my liberty. Wyatt adds this personification of liberty locked within walls. The speaker's hope denies him the liberty of breaking off the relationship; his dread denies him the liberty of pursuing the lady more boldly.

9 *disdainful*] *W, T*; that scornful *E*; the scornful *D.*

11 *comforteth.* Possibly comfort'th.

which comforteth the mind that erst for fear shook. Petrarch has 'which in part brightens the pained heart'. Wyatt, in substituting 'comforteth' for 'brightens', drops Petrarch's and his own metaphor of the beam of sunlight that brightens an otherwise cloudy sky.

14 *But such it is.* Petrarch has 'I have so much to say'.

XXVII. *E, A, T.*

In Wyatt sections of *A* and *T*.

The idea for this sonnet may have come from a *strambotto* by Marcello Filosseno (1450–1520), *Pareami in questa nocte esser contento* (*M & T* 318). But Petrarch wrote dream poems, and his imitators sometimes described erotic dreams. *T* entitles the sonnet: 'The lover having dreamed enjoying of his love, complaineth that the dream is not either longer or truer.'

F argues that this sonnet was written in Spain in 1537 on the grounds that it occurs in *E* after a poem about going to sea (LXXXIX) and shortly before a poem (XLVI) about being in Monzòn, Spain. The discovery of the source of XLV in a Spanish manuscript by J. G. Fucilla (see *FR*) offers some support to *F*'s hypothesis that *E*'s poems are transcribed in the order of their composition.

With the possible exception of *T*, editors and commentators have not acknowledged the obscurity of this poem. Particular problems are noted below. But the general problem is the meaning of events in the second quatrain and the relationship of those events to the rest of the poem. Is the speaker describing a waking or dreaming state in ll. 6–8? Does the condition described in ll. 9–10 follow temporally and perhaps psychologically on the state in ll. 6–8? Or do ll. 9–13 recapitulate the events from the time the speaker begins to dream until he reaches the condition of wakefulness described in the first quatrain?

I think it makes best sense to take the second quatrain as describing, in a tone of heavy sarcasm ('good respect . . . dangerous case'), how the dream wakes the speaker ('madest my sprite live') in spite of his plea – in the first quatrain – that the dream prolong itself. He awakens to a condition of loneliness in which his body is embracing a lady that is not there ('my body [to be] in tempest'). Line 6 then means that, while the lady was once present in the dream, she disappears ('Thou brought'st not her') just before he wakes ('into this tossing mew'). Lines 9–13 recapitulate the events: the dream in which the speaker's spirit delights in the lady's presence ('his desire'), and the return to the 'fire' of consciousness.

T's change of 'mew' to 'seas' in l. 6 may have been an attempt to deal with the problem of the second quatrain in a different way. Taking a cue from 'Unstable . . . according to the place', *T*'s editor might have located the speaker on a ship in 'a dangerous case' and had him expressing gratitude for the lady's being present only in a dream rather than in reality.

1 *according:* appropriate. The dream's unstable character is appropriate to the 'place' where it is dreamed: either the speaker's mind or his bed ('mew', l. 6). I prefer the first.

2 *Be steadfast once:* endure on at least this one occasion.

at least be true: (?) come true by making my lady physically present; *or* be true to the fact that my lady is not really present. I prefer the second; 'at least' is an odd qualifier to attach to the lady's physical presence. The speaker would rather dream about the truth than suffer the pain of waking from a *brief* dream about that which is 'false' and 'feigned' (l. 4) – his lady's presence.

4 *feigned.* Probably feignèd.

3–4 *By tasted sweetness make me not to rue/The sudden loss of thy . . . grace:* do not force me to regret [by bringing this dream to a sudden close] the sudden loss of your grace – a grace [I have experienced] as a result of having tasted your sweetness. I think the speaker implies that it would have been better not to have dreamed of his lady's presence at all rather than be suddenly deprived of it after a brief 'taste'.

5 *By good respect:* as a result of proper consideration.

in such a dangerous case: (?) in a situation so dangerous [to the lady, presumably her chastity]; *or* in a situation so dangerous [to the speaker, presumably because he would be unduly gratified if he had a long taste of the lady's dream-image]. I prefer the second, read with sarcasm.

6 *brought'st*] *ed.*; broughtes *E.*

mew] seas *T.*

mew: a cage in which hawks or other fowl are kept for moulting, fattening, or breeding; here, figuratively, for either the speaker's bed, on which he tosses restlessly, or the speaker's mind as, in agitation, it moves towards waking. I prefer the second.

Thou brought'st not her into this tossing mew: (?) you did not bring the lady physically to this bed [and, as a consequence, did not make my dream 'true' in one of the possible senses of l. 2]; *or* you did not bring a dream-image of the lady to my mind at all; *or* you did not bring the dream-image of the lady to my mind just as I was waking [though her image had been present before and its disappearance contributed to my waking]. The third, though perhaps strained, seems to me preferable. It is difficult, in the case of the first reading, to see how a dream could bring the lady physically to the speaker's bed – though John Donne later finds a way in 'The Dream'. The second reading does not explain the 'tasted sweetness' (l. 3) or the sprite's having 'his desire' (l. 9).

7 *madest my sprite live:* (?) made me dream; *or* made me wake up.

8 *My body in tempest her succour to embrace:* (?) [you, the dream, made] my body, in a state of great passion, embrace the lady in the dream; *or* [you, the dream, made] my body [to be] in a state of great desire to embrace the lady [just as I awoke to find her absent]. I prefer the second: his spirit's care (l. 7) would probably not be renewed if, in his dream, his body were embracing the lady.

9 *The body dead, the sprite had his desire.* (?) It is conceivable that the body's 'death' in a dream might result from a dreamed embrace in l. 8. But such sexual detumescence is probably not compatible with the spirit's continuing to have 'his desire' and to be in a state of 'delight' (l. 10). It therefore seems likely that the state described in l. 9 does not follow from that in ll. 7–8 but refers instead, by way of recapitulation, to the early stage of the dream. If so, 'dead' means 'asleep' and the spirit's delightful desire is sexual.

11–13 *Why ... did it not keep it right,/Returning to leap into the fire,/And where it was at wish it could not remain?:* Why did the spirit not keep itself where it belonged – in the dream – instead of returning to painful consciousness ('fire')? [Why] could the spirit not remain where it was as a result of its wish?

14 *Such mocks of dreams they turn:* such mocking dreams turn.

XXVIII. *E, A, T.*

Attributed to 'Tho.' in margin of *E*; in Wyatt sections of *A* and *T*; revisions in Wyatt's hand.

The first six lines of this sonnet may owe something to Petrarch's *Rime* 224 (*M & T* 278), translated closely in XIII. If there is a debt it is in structure – the suspension of the main clause through a series of 'if' clauses – and some of the symptoms of love.

T entitles the poem: 'The lover confesseth him in love with Phyllis.'

If Brunet is Anne Boleyn (see note to ll. 7–10), this poem was composed after Anne's disgrace and death in 1536.

1 *waker:* wakeful; vigilant.

2 *with little speech to plain:* to complain with few words [because the 'many sighs' are consuming all his breath].

3 *if they my cheer distain:* if joy and woe stain my face [presumably with blushing and growing pale].

4 *For hope of small, if much to fear therefore:* if to fear much in the hope of little; 'therefore' seems redundant.

5 *less or more.* Probably refer to 'haste' as well as 'slack'.

6 *Be*] *T*; by *E, A.*

8 *roar:* tumult; disturbance.

Brunet that set my wealth in such a roar] *W*; Her that did set our country in a roar *E.*

9 *Th'unfeigned.* Probably th'unfeignèd.

8–10 *Brunet . . . Phyllis . . . Brunet.* Brunet was probably Anne Boleyn; see E. K. Chambers, p. 139 (*FR*), for a consideration of the evidence. Wyatt's alteration of l. 8 in *E* may have been an attempt to obscure the identification. Chambers (pp. 140–5) rejects the unsubstantiated suggestion by *F* that Phyllis was Mary, Duchess of Richmond, sister of Henry Howard, Earl of Surrey. He suggests Elizabeth Darrell, Wyatt's mistress in his later years.

11 *from myself:* alien to myself; beside myself, out of my wits. The theological metaphor pervading the last four lines is here most explicit. As the saved sinner is to God, the speaker is to Phyllis: he is 'alien to himself' in that he is worthless, and he is 'beside himself' with a love for the lady that results from her holding him ('hath me') in her 'grace'. Here 'grace' is Protestant in character – God's loving kindness directed to sinners without regard to their worthlessness.

13 *My heart alone well worthy she doth stay:* she alone – a person of genuine worth – sustains and comforts my heart.

14 *scant:* scarcely, barely.

XXIX. *A, T.*

In Wyatt section of *T.*

This sonnet freely imitates Petrarch's *Rime* 269 (*M & T* 429), a lament for the death of his patron, Giovanni Colonna, and of Laura. *T* entitles the sonnet: 'The lover laments the death of his love.'

Modern scholars, following the lead of *N*, have suggested that this is not a love poem but Wyatt's lament for the execution of his patron, Thomas Cromwell, Earl of Essex, on 28 July 1540. *Mason* (197) gives strong evidence of the affection between Wyatt and Cromwell. But the conjecture about the poem's occasion depends on: 1) the assumption that Wyatt knew the occasion of Petrarch's poem and, finding it parallel to his own situation, imitated the poem for that reason; and 2) the argument that Wyatt's departures from Petrarch, especially in ll. 7–8 and 12–14, indicate his fear for his life as a result of Cromwell's fall (*Tillyard* 172), perhaps even his imprisonment in the Tower early in 1541 which resulted from the schemes of his and Cromwell's enemies (*M & T*). Working against the conjecture is the statement of self-hatred in l. 13: Wyatt was not responsible for Cromwell's fall. But perhaps 'the failure of his mission in Spain (1537–9) or his service in France (1539–40), in which he had to collaborate with Cromwell's enemy

the Duke of Norfolk, made him feel that he had indirectly contributed to it'
(*M & T* 430).

There is another translation of this sonnet in *H*, fol. 47.

1 *The pillar perished is whereto I leant.* Petrarch has 'The tall column is
broken and the green laurel'; *colonna* puns on the name of Petrarch's patron
Colonna and *lauro* puns on Laura.

3–5 *The like of it no man again can find . . ./To mine unhap:* to my mis-
fortune, no man can find the like of it.

8 *till death do it relent:* until death dissolves my misfortune ('it').

7–8 *And I, alas, by chance am thus assigned/Dearly to mourn till death do it
relent.* Petrarch has: 'And not earth nor political power nor oriental jewel
nor force of gold can restore it' (the 'treasure' of the life that death has taken).

14 *cease*] *ed.*; cause *A*; ease *T*. The word 'cease' could easily be misread
as 'cause', 'ease' not so readily.

12–14 *My mind in woe, my body full of smart,/And I myself myself always to
hate/Till dreadful death do cease my doleful state.* Petrarch has 'O how
beautiful our life is in prospect, how easily one loses in a morning what in
many years is acquired in great pain'.

XXX. *E, D, A, T.*

Attributed to 'Tho' in margin of *E*; in Wyatt sections of *A* and *T*.
T entitles the poem: 'Of change in mind.'

1 *device:* 1) purpose, inclination, desire; 2) stratagem [in dealing with
other people].

2 *on my faith:* an oath on his Christian faith (ironic in the context of a
statement justifying infidelity to people?).

3 *purpose*] *A, T*; propose *E*.
   like after: in the manner, or imitation, of.

2–3 *good reason/To change purpose . . . season.* Echoes the proverbs 'A
wise man need not blush to change his purpose' and 'A wise man changes
his mind, a fool never will'; see *Tilley* M431 and M420.

4–5 *in every case . . . one guise . . . wise.* Contradicts proverbs alluded to
in ll. 2–3.

6 *manner condition:* kind [of] character or mental disposition.

8, 9 *diverseness*] *D, A, T*; diverness *E*: inconsistency.

7–10 *after a diverse fashion . . . after one rate:* inconsistently . . . consist-
ently.

XXXI. *E, A, D, T.*

Attributed to 'Tho.' in margin of *E*; in Wyatt sections of *A* and *T*.
   T entitles the poem: 'A renouncing of love.'
   The following is the *D* version of the poem – a good example of the way
in which *D* differs from *E*. *D*'s readings probably represent a version of the
poem earlier than that of *E*.

D version of xxxi

Now farewell love and thy laws forever.
Thy baited hooks shall tangle me no more.
Too sore a proof hath called me from thy lore
To surer wealth my wits to endeavour.
In blind error whilst last I did persevere,
Thy sharp repulse that pricketh so sore
Hath taught me to set in trifles no store
But scape forth for liberty is lever.
Therefore farewell. Go trouble younger hearts
And in me claim no more authority.
With idle youth go use thy property
And thereupon go spend thy brittle darts:
For hitherto I have lost my time;
Me list no longer rotten boughs to climb.

3 *Senec:* Seneca (*c.* 4 B.C.–A.D. 65), one of Wyatt's favourite authors. He urged his son to study Seneca (*L* 43) and translated a passage from Seneca's *Thyestes* (XLIX). There is no evidence that Wyatt knew Plato directly (*M & T*) or that he could read any Greek writers in the original, though *F* suggests that he might have begun the study of Greek at Cambridge in 1518.
4 *To perfect wealth my wit for to endeavour:* to exert my wit toward a state of well-being that is free, or relatively free, from imperfection. Implicitly contrasted with the imperfect and hence fragile pleasures of sexual love is the content of the mind detached from a concern for such unstable goods (Seneca) and directed to the contemplation of goodness itself (Plato and, analogously, Christian teaching).
5 *blind error:* the lover, like the blind god of love (Cupid), cannot see what is genuinely of value.
6 *repulse that pricketh:* the act of repelling that wounds. The lady's, or Love's, rejection of the lover's advances is described in military terms.
8 *lever:* liefer, dearer, preferable.
11 *property:* 1) instrument (bow?); 2) characteristic quality.
14 *no longer rotten boughs to climb.* Alludes to the proverb 'Who trusts to rotten boughs may fall'; see *Tilley* B557 (*Da*).

XXXII. *E, A* (2 versions), *D, B, T.*

Attributed to 'Tho.' in margin of *E*; in Wyatt sections of *A* and *T*.

T entitles the poem: 'The abused lover seeth his folly, and intendeth to trust no more.' In *D* the poem is headed 'To my.' *F* (II, 35) says the 'whole tenor of the poem expresses the deceiving of one who has formerly deceived in his youth, and has since repented'.

1 *There was never file half so well filed*] Was never yet file half so well filed *D*.
1–2 *file:* 1) the metal instrument for smoothing surfaces; 2) an artful, shrewd person.

2 *every*] any *A, D, B, T*.

smith: one who works in metals.

4 *to frame*: 1) to make ready for use (although *OED* restricts this meaning to Middle English); 2) to shape (*OED* records first use in 1543). 'Manipulation' and shaping for future 'use' seems the sense demanded by the context; 'frame' probably continues the metaphor of the 'file'.

while: (?) until, up to the time that; *or* during the same time that. The meaning of the poem turns largely on the meaning of this word. With the first meaning, the speaker is saying that he deceived others until he was deceived by another and discovered that fact. With the second meaning, he is saying that he was being deceived at the same time as he was deceiving others.

beguiled: over-reached with guile or deceit; deceived; cheated [of my hopes]; disappointed; foiled.

1–4 The conceit and its implications are not entirely clear to me. The speaker compares himself to a 'file' (l. 1), or 'filing instrument' (l. 3), which was itself 'filed' (l. 1) so that it could in turn 'file a[nother] file' (l. 2) or 'frame other' (l. 4) for use by a 'smith'. I should paraphrase the tenor of the comparison as follows. The speaker was shaped, smoothed, and polished by undefined forces (the first file in the process), presumably his education of himself as well as the influence of others. As a result he became an artful, shrewd person (the second file, here in the second sense of the word) who could deceive, manipulate, and shape another person (the third file) for use by the speaker and others (assuming that the speaker is one of the 'smiths').

If 'while' means 'until', the speaker continued his deceitful manipulation of others until at least one of his victims learned from the manipulator, became an artful and shrewd person in his or her own right (the third file in the second sense of the word), and over-reached the speaker's deceitful manipulation with a deceit of his or her own ('I was beguiled'). In one situation possibly implied by this construction of the lines: an artful man seduces the woman he loves by a promise of marriage, only to renege on the promise; she learns from his lie and fools him into thinking she is faithful while in fact loving another man; when the first lover learns of her deceit, the pain it causes him leads him to stop deceiving others.

If 'while' means 'during the time that', the speaker deceives or manipulates his victims while at the same time being deceived or manipulated by at least one of them. Again, in a situation possibly implied by this construction of the lines: an artful man seduces a woman to whom he swears fidelity but to whom he is unfaithful; she too swears fidelity but is at the same time making love to another man.

5 *reason*: the faculty which enables a man to understand a matter and make moral evaluations.

6 *pardoned*] *D, G, T*; pardons *A, B*; pardon *E*.

7 *Of my lost years*] My little perceiving *D*.

years. Spelled 'yeres' in *E* and possibly to be pronounced as two syllables.

8 *guiled*] *D*; guided *E*: beguiled, deceived.

9 *this trust I have:* I have this [following] object of my trust or belief; I have this [following] belief.

of full great appearance: of very great likelihood. 'I believe that the following statement is very probably true.'

11 *Of very force:* of true necessity; absolutely.

10–12 *Since ... recompense:* since deceit can always be reciprocated, it is absolutely fitting that the repayment for being deceived be made with deceit ('therewithal').

13 *guile beguiled:* deceit over-reached by deceit; deceit matched by deceit.

14 *the reward little trust:* the rewarding consequence [of having one's deceit over-reached or matched by deceit] is learning to have little trust [of anyone]. The speaker's cynicism results from knowledge of his own potentiality for deceiving as well as from his experience of being deceived.

13–14 *Then guile beguiled plained should be never/And the reward little trust forever.*] And guile's reward is small trust forever,/Guile beguiled should be blamed never. *D.*

XXXIII. *E, A, T.*

Attributed to 'Tho.' in margin of *E*; in Wyatt sections of *A* and *T*.

This sonnet contains several echoes of Chaucer. *T* entitles the poem: 'The lover unhappy biddeth happy lovers rejoice in May, while he waileth that month to him most unlucky.'

2 *lust:* pleasure.

lust and ... jollity. Compare Chaucer, *Complaint unto Pity,* 39 (*M & T*).

3 *sluggardy:* laziness.

do away your sluggardy. Compare Chaucer, *CT* I (A), 1042: 'For May wole have no slogardie a-nyght' (*M & T*).

4 *Arise ... do May some observance!* Compare Chaucer, *Troilus* II, 111–12: '... rys up, and lat us daunce,/And lat us don to May som observaunce' (*M & T*).

5 *in mischance:* in a condition of bad luck.

7 *me betide:* happen to me.

6–7 Wyatt was imprisoned in the Fleet in May 1534 for fighting in the London streets. He was again imprisoned in May 1536 because of a quarrel with the Duke of Suffolk at the time of the disgrace of Anne Boleyn. Anne was tried and executed in May 1536.

8 *avance:* advance.

As one whom love list little to avance. Compare Chaucer, *Troilus* I, 518: 'Of hem that Love list febly for to avaunce' (*M & T*).

9 *Sephame*] *M & T*; Sephances *E.*

Sephame. Possibly an Edward Sephame, who cast a horoscope for Edward VI (*M & T*).

10 *Mischanced was with:* was unfortunate with respect to.

11 *of that the verity:* the truth of that [unlucky relationship to May].

XXXIV. *A, T.*

In Wyatt section of *T*.

T entitles this double sonnet: 'The lover describeth his restless state.' But Wyatt probably wrote the poem in prison in 1541 and is alluding to his condition as a prisoner: illness of body and spirit (ll. 1–12) and that other 'wound' of disgrace which, however ill deserved, will remain with him (ll. 13–23). This conjecture is supported by Wyatt's other uses of the proverb about the scar that cannot be erased (l. 14): in LXII, which *T* entitles 'Wyatt being in prison, to Brian', and in his defence against the charges that led to his imprisonment in 1541.

The rhyme scheme of the two sonnets, which approximates the 'Shakespearean', is unique in Wyatt's verse.

6 *Do feel some force:* (?) *N* (543) suggests: 'My eyes must have some secret spring or cause which supplies them with water . . .' In northern dialect 'force' can mean 'waterfall' or 'cascade', though the *OED*'s first recorded instance is 1600. The general tenor is clear: some special cause must explain his crying so much.

8 *tell:* make out, understand.

7–8 *The wasted flesh of colour dead can try/And something tell what sweetness is in gall:* though my flesh is emaciated and the colour of a dead body, I [am still sufficiently sensitive] to discover and understand something about the pleasure mingled with the pain. The tone, I think, is ironic, implying that there is no pleasure mingled with the pain; but he is still sensitive to the pain.

10 *can force:* can be of consequence, can matter.

12 *no force:* no matter; it is of no consequence.

13–14 In Wyatt's defence against the charges of Bishop Bonner that led to his imprisonment, he writes: 'These men thinketh it enough to accuse and, as all these slanderers, use for a general rule: "Whom thou lovest not, accuse. For though he heal the wound, yet the scar will remain." ' (*L* 193). Compare *Tilley* W929 (*Da*).

15–16 *you . . . can best be judge.* Wyatt's friend has also experienced imprisonment.

18 *there is no great desert:* there is nothing of importance that I have done to deserve this punishment.

20 *Of fortune saw the shadow that you know:* (?) saw the shadow of ill fortune that you continue to experience.

21 *trifling*] *T*; *tasting A*. The obvious contrast is between the 'weighty matters' for which Wyatt's friend had suffered and the 'trifling things' for which Wyatt has been imprisoned.

22 *doth wound:* (?) gives pain [to me].

23 *save on the second day:* (?) except every other day.

25 *she list assign:* she (my fever) wishes to assign (for my being in burning heat).

22–25 *That, ... list assign:* his only companionship is his heart and his fever.

27–8 *provoke/To have:* (?) call forth [on himself the fate] of having.

xxxv. *D.*

In Wyatt section of *D.*

1 *To rail:* (?) to utter abusive language; *or* to jest. Though the second meaning makes 'jest' redundant, I think it more likely. The speaker is insisting that, while he sometimes finds human conduct worthy of laughter, he is not given to jesting, and especially not in this business of the lady's infidelity. This protestation of seriousness establishes the (slyly and sarcastically?) serious tone in which he recommends that she continue unfaithful.

I use it not: I do not make a practice of (jesting).

5 *if ye were to me as ye are not:* if you really loved me as in fact you do not. The speaker implies that her 'love' has always been feigned (l. 11).

6 *unkind:* without kindness, with a pun on 'unnatural'. That which the lady does by reason of her fallen and defective individual nature (l. 7) violates the natural law.

10 *of right:* as a matter of justice.

xxxvi. *D, T.*

In Wyatt section of *T.*

T entitles the poem: 'The lover abused renounceth love.' The poem shifts from the third person to direct address in l. 9; *T* eliminates the need for that shift by emending 'me' to 'you' in l. 2 and 'her' to 'your' in l. 8 (l. 4 is not in *T*).

1 *took scorn:* scorned. The expression is difficult – perhaps analogous to 'thought [it] scorn' or 'took pleasure'. *T* and *N* emend 'took scorn' to 'to scorn', and 'Wherein' (l. 2) to 'Therein', changing completely the sense of ll. 1–2 (and of the whole poem): I thought it was cruel for her to scorn my love but to retain my service.

2 *used.* Probably usèd.

4 *which:* who.

5 *care:* mental suffering, sorrow, pain [caused by the lady].

7 *not*] as *original D*; nor *T, N*: [and] not.

8 *That, as I was, her man I might remain:* that I might remain her man (now and in the future) as I was (her man in the past). *M & T* gloss ll. 7–8: 'Giving me no choice not to agree with her that I might remain her man.' Wyatt's mistress, they suggest, 'while scorning his love, wanted to keep him in her clutches.' This reading is more compatible with *T*'s and *N*'s 'to scorn' in l. 1 than with *M & T*'s 'took scorn'.

11–12 *Displease thee not my doting days be past /And with my loss to live I must agree:* [let it] not displease thee [that] my days of doting [on you, and hence suffering], are past and [that] I must consent to live with my loss [and, because out of love, without pain].

14 *to assuage*] *T*; t'assuage *D*.

XXXVII. *T*.

In Wyatt section of *T*.

T entitles the poem: 'To his lady cruel over her yielden lover.'

Each of the three quatrains rhymes abab – a scheme unique in Wyatt. *F* suggests that Wyatt simply doubled the first six lines of his *ottava rima* stanza to form the first twelve lines of the sonnet.

3 *A'inst:* against.
4 *yielden:* yielded.
6 *prest* could be either the past participle of 'to press' or an adjective meaning 'ready'.
8 *it:* malice (redundant).
11 *my*] *N*; me *T*.
13 *execrable:* accursed.
14 *For that they hate are made most miserable:* because they hate, they are made most miserable (that is, even more miserable than the other 'execrable' furies).

EPIGRAMS

Poems XXXVIII–LXXII are epigrams. An epigram is a short poem, witty in character and usually ending with an ingenious, often barbed remark. Though the epigram is classical in origin, and of varying length, Wyatt's models are mainly *strambotti* by Serafino d'Aquilano and hence in the eight-line stanza rhyming ababababcc (*ottava rima*). *F* suggests that, though Wyatt's models were Italian, he wrote epigrams largely because they were in vogue at the French court where he spent some time between 1528 and 1532. There the fashion had been set by Clément Marot (1496–1544) and M. de St Gelais (1466–1502).

XXXVIII. *E, A, T*.

Attributed to 'Tho.' in margin of *E*; revisions of *E* in Wyatt's hand; in Wyatt sections of *A* and *T*. The text of *E* was 'revised' by an unidentified editor as well as twice by Wyatt (Wyatt's revisions in ll. 1 and 7 are in faded brown ink, like that of the scribe; the others are in black ink).

This epigram freely imitates a *strambotto* by Serafino (*M & T* 303).

T entitles the poem: 'To his love whom he had kissed against her will.'

1 *stealing*] *W, A*; robbing *E*.
2 *there*] *W*; then *E1*; therein *E2, A, T*.
5 *next:* nearest.
Then revenge you, and the next way is this] *W, A*; Revenge you then and sure you shall not miss *E*.
6 *Another kiss shall have my life ended*] *W2*; Another kiss shall have my life

through ended *W1, A* (*W* inserted 'through' and then apparently deleted it, though the deletion is not perfectly clear); To have my life with another ended *E*.

7 *first*] *W, A*; t'on [the one] *E*.
8 *next shall clean*] *W, A*; t'other shall *E*.
7–8 *the first my heart did suck ;|The next shall . . . it pluck*. Neo-Platonists sometimes suggested that souls (*spiritus*, breath) were drawn up to the mouth and united by a kiss; see B. Castiglione, *The Book of the Courtier*, trans. Charles Singleton (1959), pp. 349–50. Demonologists thought that the incubus – a devil in human form – could suck out its victim's soul with a kiss; see Marlowe, *Doctòr Faustus* V, 1, 110. The lines may be playfully mixing the two views of the kiss. Wyatt's 'heart' translates Serafino's '*spirto*' and can mean 'spirit', 'soul', and the 'seat of love'.

XXXIX. *E, D, H, T, NA.*

Attributed to 'Tho.' in margin of *E*; in Wyatt section of *T*; a correction by Wyatt.

The poem turns on the image of the man who encounters a snake. That image, classical in origin, was a commonplace by Wyatt's time (*M & T*).

T entitles the poem: 'Of the jealous man that loved the same woman and espied this other sitting with her.'

1 *gadling*: fellow; vagabond.
  tide: time.
2 *retchless*: reckless.
4 *Despite*: spite, evil feeling, anger; 'jealous Despite' is a personification.
6 *crop*: top of a plant; 'crop and root' means the whole of a thing. Compare Chaucer, *Troilus* II, 348 (*N*).

XL. *E, A, T.*

Attributed to 'Tho.' in margin of *E*; in Wyatt sections of *A* and *T*.

This epigram translates a *strambotto* by Serafino (*M & T* 306).

T entitles the poem: 'To his love from whom he had her gloves.'

1 *threnning*: lamenting (presumably formed from the noun 'threne' or 'dirge').
3 *mind*: intention. The Italian has 'fault'.
4 *fair*. Wyatt's addition.
  display. The Italian has 'despoil', 'rob', 'undress'.
  Nor causeless your fair hand did I display: and I did not exhibit your hand [by removing your glove] without a reason ('cause').
5 *meet*] find *T*.
  or else whom next we meet: Wyatt's substitute for the Italian '[love] which I desire'.
6 *both hear what*: hear what both.
8 *if th'one be worth th'other*: if my heart is worth as much as her glove, and *vice versa*.

XLI. *E, A, D, T.*

Attributed to 'Tho.' in margin of *E*; revisions of *E* in Wyatt's hand; in Wyatt sections of *A* and *T*.

See the head-note to LIII for an analogue or possible source by John Skelton (*c.* 1460–1529). *F* suggests that another analogue or source is a *dizaine* by Maurice Scève (*c.* 1501–*c.* 1564) (*M & T* 309). *T* entitles the poem: 'Of his love that pricked her finger with a needle.'

3 *in*] *W*; and *E*.

4 *sampler:* a piece of canvas embroidered by a beginner as a specimen of her skill, usually containing the alphabet, mottos, and decorative devices.

7 *Made her own weapon do her finger bleed*] *W*; With her own weapon did make her finger bleed *E, D*.

8 *indeed*] *W*; a deed *E*.

XLII. *E, D, H, NA, T.*

Attributed to 'Tho' in margin of *E*; revisions of *E* in Wyatt's hand; in Wyatt section of *T*.

This epigram translates a *strambotto* by Serafino (*M & T* 311). *N* conjectures, on the basis of the more personal note in the first version of l. 1, that Wyatt wrote the poem about his imprisonment of 1541. *F* relates it to Wyatt's imprisonment in 1534. *T* entitles the poem: 'The lover hopeth of better chance.'

1 *He is not dead that sometime hath a fall*] *W*; I am not dead although I had a fall *E, D, H*. The Italian has: 'Even if I have fallen to the ground, I am not dead.' Wyatt's later version generalizes the more particular and personal earlier version into a statement which echoes the proverb 'He that falls today may rise tomorrow'; see *Tilley* F38 (*Da*).

2 *The sun returneth that was under the cloud.* Proverbial; see *Tilley* C442. Since 'under a cloud' is itself a proverbial metaphor for 'out of favour' (see *Tilley* C441), Wyatt's line can refer to being restored to the favour of an important person or to prosperity generally.

5 *into haven fall:* reach port.

5–6 *ship . . . after the storm.* Echoes the proverb 'As broken a ship has come to land'; see *Tilley* S344 (*Da*).

7–8 *the willow that stoopeth . . . greater wood doth bind.* Alludes to the proverb 'Willows are weak yet they bind other wood'; see *Tilley* W404 (*Da*).

XLIII. *E, A, T.*

Attributed to 'Tho.' in margin of *E*; revisions of *E* in Wyatt's hand; in Wyatt section of *T*.

This epigram freely imitates a *strambotto* by Serafino (*M & T* 312). *T* entitles the poem: 'The lover compareth his heart to the overcharged gun.'

1 *The furious gun*] *W2*; Like as the bombard *W1*; Like as the canon *E*. The Italian has 'a large bombard (or canon)'. Wyatt's final version intensifies the personification of the gun already present in 'raging ire'.

2 *ball :* the solid round missile shot from the gun.

rammed. Probably rammèd.

3 *And that the flame*] *E*; And it the same *A*.

the flame cannot part from the fire. The line is unintelligible to me in terms of the technical meanings of 'flame' and 'fire' current in Wyatt's time. The 'flame' might refer to the fire used to ignite gun powder (*M & T*), but it makes little sense to say that such fire cannot part from the thing to be fired; 'fire' might be a shortened form of 'fire-ball' (*M & T*), but the *OED* does not record such a shortened form and first records 'fire-ball' in 1555. *A*'s reading – 'the same' (the ball) for 'the flame' – makes sense of the line: 'the ball cannot part from the burning gun-powder (fire).' But it is probably wrong to emend a text in which Wyatt himself made four revisions. I can only suggest a reading in which 'flame' and 'fire' are used very loosely: 'the burning gun-powder cannot eject that which is to be fired.'

5 *shivered :* splintered.

6 *Whose flame*] *W*; Which daily *E*.

7 *Which to let out*] *W*; Whose flame to open *E*.

to let out : to express [and thereby diminish the intensity of] desire ('flame').

8 *inward*] *E*, *T*, *N*, *M*; now hard *F*, *M & T*, *Da*; that of *A*. There is controversy about *E*'s reading; with *M*, I see 'inwhard', not 'now hard'.

all to-break : completely break in pieces. Both 'all' and 'to-' intensify the verb.

XLIV. *E*, *D*, *H*, *H78*, *Cam*, *NA*, *T*.

In Wyatt's hand in *E*; attributed to 'Tho' in margin of *E*; in Wyatt section of *T*; headed 'Sir T.W.' in *H78*.

This epigram translates a *strambotto* by Serafino (*M & T* 317). *T* entitles the poem: 'That pleasure is mixed with every pain.'

1–2 *Venomous thorns . . . flowers.* Proverbial; see *Tilley* R179 (*Da*).

2 *fair and fresh of hue.* Wyatt's addition.

3–4 *Poison . . . causeth health.* Alludes to proverb 'One poison expels another'; see *Tilley* P457 (*Da*).

5 *Fire that purgeth all thing that is unclean*] The fire eke that all consumeth clean *H*, *NA*; Fire that all thing consumeth so clean *D*. In the *E* version Wyatt departs from the pattern, established in ll. 1 and 3 and the earlier versions of l. 5, of emphasizing harmful qualities before stating the salutary.

5–6 *Fire . . ./May heal and hurt.* Presumably fire heals by cauterizing a wound. The lines echo the proverb 'Fire is as hurtful as healthful'; see *Tilley* F258 (*Da*).

8 *joined.* Probably joinèd.

every woe . . . wealth. Proverbial; see *Tilley* W188 (*Da*).

XLV. *E, T.*

In Wyatt's hand in *E*; attributed to 'Tho.' in margin of *E*; in Wyatt section of *T*.

This epigram translates an anonymous Italian *strambotto* (*M & T* 319) found in a Spanish manuscript by J. G. Fucilla (see *FR*). In the manuscript the poem is ascribed to Leone Ebreo, a Jewish Neo-Platonist, but there is doubt about his authorship. The story comes ultimately from Josephus, *The Wars of the Jews* VI, iii, 4 (ed. Whitson (1825) II, pp. 465–6), which was taken for Wyatt's source before Fucilla's discovery. Josephus tells the story of Mary, daughter of Eleazer, who killed and ate her son during the siege of Jerusalem in A.D. 70. She had several motives: her own hunger; the desire to save her son from Roman slavery, death by famine, or death in civil discord; and her desire to appal the Jews whose dissension had weakened Jerusalem. Although Wyatt alters his Italian source only slightly, he does so in order, apparently, to elicit more sympathy for the mother.

1–2 *In doubtful breast whilst motherly pity/With furious famine standeth at debate.* The Italian has: 'While in the hard and pitiless breast anger struggles against hunger and fury.' Wyatt emphasizes the mother's doubt, makes her pitying rather than pitiless, and creates a conflict between her pity and her hunger. He omits her anger and ascribes her fury to the famine (*M & T*).

5 *made unto thee:* caused you to possess.

6 *And enter there where thou wert generate.* The Italian has: 'So, as they were made by me, they may be unmade by me.'

8 *must.* 'Wyatt's addition, perhaps intended to suggest the mother's compulsive action, as distinct from the willed action of the Italian *farò*' (I will make) (*M & T* 320).

sepulture. Probably sepúlture; burial place, grave, sepulchre.

XLVI. *E, T.*

In Wyatt's hand in *E*; attributed to 'Tho' in margin of *E*; in Wyatt section of *T*.

Wyatt owes some debt to Petrarch's *Rime* 103 (*M & T* 320) or an earlier imitation of that poem. Wyatt translates the first two lines and, like Petrarch, applies the story of Hannibal to a contemporary instance: in Wyatt's case, his embassy to Spain in 1537. This epigram can be dated with unusual precision because of the reference to Monzòn (Mountzon) in l. 8. Wyatt wrote to Lord Lisle, the Deputy of Calais, from 'Barbastra, besides Mountzon' on 16 October 1537. Since Wyatt's only recorded visit to Monzòn occurred in 1537 while the Emperor Charles V held his court there, the poem very probably dates from that year (*L* 47).

The poem is obscure in phrasing and in its reference to events. Wyatt is probably referring to his objectives as an ambassador, especially that of preventing an alliance between the Emperor, France, and the papacy against England. Crucial to this goal was the war between the Emperor Charles V and Francis I of France for Milan. The war began in the 1520s when Henry VIII was allied with Charles and Pope Leo X against France; it was stopped for a time in 1526; but it was renewed in 1536. Henry, while offering himself as a mediator, was probably interested in prolonging the conflict (L 63, 73) or, at the least, ensuring that a treaty or truce did not work to England's disadvantage. It was Wyatt's mission to implement that strategy. While Wyatt won the esteem of the Emperor, he may have realized already in the autumn of 1537 that events were out of his control and were drifting in an unfavourable direction. In May 1538 Charles and Francis agreed on a truce which did not serve England's interests. This situation might explain ll. 6–7: his peace of mind was hanging in the balance of other people's decisions whether to continue or end the war; and that lack of control over his own peace of mind was the only reward for all of his efforts as a diplomat.

On the other hand Wyatt may be referring to events in his private life. He had rejected his wife before leaving England in the spring of 1537 and he had probably formed his liaison with Elizabeth Darrell. This situation might explain the allusion to 'conquest' in l. 4; it would make ll. 6–7 refer to his peace as a private man which depended on his return to England – a move which also could be seen as hanging in the balance of the negotiations over the war.

T entitles the poem: 'Of disappointed purpose by negligence.'

1 *of Carthage he:*   the man from Carthage (Hannibal).

2 *Could overcome but could not use his chance:*   could win individual battles but could not take advantage of the chances which these victories gave him (*O*). Hannibal, in the Second Punic War, won great victories in Italy in the years 218–216 B.C., especially at Lake Trasimeno in 217 and Cannae in 216. But he did not follow up these victories with an attack on Rome itself, which, according to Livy (*History* XXII, 51), might have succeeded.

3 *of . . . my . . . endeavour:*   (?) during my endeavour, on the analogue of 'of recent years'.

4 *sharp:*   (?) acute, clever, keen-witted; *or* intensely painful.
conquest.   Possibly conquést.

3–5 *And I . . ./The . . . conquest though fortune did advance/Could not it use:*   and I – though fortune aided my conquest – could not use the opportunity it gave me. The referent is obscure. See the head-note for one suggestion related to Wyatt's 'conquest' of a mistress before he was dispatched to Spain. *F* implies that the lines refer to Wyatt's 'conquest' of the Emperor's esteem and his overcoming of Charles's dislike of England only to find that he could not put his personal standing to any diplomatic use.

6 *balance.*   Possibly balánce.

5–6 *The hold that is given over/I unpossessed:*   (?) I did not possess, or I lost, the control [over events] that has now been [completely] abandoned.

6–7 *So hangeth in balance/Of war my peace, reward of all my pain.*   See head-note for two possible meanings.

8 *rest:*   abide, stay.

XLVII. *E, B, T.*

In Wyatt's hand in *E*; attributed to 'Tho.' in margin of *E*; in Wyatt section of *T*; subscribed 'W' in *B*.

The comparison of love to a river occurs frequently in Italian. The poems that have been suggested as sources (*M & T* 332–3) are more probably analogues. *T* entitles the epigram: 'Comparison of love to a stream falling from the Alps.'

On the grounds that this poem occurs in *E* between XLVI, in which Wyatt refers to his being in Monzòn, Spain, and LXXVI, entitled 'In Spain', *F* implicitly dates the poem during Wyatt's embassy in Spain (April (?) 1537 to June 1539) and identifies the 'high hills' as the Pyrenees.

2 *trilleth :* to roll, to flow in a slender stream, the particles of water being in constant revolution.

still] small *E.*

still : 1) quiet, barely audible; 2) flowing imperceptibly.

3 *Of this and that it gathers :* it gathers water from this and that tributary source.

4 *Till it have just off flowed the stream and force :* (?) until it has just flowed over the waters of the stream near its base and over the falls. See XXXIV, 6 and note.

5 *at the foot :* (?) at the base of the falls.

6 *ta'en a source :* taken a beginning; 'source', as in 'source of a river', means 'spring' and continues the comparison.

1–6 *as . . ./So.* The poem is an extended simile.

7 *His rein is rage :* Love's only restraint is rage. Implicitly, then, love endures no restraints at all.

none : nothing.

8 *The first eschew is remedy alone :* to avoid ('eschew') love from the beginning is the only remedy. Compare Chaucer, *Parliament of Fowls* 140 (*Da*).

7–8 *His rein is rage; resistance vaileth none ;/The first eschew is remedy alone*] His rein is rage; then booteth no deny;/The first eschew is only remedy *E*. Wyatt perhaps made the revision to improve the rhyme of 'deny' and 'remedy'.

XLVIII. *E, H78, T.*

Headed in *H78* 'A Riddle Tho. W.'; in Wyatt section of *T*.

Harrier (10–11) argues that the poem in *E* is in an italic hand sometimes used by Wyatt. I think it far more likely that *S* (163) is right in his interpretation of the hand as not Wyatt's but a scribe's which appears elsewhere in the MS only in a transcription of two letters sent by Wyatt to his son during his embassy to Spain. The poem was probably copied late from *T* (*M & T*), with which it agrees in all substantive readings. The *E* version therefore lacks its usual authority and is, I think, since it lacks even a syllabic metrical pattern, manifestly corrupt. But *H78*, while preserving a superior reading in l. 4, is also corrupt. Wyatt's text is therefore irrecoverable at this point.

This riddle has the brevity and ingenuity of an epigram. The first six lines of the poem are a translation of an unidentified version of a Latin riddle which appears in an allegorical dialogue, *Bombarda*, by Pandolfo Collinutio, an early sixteenth-century ruler of Siena (*N* cxxvii–cxxviii, 555). Wyatt's source probably differed slightly from both the original and the version given after Wyatt's translation in *H 78(M* 38). *T* entitles the riddle: 'Description of a gun.'

1–3 *Vulcan . . . Minerva . . . Nature . . . Craft . . . Three bodies . . . naught.*
In Pandolfo's dialogue, Phronimus, the builder of a city, is seeking the best defence for the city. Puzzled by enigmatic suggestions of Heraclitus and Diogenes to examine an egg and a chestnut, he is given this riddle by Pallas (Minerva), who, in her wisdom or shrewdness, therefore 'taught' the making of the gun or cannon. Unable to solve the riddle, Phronimus consults Hercules who interprets it in terms of a struggle between Vacuum ('naught') and Juno. Vulcan advises Vacuum to present Juno with the gift of a window-less house made of brass (the chamber and metal tube or barrel of the gun). Its passage should be filled with stones (cannon-balls) and it should be stored with 'three' foods – the saltpetre, sulphur, and charcoal which constitute gun-powder. When Juno enters, Vulcan and Vacuum steal in at a back-door to expel her – that is, fire (Vulcan) ignites the gun-powder in the chamber of the gun from which air is excluded (Vacuum) to cause an explosion which propels the cannon-balls; and Nature, coming to Juno's aid, fills the house with a thunderous noise, destroys Vacuum, and confines Vulcan to a flint. When Phronimus is as puzzled by the explanation as by the riddle, Hercules tells him how to make a gun (*N* cxxviii).

In Wyatt's version, Nature is the mother and Craft the nurse in that the raw materials for the gun are derived from nature but they are combined in increasingly sophisticated ways by human art.

4 *Slaughter*] *H78*; Anger *E.*

XLIX. *A, T.*

In Wyatt section of *T.*

The poem translates Seneca's *Thyestes*, 391–403 (*M & T* 431). Compare Andrew Marvell's translation beginning 'Climb at court'. *T* entitles the poem: 'Of the mean and sure estate.' *T*'s version of this poem differs from *A*'s in ways more radical than can be explained by *T*'s usual regularizing and may represent a different stage of composition:

> Stand whoso list upon the slipper wheel
> Of high estate, and let me here rejoice
> And use my life in quietness each deal,
> Unknown in court that hath the wanton toys.
> In hidden place my time shall slowly pass;
> And when my years be passed withouten noise

> Let me die old after the common trace.
> For grips of death doth he too hardly pass
> That known is to all, but to himself, alas,
> He dieth unknown, dazed with dreadful face.

1 *slipper:* slippery.

3 *use me quiet without let or stop:* comport myself quietly without hindrance or impediment from others.

4 *brackish:* being spoiled to the point of being nauseous by the mixture of the salty with the fresh.

   that hath such brackish joys. Wyatt's addition to the Latin.

7 *after the common trace:* 1) on the common way or path; 2) like other people. The Latin has 'a common man'.

8 *For]* T; *From* A.

   crop: 1) bird's neck; 2) throat.

   For him death grip'th right hard by the crop. The Latin has 'Death lies heavy on him'.

10 *dazed:* 1) bewildered, stupefied; 2) benumbed with cold.

   dazed, with dreadful face. Wyatt's addition to the Latin.

L. *D, T.*

In Wyatt sections of *T* and *D*.

This epigram translates a *strambotto* by Serafino (*M & T* 421). *T*, whose 'look' in l. 1 changes the meaning, entitles the epigram: 'To his lover to look upon him.'

1 *sight]* look *T*.

   thy sight: the sight of you (*O*).

2 *hidest.* Probably monosyllabic (hid'st).

4 *stick:* hesitate.

   madest. Probably monosyllabic (mad'st).

   Why dost thou stick to heal that thou madest sore? The Italian has: 'Why do you nevertheless flee, flee one who adores you?'

7 *the heart]* ed.; thy heart *D*.

8 *thou]* *T*; then *D*.

6–8 *For if I die, . . ./Since t'one by t'other . . . thou also with my smart]* And if I die thy life may last no more,/For each by other doth live and have relief,/I in thy look, and thou most in my grief *T*.

LI. *T*.

In Wyatt section of *T*.

This epigram probably imitates a four-line Latin epigram by Ausonius (*M & T* 435). The latter was derived ultimately from a couplet ascribed to Plato which Coleridge translates:

> Tom, finding some gold, left a rope on the ground.
> Jack, missing his gold, used the rope which he found. (*F* II, 74–5).

T entitles the poem: 'Against hoarders of money.'

1 *shamefast:* ashamed.
  harm: (?) evil or hurt suffered or done to another; *or* grief.
  need: (?) violence upon or by another person; *or* condition of distress or need.
  For shamefast harm of great and hateful need: (?) because of a grief of which he was ashamed, a grief due to a condition of deep and odious need.
3 *With ready cord out of his life to speed:* with a rope for hanging ready to hurry him out of his life.
5 *this deed:* the act of suicide by hanging.
6 *tho:* (?) then; *or* abbreviated form of 'though'.

LII. *E, A, T.*

Attributed to 'Tho.' in margin of *E*; in Wyatt sections of *A* and *T*.

This poem, LIV, and LXXI are the only epigrams attributed to Wyatt that have seven lines, and the rhyme scheme of this poem is unique among the epigrams. *N* suggests that a line has been omitted after l. 4. *T* entitles the poem: 'Of the feigned friend.'

1 *full yore ago:* a very long time ago.
2 '*Take heed of him that by thy back thee claweth*': be wary of the man that scratches your back to flatter you. Proverbial; see *Tilley*, B17.
4 *they seem*] he seem *T1*; the[e] seem *T2, M.* Though the plural 'they' does not fit well with the singular referents elsewhere, it makes adequate sense, and I do not see how it could have resulted from a misreading of 'he' or 'the[e]'.
4 *all thing:* [seem indeed] everything.
5 *know it well that ... creepeth.* Echoes the proverbial warning against nourishing a snake in one's bosom; see *Tilley* V68, and compare Chaucer' *CT* III (D), 1992-5 (*Da*).
6-7 *For many a man such fire oft kindleth/That with the blaze his beard singeth.* Perhaps a variation on the proverb 'That fire which lights us at a distance will burn us when near' (*Tilley* F281).

LIII. *E, A, D, T.*

Attributed to 'Tho' in margin of *E*; revisions of *E* in Wyatt's hand; in Wyatt sections of *A* and *T*.

F suggests that Wyatt derived his idea for this epigram from John Skelton's *Philip Sparrow* 26-9, 35-43. There, the lady is stitching an image of her sparrow; he seems to cry out when she stitches his head and causes her to prick her finger; she at first takes the blood to be his. *T* entitles this poem 'Of the same' because it follows the poem XLI entitled 'Of his love that pricked her finger with a needle'.

1 *cruelty*] *W*; tyranny *E, D*.
2-3 *remembered her my woe/That caused it:* reminded her – who caused my woe – of my woe.

LIV. *E, A, T.*

Attributed to 'Tho.' in margin of *E*; in Wyatt sections of *A* and *T*.

This riddle shares with the epigram brevity and an ingenious, in this case paradoxical, ending. A hand later than the scribe's has written 'Anna' above the poem. *T* entitles it: 'Of his love called Anna.' He also substitutes 'Anna' for 'answer' in l. 3. 'Anna' is the solution to the riddle because the name remains the same when spelled backwards ('turned') and roughly so when divided 'in twain', provided the second syllable is also 'turned': 'An, An.' *N* suggests that the poem is about Anne Boleyn.

3 *answer:* solution to the problem [of my pain]. Though the *OED* records no instance of this sense prior to 1592, no other sense fits the context. The word is probably also a pun: 'Anne, sir'.

5 *It love rewardeth*] *ed.;* A love rewardeth *E*; Who love rewardeth *N*.

5, 6 *It:* the word.

6 *What would ye more?:* 1) what additional hints would you like? 2) what more would you have a lover do [besides continue to love someone who disdains his love]?

LV. *E, A, D, H78 (1–4), T.*

Attributed to 'Tho' in margin of *E*; a revision of *E* in Wyatt's hand; in Wyatt sections of *A* and *T*; headed 'Tho. W.' in *H78*; subscribed 'Wyat' in *D*.

N (xxiii) and *S* (43) suggest that the occasion of this epigram was the visit paid by Anne Boleyn and Henry VIII to Francis I at Calais in October 1532, just before their marriage. *N* conjectures that Wyatt was in the train of Anne and that the poem is about his changed feelings toward her. *T* entitles the poem: 'The lover that fled love now follows it with his harm.'

1 *Sometime:* in the past.

brent: burnt.

2 *By sea, by land*] *W;* by hills and dales *E, D*.

3 *quent:* quenched.

4 *against my mind:* with reluctance.

5 *sprung and spent:* excited and then exhausted. The metaphor of the fire giving way to quenched coals may still be latent in these participles.

6 *whilom:* once upon a time.

7 *he laugh:* he [may] laugh.

8 *to-torn:* torn to shreds; 'to' is an intensive prefix (*F*).

Meshed in the briers that erst was all to-torn: formerly torn by the briers, [he finds himself] now enmeshed in them; 'in the briers' is proverbial for 'in trouble' or 'in danger'. See *Tilley* B672, B673 and *ODEP* 359 (*M & T*). The speaker comments on the irony that he is now thrown into intimacy with the person whom he once loved but no longer loves, and whom he sought, while in love, to flee, because a relationship with her was so dangerous and painful. *Daalder* construes ll. 7–8: 'now he laughs who formerly was torn to pieces while entangled in the thorny bushes of passion.'

LVI. E, T.

Attributed to 'Tho.' in margin of E; a revision of E in Wyatt's hand; in Wyatt section of T.

This epigram may be a translation, but there is no known source. T entitles the poem: 'The lover complaineth that deadly sickness can not help his affection.'

4 *fever.* Presumably a fever of the body caused, in part at least, by the speaker's feverish love.

    clean: wholly, absolutely.

5 *despair:* despair of the speaker's love being reciprocated and therefore of mental and physical health being restored.

7 *strake:* struck.

8 *drave:* drove.

    And drave the first dart deeper more and more. I do not understand the psychology and physiology of this statement. Perhaps the increase of physical illness – an increase which results from not struggling against the illness – lays the speaker open to a greater feeling of the pain of unrequited love. The poem is then about the way in which the 'fever' of the body and the 'fever' of love intensify each other.

LVII. E, D, B, H78, T.

Attributed to 'Tho.' in margin of E; revisions of E in Wyatt's hand; in Wyatt section of T; ascribed 'Sir T.W.' in H78.

T entitles the poem: 'How by a kiss he found both his life and death.'

1 *feat:* adroit.

    grace: 1) gift; 2) pleasing ability.

2 *find*] W, H78; get E, D; fetch B;

    of: in.

3-4 *Hath taught the spider out of the same place/To fetch poison.* A common belief. F cites a passage from George Gascoigne (1539?–77) (*Works*, ed. J. W. Cunliffe (1907), I, 6): 'I had alleged of late by a right reverend father that, although indeed out of every flower the industrious bee may gather honey, yet by proof the spider thereout sucks mischievous poison.' Rollins cites four instances from Elizabethan texts.

4 *by strange alteration:* by (Nature's) strange alteration [of the relationship between bee, flower, and honey].

6 *operation:* power; action.

5-6 *stranger case ... secret operation.* There seems to be an implication that her kiss is more mysterious than Nature and her power greater than Nature's – hence 'supernatural' and possibly magical.

7 *Both these:* honey, because her lips are sweet and entice to love; poison, because they make the speaker weak with love.

8 *change:* exchange.

    I leave my heart behind. Compare XXXVIII, 7–8, for two views of the power of the kiss over the soul ('heart'): 1) the Neo-Platonists' view that the kiss draws the souls of two lovers to their lips and unites them; 2) the demonologists' view that the incubus – a devil in human form – can suck out its victim's soul with a kiss. These two views may be implied in 'honey' and 'poison'.

LVIII. *E, D, T*.

In Wyatt's hand in *E*; attributed to 'Tho' in margin of *E*; in Wyatt section of *T*.

Assuming that *D* is an earlier version by Wyatt, we can identify two stages of composition prior to the version I have printed, which incorporates Wyatt's revisions of his own final *E* version.

D

Cruel desire, my master and my foe,
Thyself so changed for shame how mayst thou see?
That I have sought doth chase me to and fro;
Whom thou didst rule now ruleth thee and me.
What right is to rule thy subjects so
And to be ruled by mutability?
Lo, where by thee I doubted to have blame
Even now by dread again I doubt the same.

E (in Wyatt's hand before revisions)

Desire, alas, my master and my foe,
So sore altered, thyself how mayst thou see?
Whom I did seek now chaseth me to and fro;
Whom thou didst rule now ruleth thee and me.
Tyrant it is to rule thy subjects so
By forced law and mutability.
For where by thee I doubted to have blame
Even now by hate again I doubt the same.

T entitles the poem: 'The lover blameth his instant desire'; ('instant' is probably a misprint for 'inconstant').

1 *Desire ... my foe.* Desire is the speaker's foe because, with his counterpart 'revulsion', he leads the speaker into the relationships of unrequited love that the poem describes.
2 *So sore altered, thyself how mayst thou see:* how can you recognize yourself when you have changed so completely [to revulsion].
4 *ledst ... leadeth:* you guided by persuasion [the woman] who [now] guides by persuasion.
3–4 *Sometime I sought that drives me to and fro;/Sometime thou ledst that leadeth thee and me:* In the past I sought that woman whom now [I would shun but who, in seeking me], drives me to and fro; in the past you, desire, used persuasion on that woman who now uses persuasion on you and me.

In all three versions the speaker *in the past* desired a woman whom *now* he hates (l. 8), while that woman, who *in the past* hated the speaker, has *now* come to desire him. *T*, missing the contrast between past and present, construed 'ledst' as present tense and made 'sought' conform by changing it to 'seekest'. *N* followed *T*.

5 *What reason is to rule:* what reason is [there for you] to rule.

6 *forced.* Probably forcèd.

forced law and mutability: a law forced on the subjects and then changed. Desire imposes affection on the human heart and then changes affection to hate. The submerged metaphor is that of the tyrannical ruler which was explicit in the first *E* version of l. 5.

7-8 *For where by thee I doubted to have blame,/Even now by hate again I doubt the same:* for where in the past I feared to have [the woman's] blame because of my desire for her ('by thee'), now I fear to have her blame ('the same') because of my hatred of her.

LIX. *E.*

Attributed to 'Tho' in margin of *E*.

N does not include the poem in the canon of Wyatt's works. The unintelligibility of ll. 3, 5, 6 in *E* warrant, I think, the emendations I have made.

The reading and interpretation of 'afar voids' in l. 2 were suggested by H. A. Mason, 'Editing Wyatt', *SR*, LXXXIV (1976), 682. *E* reads 'offerre voydes'.

2 *voids joyfulness:* joy goes away, vanishes.

3 *Sore chargeth me unrest*] ed.; So changeth unrest, *with* re *inserted between the last two words E.*

Sore chargeth me unrest that naught shall fade: unrest, that nothing shall diminish, painfully burdens me.

4 *despite:* disdain.

6 *is*] ed.; in *E*.

5-6 *Ago long, since that she hath truly made/Disdain for truth, set light is steadfastness:* because she, from a time long gone, has shown genuine contempt for loyalty, abiding commitment is widely regarded as unimportant. The verbal paradoxes – 'truly disdain truth', 'set light that which stands fast' – suggest that these two lines comprise a syntactic unit.

8 *Plain or rejoice who feeleth weal or wrong:* let the person who feels a wrong complain; let the person who feels happiness rejoice.

LX. *E, T.*

In Wyatt's hand in *E*; in Wyatt section of *T*.

This epigram is entitled 'In Spain' in *E*. It very probably refers to Wyatt's departure from Spain in early June 1539 at the end of his embassy there. *T* entitles the poem: 'Of his return from Spain.'

1-2 The sands of the Spanish river Tagus were famous for looking like grains of gold already refined. Chaucer (*Boece* III, Metrum 10) refers to

'Tagus ... his goldene gravelis' (F). In *Philip Sparrow* 875–81, John Skelton writes:

> Of Tagus, that golden flood
> That passeth all earthly good;
> And as that flood doth pass
> All floods that ever was,
> With his golden sands ...
>
> (*M & T* 343)

4 *Gainward the sun:*   against the sun, that is, towards the east.

her wealthy pride: the pride of the Thames based on the rich fullness of the river and possibly the prosperity of London. The wealth of the Thames is contrasted with the gold of the Tagus.

5 *the town which Brutus sought by dreams:*   London. According to the legend which probably originated with Geoffrey of Monmouth, Brutus, the descendant of Aeneas, was instructed by Diana in a dream to sail to the cliffs of Albion and build another Troy. Brutus landed at Totnes, proceeded inland, and eventually founded, on the north bank of the Thames, Troynovante, which became London.

3–6 *With spur ... /Gainward the sun ... her lusty side:*   for, with spur and sail, I go seek the Thames that displays its wealth flowing east and lends a crescent-shaped bank to London. The Thames, which flows east, is contrasted with the Tagus, which flows west.

7 *alone for from I live*]   for whom only I live *E1*; for whom alone I live *E2*.

7–8 *My king, my country, alone for whom I live,/Of ... love the wings for this me give:*   my king and country, for whom alone I live, give me the wings of love for this journey; '... love of king and country gives me wings for my journey' (*Tillyard* 170). It is surprising for a Christian poet to say he lives only for king and country. *Mason* (200–1) wonders what Wyatt was thinking of both his God and his king when he wrote these lines.

LXI. *E, T.*

In Wyatt's hand in *E*; in Wyatt section of *T*.

Both *N* and *F* suspect this epigram is a translation, but an original has not yet been found. *T* entitles the poem: 'Why love is blind.'

1 *Of purpose:*   on purpose.

Love: Cupid, the blind god of love, traces his history back to Anacreon, a Greek lyric poet who flourished in the middle of the sixth century B.C.

chose]   *ed.*; chase *W*.

2 *For he with sight of that*]   For if he might have seen *E*.

that that: that beauty which.

3 *Vanquished had been against all godly kind:*   had been conquered, which is contrary to the nature ('kind') of gods.

4 *His bow your hand*]   Your hand his bow *E*.

His bow your hand and truss should have unfold : your hand and garment should have straightened out or relaxed his bow.

5 *he with me to serve had been assigned :* he, like me, would have been made to serve you.

6 *he blind and*] because he *E.*

6–8 *for he blind ... would him hold/And ... by chance his ... strokes bestow,/With such as see I serve and suffer woe :* because he would keep himself blind and shoot his arrows randomly, I [have been struck by his arrow – your beauty – in my eye, and thus] with those who see [beauty – as opposed to being blind to it like Cupid –] serve you in love and suffer the pain [of your not reciprocating my love].

LXII. *H78, T.*

In Wyatt sections of *H78* and *T.*

The poem was probably written during Wyatt's last imprisonment between January and March 1541; compare XXXIV. In *H78* the poem is entitled: 'Tho. W. to Brian'; in *T* it is entitled: 'Wyatt being in prison, to Brian.'

For Sir Francis Brian, see the head-note to CLI. Brian collected proverbial sayings; the one quoted in the couplet might well have been in his collection. For another allusion to his proverbs, see CLI.

1 *drink*] also drink *M. M* (102–3) argues that l. 1 and l. 3 should be expanded to ten syllables because the remaining six lines are decasyllabic. But since ll. 6 and 7 are both eleven syllables, the number of decasyllabic lines is equalled by those which are not decasyllabic and therefore do not present a standard to which the others must be accommodated.

2 *such music would crave :* (?) would call for the music of sighs and weeping (although the sound of weeping is not alluded to in calling the tears 'drink').

6 *assaulted*] assaulteth *Maxwell.*

save] *M;* have *H78, T.*

Malice assaulted that righteousness should save : (?) malice has assaulted that person – that is, the speaker – whom righteousness (the speaker's own) should save. Wyatt implies that the charges of Bonner which led to his imprisonment were false and inspired by malice.

7–8 *this wound shall heal again/But yet, alas, the scar shall still remain.* Proverbial; see *Tilley* W929 and *ODEP* 735 (*M & T*). Wyatt's is the first recorded instance of the saying (in his *Defence,* 1541, quoted in *L* 193); see also XXXIV, 13–14. Surrey alludes to Wyatt's use of the proverb, probably in the *Defence* (*Rollins*).

LXIII. *Raw, A, T.*

In Wyatt sections of *A* and *T.*

I have adopted *Raw* as copy-text because it comes closest, in its version of l. 6, to realizing the probable intention of concluding the poem with four

8-syllable lines. I have emended l. 3 because it seems likely that the first four lines should have 10 syllables. The first four lines seem to have a 4-beat rhythm: for example,

> A lády gáve me a gíft she hád not
> She gáve it wíllingly yét she wóuld not.

The last four lines seem to have a 3-beat rhythm: for example,

> If she gáve it me I fórce not
> For Í am fast swórn I máy not.

This riddle shares with the epigram the qualities of brevity and wit. Compare LIV. Both *Raw* and *T* entitle the poem: 'A riddle of a gift given by a lady.' A marginal note in the 1587 edition of *T*, attributed by *N* to Selden, says: 'I think it is a kiss' (*Rollins*). Editors frequently cite what they call an 'imitation' by George Gascoigne (1539?–77) to support this solution to the riddle:

A Riddle

> A lady once did ask of me
> This pretty thing in privity:
> 'Good sir,' quod she, 'Fain would I crave
> One thing which you yourself not have
> Nor never had yet in times past
> Nor never shall while life doth last.
> And if you seek to find it out
> You lose your labour out of doubt.
> Yet if you love me as you say
> Then give it me for sure you may.'

But *Rollins* relates the story of Peter Motteux who asked the readers of the July 1692 issue of *The Gentleman's Journal* for help with the riddle and reached the tentative conclusion that the solution was the lady's virginity. One might also construe it as the lady's vagina – a 'negative' entity – in the act of sex.

3 *She gave it willingly, yet she would not*] *ed.*; She gave it me willingly and yet she would not *Raw, A, T.*

willingly, yet she would not: she wanted to do what she was ashamed of doing.

5 *gave*] give *A, T.*

6 *If she take again, she cares not*] And if she take it again she cares not *A, T*: if she takes back what she has given, she does not care for me.

8 *may not*: may not tell.

LXIV. *D, B, T.*

In Wyatt section of *T*, who entitles the poem: 'Of sudden trusting.' The trust might be of a political or an amatory nature.

3 *to speed*: to be successful.

6–7 *whoso trusteth ere he know . . . foe*. Alludes to proverb 'Try before you trust'; see *Tilley* T595 (*Da*).

LXV. *D*.

In a Wyatt section of *D*.

Compare XVII, XX, and CXIII for Wyatt's explorations of the 'contraries of love'.

3 *he*: Despair.

7 *Tantalus*: in Greek mythology, a son of Zeus, who, having aroused his father's anger, was doomed to the eternal punishment of feeling great hunger and thirst and being surrounded by food and drink he could not reach.

8 *Amids my help*: implying, perhaps, that the speaker 'is close to obtaining his desires, though always cheated of them' (*M & T* 421).

that] *N*; and *D*.

LXVI. *B*, *T*.

In Wyatt section of *T*.

This poem is an acrostic, with the first letters of the lines spelling 'Anne Stanhope'. Lady Anne Stanhope was the wife of Sir Michael Stanhope, a Nottinghamshire man much favoured by Henry VIII. *T*, who spoiled the acrostic with emendations in ll. 2 and 3, entitled the poem: 'The lover suspected of change prayeth that it be not believed against him.'

9 *depart*: divide.

12 *Except thou mind*: unless you intend.

LXVII. *B*, *H*, *NA*, *T*.

In Wyatt section of *T*, who entitles the poem: 'A description of such a one as he would love.'

E. K. Chambers (*FR*) suggests that this might be a portrait of Elizabeth Darrell.

2 *comely*] lovely *H*, *NA*, *T*: having a homelier style of beauty than the 'fair' woman.

6 *crisped*. Probably crispèd.

7 *might chance I might be tied*] perchance I might be tried *T*; may chance I to be tied *M*. *M*'s statement (136) that the reading of the manuscript is clearly wrong overlooks, I think, the gain in tentativeness from the impersonal construction and double 'might'; '[it] might just chance that I might be tied.'

8 *And knit again the knot that should not slide*. The phrase may echo the proverb 'Where the knot is loose the string slips' (*Tilley* K169 and *ODEP* 343). But the recorded instances of that proverb are later than Wyatt's phrase. Compare: LXXVII, 7, XCI, 24, XCIII, 26–7, CCXVII, 34, CCXXXIV, 23, and CCXLIX, 28.

LXVIII. H, NA, T.

In Wyatt section of *T*, who entitles the poem: 'Of such as had forsaken him.'

The poem was probably written after the death of Cromwell in July 1540 and before or during Wyatt's subsequent imprisonment from January to March 1541.

1 *Lucks.* Probably the proper name of a falcon, with a pun on luck and *lux* (light).

2–3 *How well pleasant it were your liberty!/Ye not forsake me that fair might ye befall:* how very pleasant would your liberty be to you, and yet you do not forsake me so that fair or pleasant things might happen to you.

6 *proof in light adversity:* test of their friendship in merely light adversity.

LXIX. T.

In Wyatt section of *T*.

This poem is not like most of Wyatt's epigrams in that its ending does not 'cap' the preceding lines in ingenuity. *T* entitles the poem: 'The lover professeth himself constant.' The title is not particularly apt, since the poem seems rather a catalogue of the vices that the good lover or friend would avoid.

2 *Of gentle minds the freedom for to lose:* to lose that detachment from obsession, that self-possession, which characterizes truly human, virtuous minds. It is this 'freedom' which prevents the possessiveness that leads to jealousy and cruelty in love and friendship.

4 *a forger, faults for to disclose:* one who fabricates a tale about another person in order to reveal that person's faults.

5 *to gloze:* to veil with specious comments; to explain away.

6 *To set a gloss upon an earnest pain:* to cast an appearance of unimportance on a pain that deserves to be taken seriously. The pain can be, presumably, either one's own or another's.

8 *That list to blow retreat to every train:* who wish to withdraw from every enterprise [of, for example, love or friendship].

LXX. T.

In Wyatt section of *T*, who entitles the poem: 'Of dissembling words.'

3 *good cheap:* a good bargain. The cheapness of words is proverbial; see *Tilley* W808 and W804 (*Da*).

4 *Their substance is but only wind.* Proverbial; see *Tilley* W833 (*Da*).

LXXI. T.

In Wyatt section of *T*, who entitles the poem: 'The courtier's life.'

1 *decked.* Probably deckèd.

6 *joys ... to hold:* enjoys sustaining.

7 *In prison joys:* feels joy in prison.

LXXII. *T*.

In Wyatt section of *T*, who entitles the poem: 'That speaking or proffering brings alway speeding.' I find the poem obscure because of the difficulty of identifying the possessors of the 'will', 'power', and 'need'. I offer the following paraphrase with tentativeness: 'State your request to another and succeed in getting what you ask if either the other person's willingness to assist you or your own power can be of any help. Where your power is lacking, the other's willingness to help must [usually] be secured by bribing him with your money. For the other person's need for money will make your suit successful even when his will is not so generously inclined as it should be by nature. And your offer of money will cause you to discover that your foes are your friends. For a mere suit or request will obtain anything from a good man, and the offer of gold as a bribe will obtain anything from a bad man.'

1 *Speak . . . speed.* Proverbial; see *Tilley* S719 (*Da*).
5 *suit and gold, what do not they obtain?* Alludes to the proverb 'What will gold not do'; see *Tilley* M1102 (*Da*).

CANZONI

The Italian *canzone* is usually a long poem arranged in stanzas with a complicated rhyme scheme and, often, with lines of irregular length. In this group I have included poems that imitate the Italian *canzoni* in subject matter and, at least to the extent of being of some length, in form. CLIII and CLXI have been excluded, despite their debt to *canzoni*, because they are short. But they, along with CLXXIV, CLXXV, and CLXXVI, should be compared with the following poems as examples of different ways of handling the Italian form.

LXXIII. *E* (22–147), *A* (1–79), *T*.

In Wyatt sections of *A* and *T*.

Because of a missing folio, *E* lacks ll. 1–21. I have used *A* as a copy-text for those lines. *A*, like *T*, seems to have been frequently emended in order to make the meter approximate iambic pentameter. *Hughey* (II, 191–2) notes and exemplifies the 'exceptional number of lines in a free rhythm' in *E*: for example, ll. 23, 25, 29, 34, 35.

The poem translates Petrarch's *Rime* 360 (*M & T* 267–72), a *canzone*. Petrarch personifies the lover's love and has the lover call his Love to trial before Reason for judgement of Love's worth. The ensuing debate between the lover and Love weighs two aspects of Petrarch's love against each other. The lover emphasizes the pain of a love inclined to be possessive, passionate, and sexual but unreciprocated by the woman with comparable passion and sexual desire. The personified Love insists on the spiritual benefits of the relationship: the lover's love of a uniquely virtuous woman (Laura) has inspired him to shun vice and cultivate virtue in order to please her; to write great and famous poetry about his love instead of trivial and false verses; and to climb the Neo-Platonic ladder from love of the woman to love of God. In a last sharp exchange we learn that the lover's pain is in part a response to the death of his beloved.

While Wyatt for the most part attempts a close translation of Petrarch's poem, he departs from the original in a few important ways. He omits all of Petrarch's allusions to poetry and his fame as a poet, sometimes substituting an insistence on Love's teaching virtue (ll. 81, 99–105); he thereby avoids attributing to himself excellence and fame as a poet. He heightens the lover's abuse of Love (ll. 41, 55, 139 and notes) and Love's abuse of the lover (ll. 111–12 and notes to ll. 111–12 and 124–6). He dilutes Petrarch's Neo-Platonism, again emphasizing the temporal and moral benefits of this love (ll. 129–33). He tempers Petrarch's praise of the lady (note to ll. 118–19) and replaces the allusion to Laura's death with what is probably a suggestion that the lady has given herself to another man because of his wealth (ll. 138–40). Finally he scales down the stature of the lover (ll. 92 and notes to ll. 92, 4, 16, 36). The general effect of these changes and most of the changes not due merely to difficulty with rhyme is to make more mundane the relationship analysed and judged in the poem.

Petrarch's *canzone* consists of ten fifteen-line stanzas, rhymed abbcbaacc ddeeff, ghhihggiikkllmm etc., and a seven-line coda rhymed wxxyyzz. The stanzas and coda interweave five-beat and three-beat lines. Here Wyatt makes no attempt to imitate Petrarch's stanza. Instead he uses the stanza form of Chaucer's *Troilus*: lines usually of ten syllables rhyming ababbcc. He uses two stanzas for each of Petrarch's stanzas and one for the coda.

T entitles the poem: 'Wyatt's complaint upon Love, to Reason, with Love's answer.'

2 *Queen:* Reason.

    accited: summoned.

4 *like as gold in fire he might be tried* ... Petrarch has: 'like gold which becomes pure in the fire, I present myself.' Wyatt deflects the comparison with gold away from the lover and to Love.

5 *Charged.* Probably chargèd.

7 *wrongful ... alway.* Wyatt adds these two words which reveal the lover's self-esteem but not necessarily his stature.

8 *left foot.* Probably symbolic of the appetite which moves the soul in the realm of earthly love (*M & T*), or, less definitely, an important but weak aspect of the human person.

13 *oppressed.* Probably oppressèd: hard-pressed; overwhelmed. Petrarch has 'unlimited'.

    past: surpassed, exceeded. His suffering was too great for his patience.

16 *ways profitable.* Petrarch has 'useful, honest paths'. Wyatt's lover does not claim 'honesty'.

18 *deceivable:* deceitful.

19 *prest:* ready; lively.

19–20 *What wit have words ...|That may contain my ... mishappiness:*

what mind has the words that can adequately express my unhappiness, my state of ill fortune.

22–8 *O small honey*... Petrarch has: 'O small honey, much aloe with gall! To such great bitterness has my life become accustomed, along with his false sweetness, which drew me to the amorous company – me, who, if I do not deceive myself, was prepared to rise high from the earth. And he took me from peace and set me in war.'

22–3 *aloes and gall*... *have my*... *life tasted*: (?) my life has tasted aloes and gall; *or* aloes and gall have imparted a taste to my life. *OED*'s first recorded instance of 'tasted' in the second sense is 1577.

24 *that turneth as a ball*: that is changeable like the ball or wheel of fortune. Wyatt's addition. Allusion to the proverb 'The world turns as a ball'; see *Tilley* W901 (*Da*).

25 *traced*: (?) harnessed in traces – the pair of ropes, chains, or straps by which the collar of a draught animal is connected with the splinter-bar. *OED*'s first recorded use of the verb in this sense is 1602.

26 *araced*] *A*, *T*; ataced *E*; araised (raised, lifted up) *N*.
araced: pulled up by the roots; torn away.

28 Wyatt changes Petrarch's 'peace' and 'war' to 'rest' and 'wandering', probably because the latter are more clearly psychological states.

35 *whetstone, tempered with fire.* Petrarch has: 'whetstone whence I hoped for repose from his cruel and iron yoke.'

36 *wit.* Petrarch has 'bright, proud wit'. Wyatt does not praise the lover's wit.

36–9 *where*... *had I ever wit*/... *given me*... /*That sooner shall change my*... *sprite*/*Than*... *will*: why have I been given wit if my spirit shall change sooner than my will (*O*).

41 *wicked traitor.* Petrarch has the less strong 'cruel one'.

42 *That bitter life have turned me in pleasant use*: that my bitter life has become for me a pleasant habit (*O*).

45 *strait pressions*: (?) tight pressures. Perhaps the phrase refers to a 'press' or crowd of people.

43–9 Wyatt's description of the lover's travels is more generalized than Petrarch's.

50 *nother*: neither.

52 *timely death*: (?) 1) early; *or* 2) opportune, well-timed death. Petrarch has 'cruel and hard death before my time to die'.

54 *slake*] *G*, *A*, *T*; shake *E*.

55 *his cruel extreme tyranny.* Petrarch has 'tyrant'.

54–6 *The heavenly goodness of pity do it slake*/*And not this*, ... /*That feedeth him with my*... *misery*: [the reason death has not overtaken me is that] heavenly goodness, out of pity, abates my movement towards death, and the reason has nothing to do with this tyranny of Love who feeds himself with – that is, delights in – my misery [and therefore would like to see me die].

58–9 *the wakey nights*,/*The banished sleep may no wise recover*: the wakeful nights may in no way recover banished sleep (*O*).

68 *the languishment:* the pining away or sickness. Wyatt's addition.

73 *That:* So that.

74 *ere*] G, T; here E.

76 *maketh a clattering knight.* Petrarch has 'even selleth lies'.

79 *pleasant game:* delightful amusement (as opposed to the painful satisfaction of his lustful desire).

80 *desire that might have been his pain.* Petrarch has 'desire which often his wickedness willed'.

81 *Yet only thereby I brought him to some frame:* yet only through restraining his desires did I bring him to a position of some moral benefit. Petrarch has 'having climbed to some fame only through me'. Wyatt suppresses all attribution of fame to himself. Compare ll. 99-105.

84 *dastard:* dullard.

85 *Atrides:* Agamemnon, son of Atreus.

86 *troublous.* Probably trisyllabic: troublesome.

88 *Scipion:* Scipio Africanus Major, who defeated Hannibal.

90 *fame and honour.* Petrarch has 'stars'.

92 *no deals:* no part; in no way.

though he no deals worthy were. Wyatt's addition.

95 *Of wisdom, womanhood, and discretion.* Wyatt's addition.

96-8 *of my grace ... fashion ... a way ... to teach ... reach.* Petrarch has: 'I gave her so sweet a language and a way of speaking so delightful that base or low thought could never endure in her presence.' Wyatt renders the lady's speech more vaguely but then makes her, more concretely, a moral teacher of the lover himself.

99-101 *to content his mistress,/That was his only frame of honesty,/I steered him still toward gentleness:* I guided him always towards gentleness so that he might content his mistress – and that effort to content her was the only support of his honesty.

99-105 Wyatt leaps ahead to Petrarch's ll. 110-20. But Wyatt's speaker learns virtues in the school of love, while Petrarch learns, through the influence of a unique woman, to write famous, important, and lasting poetry instead of the insignificant verse for the common people that he would have written without the influence of Laura and his love for her. Compare l. 81.

106-112 Wyatt returns to Petrarch's ll. 105-9.

107-8 *torment .../Sweeter than for to enjoy any other in all:* the torment inflicted by love of this woman is sweeter than the total enjoyment of any other woman.

109 *Of right good seed ill fruit I gather.* A variation of the Italian and English proverb 'Such is the tree, such is the fruit'; see *Tilley* T494, T486, T497 and *ODEP* 670. Compare XX, 14.

111-12 *I nourish a serpent ... to sting.* Wyatt's addition heightens Love's abuse of the lover. Echoes proverbial warning against nourishing a serpent in one's bosom; see *Tilley* V68 and compare LII, 5 (*Da*).

113 Wyatt moves foward to Petrarch's l. 121

118-19 *Doubting report that should come to her ear./Whom now he accuseth he wonted to fear.* Petrarch has: 'after he had become her liegeman, so that a noble image was impressed on his heart and made its likeness there.' Wyatt makes more social and psychologically ordinary the mode of the lady's influence and thereby mutes some of Petrarch's praise of her.

122 *nightly phantom:* dream (notoriously erroneous).

124 *striveth ... bit.* Varies the proverb 'He takes the bit in his teeth'; see *Tilley* B424 (*Da*).

126 *remain:* to stop, cease.

124-6 *he striveth ... remain.* Petrarch has: 'he who is in grace with God and man from the time that he knew us; this his pride laments and regrets.'

129 *honour and fame.* Wyatt's addition emphasizes the possible temporal and earthly benefits of love.

130-3 *mortal things. . . above.* Petrarch elaborates the Neo-Platonic ladder to God with: 'mortal things which are the ladder to God . . .; so that, considering very intently how many and what powers were in that hope of his, he might rise from one appearance to another to the great first cause.'

131-3 *Considering the pleasure that an eye/Might give in earth by reason of his love,/What should that be that lasteth still above:* considering the pleasure that comes from loving contemplation of the beloved on earth, how much greater will be the pleasure of loving contemplation that lasts forever in heaven.

134 *same ... hath said.* Petrarch has: 'has said it sometime in verse.'

137 *shright:* shriek.

139 *That woe worth thee:* for that, may evil happen to you. Wyatt's addition.

140 *'Not I,' quod he, 'but price that is well worthy':* (?) the honour or reward very much deserved by her at death was the reason for her removal from you in death; *or* the honour or reward at death that is of very great value was the reason for her removal from you in death; *or* the price that a very worthy rich rival paid for her is the reason for her separation from you. The first two glosses are supported by Petrarch who has 'Not I, but he who desired her for himself'. The third gloss may be supported by 'price' in CCIV, 24. H. Howarth suggests that 'Price' is a cipher for Prince or King Henry who took Anne Boleyn and that the line means that Henry 'has filched her' (see *FR*). I think the third gloss is most probable.

147 *longer time doth ask resolution:* resolution requires longer time.

LXXIV. *E, A, D, B.*

Attributed to 'Tho.' in margin of *E*; in Wyatt section of *A*; subscribed in *D* 'Finis. Quod Wyatt' ('Quod' designates the author).

In *B* the stanzas are printed in the following order: 3, 1, 2, 4.

The variants in ll. 7, 15, 16, and 18 make the *D* and *B* versions about love. That is not so clearly the case in *E*, where the use of 'they' instead of 'she' makes it possible for the poem to refer to various kinds of friends – political, for example, as well as amatory – who have turned into enemies.

I have punctuated ll. 1-2 and 7-8 to make 'Patience' in the first two stanzas mean what it clearly does in the last two: 'I must (or will) have patience.' But different punctuation of the first two stanzas could make 'Patience' a personification addressed by the speaker and link syntactically ll. 1–2 with ll. 3–4 and ll. 7–8 with ll. 9–10:

> Patience! Though I have not
> The thing that I require,
> I must . . .
>
> Patience! Do what they will
> To work me woe or spite,
> I shall content me . . .

Compare LXXV, CLXI, and CLXXV. These poems share with LXXIV the theme of patience, metrical pattern, and rhyme scheme. LXXV may have been conceived as a response to LXXIV in its *D* version. These four poems – sometimes along with LXXVIII which shares with them theme and rhyme scheme – have often been taken by critics as a group and as perhaps having Serafino's *Canzona de la Patientia* (*M & T* 300–1) as an inspiration. LXXIV, 19–20, and CLXXV, 1–2, translate the first two lines of Serafino's poem; otherwise the poems diverge markedly from Serafino's. He affirms his trust in God in corrupt times that might otherwise drive him to despair.

7   *they*] she *D*; ye *B*.

14   *naught:* not.

15   *I know they know the same*] I know she knows the same *D*; I wish she know'th the same *B*.

16   *they . . . their*] she . . . her *D, B*.

18   *it*] she *B*.

19   *Patience of all my harm:* patience in the face of all the harm done me.

LXXV. *D, E, A* (1–8), *B*.

In Wyatt sections of *A* and *D*.

The poem is a possible companion-piece to LXXIV; before the poem in *D* is the following note, which begins by quoting LXXIV: 'Patience though I had not the etc./to her that said this patience was not for her but that the contrary of mine was most meetest for her purpose.' If the poem is related to LXXIV, it is probably related to the *D* and *B* versions of LXXIV, which are about love, not to the more general version in *E* (see the head-note to LXXIV). But if *E* is Wyatt's final version of LXXIV, then LXXV may not be by Wyatt: would he have revised LXXIV to make it less compatible with the 'response' in LXXI if that 'response' had been his originally? More probably LXXV is by someone who had shown LXXIV to a lady as 'his' poem.

With a few emendations, I have printed the *D* text of LXXV rather than *E*. *E* is unintelligible to me; furthermore, if the poem is not Wyatt's, *E* has no special authority because the hypothesis by which it has authority in any poem not in Wyatt's hand is that Wyatt took an interest in the *E* text of poems by him.

The poem, even in *D*, makes sense to me only if we accept the suggestions of *N* and *Simonds* (120) that it is a dialogue between the discarded lover and his former lady. The note preceding *D* suggests that the lady espouses a kind of patience which is 'contrary' to that traditional kind which the lover enjoins on himself in LXXIV. If I understand ll. 23-4 correctly, the lady ultimately defines her kind of 'patience' as 'bearing another's body' or 'submitting to another's lust', a patience which has caused her gown to need brushing (l. 14) and which she practises with 'a good will' (l. 23). She is, then, the speaker of stanzas 2 and 4 and is addressed in stanzas 1 and 3 by the lover just after, apparently, she has been found 'bearing' another man.

See the head-note to LXXIV for the suggestion that LXXIV, LXXV, LXXVIII, CLXI, and CLXXV constitute a group and have Serafino's *Canzona de la Patientia* as inspiration.

1 *device*: 'heraldic device bearing the motto "Patience," or the motto alone' (*M & T* 302).

3 *contraries*] *E*; contrary *D*.
   guise: style of personal adornment, in this case the 'device' of l. 1.

4 *Must needs be*] Is ever the *E*.
   overthwart: opposite.

1-6 *Patience for my . . . contrary for you*. The lover equates fidelity ('true') with patience and thereby reasons that his unfaithful lady is impatient. He does not define the barriers to their union which cause him to associate fidelity with patience.

8 *Yours hath*] You have *E*.

7-8 *Patience, a good cause why!/Yours hath no cause at all*: you have good reason to talk about your patience (spoken in an ironic tone)! Your patience has no cause whatsoever [because you have really suffered nothing].

9 *Trust me that stands awry*] Therefore your standeth awry *E*.

10 *Perchance may sometime fall*] Perchance sometime to fall *E*.

11 *then*] *E*; the *D*.
   say and sup] then take him up *E*.
   sup: sip.

9-11 *Trust me, that stands awry . . . may . . . fall./'Patience' then say*: believe me, whoever stands at an angle may fall [and your moral posture is as crooked as mine]. When you have fallen [like me], then talk of 'Patience'. The lady here, as in ll. 7 and 12, implicitly defines patience as 'suffering', one of the meanings of the Latin *patior*, but without the word's traditional emphasis on calm and composure in suffering. She shifts her etymological definition in ll. 23-4 to 'bearing', another meaning of *patior*.

12 *A taste*] And drink *E*.

13 *Patience! No force for that*: have patience. No matter about [the nonsense] that you have just been speaking.

15 *Spurn not thereat*: do not kick against patience.

16 *pain:* (?) the pain of having sex with the other man; *or* the pain of being discovered by her former lover just after having sex with the other man.

Lest folks perceive your pain] Let no man know your pain *E*.

17-18 *Patience at my pleasure/When yours hath no measure:* have patience because I tell you to in the aftermath of your having indulged your desire for pleasure excessively. The lover puns on 'pleasure': his will or discretion, and the lady's sexual pleasure.

19 *The t'other was for me:* [You said at first that] impatience ('The t'other') was my characteristic [so stop prattling on about patience].

20 *This patience is for you:* this patience [that you keep talking about] is the virtue you espouse [and I am now giving you a chance to exercise it by showing you I have a new lover (l. 22)].

21 *let see.* Probably an exclamation meaning 'come!', 'go to!' (*M & T*).

23 *Patience:* 1) your bearing of a pain; 2) my bearing of another man's body (a common usage of the Latin verb *patior* from which 'patience' derives).

good will: 1) willing determination; 2) strong sexual appetite.

24 *fulfil:* achieve; exercise. A virtue, like patience, is a habit achieved through repeated action and thereafter exercised in actions.

23-4 *Patience with ... fulfil.* If the lady at first felt pain in her fall to another man (ll. 9–12, 16), she no longer does so, or at least protests to that effect.

LXXVI. *In Spain. E, A, D, T.*

In Wyatt's hand in *E*, with many revisions by Wyatt, two of which (ll. 15, 99) involve rhyme words, which show that he was composing at least parts of the poem in *E*; in Wyatt sections of *A* and *T*.

Wyatt's own title, 'In Spain', places the composition of the poem between June 1537 and June 1539 when he was ambassador to Spain. His revision of l. 88 to blame an 'other will' for his 'long abode' probably refers to the will of King Henry that he remain in Spain despite his desire to return to England. It is likely that he made that revision early in 1539 when he was pressing hardest for recall (*L* 86–7).

The poem translates Petrarch's *Rime* 37 (*M & T* 335–7), a *canzone*. Petrarch's *canzone* consists of seven sixteen-line stanzas and an eight-line coda, irregularly rhymed; the stanza pattern is created by the interweaving of five-beat and three-beat lines. Wyatt partly imitates Petrarch's division into stanzas and coda by grouping the lines into sections (14 + 14 + 14 + 12 + 14 + 12 + 14 + 6). But for Petrarch's complex metrical scheme he substitutes poulter's measure: rhyming lines of six and seven iambic feet respectively, making a couplet of thirteen feet (a poulter's dozen). Wyatt may have chosen this measure because, like Petrarch's stanza, its lines vary in length (*M & T*) or because its movement seemed to him, as to poets later in the century, particularly appropriate to the mood of 'complaint'.

For Wyatt the metrical norm of poulter's measure apparently included a

caesura in the first line after the third foot and in the second line after the
second and fourth feet; for example:

> But if my hope sometime/rise up by some redress,
> It stumbleth straight/for feeble faint,/my fear hath such excess (89–90).

Wyatt did, however, sometimes depart from this norm (for example, ll. 4, 15,
17, 83), and enjambment often defies one's expectation of a major pause
after the first line (for example, ll. 1–2, 5–6). Wyatt marked the caesuras in
thirty-five lines of *E*.

Prior to the coda, Wyatt translates Petrarch closely. He sometimes expands
to make clear the implications of the Italian (ll. 17–20, 42), to enrich his
Petrarchan manner with 'contraries' (ll. 72, 91), or to fill up his long lines
(ll. 3, 21, 64–5). He multiplies references to the lady's effect on his attitudes
and behaviour (ll. 77, 82–3, 85–6) and states that absence from her is the
result of another's will, presumably the king's (l. 88). Untypically, he adds a
reference to the classical myth of the Fates (l. 4) and calls the sun by classical
names (ll. 40, 69).

Wyatt departs strikingly from Petrarch only in his equivalent of the coda.
Petrarch is not certain the song will reach the lady; if it does and if she shows
herself willing to receive it, it should nevertheless cast itself reverently at her
feet. Wyatt's speaker is confident the song will reach the lady and is 'more
expectant of an ordinary womanly response' (*M & T* 338).

T entitles the poem: 'Complaint of the absence of his love.'

2 *plight:* 1) condition of being; 2) danger.

4 *running spindle of my fate.* Recalls the 'thread' of l. 1 and redefines it as
the fibre of individual fate or destiny woven and eventually cut by the Fates.
Petrarch has: 'my heavenly life may soon flow to the shore [of the river of
death].'

5 *Since*] For since *E*.
   th'unhappy. For the apostrophe, compare l. 14 and note.
   did me: caused me.

6 *apart:* separated from ('my sweet weal').

7 *persuade such words unto my . . . mind:* inculcate the following words in
my mind; urge the following words as credible to my mind.

10–11 *if thy return be for thy most delight/Or . . . thy loss if thou once mayst
recover:* if there may [not] be in store for you a return that will give you the
greatest delight, or if you may [not] at some time recover what you have lost
(*O*).

12 *rape:* take away; take by force.
   cover: 1) protect; 2) restore, heal. The first meaning, along with
'defend', elaborates a military metaphor submerged in 'rape'. Time may
become an ally, forcibly remove the enemy 'woe' from the lover, and
thereafter defend and protect him.

14 *see'it.* The purpose of Wyatt's apostrophe is unclear. Perhaps, if he
intended the 'ed' of 'trained' to be pronounced, he was trying to create the
appearance of the metrically correct number of syllables (14), whatever the

elision's impact on the rhythm of the line. Line 59 seems to reinforce that possibility. But l. 5's 'th'unhappy' and l. 39's 'me'and', if taken as elisions, render the lines one syllable short of the required twelve.

15 *bend*] fly *E*.

th'hours . . . bend. 'Petrarch describes the "voyage" of the "hours", i.e. of the sun through the zodiac. Hence Wyatt's *bend* doubtless means "incline", and he, too, uses "hours," poetically, for the sun' (*M & T* 339). Alternatively 'bend' might mean 'proceed', a sense suggested by Wyatt's original 'fly'; but *OED* exemplifies this sense only with indications of direction (to, toward, thither, this way).

16 *space:* time.

18 *straight*] self *E*: straightway, immediately.

19 *as fast*] again *E*.

path awry: oblique path. Wyatt refers to the sun's journey through the zodiac (*M & T* and note to l. 15). Or he may refer to the path of the winter sun, low on the horizon.

31 *whilst I enjoyed that grace.* Petrarch has 'while it pleased God'. Wyatt transforms God's grace into the secular gift of the lady's presence.

32 *that*] *E*; where *W*.

that: would that.

34 *watch:* the state of being awake.

32-5 *My pleasure past, my present pain that I might well embrace!/But for because my want should more my woe increase,/ . . . my will doth never cease/That thing to wish:* my pleasure, derived from her presence, is in the past; my present absence from her results only in pain – would that I might accept that pain! Instead, in order to make my missing of and desire for her ('want') increase that pain, I choose never to stop wishing for her presence. This masochistic delight in the intensification of pain is voiced again in ll. 53-62 and 80-1. Wyatt adds l. 32 to the Italian.

37 *mete:* 1) measure size; 2) traverse in imagination.

38 *them entremete:* interpose themselves.

39 *me'and.* Compare l. 14 and note.

shining lights: the lady's eyes.

40 *Phoebus' sphere:* the sun. *Hughey* thinks Wyatt intended 'spear' on the grounds that the spelling of *E* and *D* is 'spere'; the reference would then be to a spear-like ray of light from the sun. But 'spere' is a normal spelling of 'sphere' well into the sixteenth century; and Phoebus Apollo's characteristic weapon is a bow and arrow.

42 *record:* recollection, memory.

bate: abate, decrease, diminish.

41-2 *It teacheth me also what was my pleasant state,/The more to feel by such record how that my wealth doth bate:* my uneasy life (l. 37) also teaches me by contrast how pleasant was my past state; and as a result of that recollection of my pleasant past I feel even more intensely how my well-being is diminishing in the present.

43 *inflamed.* Probably inflamèd.

45 *let:* (?) hindered, obstructed.

45–7 *If love forget himself, by length of absence let,/Who doth me guide ... unto this ... net/Where doth increase my care?:* if it be true that love, hindered by long absence, forgets the partner in love, who leads me into this trap of remembering my partner in love, a trap that increases my sorrow?

48 *all thing forgot, still*] to think on naught and *E.*

50 *bewray:* reveal, show.

51 *accumbered:* oppressed, overwhelmed.

thoughtful throes discover: reveal profound, moody spasms.

53 *ever more:* ever greater, always increasing.

53–4 *Out by these eyes it shew'th that ever more delight/In ... tears to seek redress:* the spirit ('it') shows through [weeping] eyes its always increasing delight in seeking relief through tears.

55 *new kinds of pleasures:* the masochistic pleasures derived from feeling pain. Compare ll. 32–5.

most] all *E.*

58 *sits:* suits.

me seems me: it seems to me.

59 *to'assay.* For the apostrophe, compare l. 14 and note.

60 *Like as*] Since that *E.*

61–2 *And for because thereto of those fair eyes to treat/Do me provoke, I shall return, my plaint thus to repeat:* and because treating the subject of those fair eyes moves me to tears ('thereto'), I shall return to that subject in order thus to repeat my grieving.

63–4 *within/Where they rule all, and I ... naught but the case:* in my spirit where the lady's eyes rule everything, and I rule nothing except the body.

68 *That were the guides that did it lead:* [mine eyes] that were the guides that did lead my heart.

69 *crisped.* Probably crispèd.

70 *streams*] *A, T;* strenes (strains?) *W, D. Hughey* and *M & T* construe 'strains' as 'light from stars', but I cannot find that literal sense in *OED* and do not see a metaphor; 'strenes' could easily have been an error for 'stremes' ('streams') which fits the metaphor 'glide'. The reference is to the lady's eyes.

71–2 *beams of love .../Which yet so far touch me so near in cold to make me sweat:* loving glances which, though so far away, touch me so intimately that they make me feverish, that is, sweat while feeling chills.

74 *such*] erst *E.*

73–4 *The ... talk, so rare or else alone,/That did me give the courteous gift that such had never none:* the lady's conversation, so unusual or perhaps even unique, that was given as a courteous gift to me who had never before received such a gift; 'talk ... that did ... give ... gift' apparently translates the Italian's 'words that did give the gift of themselves'.

76 *forbear:* endure the absence of; spare.

78 *wonted ... in kindled will to virtue me to train:* was accustomed to

draw me to virtue in my will, inflamed [by the love of her and hence by the desire to please her with my virtuous behaviour].

80 *My comfort scant, my large desire in doubtful trust renews:* the small comfort [I derive from news of the lady] makes me think again that my great desire might be satisfied ('trust') but also might not be satisfied ('doubtful'). The Italian has: 'I do not think I will ever hear a thing that comforts me without making me sad.'

81 *with more delight to moan my woeful case:* to bemoan my painful situation with even greater pleasure. Compare the lover's taking pleasure in his pain in ll. 32–5 and 53–62.

82 *complain:* lament, bewail [the absence of].

firmly do embrace] do embrace E.

82–3 *that ... do embrace/Me from myself:* that take me out of myself; that make me unconscious of myself. N cites as the source Horace, *Odes* IV, xiii, 20.

84 *The sweet disdains, ... the lovely strife.* Wyatt substitutes 'pleasant wraths' and 'lovely strifes' for Petrarch's 'youthful heart' and 'towering intelligence'.

85 *tune:* put in tune; bring to a desirable condition.

temper: a proper balance of the four humours that determine temperament; the mental and emotional composure resulting from that balance, including the control of anger.

just and meet: proportioned and appropriate to the situation rationally judged.

86 *undiscreet:* lacking in sound judgement.

84–6 *lovely strife ... furor undiscreet.* The lines probably refer to the lover's fury at the lady's resistance to his demands, and her ability to resist in such a kind way that, finally, his rage was subdued.

87 *cragged.* Probably craggèd.

88 *At other will]* My fainting hope E.

long abode] brittle life E.

my deep] welling E.

At other will my long abode my deep despair fulfils: my lengthy residence [away from the lady], in obedience to the will of another person, makes my despair full and complete. See the head-note.

90 *faint:* faintness.

91 *sort:* 1) kind, species, with a possible pun on 2) divination of the future by casting a sort or lot.

91–2 *Such is the sort of hope, the less for more desire,/Whereby I fear and yet I trust to see:* this is the kind of hope – growing less as my desire increases – that makes me fear that I shall not see and yet have confidence that I shall see. Compare l. 80.

96 *May chance thee have:* it may chance that you have.

99 *tell her that]* say E.

she shall me shortly see] for here I may not tarry E.

100 *this]* my E.

LXXVII. *D, B, T.*

In Wyatt section of *T.*

The poem freely imitates Petrarch's *Rime* 206 (*M & T* 406–7), a *canzone*. Petrarch's *canzone* consists of six nine-line stanzas and a five-line coda. Only three rhymes are used throughout, in an intricate pattern that changes three times in the stanzas and again in the coda. The stanzas interweave six-beat, five-beat, and three-beat lines; the coda frames three-beat lines with two five-beat lines. Wyatt has the same number of stanzas and three rhymes in each. But he does not restrict himself to three rhymes in the entire poem and does not alter the length of the lines.

In both poems the lover is protesting against the charge that he has said he loves another person. The first four stanzas of both poems are a series of conditional curses in the form: 'if x, then may y happen'. In some cases Wyatt's 'may' is only implied (ll. 5, 23, 27). Both poems turn in the fifth stanza to denial of the charge. Wyatt's sixth stanza compresses Petrarch's sixth and his coda. Petrarch's lover addresses 'Love'; Wyatt's addresses his lady directly. Petrarch's poem is longer (59 lines) and more impassioned than Wyatt's. Wyatt uses only two of Petrarch's curses (ll. 17–20, 25–8) and invents the rest. The counter-accusation in Wyatt's fifth stanza – that the lady has invented this rumour of infidelity to give the lover pain – has no analogue in the original; and the demanding tone of that stanza differs markedly from the tone of the humble suppliant in Petrarch's.

Compare XCI.

T entitles the poem: 'The lover excuseth him of words wherewith he was unjustly charged.'

7 *slack the knot.* See LXVII, 8, and the note.
8 *straiter:* [but make it] tighter.
13–14 *Report may . . . ring/Of shame of me:* report of me may ring with shame.
24 *lust:* pleasure.
33 *fro*] *F*; for *D*; from *B, T*; of *M* conjectures.
    clear fro thought: free of evil intent.
35 *sought:* sought out, with the implication that the rumour is invented ('wrought', l. 37).
40 *Such*] *B, T*; Your such *D.*
45–6 *Rachel . . . Leah.* Jacob served Laban seven years for Rachel, Laban's younger daughter, whom Jacob loved. On the night of the marriage, Laban substituted Leah, the older daughter, for Rachel. Until daylight, Jacob did not realize a trick had been played on him. See Genesis xxix, 1–30. Wyatt may be punning on Rachel/Rakehell and Leah/liar (*M & T*).

LXXVIII. *T.*

In Wyatt section of *T*, who entitles the poem: 'The lover determineth to serve faithfully.'

Compare LXXIV, LXXV, CLXI and CLXXV. See the head-note to LXXIV for the suggestion that these poems constitute a group and have Serafino's *Canzona de la Patientia* as inspiration.

10 *pine*: torment; exhaust by suffering; starve.
28 *writhe away*: turn away with a writhing or twisting motion.

BALLADES

A ballade, strictly defined, is a poem containing one or more triplets of seven- or eight-lined stanzas, each with the same final line as a refrain, and concluding with an 'envoy'. None of the poems which follow complies exactly with that definition, but, apart from the absence of the envoy, LXXXI, LXXXV, and LXXXVI are close approximations. In grouping the following poems, I have assumed the extended sense of the term: a poem divided into stanzas of equal length, usually of seven or eight lines. I have used this rather loose definition to distinguish, I hope usefully, these poems of longer stanzas from the poems of shorter stanzas, which I have called 'songs', in the next section. Many of these ballades, as I have defined the term, are in the stanza form of Chaucer's *Troilus*: lines usually of ten syllables rhyming ababbcc; see, for example, LXXIX or LXXX.

LXXIX. *E, D, T.*

Attributed to 'Wyat' in margin of *E*; in Wyatt section of *T*.

The poem may have been inspired by Serafino's *strambotto*, *L'aer che sente il mesto e gran clamore* (*M & T* 283). If so, Wyatt expands on the eight-line poem by adding hills, vales, rivers, rain, and oaks to Serafino's air and trees, and by concluding with a stanza of explicit complaint.

T entitles the poem: 'The lover complaineth that his love doth not pity him.'

1 *Resound*: echo. Best construed as an imperative addressed to 'woods'. *OED*'s first recorded usage in this transitive construction is 1579.
2, 4, 5 The 'ion' of 'reflection', 'compassion', and 'exclamation' is probably to be pronounced as two syllables with a stress on the second.

causing reflection: causing the throwing back [of my voice] after impact. Probably a metaphorical extension of reflection of light.
3 *record ye of*: you be mindful of, you recollect. Like 'Resound' (l. 1), best construed as an imperative.
3–5 *my pain,/Which have ye oft forced by compassion/As judges to hear mine exclamation*: the pain of me who have often forced you – by appealing to your compassion – to hear, as judges, my loud, articulate expression of pain.
9 *to express*: to show its opinion.
13 *hugy*: huge.
roared. Probably roarèd.
12–13 *Which causeless to suffer without redress/The ... oaks have roared*: (?) the oaks have roared [at my having] to suffer, without cause and without

remedy, heaviness of heart ('which'). *N* follows *T* in emending l. 12 to 'causeless I suffer', thereby leaving the roar of the oaks unexplained.

14 *in:* according to.

18–19 *stony heart, how hath this joined thee,/So cruel that art, cloaked with beauty:* how has this [person], covered with such beauty, come to be joined to thee, stony heart, that art so cruel. Wyatt 'is amazed that a heart so cruel can be accompanied (and disguised) by a woman so beautiful' (*Da*).

21 *meed:* wages, hire, recompense, reward.

20–1 *No grace to me from thee there may proceed ;/But, as rewarded, death for to be my meed:* no gift [of love or mercy] may come to me from you there ⌐in your heart⌐; but, as one rewarded, death is to be what I earn. Wyatt probably intends an ironic theological metaphor in the opposition of 'grace' and 'rewarded'. The lover addresses the lady as the God who denies the sinner grace and treats him according to his merit – in this case, 'rewarding' him with death. But the lover – despite the posture of humility implicit in his definition of death as a 'reward' for his merit – does not really think it an appropriate response to his conduct; and he thinks that, at the least, he should be granted grace. He is therefore judging this 'God' as defective by both Catholic and Lutheran standards.

LXXX. *E, D, T.*

Attributed to 'Tho.' in margin of *E*; in Wyatt section of *T*.

The poem may owe some of its details, particularly of the erotic situation in stanza 2, to Ovid, *Amores* III, 7, and I, 5 (see C. E. Nelson in *FR*).

This poem has been much discussed by critics. See, for example, in *FR*: A. Stein, A. Berthoff, L. E. Nathan, and D. M. Friedman. See *M & T* (299) for bibliography of criticism of this poem.

T entitles the poem: 'The lover sheweth how he is forsaken of such as he sometime enjoyed.'

2 *stalking:* 1) walking softly; 2) pursuing game by the method of stealthy approach.

5 *danger:* 1) in my power; 2) in peril.

1–7 The phrase 'take bread at my hand' confirms the metaphor in the first stanza which identifies women with gentle animals; 'stalking' in its second sense establishes the unusual relationship between these 'animals' and the speaker – until l. 6 they are stalking towards him, he is not stalking towards them. The speaker's unconventional passivity is a dominant *motif* throughout the poem: in the lady's advance to him in stanza 2; in his 'gentleness' (l. 16) which enables her to present her forsaking of him as a favour to him – as if she were releasing him from an unwelcome bondage (ll. 17–18); and in his being 'served' by the lady (l. 20). The animal metaphor also establishes the dream-like atmosphere which pervades the encounter in stanza 2 and is denied in l. 15.

9 *Twenty times better:* more than twenty times.

10 *In thin array after a pleasant guise:* in a thin gown made in a pleasing fashion.

18 *of her goodness:* as a result of her goodness to me.
19 *newfangleness:* novelty in her relations with men; inconstancy.
20 *kindly:* 1) with kindness (ironic); 2) in keeping with the law of kind or nature – in this case, the unfaithful nature of women.

LXXXI. *D, E* (an 8-line version), *T.*

Followed in *D* by 'Finis. Quod Wyatt' ('Quod' designates the author); in Wyatt section of *T.*

F argues that the eight-line version of the first stanza in *E* is a revision and condensation of the entire poem in *D.* Perhaps Wyatt intended but did not complete a revision of the whole poem in which he would have changed the stanza form of Chaucer's *Troilus* to *E*'s ababbacc.

The first stanza may be a very free imitation of Petrarch's *Rime* 234 (*M & T* 417); or Wyatt may have found the common Petrarchan problem of the lover's sleeplessness treated in some earlier imitation of Petrarch's sonnet. Wyatt expands Petrarch's antithesis (between haven in emotional storms and the fountain of tears) into a catalogue of antitheses that makes the first stanza resemble XVII. He may derive his refrain from Petrarch's references to tears and to fleeing a bedroom and a bed where he once found privacy and rest. *T* entitles the poem: 'The lover to his bed, with describing his unquiet state.'

1–8] O restful place, renewer of my smart,
   O labour's salve, increasing my sorrow,
   O body's ease, O troubler of my heart,
   'Peaser of mind, of mine unquiet foe,
   Refuge of pain, remembrer of my woe,
   Of care comfort, where I despair my part,
   The place of sleep wherein I do bout wake,
   Besprent with tears, my bed, I thee forsake. *E.*

5 *Forgetter ... remembering:* causing me to forget ... to remember (*Da*).
7, 14 *Besprent:* besprinkled (modifying 'bed', 'I', or both).
10 *pains.* Spelled 'paines' in MS and possibly disyllabic.
 to ease my pains meet: suitable to easing my pain.
13 *overthwart affects:* opposed feelings (like hot and cold); mental conditions that yield the opposite of what is expected (cure causes more care).
19 *Yet that I gave I cannot call again:* but the heart, or love, that I gave I cannot call back again.

LXXXII. *T.*

In Wyatt section of *T.*

T entitles the poem: 'The lover lamenteth his estate with suit for grace.'

1 *will:* the power to will myself out of love.
2 *Under colour of soberness:* while pretending to temperance and gravity.
3–4 *Renewing ...|My wanhope with your steadfastness:* renewing my despair in the face of your steadfast rejection of me.

5 *Awake ... of gentleness:* out of kindness begin to heed my pain.

6 *at length:* fully.

7 *swelting:* burning slowly, so as to cause me to perish.

8 *Betimes who giveth willingly:* the person who gives early and willingly.

8–9 *Betimes who giveth .../Redoubled thanks ... deserve.* Alludes to the proverb 'He that gives quickly gives twice'; see *Tilley* G125 and compare Chaucer, *Legend of Good Women* G, 441–2 (*Da*).

22 *incontinent:* immediately.

24 *As waste of fire which doth relent:* (?) like that which is laid waste by a fire which melts it; *or* like the wasting away of a fire which diminishes in strength.

27–8 *me .../Which:* me, the person who lacks.

LXXXIII. *T.*

In Wyatt section of *T*, who entitles the poem: 'The lover complaineth and his lady comforteth.'

3 *point:* matter of importance.

4 *convert:* change your attitude.

5 *ire.* The fire of passion seems angry in its attack on his heart.

10 *that I may not:* that which I may not give.

13 *whatso thy words have meant:* whatever your words have intended to accomplish by way of allaying my grief.

16 *I see no time to answer:* (?) I do not see this time as right for an answer.

20 *Thou wouldest:* you will or intend.

25 *good:* good one, good friend.

32 *Thus ... and moan.* This line is either an aside of the lover's or the poet's commentary on the dialogue and its result; 'hearts' is an ironic euphemism for what has in fact been won; ll. 12–14 show that the lady had already given him her heart.

LXXXIV. *T.*

In Wyatt section of *T*, who entitles the poem: 'He ruleth not though he reign over realms that is subject to his own lusts.'

The poem is based on three passages from Boethius's *De Consolatione Philosophiae* (The Consolation of Philosophy), Book III, metres 5, 6, 3 (*M & T* 436). 'Philosophy' is distinguishing between false and true goods. In the first two passages she implies the lack of genuine value in power and in the glory derived from being of noble family and asserts that true power and nobility reside in the control of the passions. In the third passage she explicitly attacks riches as a false good and implicitly praises the spiritual calm in life and death that comes in part from detachment from wealth.

Wyatt translates the first and third passages fairly closely, though he changes the third person to the second person and adapts the matter to the *Troilus* stanza. He does a much freer imitation of the second passage: by omitting Boethius's explicit reference to boasting about noble family and ancestors, Wyatt generalizes the kind of nobility to which the mind might aspire.

Wyatt may have made use of Chaucer's *Boece*, his translation of Boethius, and had as a model Chaucer's poem 'Truth' or 'Balade de Bon Conseyl' in which he condenses much of Boethius's wisdom; see P. Thomson, 'Wyatt's Boethian Ballade' (*FR*).

2 *will:* self-will.

4 *Indian sea.* India was regarded as the most remote corner of the world; compare Chaucer, *CT* VI (C), 722.

5 *Thule.* Probably Thulè; the ancient Greek and Latin name for a land six days' sail north of Britain, supposed by Polybius to be the most northerly region of the world; the type of the extreme limit of travel, discovery, and rule.

8, 10 Wyatt appears to be rhyming pronounced but unstressed 'ed' of 'moved' and 'fixed'.

17-18 *a thousand fold . . . devise.* Wyatt's substitution for Boethius's 'and though he plow his rich fields with a hundred oxen'.

19 *Ycharged:* Probably ychargèd.

20 *busy biting:* state of mind busy about money – that is, a constant preoccupation with money – which is biting or a cause of anxiety. Chaucer literally translates Boethius's *cura mordax* 'bytynge bysynesse' (biting busyness).

20-21 *busy biting yet should never let/Thy wretched life, ne do thy death profit:* (?) yet anxious concern for money should never prevent thy wretched life – that is, prevent thy life from being wretched – nor be profitable to you in death. Boethius has: 'biting busyness about money will never leave him while he lives and his light riches do not accompany him when he is dead.' *Rollins* follows *T* in placing the comma after 'let' and in construing the lines: 'sharp corroding desire yet would never cease, nor your death be any profit to your wretched life.' With *Rollins's* punctuation, a more likely reading of the final line might be: 'nor should thy wretched life do profit [to] thy death.' *N* finds the lines unintelligible and suggests they be emended to read: '. . . yet should never let/Thy death, ne do thy wretched life profit', with 'let' meaning 'prevent' or 'retard'. I think my punctuation and reading are supported by the original and by Chaucer's translation: 'nevere ne schal his bytynge bysynesse forleeten [forsake] hym whil he lyveth/ne the lyghte richesses ne schal nat beren hym companye whan he is deed.'

LXXXV. *E, B, T.*

Attributed to 'Wyat' in margin of *E*; in Wyatt section of *T*.

Most of the lines divide into balanced half-lines that reinforce the sense of the speaker's indecisiveness. *T* entitles the poem: 'The lover, taught, mistrusteth allurements.' But notice that love is not mentioned. The assurances, therefore, could be other than amatory; they might, for example, be political or financial.

2 *doubt:* have doubts about the matter (relationship, assurances given) and therefore fear betrayal.

5 *windy words:* words 'vain and light as the wind' (*N* 547). Proverbial; see *Tilley* W833 (*Da*).

quaint: clever, cunning, crafty.

6 *maketh.* Probably monosyllabic (mak'th).

7, 14, 21 *For dread to fall I stand not fast:* 1) for fear of falling I do not take up a fixed position in that place (that is, commit myself to trusting a particular person or assurance); 2) for fear of falling I will fall (that is, the very fear of being betrayed will insure that I will be betrayed because the fear will prevent me from making that commitment of trust that just might save me).

9 *seek*] *T*; seeketh *E*; seeks *B*. *E* and *B* probably took 'maze', instead of 'I', as the referent of 'seek' and made the verb agree.

two contraries: the hope that the promises will be kept (a hope which inclines the speaker to commit himself to the maker of the promises), and the fear that they will not be kept (a fear which deters the speaker from hazarding a commitment).

10 *haze:* (?) hazard. *N* suggests emending *E*'s 'hase' to 'halse' (to embrace); but 'halse' does not rhyme with 'maze'. *M & T* suggest that 'hase' means 'has' – a meaning rejected by *N* on the grounds that Wyatt does not say 'I has'. I think 'hase' is Wyatt's abbreviation of 'hasard', 'hazard', which fits the context and supplies the rhyme. But he does not use 'hazard' elsewhere.

11 *Imprisoned.* Almost certainly imprisonèd.

Imprisoned in liberties: the liberties that result from making no decision are in fact a prison of uncertainty and fear which makes decision impossible.

13 *Always thirsty yet naught I taste*] *ed.*; Always thirsty and yet nothing I taste *E*. *E*'s reading produces the only line that exceeds by more than one syllable this poem's norm of eight syllables to the line. I suspect that Wyatt first wrote: 'Always thirsty and nothing taste' and then revised to the reading in the text. The scribe of *E* might easily have conflated the two versions, especially given the difficulties created by Wyatt's line-outs and inter-linear corrections. *B* has 'naught' for 'nothing'.

15 *Assured I doubt I be not sure:* 1) assured, I doubt; I am not sure; 2) assured, I fear I am not sure. Any internal punctuation would eliminate the probably deliberate ambivalence of this line (*S* 75).

16 *surety:* pledge given for the fulfilment of an undertaking.

17 *put the proof in ure:* put the testing of its reliability into practice.

18 *trusty:* trustworthy.

LXXXVI. *E, T.*

Attributed to 'Tho.' in margin of *E*; in Wyatt section of *T*.

T entitles the poem: 'The lover rejoiceth against fortune that, by hindering his suit, had happily made him forsake his folly.' Clearly *T* has made love the poem's context without evidence. From the poem's own terms we know only that the speaker has somehow profited – possibly through the exercise of his mind or virtue (ll. 10–12) or simply through a surprising outcome of events (ll. 15–18) – from an unexpected change in fortune which at first threatened to harm him.

1 *not well*] *Mason, Maxwell*; wot not well *E*.

2 *wondrous.* Possibly trisyllabic.

3–6, 19–20 To be in the chain or coil of Fortune (ll. 6, 20) is to allow one's happiness to depend on chance events and their consequences. In this poem Fortune's creation of real prosperity in seeming ruin seems at first the result of whim (ll. 4–5), then of incompetence (l. 19). *N* sees in l. 3 an allusion to Horace's description of Fortune as delighted with her savage business (*Odes* III, 29).

4–5 *That causeth joy full dolourous/And eke the same right joyous*] *N*; That causeth joyful dolours/And eke the same right joyous *E*. *E*, while redundant nonsense, points to the intended meaning of 'the same' as 'dolours'. The lines intend a contrast between apparent joys that are in fact dolorous and apparent dolours that are in fact joyous. *N*'s emendation, adopted in the text, has the virtue of being closest to *E* in 'causeth'; but it creates the danger of misconstruing the contrast as one between dolorous joy and joyful joy.

7, 14, 21 *Spite of thy hap, hap hath well happed:* in spite of your attempt to determine events [malignly], the event, superficially unfortunate, has turned out well.

8 *me set for a wonder:* set me up as someone whose misfortune will fill onlookers with awe.

13 *have me trapped*] *T*; have trapped *E*.

16 *made a gap where was a stile:* made a gap in the fence or hedge to pass through easily where previously there had been a stile on which one had to climb. To maintain the parallel with furthering while trying to hinder (l. 15), one must assume that Fortune removed the stile in order to prevent even passage of some difficulty but, in so doing, left a gap that made passage easier.

17 *Cruel.* Probably disyllabic.

18 *lour.* Possibly disyllabic.
Weening to lour: intending to frown.

20 *lapped:* coiled; implicated, entangled.

LXXXVII. *E*.
Attributed to 'Tho.' in margin of *E*.

The last line of each stanza is repeated at the opening of the following stanza – a form that Wyatt liked.

In this poem Fortune produces unhappiness in a situation apparently promising happiness. Contrast LXXXVI where Fortune creates real prosperity in seeming ruin. Love is not mentioned in either poem, and it need not be the subject of LXXXVI. But this poem's reference to the lover's 'contraries' of feeling (ll. 17–18) and the need to 'refrain' (ll. 28–9) make clear that at least the primary subject is the emotional and moral dilemma of the courtly lover whose lady returns his love but refuses to satisfy his sexual passion. The speaker says that he regards this perennial predicament as unique – a new kind of unhappiness (l. 5) never before experienced by a true lover (l. 2) – and that he does not know how to describe it (ll. 6-7).

1 *happed.* Probably happèd.

3-4 *At me Fortune list to begin/To shew that . . .:* Fortune wishes to begin with me to show that which . . .

10-14 *But why I have not help again,/That know I not unless I sterve/For hunger still amidst my food – /So granted is that I deserve/To do me good:* but I do not know why I receive no help in my pain unless, like Tantalus, I am being made always to starve in the midst of my food – [and] the food I deserve is being given to me in this [peculiar] way in order to do me a good [that I do not understand].

16 *deserve:* (?) have a right (intransitive); *or* serve (transitive).

For I deserve and not desire: (?) for I have a right [to my lady and, in that sense, possess her, and therefore need] not desire her; *or* for I serve [my lady] and do not desire her. The speaker seems either sophistic or self-deceiving.

18 *raked.* Probably rakèd.

17-18 *cold . . . fire:* the chill of sexual frustration . . . the fire of sexual passion. These conventional 'contraries' of feeling more often describe the lover's fear and hope.

19-20 *For though I have . . ./In hand to help that I require:* for though I have in hand what I need to help me [that is, the lady].

25 *that I have, to crave:* to crave what I already possess.

26 *lust:* 1) desire; 2) sexual desire (?). Is the speaker willing to admit or name the second, given that he 'cannot express' the thing he means (ll. 6-7) and the claim that he does not 'desire' his lady (l. 16)?

27 *ask and have.* Proverbial; see Tilley A343 (*Da*).

30 *'So hawks be taught':* hawks are trained by being deprived of light and food (*F*).

31 *layeth.* Probably monosyllabic (lay'th).

clause: 1) a short sentence; 2) a proviso in a legal document. The word 'case' supports the second reading. Both refer to the 'saying' about hawks.

32 *such craft:* the kinds of tricks used 1) to train hawks; 2) by lawyers.

33 *and good cause why:* and there is good reason why [I should say it].

34 *raught:* reached.

LXXXVIII. *E, D, A.*

In Wyatt sections of *A* and *D*.

3 *Lust:* pleasure.

refused: abandoned; left.

5 *Too much advancing slacked my speed:* moving [at first] too far and too

quickly [ultimately] slowed my speed, reduced my success. Echoes proverb 'The more haste, the less speed'; see *Tilley* H198 (*Da*).

8-9 *Whereto did I assure my thought/Without displeasure steadfastly:* (?) for what reason did I steadfastly fix my opinion or expectation of the other person without [misgivings of] displeasure.

11 *revolted:* turned.

12 *wonderly:* in a manner that causes wonder or awe.

13 *thought*] *D, A*; though *E*.

thought naught but faithfulness: expected nothing but fidelity [from the other person].

15 *cheer.* Presumably that of the other person.

19 *Should not from truth be set apart:* should not even consider the possibility of being unfaithful.

20 *my*] *D, A*; me *E*.

Since truth did cause my hardiness: (?) since the other person's [initial] fidelity caused my boldness; *or* since my fidelity caused me to think I had a right to be bold.

23 *led*] *D*; leds *E*.

24 *among:* (?) from time to time; *or* all the while.

26 *happed.* Probably happèd.

27 *Assurance:* confidence; subjective certainty.

caused] *M*; causeth *E*. Probably causèd.

29 *note:* 1) characteristic feature; 2) music, melody, tune. The pun is continued in l. 31.

31 *burden:* 1) load of sorrow; 2) bass part or undersong; 3) refrain of a song.

33 *No pleasure hath still steadfastness:* a calm, quiet 'standing-fast' in a relationship involves [or obtains?] no pleasure.

LXXXIX. *E, B.*

In *E* after a poem attributed to 'Tho.' and before a poem in the Wyatt sections of *A* and *T*. But because this poem does not have an explicit attribution, I should have placed it in the second section of poems attributed to Wyatt after the sixteenth century.

There is a problem in determining the person addressed throughout the poem. The first stanza is clearly addressed to Venus. But 'thy sight' in l. 15 refers most naturally to the sight of the lady: she is more easily hidden from sight by sea and hills than is the planet Venus; and the lover would more probably occupy the night recalling her 'wonted grace' (l. 16) than that of Venus or the planet. The second stanza, on the other hand, could be addressed to either Venus or the lady or both. Addressing both seems to me a device in keeping with Wyatt's fondness for riddles and puzzles. If both are addressed there, the second stanza is a transition from Venus as the sole person addressed to the lady as the primary person addressed – 'primary' because Venus is still a possible addressee in the third and especially in the fourth stanza.

1 *this thy port*] *B*; this port *E*; this the port *N*. Lines 1–4 seem to relate every aspect of the speaker's situation to Venus; hence *B* seems most plausible: 'Though this is *thy* port and I am *thy* true servant . . .' On the other hand I have not been able to find any port dedicated to Venus, and *B* suggests that kind of specificity.

3 *chief house*. In astrology the sphere of the fixed stars, or firmament, is divided into two sets of twelve houses. The zodiacal houses are twelve divisions of a narrow horizontal band of the firmament through which the planets are seen to move. Taurus is the chief house of Venus in the zodiac; her presence there promises love's joys and pleasures. A second set of houses results from dividing the entire firmament into twelve equal parts by six circles passing through the north and south poles of the firmament. Each of these houses is associated with certain advantages or disadvantages. The first, reckoned from the eastern horizon, and the seventh are propitious and hence 'chief'. The first is associated with life, the second with marriage. In the poem, then, Venus is either in Taurus or in the first or seventh house.

4 *Both joy and eke delight*] Joy and delight *N* conjectures.

5 *my bliss:* my lady.

6 *Cytherea:* Venus. The name was derived from an island near Crete, formerly called Cythere, now Cerigo, consecrated to Aphrodite (Venus).

6–7 '*Help . . ./My fearful trust:* 1) strengthen my trust in my lady's love, a trust which is mingled with the fear that she does not love me; 2) strengthen the grounds for my trusting my lady's love – that is, her love for and fidelity to me – a trust mingled with fear that she does not love me.

7, 14, 21, 28 *en voguant la galère:* while rowing the galley. *F* suggests that the phrase is a refrain of a French boat song. *M & T* point out that 'Et vogue la galère' is also an idiom meaning 'Come what may'.

10 *fleeteth:* journeys (by water); sails; floats.

12 *Stay that with faith:* 1) support that person (me) with faith in you, Venus; 2) support that person (me) with my lady's (your?) fidelity to me.

that faithfully doth moan: 1) that person (me) who moans with faith in you, Venus; 2) that person (me) who moans with faith in my lady (you?).

13 *And thou also givest me both hope and fear:* (?) if you give me hope as well as fear.

15 *elonged*. Probably elongèd: separated; removed.

thy sight. See the head-note.

16 *reducing:* bringing back; recalling.

20 *despair my comfort:* I would despair of my comfort.

21 *flee*] *N* conjectures; she *E*, *B*.

23 *Of any hope*] of hope *N* conjectures.

24 *do me retain:* keep me attached to her; indicate that she keeps me in her service.

25 *thy*] ed.; the *E*.

26 *my will is nothing as I would:* what I want has none of the importance that I wish it had.

XC. Parker, T.

In Wyatt section of *T*, who entitles the poem: 'Whether liberty by loss of life, or life in prison and thraldom be to be preferred.'

The poem probably 'belongs to the "lover's-dilemma type" favored by the troubadours' (*Rollins* II, 317).

2 *unsparred*: unbarred, unfastened.
4 *Whether*: which of the two.
5 *Certes*: truly, assuredly.
6 *determination*: the mental act of coming to a decision.
10 *yet*: even now.
15-16 *By length of life ... chance*] And yet me thinks, although I live and suffer,/I do but wait a time and fortune's chance *T*; *T* recognized the awkwardness of changing attitudes, without transition, within the stanza.
23 *best*] Parker, *T*; least *N*, *M & T*.
   Of two ills ... choose the best. Ironic variation on the proverb 'Of two ills choose the least"; see *Tilley* E207 (*Da*).

XCI. D, B.

In a Wyatt section of *D*. Because this poem is ascribed elsewhere in *D* to 'John', *Harrier* (45-49) thinks its inclusion in this section of Wyatt poems does not constitute an attribution.

Compare LXXVII and the *canzone* of Petrarch on which it is based.

1 *strain*: bind tightly.
24 *slip this knot*. See LXVII, 8 and the note.
34 *mind for to remove*: be mindful of removing.

XCII. D, B.

In a Wyatt section of *D*. *Harrier* (38-45) argues that the poems in this section of *D* are not all by Wyatt and excludes this poem in particular.

3 *bit not then the lip* as a sign of displeasure (*M & T*).
4 *defence of my distress*: the one who tried to keep off my distress.
16 *that*: that which.
18 *My love from her no man can let*: (?) no man can keep my love from her.
30 *In covenant*] *F*; In comenant *D*; In coumnant *B*; Incontinent *N*.
   In covenant I might find them so: would that I might find them in a real contract.
32 *Torment ... pain or woe*] *B*; *omitted in D*
35 *be*] *B*; *not in D*.

XCIII. D,

Precedes in *D* a poem that is attributed to 'Wyat' in *E* and is in Wyatt sections of *A* and *T*. It is the first in a group of ten poems in *D* in a new hand, eight of which are almost certainly by Wyatt.

2 *hold:* grasp; custody; confinement.

3 *sufferance:* pain.

11 *one happy hour:* 1) one hour governed by chance; 2) one hour governed by good luck [on behalf of some lover other than the speaker?]; 3) one hour of happiness for the unreciprocating beloved [with a lover other than the speaker?].

13 *list for to lour:* should choose to frown.

21, 22, 23, 30 *fantasy, fancy.* See the head-note to CXXVII and the poem itself for the complex set of meanings of these words.

20–1 *appeal for thy release/To fantasy:* ask your fantasy for freedom from your present love; that is, dwell on the mental image of someone else you have seen or simply imagined, thereby make yourself fall in love with that new person, real or imagined, and consequently gain freedom from your present love. Compare CXXVII.

22 *To fantasy pertains to choose:* choice relates to, depends on fantasy.

26 *no faster knot:* no firmer bond than the choice based on fantasy.

26–7 *no faster knot . . . slips.* See LXVII, 8 and the note.

27 *nice:* delicate; trivial; ephemeral; foolish; wanton.

29 *stands by change:* has change as its very nature.

30 *Fortune is frail.* Proverbial; see *Tilley* F606 and *ODEP* 221 (*M & T*).

32–4 *best to prevail,/There is no way . . ./As truth to lead though t'other fail:* there is no way better to win return of one's love than to let fidelity guide one's behaviour, even if the other person fail for a time to return one's love.

35 *thereto:* to fidelity.

XCIV. *D.*

'W' written at end of third stanza.

The poem's meaning turns in part on the defiance of expectation. Through the first three stanzas we expect the speaker to conclude: 'Blame not my lute, blame me.' But in the fourth and fifth stanzas the speaker directs the blame instead to the lady. Art and the artist, he implies, must present the truth, and the lady's infidelity is the truth.

John Hall (?–1566), poet, surgeon, and medical writer, composed a moralizing parody of this poem and provided a musical setting; see the edition of Hall's *The Court of Virtue* (1565) by R. A. Fraser (1961), pp. 164–9. Hall's work – the title of which parodies *The Court of Venus*, the earliest printed text of some poems by Wyatt – shows the hostility that the 'godly' felt in mid-century to secular love poems like Wyatt's. Compare CIX and CCVIII and head-notes.

This poem was also sung to a lute score preserved in a commonplace book in the Folger Library (MS 448.16); see J. H. Long (*FR*). The music was not composed for Wyatt's poem but adapted from an older Italian musical pattern 'that served as a neatly elastic formula for singing and playing of poetry of various kinds'; see O. Gombosi (*FR*).

2 *as liketh me:* as it pleases me.

19 *indite:* compose.

20 *Do*] *N*; To *D*.
23 *falsed.* Probably falsèd.
29 *thyself*] *N*; the self *D*.
30 *deserved.* Probably deservèd.
31 *evil.* Possibly slurred into one syllable.

XCV. *D*.

In a Wyatt section of *D*.

2 *departure.* *F* suggests that the word is to be pronounced with Romance accents, 'départúre'.
21 *undeserved.* Probably undeservèd.
20–1 *pain/That undeserved, causeless to remain :* pain that is undeserved and is to remain, though without cause.

SONGS

In one sense of the term all of Wyatt's poems are 'songs', or so he seems to imply in CXXXV when he writes:

> Me list no more to sing
> Of love nor of such thing,
> How sore that it me wring;
> For what I sung or spake
> Men did my songs mistake.

Here the word 'songs' apparently does not imply a relationship to music; it seems rather to refer to any statement in verse, sung or spoken. In fact only one known musical setting of a poem by Wyatt was made before his death: William Cornish (*c.* 1468–1523) set a version of the first three stanzas of 'Ah Robin' (CXXXIX). But in this instance Wyatt may actually have been reworking and expanding Cornish's song or the popular song on which it was based; and Wyatt's poem may have been performed to the tune of the popular song. There is no evidence that Wyatt wrote the poem for Cornish to set (*Stevens* 111, 135, 405). Wyatt may have written poems, like 'Blame not my lute' (XCIV), to fashionable tunes and expected that they might at times be sung. Extant settings of 'Blame not my lute', 'Heaven and earth' (XCIX), and 'If ever man might him avaunt' (CXLVIII), dating probably from the 1550s, and John Hall's settings or suggested tunes for moralized versions of 'Blame not my lute', 'My lute, awake' (CIX), and 'My pen, take pain' (CCVIII) in his *Court of Virtue* of 1565 perhaps give some clues to the popular tunes for which the poet might have composed those poems (later Elizabethan and Stuart settings or suggested tunes do not provide such clues). But there is no evidence that Wyatt expected his poems to be set to music or that his expectation of musical performance was an incentive to the composition of his poems or a condition of their texture. Wyatt's knowledge of music was probably quite minimal: he may have been able to 'sing a little and strum upon the lute', but all his references to music in his poems are 'vague and conventional' (*Stevens* 133–8).

I am using the term 'song', then, not to imply any necessary relationship between the following poems and music, but simply to describe poems in relatively short stanzas of six lines or fewer, usually though not always in shorter lines, and frequently with refrains. The distinction between 'song' and 'ballade' is therefore the arbitrary but, I hope, useful distinction between poems in shorter stanzas and poems in longer stanzas. I have divided 'songs' into three groups: those with lines of four or five beats in the body of the stanza, though not necessarily in the refrain; those with the shorter lines of two or three beats; and those which mix longer and shorter lines.

SONGS (1)

XCVI. *E, B, T.*

Attributed to 'Tho.' in margin of *E*; in Wyatt section of *T*.

This poem translates a madrigal by Dragonetto Bonifacio (*M & T* 297). Though Bonifacio (1500–26) left a collection of poems in a manuscript, this madrigal was first printed in an edition of about 1535, which makes it very likely that the poem was written after that date. Since madrigals differ in form Wyatt may not have recognized it as a distinct genre; here he uses four-stress lines in three quatrains, while in poem I he uses the rondeau form in translating a comparable madrigal.

T entitles the poem: 'To a lady to answer directly with yea or nay.' *E* and *B* have the following answer, probably not by Wyatt. *N* prints it in his text but doubts Wyatt's authorship. *F* prints it in a footnote.

> Of few words, sir, you seem to be.
> And where I doubted what I would do
> Your quick request hath caused me
> Quickly to tell you what you shall trust to.
>
> For he that will be called with a beck
> Makes hasty suit on light desire,
> Is ever ready to the check
> And burneth in no wasting fire.
>
> Therefore whether you be lief or loath
> And whether it grieve you light or sore,
> I am at a point, I have made a oath:
> Content you with 'Nay' for you get no more.

1–2 *withouten many words/Once I am sure ye will or no:* I will not use many words once I am sure you will or not. The original has: 'I do not know how to speak many words. Either you will or you won't.'

3 *leave your bourds.* Wyatt's addition.

5 *beck:* a gesture usually indicating assent, like a nod of the head or a motion of the forefinger.

6 *burneth.* Possibly pronounced as one syllable (burn'th).

8, 9 *yea]* *B*, *T* and *E*. The original has: 'I shall write "yes" in rhyme.'

12 *I mine own:* I will be my own man.

XCVII. *E, A, T.*

Attributed to 'Tho.' in margin of *E*; a revision probably by Wyatt; in Wyatt sections of *A* and *T*. Wyatt's first stanza may have been partly suggested by the first six lines of a *canzone* by Giusto de' Conti (*c.* 1379–*c.* 1449) (*M & T* 308).

Appended to the poem is the following statement, part Spanish, part Italian: *Podra esser che no es* (That which is not may some day be) (*Maxwell*). The tag may refer to the speaker's life or it may be unconnected with the poem.

T entitles the poem: 'The lover complaineth himself forsaken.'

2 *fet:* fetch.

8 *Fortune's friend is Mishap's foe.* Compresses a proverb; see *Tilley* T301 (*Da*).

10 *in the wind to waste my words.* Proverbial; see *Tilley* W831 (*Da*).

11–12 *Naught moveth you my ... moan/But ... you turn it into bourds:* my moan moves you not at all; on the contrary you turn it into jokes.

14 *rue] added in a hand contemporary with the scribe's, probably Wyatt's, to fill a gap in E.*

18 *that thing that was my best:* (?) my heart; my soul.

21 *sparkle in the wind:* scatter, disperse in the wind and, implicitly, thereby become wind.

22 *falsed.* Probably falsèd.

21–3 *though they sparkle in the wind/Yet shall they show your falsed faith/which is returned unto his kind.* The speaker's sparkling words show her infidelity by declaring it and by imitating it: like his words, her faith is scattered in the wind and thereby becomes mere wind, which was its nature from the start.

24 *like to like.* Proverbial; see *Tilley* L286, *ODEP* 368, and VI, 4.

32 *Without offence your heart to wreck:* [and] to gratify your [cruel] heart without my having offended you.

37–8 *it doth you grieve/And ... me my ... life:* it – my life – grieves you and me.

39 *shall naught relieve] ed.;* shall not relieve *E*.

39–40 *shall naught relieve/But death alone:* nothing but death alone shall relieve.

40 *weary] M & T;* very *E, A.*

41–3 *life ... death ... gain ... loss ... salve ... sore ... you:* the lady.

XCVIII. *D, B, E.*

Attributed to 'Tho' in margin of *E*; in Wyatt section of *D*.

Because the leaf is torn in *E* the last part of every line is missing. I have printed *D*, with some emendations from *B* in the last parts of lines. *E*'s partial lines are identical with *D*'s.

1-4 *Like as the ... you regard it not.*   Several sources have been suggested for the comparison with the swan (*M & T* 314-15), the closest being Chaucer, *The Legend of Good Women* (Dido), 1355-60. But the figure was common and proverbial; see Chaucer, *Anelida and Arcite*, 346-50, Tilley S1028 and *ODEP* 634 (*M & T*).

1   *towards.*   Probably towárds.

2, 6, 10, 14, 18   *note:*   a strain of music, a melody, a song.

6   *deadly*]   *B*; delye *D*.

10   *changed.*   Probably changèd.

15   *Melting ... death:*   melting in tears [is] a cruel death.

19   *weary*]   *B*; very *D*.
      breath: 1) breath; 2) soul or spirit.

20   *regarded*]   *B*; regard it *D*.

XCIX. *E, D.*

Attributed to 'Tho.' in *E*; subscribed 'Finis. Quod Wyatt' in *D* ('Quod' designates the author); in Wyatt section of *D*.

Wyatt may have derived the idea in ll. 1-2 – that heaven and earth hear and understand the lover's cry – from the *strambotto* by Serafino which also may have inspired LXXIX (*M & T* 283); less probably from a *strambotto* by Filosseno in which nature is not compassionate (*M & T* 315). He may owe the device of repeating the last word of each stanza to either Serafino or Filosseno (*M & T*).

6   *Forbear:*   be patient.
      slake: 1) relax; 2) burn less strongly, die down (with the submerged metaphor that surfaces in 'fire' in l. 7).

11   *force:*   compulsion of strong feeling.

17   *not:*   not only.

18   *as to my power and might:*   as much as my power and might have enabled me.

24   *my mind*] *N*;   me mind *E*.

25   *to you unware:*   unknown to you.

29   *my tears*] *D*;   tears *E*.

32   *Hard of belief it doth appear, appear:*   it appears [that you find it] hard to believe.

34-5   *Therefore when ye hear tell, / Believe it not although ye see my grave:*   [you demand such extraordinary proof of my death that], when you hear my death mentioned, do not believe it even though you see my grave.

c. *E, A.*

Attributed to 'Tho' in margin of *E*; in Wyatt section of *A*.

The poem probably owes the image of the water breaking the stone to Petrarch's *Rime* 265, to Serafino's sonnet 103, or to one or several of the latter's *strambotti* (*M & T* 321–3). The comparison of the lady with fierce animals probably also comes from the sonnet or *strambotti* by Serafino.

2 *water ... soft/Doth pierce ... stone ... from aloft.* Proverbial; see *Tilley* D618 (*Da*).

6 *stilling:* distilling; trickling down in drops.

10 *out of frame:* out of order.

9–12 *So cruel ... is naught alive, .../But some way ... may so contrive ... the wild to temper:* nothing that lives is so cruel but that some method may contrive to temper its wildness.

13–14 *sought ... for some lucky day:* sought ... the lucky day [in which I shall be able to seize and tame her].

16 *pray:* ask; probably with a pun on 'prey', seek to possess as prey.

15–16 *This fierce tiger, less I find her meek/And more denied:* I find her, this fierce tiger, less meek and am more denied by her.

18 *boot*] *N; rhyme word missing in E, A.*

Forbears that sueth meekness, for his boot: (?) spares, as a reward to him, the person who practises the virtue of meekness.

19 *in extreme dolour.* Sense dictates that 'in extreme dolour' refers to the speaker's heart, although the phrase parallels the lion's (lady's) 'raging furor' in rhetorical structure.

20 *treads under foot*] *ed.*; treads under thy foot *E.*

23–4 *And yet the humble to help at need –/Naught helpeth time, humbleness, nor place:* (?) and yet for you to help the genuinely humble person [like myself] when he is in need – in fact neither time, humility, nor place helps at all [to elicit such aid from you].

CI. *E.*

Attributed to 'Tho.' in margin of *E*.

The phrase 'to year' or 'this year' in the refrain suggests that the poem may be of the kind that sometimes accompanied New Year's gifts (*Stevens* 209–10).

The theme of the heart's superiority to material riches as a gift is common to several of Serafino's *strambotti* (*M & T* 324–5), from which Wyatt may also have derived some of the diction in the second stanza. Wyatt expands on the theme more fully than Serafino, affirms the worth of his gift more confidently and insistently, and gives the poem an element of suspense by naming the gift only in the last line.

2 *clive:* cliff overhanging the sea, a lake, or a river.

3 *Ind.* India was regarded popularly as the end of the earth; see LXXXIV, 4.

4–5 *Is none a greater gift to give,/Less set by oft:* there is no greater gift to give, put aside less often.

5 *lief:* precious.

6, 12, 18, 24 *to year:* this year.

9 *Perrie:* precious stones or gems considered collectively; jewelry.

orient: applied to pearls of superior value and brilliance, as coming from the East in ancient times; lustrous, radiant.

14 *nar:* nearer.

16 *mistrust to bar:* to prevent mistrust.

CII. *E.*

Attributed to 'Tho' in margin of *E*.

The last eight stanzas are in a different hand from that in which the first four stanzas are written. If the other party to this stanza by stanza dialogue, in addition to the heart, is the person who possesses the heart, then the heart's stoic resolve is not shared by the entire person and the tension within the poem reflects a continuing tension within the person.

Lines 33–6 suggest that the poem is about political failure and its consequences, perhaps in Spain (*F*) or in prison in 1541 (*N*), rather than, as *M & T* suggest, about love.

The refrains of the heart's stanzas are derived from Chaucer's *Fortune* 25: 'No man is wrecched, but himself it wene'; Wyatt acknowledges that debt in ll. 31–2, where he attributes the refrain to Chaucer, the one that knows 'what is what'. *F* thinks the entire poem imitates Chaucer's poem. But the negative side of Wyatt's argument is much more intense than Chaucer's; and Chaucer divides the attack on Fortune between the plaintiff against Fortune and Fortune itself; and he also gives Fortune some of the crucial lines about stoic self-possession.

6 *no moe:* no more or no other persons.

7 *I myself have at my will:* I have myself under my own control.

8, 16, 24, 32, 40 *he is wretched that weens him so:* he alone is wretched who thinks himself so.

13 *new:* anew.

15 *through it]* *Tillyard*; through *E*; therewith *N*.

it: the loss.

23 *Who hath himself shall stand upright.* Chaucer has 'he that hath himself hath suffisaunce' (*Fortune*, 26).

26 *His trust is like as he hath sped:* his confidence in himself is [or should be] the same as his success – that is, non-existent.

27 *Against the stream thou mayst not dure.* The line echoes the proverb 'It is hard to strive against the stream' (*Tilley* S927 and *ODEP* 627). Compare CVII, 5–6, and CCXXVI, 13 (*M & T*).

31–2 See head-note.

32 *saith]* *ed.*; sayeth *E*.

43 *unhap:* bad luck, misfortune.

47 *in store:* awaiting the future.

CIII. *D.*

Followed in *D* by 'Finis. Quod Wyatt S' ('Quod' designates the author).

The first two stanzas – except for their emphasis on sighing and groaning – may imitate Ovid's *Amores* I, ii, 1–4; and the refrain may translate the first words of that poem, '*Esse quid hoc dicam*' (see C. E. Nelson in *FR*).

1   *means*]   *ed.*; meaneth *D*. One structural principle of this kind of poem is its beginning and ending with the same words. Compare **CXVIII.**

3   *as hard as stone.*   Proverbial; see *Tilley* S878 (*Da*).

13   *A mornings :*   in the mornings.

14   *I turn unto my wonted guise :*   I return to my customary way of behaving [but that is only a matter of appearance].

15   *devise :*   conjecture; think; deliberate; consider.

20   *means*]   *ed.*; meaneth *D*.

30–1   *though naught appear/But most of that that most I fear :*   although nothing comes from that passage of time except the greatest amount of that frustration of my love, that frustration which I most fear.

CIV. *T.*

In Wyatt section of *T*.

The poem may be a free imitation and expansion of a sonnet by Antonio Tebaldeo (1463–1537), (*M & T* 434). If so, Wyatt derived the material for his first stanza from the sonnet's octave, and the movement in the fourth stanza to the internal faculties from a similar movement in the sonnet's sestet. The cases for and against the source are argued in *M & T*.

T entitles the poem: 'The lover curseth the time when first he fell in love.'

12   *no deal to go :*   to move not a bit; to move not at all.

18   *I each foot a hand had seen :*   I had seen each foot become or be a hand [so I would not have been able to walk].

20   *fancy's will:*   choice inspired by my fantasy, my inclination to love. For the negative implications of 'fancy' that may pertain here, see the head-note to **CXXVII.**

21   *relent :*   yield.

CV. *E, T.*

In Wyatt section of *T*.

Note the internal rhyme of the fourth syllables of successive lines (for example, 'reign'/'pain', 'bought'/'thought').

T entitles the poem: 'A renouncing of hardly escaped love.' But love is not mentioned in the poem, so the pleasure forsaken might be of a different character.

3–4   *shall surety/Conduct my thought of joys needy:*   [my desire for] certainty and security shall hereafter guide my notion of what joys (pleasures) I truly need.

5   *Of force:*   necessarily.

6 *just:* just, because woe will punish his forsaking of pleasure [as if that were a crime].

7–8 *woe which . . ./Shall therewith go:* woe, which shall be experienced along with the forsaking of pleasure.

8 *me to recure:* to cure me [of my taste for pleasure].

9 *fleeth.* Pronounced as two syllables.

10 *he]* *T*; that *E*. It is just possible in Wyatt's hand for 'he' to be misread as 'y'.

14 *a part]* *T*; apart *E*.

13–14 *rejoice . . ./Thus to sustain of each a part:* rejoice that you are thus able still to experience a part of joy and a part of pain – the new joy ('glad', l. 10) of not being enslaved to unreliable pleasure, and the new pain of escaping that pleasure, being without it, and fearing to be caught up in it again.

15 The speaker is apparently telling his heart not to give over the psychological state described in this song (in favour of renewed enslavement to that old pleasure).

15–16 *this song . . ./Welcome among my pleasant smart:* (?) this song [which is] welcome to me in my condition of pleasurable pain.

CVI. *E, D, A.*

Attributed to 'Tho' in margin of *E*; revisions in Wyatt's hand in *E*; in Wyatt sections of *A* and *D*.

9 *Is that ye would vouchsafe]* Is that ye would at last vouchsafe *N*'s suggested emendation to preserve the four-stress pattern in the third and fourth lines of each stanza.

11 *deserved.* Probably deservèd.

11–12 *I have not deserved to obtain/So high reward, but thus to serve in vain:* I have not deserved to obtain such a rich reward [as your love or favour] but only to serve you in vain as I do now.

16 *But]* *W*; For *E, D*.

18 *least]* *ed.*; lest *E*; last *N*. Both 'least' and 'last' fit the context, but 'lest' in Wyatt's own hand means 'least' (see CLIV, 69; CXLIX, 600); 'last' he spells with an 'a' (see CLIV, 61; CXLIX, 580, 621).

20 *Rejoice not at]* *W*; To rue upon *E, D*.

CVII. *E, D, A.*

Attributed to 'Tho.' in margin of *E*; in Wyatt sections of *A* and *D*.

2 *sue:* pursue.

5 *day]* inserted later by a hand other than the scribe's.

5–6 *strive . . ./Against the stream.* Proverbial, with the implication that such action is not only hard but foolish; see *Tilley* S927 and *ODEP* 627. Compare CCXXVI, 13, and CII, 27 (*M & T*).

11–12 *If then I burn to plain me so,/What may it avail me:* (?) If then I passionately desire to complain in this way, what good can it do me to complain; *or* if I burn then as a result of wanting to stay in the fire, what good can it do me to complain in this manner? The second reading depends on putting the comma after 'burn' rather than 'so'. I prefer the first reading because no other stanza has a third line with an internal caesura.

27 *treat*] entreat *D*, *A*.

33 *For in despair there is no rede:* (?) for a person in despair there is no effective counsel or help; *or* from a state of despair comes no good counsel or plan of action; 'Despair is a bad counsellor' (*M & T* 311). In either case the speaker apparently refers to his own despair.

34 *To want of ear speech is no speed:* speech is no use to one who lacks an ear. Presumably, if the meaning parallels that of l. 34, the speaker refers to himself as lacking an ear rather than to 'the causer' of his grief (l. 22).

35 *alive as dead:* alive but as if I were really dead.

CVIII. *E, D1, D2, T, NA.*

Attributed to 'Tho.' in margin of *E*; in Wyatt sections of *D* and *T*.

This poem may be an extended pun on the speaker's 'most' or greatest desire. The key phrase is 'dear heart' in l. 5. At first glance it refers to the speaker's lady and her love for him. But it also might refer to the speaker's own heart – his desire, his inclination to love – which he would have 'evermore' in his own power so that he would never again fall in love. The notes indicate that every phrase defining the speaker's 'most desire' can bear these two meanings. If I am right, the poem gives a pleasure like that of a riddle, except that we are challenged to find, not 'the meaning', but two contradictory 'meanings'.

T, like Wyatt's other editors, sees only one meaning. He entitles the poem: 'The lover rejoiceth the enjoying of his love.' He also restricts the poem to that meaning by emending l. 5's 'my dear heart' to 'my lady's heart'.

3–4 *it . . . to set my heart in rest:* 1) his lady's love; 2) the power to detach his heart from the earth's goods – as opposed to desiring and loving them.

5 *asked.* Probably askèd.
   naught but my dear heart] naught but my lady's heart *T*.
   my dear heart. See head-note.

8 *to moan*] *D1, D2, T, N;* moan *E*.

9 *a stormy blast:* 1) his lady's [temporary] rejection of him; 2) a newly intense desire of his lady and her love – the opposite of the detachment he wishes.

11 *seemed.* Probably seemèd: it seemed.

14 *revived.* Probably revivèd.

15 *sheweth.* Possibly pronounced as one syllable (shew'th).

Now Fortune sheweth herself . . . fair: 1) Fortune grants him his lady and her love; 2) Fortune grants him detachment. In terms of the poem's second meaning the speaker's emphasis on Fortune here and in ll. 1, 11, and 25 reveals his moral weakness. He desires to be detached from the goods which are governed by Fortune; but it is only Fortune, or chance, that yields that detachment. He rightly fears that such a detachment – as opposed to a genuine one resulting from stoic self-discipline – may not last (ll. 23–4).

16 *wonderly:* in a manner causing the speaker to feel wonder or awe.

17 *My most desire my hand may reach:* my hand may reach my greatest desire – that is, 1) my lady, 2) my heart, over whose desires I have control.

18 *My will:* what I desire – that is, 1) my lady, 2) the faculty of rational choice by which I assent to or dissent from my heart's desires.

20 *Her that hath power me to command:* 1) my lady; 2) my will.

22 *at my will:* at my command – that is, 1) my lady; 2) my desires.

24 *Save, that I have, to have it still:* except to have always that which I have now. See note to l. 15.

27 *sufferance:* patient endurance; suffering.

redress: compensation, reparation (the lady's love); remedy, relief (the power to detach his heart from the earth's goods).

CIX. *E, D, B, Stark, Folger, T, NA.*

A revision possibly in Wyatt's hand in *E*; attributed to 'Tho' in margin of *E*; subscribed 'Finis. Quod Wyatt' in *D* ('Quod' designates the author); in Wyatt sections of *D* and *T*; but attributed to Lord Rochford in *NA*.

John Hall composed a religious parody of this poem and suggested that it be sung to a musical setting he provided for his imitation of CCVIII; see Hall's *The Court of Virtue* (1565), ed. Fraser, pp. 169–72. Compare XCIV and CCVIII and head-notes.

T entitles the poem: 'The lover complaineth the unkindness of his love.'

7–8 *As lead to grave in marble stone/. . . as soon:* as soon as lead (the softest metal) is able to engrave [something] on a marble stone.

13 *affection.* Probably affectión (*Da*).

15 *Whereby:* as a result of which; wherefore.

19 *Think not he hath his bow forgot.* The lover is apparently predicting that Cupid will make the lady experience an unrequited love and thereby wreak vengeance on her (l. 21).

22 *makest.* Possibly pronounced as one syllable (mak'st): make fun of.

24 *Unquit:* unrequited; not repaid; without punishment.

26 *May chance thee lie*] *B, T;* thee lie *possibly W;* Perchance they lay *E.* Whoever changed *E*'s plural to a singular referent apparently overlooked the consequent need to revise 'Perchance'. There are no instances of 'perchance' used as a verb in *OED* or elsewhere in Wyatt. The sense is clearly parallel to l. 31: 'It may chance thee to.'

27 *nights*] *D, B, T, NA;* night *E.* 'Night' as an uninflected plural form was still used by Chaucer, but I cannot find any fifteenth- or sixteenth-century instances.

The winter nights: in or during the winter nights.

38 *ended is that we begun*] end that I have now begun *M*.

CX. *E, D.*

Attributed to 'Tho.' in margin of *E*; a correction possibly in hand of Wyatt; in Wyatt section of *D*.

4 Compare CIX, 7.

5 *But hap and hit or else hit not:* but luck and hitting or not hitting the target [are].

6 *As uncertain as is the wind.* Proverbial; see *Tilley* W412 and *ODEP* 695 (*M & T*).

10-11 *With pity when I first began/Your ... heart for to constrain:* when I first attempted to move your heart by eliciting your pity.

13 *of your goodness:* as a result of your goodness. Compare LXXX, 18.

19 *do revert:* come back.

18-20 *Trust me I trust to temper it so/Not for to care which do revert :/All shall be one in wealth or woe:* believe me I intend to compose my complaint and the heart from which it flows in such a way that I shall not care what responses of yours come back to me as a result: it will not matter to me if our relationship ends in well-being or woe.

21 *fancy.* See the head-note to CXXVII and the poem itself for a definition.

21-2 *fancy ruleth though right say nay,/Even as the good man kissed his cow:* the distortions of fancy rule our affections though our sense of what is genuinely valuable says 'no', a truth demonstrated by the fact that an otherwise good man was led by his fancy to kiss his cow. The lines allude to the proverb 'Every man as he loves, quoth the good man, when he kissed his cow' (*Tilley* M103 and *ODEP* 178). (*M & T*)

23-4 *None other reason can ye lay/But as who sayeth, 'I reck not how':* [because fancy rules you] you can offer no other reason for your affections except to say, 'I do not know how [it is that I love one person rather than another'].

CXI. *D*, *E*.

In Wyatt section of *D*.

Because the leaf is torn in *E*, the first part of each line is missing. An attribution has probably also been torn away.

I have printed *D*. *E*'s partial lines are identical with *D*'s.

The Latin tag *in aeternum* means 'unto eternity' or 'forever'; in l. 1, with a distortion of grammar, it might mean 'in eternity' or 'in heaven'.

1 *determed.* Probably determèd: determined.

1-2 *In aeternum I was once determed/For to have loved:* 1) I decided once to love someone forever; 2) in eternity I was destined [by God] to love [God? a human being?].

2 *affirmed.* Probably affirmèd.

2-3 *loved ... heart.* In *D* these words are spelled 'lovid' and 'herte' and are possibly disyllabic.

3 *confirmed.* Probably confirmèd.

9 *trace:* dance.

15 *to stand in her grace.* Compare Chaucer, *Troilus* III, 472, 1176 (*M & T*).

14-15 *That ... my troth had taken place ... to stand in her grace:* so that my fidelity to her had found a place in her favour.

18 *feeble building is on feeble ground.* Alludes to the proverb, 'Build on a good foundation'; see *Tilley* F619 (*Da*).

21–2 *In aeternum ... from my heart I cast/That I had first determined for the best :* (?) I cast the idea of 'forever' out of my heart – the idea that I had at first decided on as the best; *or* I cast out of my heart forever what I had at first decided on as the best: [that is, the idea of 'forever', the lady, or my love for her].

23 *thought :* 1) idea, attitude; 2) love (*N*).

CXII. *E, D.*

Attributed to 'Tho.' in margin of *E*; in Wyatt section of *D*.

See CCXXV for what may be another version of this poem.

4, 8, 12, 16, 20 *sighs*] *E*; sigh'st *N*.
5 *waste :* waste away.
    sighs] *D*; sight *E*.
9 *knowest.* Possibly monosyllabic (know'st).
9–10 *that no redress/Is thus to pine :* that to pine in this way is no remedy.
10–11 *to speak ... it is remedyless :* to speak is no remedy.
15 *vaileth.* Possibly monosyllabic (vail'th).
    To shake it off vaileth not to muse : 'It is of no avail to consider how the yoke may be shaken off, after it is once fastened on the neck' (*N* 577).

CXIII. *E, D.*

Attributed to 'Tho.' in margin of *E*; in Wyatt section of *D*.

The poem ridicules the Petrarchan contraries (stanzas 1 and 2) and conceit of the lost heart (stanza 3) only to affirm them in the fifth stanza as miracles of love (*M & T*).

2 *degree :* in medieval natural science, a stage of intensity of an elementary quality of bodies (heat, cold, moisture, dryness).

3 *point :* smallest portion of time; a moment.

1–5 *to agree/Two contraries in one degree/And in one point ... is impossible :* to make two contrary qualities of the same thing have the same stage of intensity at one moment in time is impossible; that is, a thing cannot be both hot in the second degree and cold in the second degree at the same time. The second stanza is a particular example of the first stanza's general proposition.

12, 17 *liveth.* Probably monosyllabic (liv'th).

11–15 Compare II, 11–15, and CXLII, 7–15.

16 *say what who saith :* let anyone say whatever he says; I don't care what anyone says.

16–18 *'Twixt life and death .../There liveth no life .../They join so near :* there can be no life between life and death since life and death come so close together in time.

CXIV. *E, A.*

In Wyatt section of A.

M (74) remarks that the emendation of l. 10 makes it clear that the poem is about trust in God during a period of political trouble, not, as *N*'s emendation to 'in her' suggests, about love. *F* notes the psalm-like quality of the language in ll. 5–6, 10, 13–14, and 18.

7 *languor:* mental distress, sorrow.
9 *despaired.* Probably despairèd.
10 *in him did*] *M*; in hid *E, A*; in heaven did *M & T*; in her did *N*.
11 *thought*] *A*; though *E*.
14 *assured.* Probably assurèd.
19 *make your hope your health retain:* enable your hope to maintain your sense of well-being.
20 *And me also*] *A*; And make me also *E*.

CXV. *E, T.*

In Wyatt section of *T*.

T entitles the poem: 'To his love that had given him answer of refusal.'
1, 11, 13 I have ascribed the lines to speakers. Lines 11–12 may begin an 'unfinished third stanza' (*N, M & T, F*). But if they are spoken by the lady, the sense of the poem is still clear.

1 *Th'answer.* Does the lady answer to this effect: 'I have never led you to think there was anything but casual friendship between us (ll. 6–7, 13–14), so don't allow your heart to suffer for love of me'? Part of the poem's interest lies in our guessing an answer which satisfies the conditions of being blameless (l. 5), 'friendly' (l. 18), and designed to save pain (l. 19) while simultaneously appalling the speaker (l. 3).
3 *appalled:* 1) made pale; 2) dismayed.
5 *Since I of blame no cause can well express:* since I cannot honestly state that you are to blame.
10 *maketh.* Possibly monosyllabic (mak'th).
9–10 *another may be glad/With that that . . . maketh me sad:* 1) another man may be made glad with your friendship, a fact that makes me sad (that is, I can't bear sharing even your friendship); 2) another man may be made glad by your love, the denial of which makes me sad. I think the second reading more probable.
11–12 *Another? . . ./Free heart may not be bound but by desert:* 1) 'Another' (one other) implies that I might have only one other friend, and why should I be limited to one other? My free heart may be restricted in giving friendship only by the presence or absence of merit in the potential friends. 2) 'Another' implies that *you* have some exclusive claim on me, probably that of a lover, and why should you think that? I shall choose to give my love only to someone who really deserves me.

15 *But*] *ed.*; and *E, T.*
  avaunt: boast.

16 *Of faithful will there is nowhere:* nowhere is there anyone of faithful will.

18 *good:* good, dear friend.

19 *slay'th*] *M*; sayeth *E.*

18-19 *call again that friendly word/That slay'th your friend in saving of his pain:* take back that seemingly friendly answer that in fact slays your friend in the process of trying to save him pain. *M & T,* retaining 'sayeth' (l. 19), find the stanza obscure, speculate that 'friendly' (l. 18) might be ironical, but finally agree with R. C. Harrier's view in *NQ* (1953), 234, that the speaker 'is asking the lady to revert to her previous attitude, before the harsh answer, when she said "I am your friend" ' (sayeth 'your friend'). But that interpretation makes no sense of l. 20 in which the speaker would have the 'friendly word' deprecated as a jest. *T,* also troubled, rewrote the lines:

> Now good then call again that bitter word
> That touched your friend so near with pangs of pain.

M (85) would retain *T*'s 'bitter' and emend 'sayeth' to 'slayeth'; but he does not explain 'saving of his pain'.

22 *doth*] *T*; not in *E.*

21-2 *Late or too soon let that not rule the gain/Wherewith free will doth true desert retain:* let not that answer of yours, either late or early in our relationship, govern the remedy [you could apply to my heart], the remedy whereby [your] free will holds on to [my] true desert – [that is, the remedy whereby you love me].

CXVI. *E.*

In Wyatt's hand.

CXVII. *E, T.*

In Wyatt's hand in *E,* with many revisions by Wyatt, most of which indicate that he was composing in *E*; in Wyatt section of *T.*

M & T analyse the variants as evidence of the stages in which Wyatt composed the poem. But the analysis does not take into account the fact that the first stanza is written in the darker ink of some of the revisions later in the poem and therefore might have been composed after the other stanzas.

T entitles the poem: 'To his unkind love.'

1-4 *What rage ... pleasant sweet*]

> What rage is this? What furor of excess?
> What pow'r, what poison doth my mind oppress?
> Within the bones to rankle doth not cesse
> The poisoned pleasantness. *E.*

5 *mine eyes*] my cheeks *E.*

6 *still away sleepless*] still sleepless away *E*: (the body), sleepless, wears itself away continually.

8 *sustain*] redress *E2*; sustain *E1*.

9 *In deep wide wound*] Into wide wound *E2*; The stroke doth stretch *E1*.

10 *To*] in *E*.

   return] to return *E*.

   cured. Probably curèd.

9–10 *In deep wide wound the deadly stroke doth turn,/To cured scar that never shall return. T* emended 'cured' to 'cureless'. *N* suggests that the wound, though cured, leaves a scar which never can be removed. But the stroke is 'deadly' and the first two stanzas and the 'plaint' of l. 14 do not suggest that the wound has been genuinely cured. *E* suggests that 'In' might mean 'Into'. If so, and if 'that' (l. 10) refers to 'wound' rather than 'scar', the sense is: 'The deadly thrust and the opening made by it turn into a deep, wide wound that never shall return to the cured condition indicated by a scar.'

11 *rejoice :* take pleasure in; feel joy on account of.

   goodly turn : (?) successful trick or stratagem in a contest; *or* good deed (meant ironically).

13 *cure*] ruth *E*.

14 *plaint*] death *E2*; woes *E1*.

15 *fell :* savage; cruel.

16 *rebel*] unkind *E*.

17 *be loved*] ed.; beloved *E*.

   Once may thou love, never be loved again : may you love someone once but never be loved again [by anyone but me, and hence not by that person you love].

19 *spites of just disdain :* the hurts that you may feel as a result of [the god of love's and your lover's] disdain for your love, a disdain that will be just because it repays your disdain of me.

20 *threat :* menace.

17–20 *Once may thou love . . . cruel heart*]

   Mightst thou so love, never beloved again.
   Mightst thou so love, and never more attain.
   Might wrathful love so threat you with disdain
      Thy cruel heart to reprove. *E2*
      (Thy cruelty to prove. *E1*)

CXVIII. D.

Subscribed 'ThW' in *D*. *Harrier* (36) reads 'TH' or scribbles.

1 *betime :* in good time; early in the day.

2 *eyes ye cannot*] ed.; I yez can not *D*; eyes can it not *N*; eye ye cannot *M & T*.

7 *cannot blind*] *F*; not blind *D*, *changed to* can te not blind.

15 *themselves but fools*] *N*; themself but fool *D*.

13–16 *Although they . . . take heed.* The present tense generalizes the past behaviour and experience of those who have been found out and will therefore betray others.

18 *leave it in your lap :* tell you plainly (*M & T*).

CXIX. D.

In a Wyatt section of *D*. Harrier (38–45) argues that the poems in this section of *D* are not all by Wyatt and excludes this one in particular.

8 *Which is:* and the result is.

14 *let to love her still:* cease to love her always.

27 *unhappy:* unlucky.

28 *above my poor degree:* above my low social position. Compare CXCVII, 53.

CXX. D, T.

Attributed to 'W' in *D*; in Wyatt section of *T*. *T* entitles the poem: 'The lover describeth his being taken with sight of his love.'

1 *unwarely:* unwarily, unexpectedly, without preparation.

5–6 *Thorough mine eye ... down unto my heart.* Compare Chaucer, *CT* I (A), 1096–7.

7 *glide*] *T*; slide *D*.

8 *face*] *T*; place *D*.

pale and wan. Compare Chaucer, *Troilus* IV, 235 (*M & T*).

11 *upon*] *T*; on *D*.

13 *stert:* started.

CXXI. D.

In a Wyatt section of *D*.

1 *will needs:* insist.

2 *Take it in worth such as I have:* be content with such singing as I have to offer.

9 *But fast at board and wake abed:* except [a sound that causes me] to do without food at table and lie awake in bed.

10–12 *Such tune the temper to my song/To wail my wrong, that I want tears/ To wail my wrong:* such hammers determine the character of my song as one in which I cry about the wrong done to me, [the result of such weeping being] that I [now] lack tears to bewail the wrong done me.

14 *decay*] *N*; decays *D*.

17–18 *though it be woe/To hear me plain:* although it be a source of woe to others to hear me complain.

19 *untuned.* Probably untunèd.

23 *strain:* squeeze; seize in claws; constrain.

27 *game.* Ironic.

CXXII. B.

Ascribed to 'T. W.' in *B*.

Apparently the lovers have been separated by fate (ll. 3–5, 8), and the speaker is enjoining a Christian resignation to the inevitable.

5 *Make thou a virtue of a constraint :*   make a virtue of necessity (*M & T*). Proverbial; see *Tilley* V73 (*Da*).

7 *Min is too much :*   (?) continuing to remember our relationship is too much to bear.

8 *for me*] *M & T*; me for me *B*.

9 *cure :*   (?) remedy for your unhappiness; *or* care, concern.

CXXIII. *B.*

If *Viat* in the Latin inscription at the head of the poem is 'Wyatt', he probably composed the poem. The name is surrounded by 'Innocence', 'Truth', and 'Faith'. Then, almost punning on the spatial 'surrounding' of the name with virtues, the adaptation of Psalm xvii, 9 (xvi in the Vulgate) says: 'My enemies have surrounded me.'

This poem was amost certainly written at the time of Wyatt's imprisonment in 1536. On 19 May 1536 he may have seen the execution of Anne Boleyn from his cell in the Tower. The poem very probably refers to her execution rather than to that of her alleged lovers, who were put to death on Tower Hill out of sight of Wyatt's cell (*M & T* 415 corrects *L* 32–5). The Latin inscription would suitably describe Wyatt's situation as he was beleaguered by his enemies despite his innocence and virtues but was at the same time protected from spiritual harm by those virtues.

The first two stanzas of the poem are a free imitation of Seneca's *Phaedra*, 1123–1140. The refrain, *circa Regna tonat*, is l. 1140 of the passage. In the play's context it refers to Jove and means 'he thunders around thrones' (*M & T*).

1–2 *Who list his wealth ... retain,/Himself let him unknown contain :*   let the person who wishes to retain his sense of well-being keep himself unknown.

4 *Where the return stands by disdain :*   where you will experience disdain as you make your forced exit.

12 *depart :*   leave [me].

13 *estate :*   high position.

14 *Who hastes to climb seeks to revert :*   who hastens to climb is in fact seeking to fall back down.

19 *For all favour, glory, or might :*   whatever one's favour, glory, or might.

22–3 *Wit helpeth not defence too yerne,/Of innocency to plead or prate :*   (?) the intelligence to plead or prattle of one's innocence does not help one's defence too well.

24 *Bear low :*   keep yourself in a humble position. Conjunction with the command to give the stern or stearing-gear of the boat to God suggests that 'Bear low' is also a nautical metaphor. Perhaps it refers to keeping the boat low in the water, though I have not found that meaning in the *OED*. *M & T* compare the line with a line from John Skelton's *Bouge of Court* (*c.* 1498–9), ed. Alexander Dyce, p. 250: 'Holde up the helme, loke up, and let God steer.' To 'hold up the helm' means to steer the boat away from rather than into the wind.

CXXIV. *BM, Folger, T.*

In Wyatt section of *T*, who entitles the poem: 'The lover prayeth not to be disdained, refused, mistrusted, nor forsaken.'

I follow *M* (86–7) in choosing as copy-text *BM*, in which the refrain of the first stanza constitutes the first words of the second, and so on, with all the refrains gathered in the final stanza. *M* also argues that the half-lines should all rhyme in -ot; I think that probably was the point of a reviser of *BM* and emend accordingly.

2   *leave*] *Folger, T*; pain *BM*.
3   *wot*] *Folger, T*; know *BM*.
4   *it not*] *M*; nothing *BM, Folger*; ye not *T*.
     honestly] *T*; honesty *Folger*; faithfully *BM*.
7   *ne*] *M*; nor *BM, Folger, T*.
     unjust] *Folger, T*; unkind *BM*.
8   *Sith*] *M*; Since *Folger, T*.

     by lot of fantasy: as a result of the chance of my amorous inclination having fixed on you as its object. For the complex meanings of 'fantasy' that probably pertain here, see the head-note to CXXVII.
9   *the careful knot*: the knot or bond of love which makes me full of care.
8–9   *Sith that by lot of fantasy/The careful knot needs knit I must*] *Folger and T substantially*; My heart is yours until I die/And that in short space ye shall it find *BM*.
17   *Ne*] *M*; not *BM, Folger, T*.

CXXV. *T.*

In Wyatt section of *T*, who entitles the poem: 'The lover blameth his love for renting of the letter he sent her.'

1   *Sufficed not*: did it not suffice. Probably sufficèd.
9   *Use*: employ, as a means to your end of being cruel.
12   *This*: (?) my death. But probably a couplet defining 'This' and perfecting a sonnet is missing.

CXXVI. *T.*

In Wyatt section of *T*, who entitles the poem: 'The lover complaineth his estate.'

3   *fee*: 1) estate; 2) office involving profit; 3) wage, salary; 4) reward.
4   *Of all my loss to have the gain*. Alludes to the proverb 'No man loses but another wins'; see Tilley M337 and R136 (*Da*).
6, 12, 18, 24   *other have that I deserve*. Echoes proverb 'One sows, another reaps'; see *Tilley* S691 (*Da*).
15–16   *I cannot find/Once to refrain*: I cannot find the strength ever to refrain from serving those who do not reward me.
28   *pensive*: gloomy, sad.

SONGS (2)

CXXVII. *E*, *A* (9-36), *D* (1-12, 17-36), *Folger*.

In Wyatt sections of *A* and *D*.

'Fancy', used interchangeably with 'fantasy', has a complex set of related meanings: 1) the faculty and process of forming in the mind images of things perceived by the senses, of combining these images (awake or in dreams), and of consigning them to and summoning them from the memory (you may exercise 'fancy' by closing your eyes and imagining an object you have just seen, one you saw yesterday, and then the two together); 2) a delusive imagining; 3) a capricious or arbitrary preference; 4) amorous inclination, love. The appetites of fallen men can influence the workings of fancy, distorting the image of what has been perceived into an image of what one wants to perceive; hence the 'delusive imaginings' and 'capricious preferences' of lovers who are 'blind' – that is, see more beauty in the beloved than anyone else can and perhaps underestimate those they do not love.

As I construe this poem, 'fancy' throughout is the lady's fancy, 'faith' throughout is the male lover's. The lover implicitly argues that the lady's promiscuous appetite for pleasure, including sexual pleasure – hinted in 'lust' of l. 17 – makes her fancy 'flit' (l. 14) from man to man, making each appear more lovable than he in fact is, and causing the lady to fall in love with each in turn. The lover, who has been neglected by her fancy, wants it to become the ally of his faith – that is, he wants her to direct her fancy ('set ... fantasy', l. 26) to making an image of *his* worth, which is proved by his fidelity ('faith') to be more genuine than that of other men. He also wants her consequent love to be 'steadfast' (l. 28).

Compare Wyatt's use of 'fancy' and 'fantasy' in this poem with the use of the terms in XCIII; CIV, 20; CX, 21; CXXIV, 8; CXCIX; CCXXVIII; CCXXXVII; CCXLIV, 11; CCL, 4; and CCLI, 1-2. For further discussion of Wyatt's use of the terms, see D. M. Friedman, 'Wyatt and the Ambiguities of Fancy' (*FR*).

2   *As I deserve and shall*]   *Folger*; As my deserving shall *E*.
    shall: shall continue to deserve.

5   *cannot attain*]   not attain *Folger*; not t'attain (know not [how] to attain) *M*.

10   *further my true heart*:   further the cause of my faithful love as an object of the lady's love.

12   *for to*] *D*; to *E*, *Folger*.

17   *at his lust*:   1) at his pleasure; 2) as a result of his desire; 3) as a result of his sexual desire, or lust.

23   *That may me only ease*:   that alone may ease me.

26   *Set once your fantasy*:   on at least one occasion direct your fancy.

28   *steadfast remedy*] *D*; steadfastness remedy *E*, *A*; help and remedy *Folger*.

29, 32   *he*] ye *Folger*. In *Folger*, the speaker addresses the lady in all of the last three stanzas. In *E*, *A*, *D* the speaker in the penultimate stanza talks about the lady's fancy, with the lady as an implied audience.

30 *undertake:* (?) guarantee to cure; *or* enter into combat with.

34 *As:* because.

CXXVIII. *E* (1–41), *B* (1–41), *D.*

Attributed to 'Tho.' in margin of *E*; revision in Wyatt's hand; subscribed 'Finis. Quod Wyatt' in *D* ('Quod' designates the author).

1 *mischief:* 1) harm done me by another; 2) a condition of distress.

2–8, 42–8. *I suffer grief,/For of relief/Since I have none/My lute and I . . ./ Shall . . . moan:* I suffer grief, because ('For') – since I have no relief – my lute and I shall moan. This strict construction of the syntax suggests that at least one of the causes of the speaker's grief is his moaning. Had Wyatt not intended this reading he could have used 'And' instead of 'For'.

13 *Mourning.* *N* (577) suggests that, 'As a contrast of situations seems here intended, we ought to read, probably, *Or mirth* or moan.'

26 *pervert:* perverted, perverse; wicked.

38 *lust:* 1) desire (the speaker's primary sense); 2) sexual desire (a sense we may perceive).

41 *Thus]* *D, B;* For *E.*

42–8 *I suffer . . . sigh and moan]* *D; not in E or B.*

CXXIX. *E, D, NA, Folger, T.*

Attributed to 'Tho.' in margin of *E*; subscribed 'Finis. Quod Wyatt' in *D* ('Quod' designates the author); in Wyatt section of *T.*

The eight-line stanza is mistakenly divided in two in *E.*

T entitles the poem: 'The lover's sorrowful state maketh him write sorrowful songs, but *Souche* his love may change the same.'

The repetition of the word 'such' in ll. 27, 29, and 31 suggests a pun on the name of Mary Souche, one of Jane Seymour's maids of honour. Holbein painted her portrait (*M & T*). In l. 29 of *E* a blank is filled by 'souche' in a hand other than the scribe's. *T* spells the word 'Souch' in each instance.

4 *proved.* Probably provèd.

15 *overthwart:* crossing [me]; unfavourable.

17–20 *no man . . . light.* Proverbial; see *Tilley* M80 (*Da*).

CXXX. *E, D, B* (1–5).

Attributed to 'Tho.' in margin of *E*; in Wyatt section of *D.*

The stanza-form is like that of **CXXVIII** except that a four-stress line replaces the two two-stress lines at the end of **CXXVIII**. *M & T*, *N*, and *F* think it is a song for the lute.

The poem's interest turns in part on three meanings of 'life' and 'liberty'. If one takes the poem as the speaker's complaint to a lady for disdaining his love, 'life' and 'liberty' mean primarily the renewed vitality the speaker will feel if he is granted the freedom to protest his love to the lady – a vitality that will enable him to endure even her cruelty (ll. 10–11) if she still refuses to requite his love. But secondarily those key words also mean the well-being the speaker will experience if he is freed from loving her – a liberty the lady can somehow help him achieve (ll. 30, 35), perhaps by not teasing him with hope. If the context is other than amorous – for example, political – 'life' is the fuller and happier existence the speaker will experience if he is set free from the restraints, perhaps those of imprisonment, currently imposed on him.

1–2 *If chance assigned/Were to my mind*: if chance were appointed to serve under my mind; if my mind had power over fortune.

7 *only*] D; *not in* E.

14 *Lacking my life for liberty*: (?) lacking my life as a result of [lacking my] liberty.

19–20 *If th'one be past/Th'other doth waste*: if liberty is gone life wastes away.

22–5 *And so I drive/As yet alive/Although I strive/With misery*: and so I suffer as one who is still alive even though I contend with misery [itself].

27–8 *Looking for death/And loss of life for liberty*: expecting physical death, and expecting complete loss of vitality as a result of loss of liberty.

CXXXI. E, D, B.

Attributed to 'Tho' in margin of *E*; in Wyatt section of *D*.

5 *enforce me so*: use force on myself in such a way.

12 *And* might mean 'if', though 'also' makes a coordinating conjunction more likely.

13 *pleased*. Probably pleasèd.

19 *yslain*] *Da*; *slain* E.
    outright. In *E* 'owte right', and probably trisyllabic.

15–19 *Unless that be too light/And that ye would ye might/See ... one yslain outright*: unless slow death be too slight a pain and you wish you might see a person killed in a single instant.

24 *express*: definite, explicit; purposeful.

23–5 *Would God forthwith ye would ... My heart oppress*: would to God you would immediately press my heart to death.

32 *mine excess*] my distress *N*.

31–2 *the excess/Of mine excess*: (?) the extreme pain of my extreme love.

34 *Defamed*. Probably defamèd.

CXXXII. E, B, Bannatyne.

Attributed to 'Tho.' in margin of *E*; l. 21 in Wyatt's hand.

The version in *Bannatyne* of lines 1–8, 33–40, 17–24, 9–16 was ascribed to a sixteenth-century Scottish poet, Alexander Scott, by George Bannatyne, who compiled the manuscript in 1568; see *The Poems of Alexander Scott*, ed. by A. K. Donald, pp. 47–8 (*FR*). The first part of this three-part argument may be a revision and expansion of the Scottish poem, but it is equally probable that the Scottish version derives from the English.

The third part seems to be a statement in the same *persona* as the first; it is not the second of two replies to the first part, as suggested by John MacQueen (*M* 118–19), nor the synthesis of a thesis and antithesis, as suggested by *M & T*.

5 *grounded*] *B*; ground is *E*; ground of *Bannatyne*: settled into the ground; firmly established.

2–5 *Learn ye* ...|*At me* ...|*No ways that may*|*The* ... *grief remove*: learn of me who may in no way remove the grief.

14 *That*: that snare or trap of love.

17 *To love and to be wise!* An allusion to a popular saying, the earliest form of which appears to be *Amare et sapere vix deo conceditur*: 'to love and to be wise is scarcely possible even for a god' (*M & T*). Compare *Tilley* L558 (*Da*).

18 *To rage with good advice*: 'to be mad, and yet govern madness with reason' (*N* 579).

23–4 *At once that can*|*To love and to be wise*: that can love and be wise at the same time.

25, 32 *diverse*: 1) different in character; 2) perverse; 3) various, several.

26 *Such pains that*] *ed.*; Such that *E, B, Bannatyne*.

37–9 *Repentance* ...|*A poor treasure*|*Without measure*: repentance is a poor reward for loving, and it is boundless.

41+ *The Answer*] *B*.

43 *ill*] *B*; evil *E*.

43–5 *Though ill with such it prove*|*Which* ... *use*|*Love to misuse*: though it proves to be an evil with those who are accustomed to misuse love.

48 *refuse*: refusal to love (though *N* (579) suggests 'for their being refused').

52 *deserts*: kinds of conduct which deserve unhappy consequences.

58, 65 *not be*] *B*; not to be *E*.

62 *chances*] *B*; chance *E*.

70 *Know them*] *B*; Know it *E*.

but that he says] *ed.*; but he that says *E, B*.

79–80 *Then* ... *the gain*] Then though ye feign/Pleasure for pain *B*.

Then though some feign|*And leese the gain*: (?) then though some pretend that the fire of love is genuinely painful and thereby lose the profits of loving; *or* then though some pretend to love and thereby lose, or destroy, the profits that come with loving.

81+ *The Answer to This*] *B*.

82–3 *Who most doth slander love*|*The deed must always prove*: the deed of loving [and its results] must always prove who it is that most slanders love, [not mere words].

84–6 *Truth shall excuse*|*That you accuse*|*For slander and reprove*: the truth [established by experience] shall exonerate me whom you accuse of slander and the act of reproving or censuring love.

87–9 *Not by refuse*|*But by abuse*|*You most do slander love*: you slander love the most, not by refusing to love, but by misrepresenting the nature of love.

94 *colour all the care:* disguise, misrepresent the pain.

100-101 *But from that taste/Ye vow the fast:* but you vow that you will fast from the food that tastes that way – that is, you will avoid loving and being unwise.

102 *syns:* sixes and fives, one of the luckiest throws in dice (a conflation of French *six-cinq,* which became in English 'sice cinque').

103 *Ambs-ace:* double ace, the lowest throw at dice; hence, bad luck.

102-4 *On syns though run your dice,/Ambs-ace may haste/Your pain to waste:* though you may be lucky in love for a while, bad luck may eventually hasten the pain you will feel in love into spiritual decay or destruction.

113 Feeleth *E.* Probably monosyllabic (feel'th).

not] N; yet *E, B.*

119-21 *Who so doth plain,/You best do feign/Such fire:* (?) whoever it is that complains about the fire of love, you are certainly the one who best pretends to feel that fire.

CXXXIII. *H48, B* (1-8, 13-20).

In *H48* follows six poems ascribed to Wyatt, with the last of which it shares a page. *Harrier* (78) thinks the absence of an explicit ascription makes its authorship doubtful.

7 *would fain:* would gladly achieve what it wills.

11 *lack of will:* (?) the beloved's lack of willingness to love in return.

13 *Foy:* faith (an exclamation).

14 *sustain:* bear up; endure.

16 *obtain:* prevail; succeed; prosper.

17 *will] B;* wills *H48.*

Thus wishers wants their will: thus there is lacking to wishers what they will.

19 *they that will not will:* those, like the beloved, who will not will the love of another.

CXXXIV. *D.*

Followed in *D* by 'Finis. Quod W.' ('Quod' designates the author).

4 *grame:* sorrow.

10 *strong:* oppressive (*Da*).

16 *Nother:* neither.

CXXXV. *D.*

In a Wyatt section of *D.*

3 *How:* however.

4 *what:* whatever.

6 *diffuse:* doubtful in their meaning.

10 *Neither of joy nor pain:* instead, as in the case of this poem, they will be exhortations to enjoy sexual pleasure while one can.

11 *sip*] *ed.*; sy *D, changed to* skip.

12 *over the lip:* (?) on the lip.

13 A line is evidently missing in this stanza, very probably after l. 12.

14 *withouten taste:* untasted (*F*).

33 *Delight shall quit the cost:* pleasure shall be a return for what you have to expend.

35 *Small labour is to climb:* it takes little effort to climb the tree to pick the fruit.

36 *treasure:* the body as a means to sexual pleasure.

41-3 *If this be under mist/And not well plainly wist,/Understand me who list:* if this text be obscure and not quite plainly understood, let the person who wishes to understand me do so.

44 *I reck not a bean:* I care not a bit. The phrase echoes the proverbs 'not worth a bean' (*Tilley* B118) and 'not to care a pin' (*ODEP* 78).

CXXXVI. *T, B.*

In Wyatt section of *T,* who entitles the poem: 'The lover's case cannot be hidden however he dissemble.'

Some of *T*'s readings (ll. 25, 26, 32, 38) cannot be explained as editorial sophistications of *B* or a common original. We therefore have two independent textual traditions, with at least some of the variants resulting very probably from revision by the poet. I print the text of *T* because its readings seem generally preferable and therefore more likely the result of revision.

1 *cast:* turned to the side.

3 *fixed.* Probably fixèd.

9-10 *Fain would ye find a cloak/Your burning fire to hide.* Alludes to the proverb 'Fire cannot be hidden in flax'; see *Tilley* F255 (*Da*).

13-14 *Ye cannot love so guide/That it no issue win:* you cannot guide or control love in such a way as to prevent it from finding a way of showing itself.

17 *For cause:* because.

22 *in*] from *B.*

Yourself in love to quit: to clear yourself in respect to love [as a charge made against you].

25 *Your sighs*] Causes *B.*

Your sighs you fet from far: you fetch [explanations for] your sighs from distant causes.

26 *wry*] wrap *B:* spread a cover over; hide.

27 *ne'er the nar:* never the nearer to [hiding your woe].

32 *Who puts your heart to pain*] the cause of all your pain *B.*

38 *such frowning*] dissembling *B.*

CXXXVII. B, T.

In Wyatt section of *T*, who entitles the poem: 'The lover sendeth his complaints and tears to sue for grace.'

N suggests that Wyatt may have had in mind Petrarch's *Rime* 153 (*M & T* 282), which is the source of III.

4 *reverse:* send back.

12 *nourished.* Probably nourishèd.

9–12 *For though . . . and fed.* From Virgil's *Aeneid* IV, 366: 'The bristling Caucasus gave birth to you amid hard rocks, and the Hyrcanean tigers gave you suck' (*N*).

18 *of*] or *T*.

17–22 *as the water soft . . . /Hard stones doth pierce . . . /So in her stony heart/ My plaints . . . shall grave.* The allusion to water's piercing stone is proverbial; see *Tilley* D618. The comparison comes ultimately from Petrarch's *Rime* 265, ll. 9–14 (*M & T* 322). Wyatt may have got it from Serafino (*N* 548).

32 *a*] *T*; an (?) *B*.

CXXXVIII. T.

In Wyatt section of *T*, who entitles the poem: 'The lover suspected blameth ill tongues.' But it is probably not a love poem and 'was probably written during one of the periods when W[yatt] was in danger from his enemies in 1536, 1538, or 1540' (*M & T* 435).

2 *suspect:* suspicion.

4 *once:* one day; at some future time.

3–4 *truth . . . time shall . . . detect.* Alludes to the proverb 'Time reveals all things'; see *Tilley* T333 (*Da*).

9–12 *Such sauce . . . God send them part.* Expands the proverb 'To be served with the same sauce'; see *Tilley* S99 (*Da*).

CXXXIX. E (1–16, 21–28), D (1–8), D2.

Ascribed to 'Wyat' in margin of *E*.

A slightly different version of the first three stanzas was set to music by Thomas Cornish in Henry VIII's song-book (*M & T* 309). Feste sings another version of the opening lines in *Twelfth Night* IV, 2, 78–9. This poem may therefore be an expansion of a popular song.

Réponse is 'the answer' to *Le plaintif* or 'the complainer'.

1–2 *Robin:* a common name for a shepherd-lover in English and French medieval poetry.

2 *Jolly:* young; good-looking; amorous.

3 *leman:* sweetheart.

15–16 *women's love . . . wind.* Proverbial; see *Tilley* W698 (*Da*).

17 *yet:* nevertheless.

17–20 *If that . . . thy part*] *D*; not in *E*, *with consequent confusion of speech headings.*

22 *abide their turn:* 1) wait their turn [for the lady's affection]; 2) tolerate the turning, or infidelity, of women. The two meanings in the poem are echoed in the two verbs of l. 24; the speaker 'lacks' the love of women because he cannot wait his turn; he also 'mourns' women's turning instead of tolerating it.

23–4 *can no way prove/In love but:* can find by experience no outcome in love except.

24 *lack and mourn.* See note to l. 22.

27 *others' fires*] *D2*; other fires *E*. In *D2 Réponse* suggests that *Le plaintif* have sex with the wives of other men, thereby avoiding the harm of being deserted by a lady in whose fidelity he has trusted. *E* might refer to abandoning love altogether for some other kinds of consoling behaviour; but *E* does not make sense of l. 28.

CXL. *E, H78.*

Attributed to 'Tho.' in margin of *E*, to 'T. W.' in *H78*.

The first three stanzas of the poem imitate the octave of Petrarch's *Rime* 199 (*M & T* 325) with varying degrees of freedom. The first stanza and ll. 11–12 translate the Italian fairly closely. Lines 7–9 expand Petrarch's 'sweet, open fingers'. Stanza three combines the allusion to Nature and the pearl metaphor which are not combined in Petrarch; and its first three lines probably take some inspiration from a passage in Petrarch's octave in which he describes the glove that covers the ivory and roses of the hand. The last two stanzas depart strikingly from Petrarch who has Love 'consent' to display the lady's naked hand and then, after the passage on the glove, reflects on the inconstancy of human beauy demonstrated in the death of Laura. Wyatt uses the imperative form of 'consent' to 'introduce a characteristically urgent, personal plea' to his mistress (*M & T* 325).

3 *distressed*] *ed.*; distrast *E. N* takes 'distrast' as 'distract' (pulled apart, racked); 'distressed' (subjected to severe strain) is closer to Petrarch and seems more probable.

6 *restrain:* hold in confinement.

8 *Departed right:* 'Separated in just proportion one from the other' (*N* 575).

10 *begone*] *H78*; bygone *E*.

Goodly begone. Tillyard (167) suggests 'beautifully adorned (with rings, etc.)' or 'exquisitely fashioned in itself' or themselves. Both have precedent in Chaucer, *Romaunt of the Rose*, 943; *CT* III (*D*), 606. But the following line suggests an intended contrast with 'alone': perhaps 'gracious or kind when surrounded or encompassed ("begone") by another hand and yet cruel when left alone to make gestures of rejection'.

18 *repair:* adorn, ornament.

21 *demesne:* possession (of real estate) as one's own, to do with as one wishes; 'demesne', 'service' (l. 22), and 'strain' (l. 27) are probably related in a metaphor based on feudal land tenure. The lady possesses the lover's heart 'in demesne' and therefore can do with it what she wishes. The lover has no rights in his heart, but holds it only as a villein or copyholder, that is, at the will of the lady and in return for a villein's 'service'. The lover is apparently dissatisfied with this relationship. He begs the lady, in return for his past service, to 'reach' (l. 24) or grant him her love, which would then dignify the status of his heart, probably to that of freehold property. Otherwise, he asks her to 'strain' or screw up the rent or demands for villein's service to the point where the property, his heart, will be ruined and, presumably, the villein starved to death.

24 *reach me*: grant me; extend to me.

27 *strain*: 'increase the torment so as to reduce a person to the last extremity' (*N* 575); see the note to l. 21 for a probable extension of this meaning in a feudal metaphor.

29 *suffereth*. Probably monosyllabic (suffer'th).

CXLI. *E*.

Attributed to 'Tho.' in margin of *E*. The poem is in ballad meter with a refrain.

I have used commas as opposed to full stops after the fourth line in stanzas 1, 5, and 6 because the speaker of the refrain in these stanzas might be either the narrator or the lady, with her laments governed by 'complained' (l. 3), 'speak' (l. 24), and 'groan' (l. 29).

5, 10, 15, 20, 25, 30 *Alas the while*: literally, 'Alas the time', but used as a general exclamation of grief, like 'Alas the day'.

6 *sight*] *M*; sighed *E*: sighed.

9 *loveth*. Possibly monosyllabic (lov'th).

19 *remove*: change position or place; perhaps figuratively to change feeling.

CXLII. *E*, *D* (2 versions).

Attributed to 'Tho.' in margin of *E*; revisions in Wyatt's hand; in Wyatt section of *D*.

3 *My weal, my joy, my bliss*] *W*; My worldly joy and bliss *E*.

8 *heart*: 1) love; 2) courage.

is hence: in the lady's bosom.

9-11 *bootless for to strive/Out of presence/Of my defence*: as it is pointless for me to struggle for life when I am out of the presence of my defence – that is, my courage (second meaning of 'heart' in l. 8) and my lady [whose love keeps me from death].

12 *drive*: move quickly.

13-15 *Heartless . . . I then*. Compare II, 11-15, and CXIII, 11-15.

17 *assure*: save.

19 *go*] *W*; gro (?) *E*.

CXLIII. *E.*

Attributed to 'Tho' in margin of *E.*

4 *To let :* to allow to go or escape; to set free.

5–8 *Then why should I/Hold pain within my heart/And may my tune apply/
To ease my smart :* then why should I keep the pain hidden in my heart,
especially when I can use my music to ease my pain.

11, 59 *For else all other suit :* for all other supplication else.

18 *deserved.* Probably deservèd.

23 *do go*] ed.; go *E.*

33–4 *Who shall me give/Feathered wings for to fly.* Possibly derived from
Petrarch's *Rime* 81, ll. 12–14 (*M & T* 324).

35–6, 41–4 Wanting to see the thing that grieves one and seeking a cure from
a foe are defined as perverse acts in ll. 37–40.

38 *plain*] Tillyard; pain *E.*

39 *would*] *N conjectures*; could *E.*

 beseek : beseech, beg earnestly.

CXLIV. *E, D.*

Attributed to 'Tho' in margin of *E.*

3 *fro :* away, as in 'to and fro'; away from that place.

5 *For*] ed.; From *E.*

6 *receipt :* the receptacle.

11 *mad*] ed.; made *E, D* (*a possible spelling of mad*).

CXLV. *D.*

Followed in *D* by 'Finis. Quod Wyatt' ('Quod' designates the author).

M (91) argues that the last stanza is not by Wyatt because Wyatt always
writes 'prove', never 'preve'. But if Wyatt was working with the 'believe/
leave' rhyme, it is possible that in this one instance he resorted to the
available alternative form 'preve'.

In the first two stanzas the fourth lines contain ten syllables and probably
5 stresses. In the last four stanzas the fourth lines range from eight to ten
syllables and each contains probably four stresses. *N* sees this change as sign
of corruption of an original text in which the fourth lines always had ten
syllables and five stresses and thereby maintained a stanzaic pattern in which
the second, third, and fourth lines expand from two to four to five stresses
respectively.

13 *mind :* ways of feeling.

14 *change . . . as . . . wind.* Proverbial; see *Tilley* W439 (*Da*).

17 *spy it :* (?) discern the real attitude of a person.

18 *as oft as chance on die :* as often as fortune turns or changes on the
turning of the dice.

24 *fall highest :* fall from the highest place.

27 *Whoso list believe :* to the person who chooses to believe.

28–30 *Trust . . . is possible.* Here any punctuation decides in favour of one of two possible meanings. If we take l. 29 in conjunction with l. 30, as in the text, it means 'Since men are foolish enough to wed ladies merely because they are given permission to do so, everything is possible'. If we take l. 29 in conjunction with l. 28, the two lines mean 'Trust first and afterwards discover if the trust was warranted, as men wed ladies on trust, merely because they are given permission to do so, and afterwards discover what their wives are like'.

CXLVI. *D.*

In a Wyatt section of *D*.

CXLVII. *D, E* (24–39).

In Wyatt section of *D*.

In *E*, a leaf, presumably containing ll. 1–23, is missing. The attribution may have been made on that leaf.

E's ll. 31–3 yield a rhyme scheme different from *D*'s; the latter is consistent with that of *D* in the first two stanzas. As *N* says (584) the poem's 'greatest merit' is the complicated structure of its stanza. I have therefore printed the poem from *D* except for the obviously superior *E* variants in ll. 26 and 27, which do not affect the rhyme. The missing leaf of *E* may well have contained revisions that altered, among other things, the rhyme-scheme of the first two stanzas.

13 *undeserved:* unrequited; not paid back.

22 *warm:* 1) grow warm; 2) warm me [instead of burning me with the cold flame of disdain (l. 25)].

26 *all right*] *E*; nature *D*.

27 *frowardly*] *E*; scornfully *D*. *E*'s 'frowardly', or 'perversely', clarifies the following lines: the lover has been made to repent for intentions which were not evil but which were perversely construed as such by the lady.

34 *me and mine.* *S* (174) suggests that the poem appeals to Anne Boleyn whose motto was 'Me and Mine'.

31–4 *But if your heart . . . /For me and mine*] But death shall rid me readily/ If your [   ] heart do not relent./And I know well all this ye know:/ That I and mine *E*. *E* changes the logic of the passage: ll. 34–7 state what the lady knows and why she should therefore not be cruel (ll. 38–9). In *D*, ll. 34–7 give the reason why she can slay the lover which, in turn, becomes the reason for his questioning her cruelty.

36 *assign:* determine.

37 *spill or save.* A common phrase, especially in the language of courtly love (*M & T*).

CXLVIII. *T.*

In Wyatt section of *T*, who entitles the poem: 'The lover waileth his changed joys.'

As *N* (548) points out, this title is incorrect: 'Wyatt does not complain of any change in his mistress's affections: but of the instability of fortune generally.' Compare CVIII.

1 *avaunt:* brag.

14 *That fancy might support:* that imagination might conceive and sustain.

21 *too rathe:* too quickly, with the implication that quick building is followed by quick destruction.

23 *In little space:* in a short time.

25 *turned.* Probably turnèd.

27–8 *May wail the time that I did feel/Wherewith she fed me then:* may lament the time that I did experience the pleasures with which she then fed and allured me.

31–2 *all my requests/From peril cannot save:* I cannot deliver from peril all the things I desired from Fortune.

33–6 *Yet would I well it might appear/To her, my chief regard,/Though my deserts have been too dear/To merit such reward:* (?) yet I would that it – that is, saving my requests from peril – might appear advisable to Fortune, who is still my chief object of regard, although what I have deserved and received from her in the past was too valuable to enable me to claim that I merit the reward I am asking from her now.

EPISTOLARY SATIRES

The following three poems are sometimes referred to as 'verse epistles', a generic title appropriate to their form as familiar letters to a friend and to their revelation of the character and values of the writer. They are more frequently called 'satires', a title appropriate to their attack on the false values of typical courtiers. The term 'epistolary satires' – borrowed from W. Trimpi (pp. 116–18) (*FR*) – usefully refers to a combination of these characteristics, a combination that has classical antecedents, especially in the poems of Horace. Wyatt, who introduced the form into English, knew it in the works of Luigi Alamanni (1495–1556), the Italian writer whose tenth satire was the model of CXLIX; but he undoubtedly knew it in Horace as well. Wyatt's style in these poems owes something to Horace, Alamanni, and Chaucer. Usually he maintains the intimacy of Horace's plain style. Occasionally, as in the centre of CXLIX, he moves toward the gravity and loftiness of Alamanni's more declamatory style. In CL the language of the fable seems deliberately anachronistic in its Chaucerian quality; and his idiom, which tends toward the homely and proverbial, is always English rather than Latinate.

Wyatt presumably derived his verse form – the *terza rima* which rhymes predominantly five-beat lines aba bcb and so forth – from Alamanni. Alamanni's *Opere Toscane* (Tuscan Works) were first printed at Lyons in 1532–3, so it is very probable that all three Epistolary Satires and the Penitential Psalms (CLII), which are also written in *terza rima*, were composed after 1532. *Mason* (202–6) argues that the Epistolary Satires were composed after the psalms, with CXLIX written in 1536 and CLI in 1541 at the time of

Wyatt's last imprisonment. In addition to his judgement of the satires as works of art superior to the psalms, he suggests that the 'clog' in CXLIX, 86–8 (an addition to Alamanni), is an allusion to Wyatt's restricted freedom after his release from the Tower in June 1536. He also cites a parallel between CLI, 11–13,

> To thee, therefore, that trots still up and down
> And never rests, but running day and night

and a passage from Wyatt's 'Declaration ... of his Innocence' (L 181) written in 1541,

> I, as God judge me, like as I was continually imagining and com-
> passing what way I might do best service, so rested I not day nor
> night to hunt out for knowledge of those things. I trotted continually
> up and down that hell through heat and stink from councillor to am-
> bassador, from one friend to another ...

He claims that the lines from the satire were written soon after the passage from the 'Declaration'. On the other hand, Kenneth Muir (L 251, 256 note 7) argues that the Epistolary Satires were composed before the psalms, prob- ably between Wyatt's release from the Tower in June 1536 and his departure for Spain in April 1537. Though he does not call attention to the fact, the satires occur in E several entries before LX and LXXVI, which were almost certainly composed between 1537 and 1539 when Wyatt was in Spain; the satires are also interspersed in a section of E in which Wyatt was correcting scribal copies of poems and entering and correcting poems in his own hand, so that the poems' order in the manuscript might well correspond to the chronological order of composition. Muir does suggest that Wyatt's statement in the 'Declaration' might have echoed his phrases in CLI, 11–13, rather than preceded their composition. The weight of the evidence seems to favour a date for all three epistolary satires before Wyatt's departure for Spain in April 1537.

CXLIX. *Parker, E, D, A, H, Cam, T.*

In Wyatt sections of A and T.

Lines 1–52 are omitted in E and therefore irrecoverable in what was pre- sumably Wyatt's last version. I have reconstructed the putative earlier version of these lines from the other manuscripts. There are, I believe, two families of manuscripts that witness to this version: *Parker* and *Cam*; and a family made up of D, A, and H, with H derived from A. Using *Parker* as a copy-text for ll. 1–52, I print, unless otherwise noted, the readings which appear to have greatest authority according to this family-tree or stemma.

For ll. 53 to the end I regard E as the authoritative text and hence the copy-text. E does not agree consistently with any of the witnesses to the putative earlier version; at times it agrees with one of them against the others; at times it disagrees with all of them. This fact suggests that E is either the product of Wyatt's revision or an editor's eclectic reconstruction from several manuscripts. The fact that the poem is followed in *E* by a poem in Wyatt's hand (LVIII) argues that the version is Wyatt's.

The poem imitates Alamanni's *Satira X*, first published in 1532 (*M & T* 347–9). At times Wyatt translates Alamanni closely or, when varying the matter, maintains his rhetorical structure: the parallel structure of ll. 19–36 and 89–99, for example, is derived from Alamanni. At times he states Alamanni's attitudes in a different kind of language – more concrete, colloquial, proverbial, and 'anglicized' in its allusions. Sometimes he omits passages from Alamanni; sometimes he makes additions. The result is a poem in which the voice of the speaker is quite distinct from that of the source.

Wyatt imitates Alamanni's *terza rima* but, unlike the Italian, does not necessarily make the end of a tercet coincide with the end of a unit of thought.

Like Alamanni, who wrote his satire in Provence when in exile from Florence, Wyatt probably wrote this poem in the country when in exile from the court. With the exception of *N*, who dates the poem in 1541 after Wyatt's second imprisonment, critics agree, for the reasons discussed in the head-note, that it was written in 1536 after Wyatt was released from the Tower and apparently sent home to Allington Castle in Kent where, under his father's eye, he was to improve his character. Allusions early in the poem to voluntarily leaving the court – adapted from Alamanni but intensified – may bespeak Wyatt's own attitude toward his return home: he would have chosen to leave the court for the country even if he had not been ordered to do so.

T entitles the poem: 'Of the courtier's life written to John Poyntz.'

1 *John Poyntz.* Wyatt substitutes the name of his friend for Alamanni's Tommaso Sertini. Little is known about John Poyntz. His family came from Iron Acton in Gloucestershire. He was a member of the court of Henry VIII.

2 *cause*] *D, A, H, Cam*; *causes Parker.*

3 *they*] *D, A, H, Cam*; *I Parker.* The phrase 'whereso they go' may be a 'filler' for the purpose of rhyme (*M & T*); or, as *N* suggests, it may allude to the 'progresses' of the court through the countryside during the summer and its frequent movement from one palace to another at other times.

5 *wrapped.* Probably wrappèd.

wrapped within my cloak: *N* (562) suggests that the phrase alludes to Horace's 'wrapped in my virtue' (*Odes* III, xxix, 54–5); but in l. 6 the speaker says that he is still 'learning' virtue. The phrase more probably translates the Italian's 'alone', making more concrete the implication of independence and self-sufficiency.

6 *will and lust:* the faculty of rational choice and the appetites that give rise to desire. The Italian has 'great grief'.

4–6 *Rather than to live thrall ... learning to set a law.* The lines contrast the subjection of the speaker's conduct to the will of powerful courtiers with the ordering of his conduct by his own interior standard.

9 *of right to strike the stroke:* with the right to punish us.

10 *meant:* intended, purposefully tried.

11–12 *Less to esteem them than the common sort,/Of outward things that judge in their intent:* to have less esteem for the great than do the common people, who, in their minds ('intent'), judge by external appearances (*O*).

13 *Without regard what doth inward resort*] *D, A, H, Cam*; Without regard that doth inward resort *Parker*. Both readings are possible. *D*, etc.: without attention [to] what abides inside. *Parker:* without a look or glance that goes to the inside. The Italian's 'without seeing what the depth shows' supports the first reading.

15 *touch*] twitch *D*.

heart; . . . not to] *D, A, H, Cam*; heart; and . . . not *Parker*.

list] *D, A, H*; lust *Parker, Cam*. I print 'list' to conform to the presumably later usage of Wyatt in *E*.

report] *D, A, H, Cam*; repent *Parker*.

14-15 *I grant . . . my heart:* I admit that sometimes I desire the fiery brilliance of glory. The Italian has: 'I do not indeed say that the love of glory does not sometimes burn me.'

15-16 *report/Blame by honour and honour to desire:* attack honour with words and [at the same time, but secretly] desire it (*O*).

18 *colour black*] *D, A, H, Cam*; colour of black *Parker*.

That cannot dye the colour black a liar. The notion that 'black will take none other hue' is proverbial; see *Tilley* B436. The speaker is apparently comparing his own character as an honest man to the colour black; he is insisting that he cannot change his honest character into that of a liar any more than a piece of black cloth can be dyed another colour.

17-18 *But how may I . . . honour . . . attain/That cannot dye . . . black a liar?* The Italian has: 'But with what foot might I follow him who values the world, since I do not know that art of the person who agrees to climb the stairs of other men?'

19 *tune*] *D, Cam*; tongue *Parker*.

I cannot frame my tune to feign: I cannot shape the style and tone of my speech to the making of fictitious, dissembling statements.

18-19 *That cannot . . . tune to feign*] not in *A, H*.

21 *list*] *D, A, H*; lust *Parker, Cam*.

vice for] vices to *Parker*.

20-1 *To cloak the truth for praise, without desert,/Of them that list all vice for to retain:* to hide the truth in order to praise, without their deserving praise, those who desire to keep all their vices.

22-3 *sets their part/With:* commit themselves to. The Italian has 'worships'.

23 *Bacchus:* god of wine.

25 *to do*] *D, A, H, Cam*; nor do *Parker*.

such wrong] so great a wrong *D, A, H*; so much wrong *Cam*.

26 *To worship them like God on earth alone:* to worship them alone as if they were God on earth. The Italian has the classical 'the immortal gods'.

27 *like wolves.* The Italian has the abstract 'unjust, deceitful, and wicked'. Wyatt, as usual, is more concrete. Compare ll. 44, 45-6, 48-9, 67, 94-6.

silly: simple, defenceless, deserving compassion.

28 *words*] *A, H, Cam*; word *Parker*.

I cannot . . . and moan] not in *D*.

28–9 *with my words complain and moan/And suffer naught:* pretend to be suffering when not in fact suffering.

30 *Nor turn the word that from my mouth is gone:* I cannot take back, renege on, my word or promise. *N* suggests that the phrase is an adaptation of Horace's allusion to the impossibility of a writer's words, once published, ever 'returning' to an unpublished state (*Ars Poetica* 389–90). The idea is also proverbial; see *Tilley* W777 (*Da*).

28–30 *I cannot . . . mouth is gone.* The Italian has: 'I would not know how, in speaking, to cover thorns with false flowers, in [my written ?] works, having honey in the beginning and bitter wormwood in the end.' Here, untypically, Wyatt is less concrete than the Italian.

29–30 *And suffer . . . mouth is gone*] not in *D, A, H*.

31 *and look like a saint*] *D, Cam*; with look right as a saint *Parker*.

I cannot . . . like a saint] not in *A, H*.

I cannot speak and look like a saint: (?) I cannot pretend to be a saint when I am not a saint; *or* I cannot pretend to be a saint at the same time as I am using 'wiles for wit', etc. Wyatt's addition to the Italian.

32 *Use wiles for wit:* substitute an amoral cleverness for a morally guided intelligence.

make] *D, A, H, Cam*; use *Parker*.

33 *call craft counsel:* call the cunning devising of schemes a prudence in making plans.

for profit still to paint: to give a false colouring to words and acts, to behave as a hypocrite, for the sake of one's own gain. Wyatt's addition to the Italian.

35 *With innocent blood to feed myself fat.* The Italian has: 'To have such cold [heart] as, against compassion, to harm him whom I exalt in my mind.'

37 *allow the state:* approve the rule.

38 *him*] *Parker, Cam, D*; high *A, H*. The more difficult 'him' has greater authority in the stemma and precedent in Chaucer:

> For jalousie and fere of hym Arcite.
>
> (*CT* I (*A*), 1333)

> . . . she Goddes peple kepte,
> And slow hym Olofernus, whil he slepte.
>
> (*CT* IV (*E*), 1367–8)

Wyatt does not, to my knowledge, use the redundant pronoun elsewhere.

damn] *D, A, H, Cam*; deem *Parker*.

damn Cato to die: (?) condemn Cato as worthy of execution [had he not committed suicide].

39 *with*] *D, A, H, Cam*; by *Parker*.

'scape] *D, A, H*; escape *Parker*; step *Cam*.

40 *doth*] *H, Cam*; do *D, A*; did *Parker*.

42 *did his heart the common wealth apply:* his heart devoted its energy to the common well-being.

37–42 *I am not ... wealth apply.* Wyatt drops the Italian's mention of the dictator Sulla. He substitutes for Brutus and his fellow conspirators Marcus Porcius Cato of Utica, the uncle of Brutus and ally of Pompey. Cato killed himself after the disastrous battle of Thapsus in 46 B.C. to avoid falling into Caesar's hands (Epitome to Livy, *History* CXIV). Wyatt may have felt that Cato's passive resistance to tyranny was more appropriate to a poem in praise of contemplative retreat than Brutus's more active behaviour; or he may have felt that it was politically unsafe to speak highly of the assassination of monarchs.

44 *make the crow singing as the swan*] *D, A, H, Cam*; mark the singing crow as the swan *Parker*; make the crow in singing as the swan *T, N*. One need not resort to *T*'s emendation because the variants are possible: 1) make out or describe the crow to be singing like the swan; 2) notice the singing crow as one notices the swan. The first better fits the context's emphasis on specious rhetoric.

45–6 *Nor call 'the lion' ... /That cannot take ... as the cat can:* nor call the greatest of cowardly beasts [and men], who cannot catch a mouse as well as the cat can, 'the lion'.

43–6 *I am not ... the cat can.* Wyatt substitutes allusions to animal lore for the Italian's references to calling Thersites courteous, calling a disloyal person 'Aeneas', and calling a cringing man 'Hercules'.

47 *of the*] *D, A, H, Cam*; of *Parker*.

48 *Alexander:* Alexander the Great, 356–323 B.C., conqueror of most of the then civilized world, whose name was understood to signify in Greek 'helper of men' (Edward Phillips, *The New World of English Words*, 1658).

48–9 *Pan ... Apollo.* Pan's rustic music cannot compare with Apollo's heavenly music. Pan challenged Apollo to a music contest. Apollo punished Midas, the only person present to declare his opinion in favour of Pan, by transforming his ears into those of an ass (Ovid, *Metamorphoses* XI). Wyatt's addition.

49 *many fold*] *D, A, H, Cam*; many a fold *Parker*. Both phrases mean 'many times over'.

50–1 *Praise Sir Thopas for a noble tale/And scorn the story that the knight told.* Chaucer, as a character in his own *Canterbury Tales*, begins at the Host's urging to narrate the tale of Sir Thopas, a travesty of a courtly romance in a verse and a stanza form that the Host describes as doggerel. The Host stops him in mid-tale (VII, 691–935). The Knight narrates a genuine courtly romance in iambic pentameter couplets (I (A), 859–3108). Wyatt substitutes this allusion for the Italian's allusion to the difference between Maerius (mocked by Virgil and Horace) and Homer, Virgil, and Dante.

52 *counsel:* prudence.

53 *laugheth ... beareth*] laughs ... beareth *D, A, H, Cam*; laugheth ... bears *Parker*.

54 *when he is*] Parker, D, A, H, Cam; when is E.

55 *lust:* desires.

56 *these points would.* It is possible that the line should read 'these, Poyntz, would'. Or Wyatt may be punning on 'points' and 'Poyntz'.

58 *And much the less of things that greater be:* and much the less (can I learn the way) of [doing] things that are greater [vices].

59 *colours of device:* false appearances or lies that have been devised or contrived; 'colours' probably includes a reference to the colours of rhetoric, figures of speech that ornament a statement and, in Wyatt's view here, falsify it.

61 *nearest.* Possibly monosyllabic.

62 *And, as to purpose likewise it shall fall:* and, 'likewise, as it shall be opportune' (M & T 353).

60-3 *To join the mean with each extremity:/With the nearest virtue to cloak alway the vice/And .../To press the virtue that it may not rise.* Wyatt alludes to the ethical doctrine, Aristotle's in origin, that the virtuous act is that which avoids both an excessive and a deficient response to the circumstances and can therefore be called 'the mean' or middle position between 'each extremity' or vice. He defines two ways in which the mean can be joined with an extremity. First, a vice can be given the name of a related virtue (l. 61): for example, drunkenness can be called good fellowship (l. 64). Secondly, a virtue can be called a vice and, consequently, 'pressed' so that it may not 'rise' or flourish (l. 62): for example, the inability to lie can be called rudeness (l. 73). Wyatt adds this statement to the Italian and thereby makes the acts of speech described in ll. 64-75 particular instances of a general category.

64 *As drunkenness ... to call:* as, for example, to call drunkenness ...

67 *Favel:* a common medieval personification of fraud, cunning, duplicity, and flattery. The name apparently derives from a 'fallow' (pale brown or reddish yellow) horse. In the Middle Ages 'to curry favel' meant literally 'to rub down a fallow horse with a comb'. That process of 'stroking' and the pleasure presumably given thereby to the horse became a common metaphor for soliciting favour by flattery and, as 'curry-favel', a personification of such a solicitor. 'Favel' is apparently an abbreviated form of 'curry-favel'. Wyatt adds the personification to the Italian.

68-9 *cruelty to name/Zeal of justice and change in time and place:* to call cruelty in the enforcement of the law the zealous pursuit of justice and to defend it on the grounds that the time and place of the offence are different from the time and place in which the law was made. Wyatt adds the reference to change in time and place.

70-1 *he that suffereth offence without blame/Call him pitiful:* (?) call the person compassionate who permits others to commit offences without blaming them (O); *or* call the person contemptible who endures offences from others without blaming them. The first reading contrasts unwarranted silence with unwarranted railing in ll. 71-2. The second would reverse the Italian and contrast a Christ-like forgiveness with either cruelty in ll. 68-9 or railing in ll. 71-2. The second has in its favour the addition of another instance of naming a virtue a vice – a category otherwise confined to l. 73. But the *OED*'s first recorded instance of 'pitiful' as 'contemptible' is 1582.

71 *true and plain:* truthful and plain-spoken.

72 *raileth reckless to every man's shame:* utters abusive language about others without heed to consequences ('reckless'), with the result that every man who hears him has his sense of modesty and decency violated ('shame').

64–75 *As drunkenness . . . prince's reign.* The catalogue of misnamings re-arranges the Italian, adds references to drunkenness and lechery, changes Alamanni's statement that he could not lie into the reference to the truthful man being called rude, and omits Alamanni's statement that he would not know how to steal. Wyatt confines the catalogue to misnamings. Alamanni mixes them with evil acts.

79 *chance . . . wit:* fortune [opportunity to prosper?] . . . wisdom (*O*).

78–9 *Hang on their sleeves that weigh . . . |A chip of chance more than a pound of wit.* Echoes the proverb 'An ounce of fortune is worth a pound of wit'; see *Tilley* O85 (*Da*). The Italian has the more abstract 'follow those who value fortune more than wisdom'.

80, 82 *hunt . . . hawk . . . stalk:* pursue game, chase game with a trained hawk, pursue game with a stealthy approach. Wyatt's additions.

84 *lusty leas:* pleasant grassland or pasture.

In lusty leas . . . I walk. Compare Chaucer's *Troilus* (II, 750–2):

> I am myn owene womman, wel at ese,
> I thank it God, as after myn estat,
> Right yong, and stonde unteyd in lusty leese.
>
> (K. A. Bleeth, *FR*)

85 *news:* novelties [perhaps the new situation of being exiled from the court?].

of these news I feel nor weal nor woe: (?) as a result of these novel ex-periences in the countryside of Kent I feel neither any [extraordinary] sense of well-being nor any [terrible] pain, [but a moderate content].

86 *clog . . . at my heel:* a block attached to the leg to impede motion. Proverbial; see *M & T* (354): 'I am with the gaoler, with a clog upon mine heel', *Paston Letters*, No. 414, 1461. The clog here is probably a metaphor for the king's restraint on the speaker's conduct which keeps him away from the court and in the country; see the head-note to Epistolary Satires, p. 438, and to this poem.

88 *dike:* ditch (the reading of all other MSS) used as a boundary for lands or fields.

86–8 *Save that a clog . . . leap . . . full well.* Wyatt's addition to the Italian.

87–8 *No force for that, for it is ordered so/That I may leap both hedge and dike full well:* but I do not care about the clog since it is arranged in such a way that I am not inhibited from leaping over hedges and ditches when hunting. Leaping is probably a metaphor for general freedom of movement in the country.

89 *I am not now in France to judge the wine.* Wyatt omits the Italian's references to being mocked for ignorance of wines. Thus emended, Alaman-

ni's statement coincidentally applied to Wyatt's situation in 1529 when, at Calais, he was granted a licence to import wine.

90 *With savoury sauce the delicates to feel:* to perceive, sense, taste the delicious foods served with appetizing sauce. Wyatt's addition to the Italian.

94-5 *Flander's cheer letteth not my sight to deem/Of black and white:* the good cheer of Flanders, especially that resulting from excessive eating and drinking, does not prevent my sight from judging between black and white.

96 *With beastliness they, beasts, do so esteem*] *E*; With beastliness they beasts do esteem *D*; Which beastliness those beasts doth esteem *Cam*; With beastliness those beasts do esteem *Parker*; With beastliness the beasts do so esteem *A*, *H*: (?) with beastliness that they [the Flemish], who are beasts, do value so highly.

97-8 *Christ . . . at Rome*] truth . . . of some *T*. Since *T* was first published in 1557, during the reign of the Roman Catholic Queen Mary, Wyatt's attack on the Roman church was emended.

97-9 *Nor I am not where Christ is given in prey/For money, poison, and treason at Rome –/A common practice used night and day.* The Italian has: 'I am not in Rome where the person who believes in Christ and does not know how to deceive or to poison must needs return to his house sighing.'

99 *used.* Probably usèd.

100 *in Kent and Christendom.* Wyatt's substitution for Alamanni's Provence. The phrase alludes to a proverb 'in Kent *or* Christendom', derived from the fact that Kent, unlike most of England, remained unconverted to Christianity in the reign of King Ethelbert and was therefore not considered a part of Christendom; see *Tilley* K16. Wyatt's placing of Kent in Christendom is therefore partly a joke, in that it reverses the proverb, and partly a way of affirming that life in the countryside of Kent can be more genuinely Christian than life at court.

Wyatt omits the Italian's subsequent statement that the capacity of country people to act on their malice is limited by their ignorance and fear.

102-3 *Where if thou list . . . spend my time.* Substituted for Alamanni's final attack on the vices of the court.

CL. *E, A, D* (1-18), *T.*

In Wyatt sections of *A* and *T*.

Aesop's fable of the town and country mice was available to Wyatt in several versions of which we know: Horace's *Satire* II, vi, 77-117; William Caxton's fable of the 'two rats' in his translation of a French *Fables of Esope* I, xii, published in 1484; Richard Pynson's virtually identical version in an edition of 1500; and Robert Henryson's *The Taill of the Uponlandis Mous and the Burges Mous,* first printed in 1570 but possibly available to Wyatt in manuscript. But, apart from details (cited in the notes) that Wyatt may have garnered from these versions, his fable differs from them all. He may therefore have been imitating one or more of the probably numerous versions of which we have no knowledge – for example, the song of his mother's maids mentioned in the opening lines. Or he may have adapted one or more of the above versions to his own purpose. In any case, the differences between his fable and the others are crucial to the poem's meaning.

In all the known versions before Wyatt's, the fable begins with the town mouse visiting the country mouse, voicing the first attack on country life and the first praise of life in town, and inviting the country mouse to visit. Wyat t has the country mouse attack country life, praise city life, and choose to visit the city mouse who greets her in a state of mental anxiety. Likewise, in all but Wyatt's version, the fable ends with the country mouse finally escaping back to the country – whether it be from butler, dog, cat, or some undefined threat. Wyatt's country mouse does not escape the cat and may possibly be killed by it.

These unique elements in Wyatt's version are shaped by and expressive of the moral of the fable. Wyatt's known predecessors emphatically relate attitudes of mind to external conditions of life. One might generalize their morals as a preference for the simple, frugal, quiet and hence mentally and emotionally secure life of country or moderate poverty over the complicated, hedonistic, materialistic, busy and hence anxious life of town or wealth. On the other hand, Wyatt, using the categories of Christian stoicism, defines earthly happiness as a purely interior state – quietness of mind – achieved by the exercise of virtue, and defines concerns about or desires for *any* external conditions of life as mistaken means to the end of happiness and, if they become obsessive, diseases of the mind opposed to mental quiet.

Of course Wyatt's choice of the fable does imply that it is probably easier to achieve spiritual peace in the country than in the city or the court, an implication in keeping with ll. 80–103 of CXLIX and with XLIX. But, since in this poem's more radical analysis each 'kind of life' has its 'disease' (l. 80) if the mind's attitude is wrong, the mind remains the only place essential to the achievement of health.

Wyatt's fable and his long moralizing passage attack the choice of false means to the end of happiness which, along with the virtue that leads to it, is defined briefly near the end of the poem. Hence it is the country mouse who freely but mistakenly chooses the life of material wealth and pleasure which the town mouse, from experience, knows is a source of anxiety. And the country mouse is trapped in, perhaps even destroyed by the consequences of her choice, since – unlike escape into the country from city or court – there is no easy escape from anxiety of mind and heart. The moralizing passage extends the attack to power and sensual delight, broadly defined, as false and, perhaps, spiritually fatal means to the end of happiness.

For a full account of the relationship of Wyatt's fable to the earlier known versions and to the poem's meaning, see *Thomson* (259–67). *F, Rollins*, and *Mason* (229–30) emphasize the influence of Chaucer on Wyatt's language and narrative style.

T entitles the poem: 'Of the mean and sure estate written to John Poyntz.'

3 *livelood:* livelihood.
5 *endured.* Probably endurèd.

6 *souse:* drench or soak with water.

7 *swimmed.* Probably swimmèd.

9 *bare meat:* [only] simple food.

10 *dight:* put in order.

14 *when her*] *A, T*; where *E*.
'stroyed. Probably 'stroyèd.

15, 51 *wellaway:* an exclamation of sorrow.

16 *fain:* 1) obliged; forced; 2) disposed.

18 *My sister.* In Henryson's *Taill* the two mice are twin sisters. In no other known earlier version are they related.

26 *cater:* caterer.

27 *boiled bacon meat.* Horace's country mouse serves nibbled bits of bacon (l. 85) to the city mouse who barely touches them or anything else.

31 *at this journey she maketh but a jape:* she regards the journey itself as a jest or easy matter.

32 *goeth.* Possibly monosyllabic (go'th).

32-3 *trusting of all this wealth/With her sister her part so for to shape:* confident that, as a result of all this material abundance, she would be able to fashion her lot in life ('part') with her sister.

40 *asked.* Probably askèd.

42 *Peep.* Henryson's town mouse announces her arrival at the country mouse's dwelling with 'Cry peip anis' (l. 26); she later inquires after her fainted sister's condition with 'cry peip' (l. 147).

45 *by the Rood:* by Christ's cross.

46-7 *She feasted her, that joy it was to tell/The fare they had.* Compare Chaucer, *Troilus* III, 1228: 'Made hym swich feste, it joye was to seene' (*M*).

48 *as to purpose ... it fell:* as it fell or came into the conversation (*N*). Compare Chaucer, *Troilus* III, 1366-7:

> Soone after this they spake of sondry thynges,
> As fel to purpos of this aventure. (*M*)

49 *cheered.* Probably cheerèd.

50 *befell a sorry chance:* there happened by chance an event which proved a cause of sorrow. Compare Chaucer's *Troilus* II, 464: 'me is tid a sory chaunce' (*N*).

52 *looked*] *A, T*; look *E*.

53 *steaming:* gleaming. Compare Chaucer, *CT* I (*A*), 201-2:

> His eyen stepe, and rollynge in his heed,
> That stemed as a forneys of a leed. (*F*)

55 *for though th'unwise*] *M & T*; for though *E*; for the unwise *A, T*.

59 *whither*] *A, T*; whether *E*.

60 *shift:* expedient.

61 *tho:* then.

64 *silly:* poor, unfortunate, deserving of pity.

66 *caught ... by the hip.* The phrase probably echoes the proverb 'To have one by the hip' or 'in a position of disadvantage' (*Tilley* H474, and *ODEP* 296) (*M & T*).

67 *And made her there against her will remain.* Henryson's version of the mouse's fate is closest to Wyatt's. The former's cat catches the country mouse by the back, tosses it to and fro and up and down, and plays hide-and-seek with her, before the mouse makes a lucky escape between a floor-board and the wall (ll. 169-75).

68 *poor surety:* the security that came with being poor in the country.

70 *Poyntz.* For John Poyntz, see note to CXLIX, 1.

70-1 *how men do seek the best/And find the worst.* Compare Chaucer, *CT* I (*A*), 1266-7 (*Da*).

74 *Goeth.* Probably monosyllabic (go'th).

78 *halberd:* a weapon which combines a spear and battle-axe.
knife: dagger (*N*).

75-9 *no gold ... no peace ... thy head ... hooped with gold .../Cannot repulse the care that follow should.* Compare Horace, *Odes* II, 16 (*N*), especially ll. 9-12: 'For 'tis not treasure nor even the consul's lictor that can banish the wretched tumults of the soul and the cares that flit about the panelled ceilings.'

80 *him his:* it its.
disease: lack of ease, with a pun on 'sickness' and probably 'evil tendency'.

81 *lust:* desire, appetite.

82 *lust:* pleasure; the source of pleasure.

84, 90, 98 *thing:* mental peace that comes with the Christian stoic virtue of detachment from false goods and evils and acceptance of one's lot.

86 *seek grapes ... briers.* Proverbial; see *Tilley* G411 (*Da*).

88 *hay:* net used for catching wild animals, especially rabbits, being stretched in front of their holes or around their haunts.
conies: rabbits.

89 *ye set*] *A*; ye see *E*.
drag-net: net dragged along bottom of river in fishing.

93-4 *bare/From all affects:* free from all desires.

97 *Then seek no more out of thyself to find ...* Compare Persius, *Satire* I, 7: 'look to no one outside yourself' (*N*).

101-2 *Let present pass and gape on time to come/And deep yourself in travail more and more:* (?) do not concern yourself with the present life but be in awe of the heavenly life to come; and plunge yourself more and more deeply into the labour of becoming virtuous or into the labour of 'learned and religious study' (*N*); *or* forget that the present is the only moment that counts and long for the future [– that is, have the attitude toward time that makes for the mad anxiety described in l. 100 –] and plunge yourself more and more deeply into the pointless labours after false goods. *N*, *F*, and *Rollins* accept the first construction without question. But it seems to me possible that these lines define the mistaken attitude toward time and effort held by the mad ones who choose to continue in mental anxiety. Support for this interpretation might be drawn from Horace, *Odes* II, 16: 'Let the soul be joyful in the present, let it disdain to be anxious for what the future has in store' (ll. 25–6). If the second construction were accepted, a colon should follow 'sum' in l. 103 to indicate that it refers only to what follows, not what precedes.

103   *sum:*   the sum, whole, or essence of my spiritual position.

106   *to be:*   to be in; to experience.

107   *them*]   *A, T*; then *E*.

109   *Even.*   Probably monosyllabic (e'en).

105–12   *'But to the great God ... losing such a loss.*   Compare Persius, *Satire* III, 35–8: 'O mighty Father of the gods! Be it thy will to punish cruel tyrants whose souls have been stirred by the deadly poison of evil lust in no other way but this – that they may look on Virtue and pine away because they have lost her!' (*N*).

CLI. *E, A, T.*

In Wyatt sections of *A* and *T*; a revision possibly in Wyatt's hand.

T entitles the poem: 'How to use the court and himself therein, to Sir Francis Brian.' Sir Francis Brian was a courtier, diplomat, translator, and poet. He was Wyatt's senior by about ten years. Because of his intimacy with Henry VIII in the king's youth, he had a reputation for dissoluteness. He maintained Henry's favour by assisting him in his change of wives, and by his efforts as a diplomat. In this poem Wyatt presents him as the exemplar of the statesman and man of integrity. Brian also collected proverbial sayings, some of which Wyatt's *persona*, acting as devil's advocate, tries to use against him in the opening lines and in ll. 65 and 91. Brian counters with a proverb at l. 21 (*N* lxxiv, n. 1; *F* II, 78, 108–9; *Rollins* II, 82–3, 220; *Thomson* 274–5; *M & T* 355; *DNB*).

In January 1539 Wyatt made the following statement in a letter to Cromwell from Toledo:

> I thank your lordship for the giving order for my money that I lent Mr Brian. If the king's honour more than his credit had not been afore mine eyes, he should have piped in an ivy leaf for aught of me. (*L* 86)

The hostility of this reference to Brian suggests that the poem was written when Wyatt and he were still on friendly terms and therefore before 1539. This evidence accords with the other evidence given in the head-note against 1541 as the date of composition.

Wyatt's poem probably owes some debt, for manner and material, to Horace's *Satire* II, 5. In Horace's satire, the ghost of Tiresias, responding to Ulysses' question about how to recover his lost fortune, educates the impoverished adventurer in the Roman art of legacy-hunting. Wyatt, like Horace, employs dialogue. Like Tiresias, Wyatt's *persona* in the poem ironically counsels disregard for truth in the service of flattery, getting into the wills of old men or their descendants through flattery and other forms of sycophancy, and purveying female relatives to lustful men.

But the differences between the two satires are more striking than their similarities. First, Horace's mock-heroic style has no counterpart in Wyatt, who finds the language and manner of Chaucer more suitable to his purpose (*F, Rollins, Hughey*). Secondly, Ulysses is crassly willing to follow Tiresias's advice, while Wyatt's interlocutor, Brian, although at first open to suggestions on how to make money as quickly as he spends it in the service of the king, laughs at Wyatt's 'thrifty jest' (l. 80) and steadfastly refuses to compromise his moral integrity. That difference changes the quality of the irony in Wyatt's poem: Horace's moral ideal is only implied, so that we laugh with the subtle Tiresias at the morally coarse Ulysses and the advice he is willing to accept; Wyatt's moral ideal is stated by Brian, so that we share more the implied disgust of Wyatt than the laughter of Brian at the cynical counsel Wyatt places in the mouth of his own *persona*. Thirdly, whereas Tiresias subordinates particular counsels to the over-riding objective of legacy-hunting, Wyatt orders his *persona*'s advice to the objective of making money through flattery, as opposed to truth-telling, and through the vicious deeds of usury, legacy-hunting, and prostituting a female relative to one's 'better' for immediate gold. Finally, it follows from Brian's presence and character in the poem and from the more general character of its cynical counsel that Wyatt's poem is more than an attack on legacy-hunting. It is rather a praise of political responsibility and personal moral integrity and an attack on the selfishness, mainly in the form of greed, that undermines both. To the development of these themes Wyatt's experience was probably more important than a literary model.

These are the kinds of differences that led *N* to characterize the poem as

> one of those imitations which entitle to all the praise of originality. Wyatt is indebted to Horace for little more than general ideas. The particular subject to which the Satire is applied is different, and so likewise are the actors. In fact Wyatt cannot be said to have borrowed any one thought distinctly from Horace. His thoughts seem to have been rather excited by reading the Latin Satirist than taken from him. (*N* cxliv)

For further discussion of the relationship of Wyatt's poem to Horace's, see *N*(cxlvii–cxlviii) and *Thomson* (267–8).

1–2 '*A spending hand ... bringer-in as fast*'. Echoes the proverb 'Spend as you get'; see *Tilley* S738 (*Da*).

3–4 '*On the stone that still doth turn about/There groweth no moss*'. Proverbial; see *Tilley* S885 and *ODEP* 547 (*M & T*).

6 *waste*: 1) diminish; 2) destroy.

9–10 *Brian ... who knows how great a grace/In writing is to counsel man the right*. Brian wrote a poem of 184 lines 'in which he "counsels man the right" in a series of proverbial and didactic sayings' (*Rollins* II, 82, n. 1).

13 *From realm to realm*. Brian was in fact employed in many diplomatic missions. *F* (II, 110) lists one to Rome and four to France.

16 *nappy:* having a head of foam; heady, strong.

for the nonce: for the occasion.

18 *Likest.* Probably monosyllabic (lik'st).

groins: (?) grunts; or digs in the earth with the snout ('groin' can mean 'snout').

19 *chaw:* chew.

moulded: turned mouldy.

20 *drivel on pearls.* Compare Matthew vii, 6: 'Cast not your pearls before swine' (*Rollins*).

21 *Then ... do]* ed.; Then ... to *E*; So ... doth *A, T*. The word 'do' could be misread as 'to'.

Then of the harp the ass do hear the sound: then, too, the ass hears the sound of the harp [but not the melody]. Proverbial; see *Tilley* A366 and *ODEP* 16. Compare Chaucer, *Boece* I, Prose 4, ll. 2–3, and *Troilus* I, 731–5:

> Or artow lik an asse to the harpe,
> That hereth sown whan men the strynges plye,
> But in his mynde of that no melodie
> May sinken hym to gladen, for that he
> So dul ys of his bestialite? (*N*)

22–3 *So sacks of dirt be filled up in the cloister/That serves for less than do these fatted swine]* So sacks of dirt be filled. The neat courtier/So serves for less than do these fatted swine *A, T. A* and *T* altered the original because such criticism of monks ('sacks of dirt') and monasteries was not acceptable in the reign of the Roman Catholic Queen Mary (1553–8).

28–9 *but what and if thou wist/How to bring in as fast as thou dost spend?* Compare Horace, *Satire* II, 5, 2–3: 'By what ways and means can I recover my lost fortune?'

33 *truth shall ... offend.* Proverbial; see *Tilley* T569 (*Da*).

34 *it is both wealth and ease:* fleeing the truth will make for your well-being, abundance of possessions, and ease.

36 *that wind:* that wind or breath expended in the cant praise of truth.

goeth. Probably monosyllabic (go'th).

37 *now-a-days]* *A, T*; now-a-day so *E*.

42 *upon thy bare feet:* (?) silently; in quiet and stealthy ways (*Rollins*).

44 *dog]* calf *A, T*.

as to a dog a cheese. The meaning has not been discovered, with either 'dog' or 'calf'. But the general sense of ll. 43–6 is clear: 'Do not lend unless you can make a great profit from the interest.'

45 *cant:* portion.

47 *Kitson]* the Lad *A, T*.

at Kitson: of or from Kitson. *N* suggests that the allusion is to Sir Thomas Kitson, Sheriff of London, who died worth over £3000. *Rollins* thinks the wealthy bookseller, Anthony Kitson, may be the object of the attack. *A* and *T* emended the reference to an even more mysterious 'Lad', probably to avoid offence to the Kitson intended.

55 *tread out and please him so:* step on the spit [so that he will not have to see the evidence of his approaching death] and thereby please him (*N*).

54–55 *if he cough too sore,/When he hath spit, tread out and please him so.* Compare Horace, *Satire* II, 5, 106–9: 'If one of your co-heirs happens to be older than you, and has a bad cough, say to him that if he would like to buy land or a house that is in your share, you would gladly knock it down to him for a trifle' (*N*).

56–7 *A diligent knave that picks his master's purse/May please him.* Compare Chaucer's characterization of the Reeve in *CT* I (A), 587–622 (*Hughey*).

57–8 *withouten moe,/Executor is:* without doing anything more is made executor of his master's estate.

59, 67, 85 *you*] thou *A, T*.

60 *deburse:* disburse, pay.

61 *rivelled:* wrinkled.

65 *Let the old mule bite upon the bridle:* let the old woman be vexed as a result of getting nothing for her pains. For proverb 'bite upon the bridle' see *Tilley* B670 and *ODEP* 46–7 (*M & T*). Compare VII for a description of such an 'old mule'.

69 *handsome be*] *A, T*; handsome by *E*.

if handsome be her middle: if she have a fine figure.

74–7 *That in ... all his pain.* Chaucer's Pandarus did not get money from Troilus in exchange for arranging the affair with Criseyde. See *Troilus* III, 260–4, 400–6 (*N*).

78 *Be next thyself:* be your own best friend. From Terence, *Andria* IV, 1, 12: 'I am nearest to myself.'

80 *jest:* a piece of raillery or banter.

81 *Wouldest.* Probably monosyllabic (would'st).

86–7 *Content thee .../With free tongue, what thee mislikes, to blame:* content yourself to blame, with a free tongue, what displeases you.

91 *as water in a sieve.* Proverbial; see *Tilley* W111 and *ODEP* 694 (*M & T*).

A PARAPHRASE OF THE PENITENTIAL PSALMS

CLII. *E* (except ll. 100–53), *A, R, CP*.

In Wyatt's hand in *E*, with revisions that show he was composing the poem there. With the possible exception of Psalm 143, the italicized psalm numbers are in a hand and ink later than Wyatt's and possibly that of Sir John Harington (*Harrier* 13–15). Unlike *Harrier*, I see no conclusive evidence that the opening Latin words, which are from the Vulgate, are in Wyatt's italic hand.

Wyatt's most important sources for the paraphrase of the Penitential Psalms are:

1) A paraphrase of the Penitential Psalms by Pietro Aretino (1492–1556), *I Sette Salmi de la Penitentia di David* (1534).

2) A Latin paraphrase of the psalms from the Hebrew by Joannis Campensis (1490–1538), a lecturer in Hebrew at the University of Louvain, and a

Latin translation of the psalms from the Hebrew by Ulrich Zwingli (1484–1531). Campensis's paraphrase was first published in *Psalmorum omnium juxta Hebraicam veritatem paraphrastica interpretatio* (1532). It was published again, in a parallel text with Zwingli's translation, in *Enchiridion Psalmorum Eorundem ex veritate Hebraica versionem, ac Joannis Campensis e regione paraphrasim ... complectens* (1533). Wyatt almost certainly used the latter edition. See *Mason* (*TLS*).

3) An anonymous English translation of Campensis's paraphrase, *A Paraphrasis upon all the Psalms of David, made by Johannes Campensis* (1535).

4) George Joye's *David's Psalter* (1534), an English translation of Zwingli's version.

5) The Latin Vulgate.

6) Probably the English Bible of 1535, translated by Miles Coverdale.

7) Less probably *The Bible in English*, or Great Bible, of 1539.

8) John Fisher, *This Treatise Concerning the Fruitful Sayings of David the King and Prophet in the Seven Penitential Psalms* (1508).

9) William Tyndale's commentaries on the scriptures and his treatises.

Limitations of space make it impossible to print Wyatt's sources. Interspersed in *M & T*'s commentary are the verses from the Latin Vulgate (*Biblia Magna*, 1525), the passages from Aretino, and some of the passages from Campensis, Zwingli, and Joye to which Wyatt is indebted. There has been one English translation of Aretino's psalms: *Paraphrase upon the Seven Penitential Psalms of the Kingly Prophet Translated out of Italian by I. H.* [John Hawkins] (1635). John Fisher's treatise is available in *JF*. The 1535 Bible was reprinted in 1838. Tyndale's works are available in *WT*. The works of Campensis, Zwingli, Joye, and the anonymous translator of Campensis are not available in modern editions.

The seven Penitential Psalms (6, 32, 38, 51, 102, 130, and 143 in psalters used in the English Church) were recognized as a group in the Middle Ages, appearing frequently in Vulgate Latin in devotional handbooks, Books of Hours, missals, and primers. They were used by both clergy and laity in preparing for the sacrament of Penance, sometimes as an act of penitence after the sacrament, and in preparation for death. Paraphrases of the psalms were rare before the sixteenth century. The earliest extant paraphrase in English dates from 1414. Alamanni's *Opere Toscane* (1532) includes a paraphrase in which each psalm deals with one of the seven deadly sins.

Wyatt's paraphrase of the Penitential Psalms involves not only the psalms themselves but also a narrative prologue to the first psalm and six narrative links between the psalms. This narrative framework establishes the character of David as the singer of the psalms and describes his psychological and spiritual state as he begins and ends a psalm. The psalms therefore become speeches in a larger 'historical fiction' based on the story of David and Bathsheba in 2 Samuel xi–xii.

Wyatt's main source for the narrative prologue and links is Aretino's paraphrase. Wyatt translates the prologue and first two narrative links of Aretino closely, although he does depart on occasion from Aretino to make subtle changes in the theology with which he interprets David's experience. The link between the third and fourth psalms (ll. 395–426) is a freer translation of Aretino's but does not change it substantially. The last three links depart completely in substance from Aretino's, and he omits Aretino's epilogue altogether. As he progresses through the seven narratives, then, Wyatt becomes increasingly independent of Aretino.

A similar pattern emerges in the psalms themselves, but from the very beginning Campensis and other sources rival Aretino as the major inspirations for the paraphrase of the scriptural words, and Wyatt radically compresses Aretino's amplifications of the scriptures. From the third psalm to the end, Wyatt is eclectic in his use of his sources and increasingly independent of them in both paraphrasing and amplifying the scriptural words. He makes less and less use of Aretino as he progresses, until the Italian's paraphrase supplies only an occasional elaboration of points in the other sources. Campensis becomes probably his major source, but he uses the others freely.

Wyatt draws away from Aretino partly because of the Italian's verbosity: when Wyatt follows Aretino closely in the first psalm, it takes him 112 lines to paraphrase 10 verses of scripture; when he is virtually free of Aretino in, for example, the fifth psalm, it takes him 89 lines to paraphrase 28 verses. But more important, Wyatt departs from Aretino in order, I think, to create a shape for the whole work that presents a Reformed Christian's view of the individual's experience of redemption rather than a Roman Catholic's. Aretino's David vacillates between hope and a fear bordering on despair throughout the work; he thereby creates the impression that, even though he is seeking forgiveness for his sins against Uriah and Bathsheba, he is in fact caught up in the continuing cycle of sin and forgiveness and sin typical of much Roman Catholic spirituality: as he says in the last psalm, his soul dies to grace as often as it sins and therefore must be reborn each time with new acts of contrition and divine forgiveness. Wyatt, on the other hand, is trying, I think, to make David the type of the Reformed Christian who experiences the genuinely profound, almost despairing sense of his sinfulness only once before the critical act of believing that God forgives him, justifies him by imputing righteousness to him, loves him, and will make him holy. Having apprehended his justification by God's grace in the fourth psalm (Psalm 51), Wyatt's David overcomes the temptation to spiritual complacency in the link between the fourth and fifth psalms, is sufficiently freed from concern for his own salvation to identify with all other sinners and to pray, in the fifth psalm, for the salvation of the human community, soberly appraises his new relationship with God in the sixth psalm, and finally in the last psalm asks that God aid him, as a justified sinner, in temporal and material ways. I do not think Wyatt is entirely successful in imposing this pattern on his material, but I think the pattern is discernible and his own.

There are two excellent critical works on the psalms. R. G. Twombly (see FR) argues against the view presented above. He sees the poem as a psychological drama of the outcast in which there is no clear development of

David's spiritual state, although he does see David capable of a new forth-rightness after his identification with other sinners in the fifth psalm. He thinks that Wyatt is depicting the spiritual disorientation of David as he tries, in his pride, to achieve humility, and as he 'experiences overlapping emotional convolutions of hope and doubt'. The other work is *Mason* 206–21, to whom I owe my view of the poem.

The date of composition of the psalms, like the date of the Epistolary Satires, remains a matter of dispute, with 1536 or 1541 being the main competitors. The order of the poems in *E*, on which Muir relies in arguing for 1541 (*L* 256, n. 7), is inconclusive. The psalms do occur several entries after LX and LXXVI, poems composed in Spain between 1537 and 1539. But the psalms seem to constitute a special section for which space might have been reserved at any point in the use or compilation of the manuscript; and they are followed in *E* by CLIV, which may have been written in 1539. Another argument advanced implicitly on behalf of 1541 (*M & T* 357) rests on the assumption that Wyatt uses the Great Bible of 1539 for some of his lan-guage. But Mason (*M* 178–85) rightly undermines that assumption by show-ing a source in Campensis, Zwingli, or Joye for all but one word or phrase supposed by *M & T* to derive from the Great Bible (see note to l. 275 for the exception). The suggestion that Wyatt, composing and correcting the psalms in *E*, leaves them in an 'unfinished' state because he dies before he has a chance to finish his new work (*L* 256, n. 7) depends for its force on the questionable view that the psalms are indeed 'unfinished'.

On the other hand *Mason* (203–6) argues for 1536 on equally problematic evidence. His judgement that the psalms are inferior as poems to the Episto-lary Satires and therefore written before them does not take into sufficient account the possibility that the paraphrase of the psalms was a different and perhaps more difficult intellectual and poetic enterprise than the composi-tion of the satires; it also has a bearing on the date of composition only if one agrees with his, to me, inconclusive dating of the satires (see the head-note to the Epistolary Satires on pages 437–8 for a discussion of their date of composition). He further argues that a similarity in diction and phrase between two of Surrey's poems written in 1537 and Wyatt's psalms must be the result of Surrey's echoing Wyatt's earlier work because Wyatt's language was dictated 'by the necessities of his translation'. But, as Muir points out, Wyatt's words are not the only possible translation of his original, and he may indeed have been echoing the words of the younger poet.

A precise dating of the psalms seems to me impossible. If Wyatt derived his *terza rima* from Alamanni – and that seems almost certain – then CXLIX, the first satire, was probably the first poem he composed in that verse form sometime after the publication of Alamanni's works in 1532–3. The psalms, given their *terza rima*, their special position in *E*, and their dependence on Joye's psalter of 1534, could have been composed at any time after Joye's psalter and the composition of CXLIX and before Wyatt's death in 1542. Their relationship to an imprisonment in 1536 or 1541 is pure conjecture.

Mason's judgement that they are inferior to the satires as works of art – a judgement with which I concur – tells us nothing conclusive about the date of any of the works in question or the chronology of their composition.

1–72 Wyatt translates Aretino's narrative prologue closely. His few modifications seem directed towards intensifying the gravity of David's sin (ll. 31–2, 69), the humility of his posture (ll. 48, 62), and his fear of not having a genuine faith (ll. 70–1).

1 *subject hearts :* hearts subject to, under the dominion of, Love.

2 *Barsabe.* Probably Barsabè: Bathsheba.

3–4 *in a look . . . himself converts/Cruelly pleasant before King David sight :* (?) (Love) at once changes himself into a cruelly pleasant look before King David's sight (O); *or* into a look (Love) changes himself, cruelly pleasant before King David's sight.

5 *dazed :* (Love) dazed.

8 *sparpled :* scattered; cast here and there.

for the nonce : (?) for the particular purpose; *or*, more likely, a gap-filling metrical tag with no particular meaning.

10 *moist*] warm E.

lanced. Possibly lancèd: shot, thrust.

12 *branle :* a state of confusion and agitation.

he] it E. In his first version, Wyatt apparently refers to the soul; in his final version he refers to David.

tranced. Possibly trancèd: was in a state of dread and suspense.

13 *figure and the frame :* bodily shape. Here 'figure' and 'frame' are virtual synonyms. Aretino has 'effigy' or 'image'.

14 *in his presence glanced :* (?) shot into his presence (O). OED does not record 'glanced' in this transitive usage until 1656.

glanced. Possibly glancèd.

15 *form :* mental image of the lady, which answers to her bodily 'figure' in l. 13. Aretino seems to distinguish between an initial image of the lady that impresses itself on David and a new, more intensely adored image that results from his having fallen in love.

16 *things.* Spelled 'thinges' in MS and probably disyllabic.

17 *forgot :* having forgot (O).

forecast : foresight; wisdom. Wyatt's addition for the sake of a rhyme word.

the wisdom and forecast] and out of mind clean cast E1; the wisdom over all E2. These revisions involve a change of rhyme from 'all' to 'forecast' which affects the rhyme of the rest of the stanza. They, like the revisions in ll. 21–2, 26, and many other lines throughout the poem, prove that Wyatt was composing in E.

20 *doth to make :* causes.

21, 22 *Urie :* Uriah, a Hittite soldier, husband of Bathsheba.

21–2 *Urie to go into the field in haste –/Urie I say*] Under pretence of victory, in hast/Urie to go E.

22 *make:* mate, husband.

25 *out of doubt*] all alone *E*.

26 *Whom more than God or himself he mindeth*] Whom he doth love more than himself or God *E1*; Whom more than God or else himself he lov'th *E2*.

27 *after*] when *E*.

28 *And of that lust possessed himself he findeth*] Of that delight possessed himself he findeth *E1*; Of that his lust possessed himself he findeth *E2*. 'And' was probably added at the same time as 'when' was changed to 'after' in l. 27. These revisions altered the syntax of the entire stanza.

28-9 *And of that lust possessed himself he findeth/That . . . doth reverse . . . :* and he finds himself possessed of the object of his lust, a lust that reverses . . .

31-2 *He, blinded, thinks this train so blind and close/To blind all thing, that naught may it disclose:* he, blinded [by his lust], believes this trick so concealed from sight and so secret [as] to blind every being, so that nothing may discover it. Wyatt's addition.

40 *aged.* Probably agèd.

this aged woeful man] this woeful man *E*. The 'man' referred to is David. Aretino describes him as 'the good old man'.

41 *Like him:* as in the case of a person.

43 *droopeth:* sinks.

44 *he:* David.

fire manifold: fire of passion, having various forms.

47 *pall:* robe.

48 *And to the ground . . . withal.* Wyatt's addition.

49-50 *pride . . . rebates . . . humbleness:* humility brings down pride.

51 *Thinner vile cloth*] A thin cloth *E1*; A thin vile cloth *E2*.

Thinner . . . than clotheth poverty. Wyatt's addition.

54 *knowing his wickedness*] repenting his excess *E*.

53-4 *His . . . hoar beard . . ./With ruffled hair knowing his wickedness:* his white beard along with the ruffled hair on his head acknowledging his wickedness. Presumably white, the colour of the beard, is taken as a symbol of repentance. The Italian has 'reminding one of his wickedness'.

55 *selfsame repentance:* (?) repentance itself; repentance personified (*O*).

56 *worldly*] ed.; wordly *W*.

58 *his plaints, his soul to save*] the plaints and the cries *E*.

57-9 *His harp . . ./Wherewith he offer'th his plaints . . ./That from his heart distils on every side:* his harp with which he offers [to God] his complaints that condense from the still of his heart on every side.

61 *might him hide*] might hide *E*.

62 *grave.* Wyatt's addition, possibly to emphasize the spiritual death which David fears.

as in prison or grave] in prison or in grave *E*.

64 *did make*] made *E*.

did make his fault adrad: made his fault frightened; frightened his sin; frightened him in and because of his state of sin.

66 *Rof that:* took the harp.

69 *his cheer coloured like clay.* Wyatt's addition.

70 *Dressed upright:* erect in posture.

seeking to counterpoise] he tunes his God to please *E*.

70-1 *seeking to counterpoise/His song with sighs.* The Italian has 'having quieted the sound of his sighs'. Wyatt emphasizes the importance of sorrow ('sighs') and diminishes the importance of the 'song', perhaps because he sees even the song of repentance as an 'outward deed' to be distinguished from the 'rightful penitence' of the 'heart . . . contrite' (ll. 651-5).

73-184 The first Penitential Psalm. *Psalm 6. Domine ne in furore* (O Lord, not in anger). When paraphrasing the scriptural words of the psalm, Wyatt usually takes his cues from Campensis, with some reference to Zwingli and Joye; but he seems to take hints from the Vulgate at ll. 97-9 and 131-2, and he offers a compressed version of Aretino's wording at ll. 132-41. In the amplification of the psalm, he radically compresses Aretino and adjusts the theology in the direction of Reformed Christianity.

73-80 These lines translate Aretino's preamble, but with a modification in ll. 75-7 that shifts the theological attitudes in the direction of Reformed Christianity.

73-4 *in my mouth thy mighty name/Suffer'th itself 'my Lord' to name and call:* thy mighty name consents to name and call [itself] 'my Lord' in my mouth (*O*). The speaker's mouth is simply the place in which the Lord's name names and calls itself the speaker's Lord – a sign of God's favour.

75 *by the same:* because of that same fact of your willingness to name yourself as my Lord in my mouth.

77 *mercy as the thing*] ever the same thing *E*.

75-7 *hope . . ./That the repentance which I have, and shall,/May at thy hand seek mercy.* Aretino has 'hope which the heart's repentance has taken in that mercy'. Wyatt's David is more frightened than Aretino's. The phrase 'and shall' implies the fear that his repentance will not last. The hope that in his repentance he will seek only mercy implies the fear that he might regard his own repentance as having merited forgiveness (see ll. 217-24).

78 *wretched*] us *E*.

81-9 Verse 1, with ll. 81-2 and 88-9 paraphrasing the scriptural words. In ll. 81-2 Wyatt briefly abandons Aretino for a translation of Campensis who, unlike Aretino at this point, stresses the justice of God's anger. Thereafter he modifies and compresses Aretino.

83-4 *I dread, and that I did not dread/I me repent:* I fear you, and I repent that I did not fear you in the past.

84-5 *evermore desire/Thee, thee to dread:* I desire you to make me fear you always. Aretino has: 'I resolve to will to fear you.' Wyatt sees the fear of God as a divine gift to man, not as the product of the human will.

87 *bread:* breadth.

90-102 Verse 2, with ll. 92-3 and 97-9 most closely related to the scriptural words. Wyatt paraphrases Campensis in ll. 92-3 and 100 and Zwingli in

l. 99. The rest of the verse and its amplification are derived mainly from passages selected from Aretino and from Campensis and Fisher (ll. 94–5).

91 *for recompense*] prepare again *E*.

90–2 *Temper . . . the harm of my excess/With mending will that I for recompense/Prepare again:* (?) reduce the injury done to me in my departure from you ('excess') by mending my will which, in an effort to make recompense to you for my sin, I am again making ready [for your healing influence]. Aretino has: 'Temper . . . the angers which the sins I have committed have kindled in you by considering the acts of goodness which I am getting ready to perform.'

93 *clean without defence*. Wyatt's addition.

94 *More is the need I have of remedy*] And have more need of thee for remedy *E*.

95 *whole:* healthy.

94–5 *More is the need I have of remedy/For of the whole the leech taketh no cure.* Wyatt's addition to Aretino, inspired by Campensis and John Fisher's sermon on this psalm (*JF* 14).

96–7 *The sheep . . . am strayed.* Wyatt's addition.

100–53] *A*; not in *E*.

100–2 *My heart doth fear the spear –/That dread of death, of death that ever lasts,/Threateth of right, and draweth near and near:* (?) my heart fears the spear of death – [my heart feels] that dread of death, of the soul's eternal death in sin and hell, a death that justly threatens me, a death that draws nearer and nearer. Aretino has: 'My heart is wounded by the arrow which the bow of fear of its damnation has shot into it.'

103–15 Verse 3, with ll. 103–4 and 112–13 most closely related to the scriptural words. For the scriptural core of this verse Wyatt mainly paraphrases Campensis and Zwingli. He amplifies with passages from Aretino.

104 *that come as thick as hail*. Wyatt's addition. Compare Chaucer, *Legend of Good Women* F655 (*Da*).

105 *vanities*] *CP*; vanity *R*, *A*. Aretino has 'vanities'.

104–6 *assaults . . ./Of worldly vanities, that temptation casts/Against the weak bulwark of the flesh*. I take 'that' to refer to 'assaults' rather than 'vanities'. If my assumption is correct, temptation casts the assaults against the bulwark, and the assaults are worldly vanities. Aretino has: 'my soul is extremely disturbed, so many and such are the temptations that assail her. She is enclosed inside the walls of the flesh, and the weapons of worldly vanities have conspired against the flesh.'

109 *use*] vice *M*.

107–9 *the soul . . ./Feeleth the senses with them that assail/Conspire, corrupt by use and vanity:* the soul feels the senses conspire with them that assail the flesh, the senses having been corrupted by the custom or habit [of self-indulgence] and by the empty pleasures [with which they indulge themselves].

110 *shade*] *R*, *CP*; shadow *A*.

110–11 *the wretch doth to the shade resort/Of hope in thee:* the wretched soul resorts to the shade of hope in thee.

112–13 *how long after this sort/Forbearest thou to see my misery.* Wyatt conflates Zwingli's 'how long are you delaying' with Campensis's 'when wilt thou at last look on my misery'.

114–15 *Suffer me . . ./Fear and not feel that thou forgettest me:* grant that I have only a false fear and not a validly grounded feeling that you forget me. Aretino has 'Grant . . . that I imagine and do not see that you forget me.'

116–30 Verse 4, with ll. 116–18 and 126 most closely related to the scriptural words. Wyatt seems to be paraphrasing Campensis in ll. 116–18 (to 'soul') and compressing Aretino thereafter.

118 *Reduce:* restore.

121 *stirred.* Probably stirrèd.

123 *remorse so sharp'th it :* remorse is making itself so sharp or intense.

124–5 *but thou help the caitiff that bemoans/His great offence:* unless you help the wretched body that bemoans its great sin.

125 *turn'th]* M; turneth R, CP; turns A.

118–25 *be thou the leech . . . to dust.* Wyatt here compresses a passage of Aretino's that follows, in Aretino, the passage Wyatt imitates in ll. 126–30. By reordering the passages, Wyatt brings together the related issues treated in ll. 126–38.

126 *for the nonce :* for a particular purpose.

128 *Suffer no sin or strike with damnation :* tolerate no sin or strike the sinner down with damnation.

129 *want needs it must :* must necessarily want or lack.

127–30 *For if thy . . . hand . . ./Suffer no sin . . ./Thy . . . mercy want . . . must/Subject matter.* Aretino has: 'But if there may be no error, your mercy would not be what it is; and if mercy were not to exist, in what way might sinners know God?'

131–41 Verse 5, with ll. 131–7 most closely related to the scriptural words. Wyatt is apparently conflating Zwingli and the Vulgate in ll. 131–2 and compressing Aretino's version thereafter.

131] CP, R; not in A.

132 *damned.* Possibly damnèd.

131–2 *For that in death there is no memory/Among the damned.* Wyatt apparently is conflating Zwingli's 'Inter damnatos' with the Vulgate's 'Because there is not in death anyone who is mindful of you'.

137 *there:* in hell.

138 *nilt:* wish not; do not will.

140 *one]* M; a A, R, CP. Compare CLIV, 36.

132–41 *nor yet no mention/Of thy great name . . . repentance to remove.* Wyatt compresses a passage in Aretino, selecting God's mercy from a long catalogue of divine blessings that Aretino's David will praise to the people if he is not damned.

142–9 Verse 6, with ll. 142–4 and 148–9 most closely related to the scriptural words. In ll. 142–7 Wyatt is compressing a much longer passage in Aretino. Either Zwingli or the 1535 Bible is the main source of ll. 148–9.

143 *afore the day :* before the dawn of day.

145 *That :* (this flesh) that.
down : the feather-stuffing of his bed or cover.

147 *suffer'th*] *R*; suffreth *CP*; suffers *A*.

148 *By :* as a result of.
instead of pleasures old. Wyatt's addition.

149–51 *I wash . . ./To dull my sight . . . never bold/To stir my heart again to such a fall.* Campensis has: 'Mine eye is darkened by reason of overmuch sorrow; its sight is dulled for fear of this great multitude of mine enemies which covet to destroy me.' Aretino, much later in the corresponding passage, has David defend against the deceits of his enemies 'with the streams from these eyes' and by closing his ears. Wyatt may have seen the idea of purposive weeping implied in Campensis, or he may have anticipated the passage in Aretino. Whatever the source, he uses the idea of intention to create an original link between verses 6 and 7.

150–66 Verse 7, with ll. 150–2 most closely related to the scriptural words. Line 152 may translate Zwingli. Lines 153–66 are probably a free paraphrase and compression of Aretino.

154 *even.* Probably monosyllabic (e'en).
so] lo *E*.

152–4 *my foes . . . me beset even now where I am.* David's foes here and throughout the remainder of this psalm are probably vividly personified thoughts or mental images of 'worldly vanities' (l. 105) that make him 'see' pleasing sights and 'hear' pleasing sounds in the cave. It is less likely that they are human counsellors that tempt him to sin with real sights and sounds. If the former reading is correct, Wyatt is departing from the most obvious meaning of the psalm. He probably does so in response to his reading of Aretino, who is ambiguous but seems to be personifying fantasies and desires.

161–2 *shew me . . ./Triumph and conquest.* I take 'triumph and conquest' to be objects of 'shew', not, like *M & T*, governed by 'power of'.

164 *riches*] glory *E*.

167–71 Verse 8, with ll. 169–70 paraphrasing the scriptural words. Wyatt takes cues from several sources.

167–8 *And, for I feel it com'th alone of thee/That . . . these foes have none access.* Wyatt's addition, though throughout the corresponding passage Aretino does emphasize the importance of God's help.

169 *Avoid :* depart.

169–70 *Avoid . . . complaint.* Wyatt may have taken these two words from George Joye's translation of Martin Bucer's *The Psalter of David in English* (1530) (*M & T*); but he could have got 'Avoid' from Joye and 'complaint' from the anonymous translation of Campensis.

171 *engines :* plots; snares; tricks. Probably inspired by Campensis's 'all ye that plot evil against me'.

172–7 Verse 9, with ll. 172–3 paraphrasing the scriptural words. In the corresponding passage, Aretino's David exults at length in his sense of having been redeemed. Wyatt compresses the passage drastically, places the work of redemption in the future tense, and removes the tone of rejoicing.

174-5 *do make my senses . . ./Obey:* cause my senses to obey.

176 *glosing:* coaxing; deceiving; flattering.

your glosing bait. Wyatt's addition.

177 *usurp*] *A, R, CP;* usurped *W.*

176-7 *Where the deceit of your glosing bait/Made them usurp a power in all excess*] Where by deceit of your glosing venom/There hath usurped a power in all excess *E.*

178-84 Verse 10. Wyatt modifies Aretino's military imagery and concludes with his own emphasis on divine protection.

178 *Shamed.* Possibly shamèd.

179 *compass:* surround with hostile intent.

178-9 *Shamed be they . . . by missing of their prey:* let their shame derive from their missing of their prey.

182 *suggestion*] enterprise *E:* incitement to evil.

183 *That they to hurt my health no more assay:* that they shall no longer try to hurt my spiritual well-being.

185-216 Wyatt translates Aretino's narrative link closely, making slight changes in ll. 189, 196-200, 205, and 211 to keep David afraid of his spiritual state.

185 *fever*] dolour *E.*

187 *And that the fit is passed of his fervour:* and after the fit has passed its most intent heat, has passed its height.

185-8 *the sick . . ./Draw . . . sighs.* Here 'sick' is the subject of 'Draw'.

188-9 *let him, I say, behold/Sorrowful David*] with sobbing double fold/ Let him sorrowful David *E.*

189 *Sorrowful.* Aretino has 'most just'.

190 *eyes down rolled*] eyes rolled *E.*

191 *Paused.* Possibly pausèd.

192 *Faithful record . . . sharp.* Wyatt's addition.

193 *seemed.* Probably seemèd.

193-4 *of his fault the horror/Did make afeard no more his hope:* the horror that he felt at his sin no longer frightened him out of his hope.

195 *The threats whereof:* the threats to his hope posed by the horror he felt at his sin.

terror] *CP, N, M;* error *W.* The Italian has 'threats with which [the horror] used to terrify the hope'.

196 *Did hold his heart as in despair a space.* Wyatt's addition.

197 *for his succour*] for succour *E.*

198 *beknowing*] and knowledging *E:* acknowledging.

197-9 *Till he had willed . . . appease.* Wyatt expands Aretino's 'before he had resolved to cry over his sins'.

200 *Eased, not yet healed, he feeleth his disease.* Wyatt's addition, probably to keep David uncertain about God's forgiveness and thereby make more plausible the frightened pleas of Psalm 38; 'not yet healed' implies a future

healing, but that is an implication for the reader, not David, who still 'feeleth his disease'.

202 *fault for to tremble*] fault to be adrad E. See l. 64 and note.

205 *who had seen*. Aretino has David looking at the cave and deciding it is a place worthy of reverence. Wyatt's change, as in l. 200, differentiates the perspective of an onlooker, or reader, from that of David, who remains uncertain of God's forgiveness and hence of the cave's sacredness.

so kneel] so him kneel *a later addition in different ink and hand.*

grave. Wyatt's addition. Compare l. 62.

206 *assemble:* assembly.

211 *were*] R; where W.

that were dismayed for fear. Wyatt's addition.

212 *rought:* grasped, took hold of.

His harp ... rought. Wyatt's addition.

213 *Tuning accord by judgement of his ear:* tuning [his harp's strings] by ear [so that they went in] accord [in pitch and tone] – that is, capable of sounding harmonious. Aretino's David makes his voice accord with the harp.

215 *the hollow tree:* the harp. Wyatt literally translates Aretino's periphrasis for the harp.

216 *strained.* Probably strainèd: (?) exerted by abnormal effort to an abnormal degree; *or* tightened, like the strings of an instrument, to raise pitch to match that of the harp (*M & T*).

217–92 The second Penitential Psalm. *Psalm 32* (31 in the Vulgate). *Beati quorum remiss[a]e sunt* (Blessed are they whose sins are forgiven). When paraphrasing the scriptural words of this psalm, Wyatt is more eclectic than he was in the first psalm. Here he draws frequently on Aretino (ll. 217–36, 271, 282–6, 290, and perhaps 263–9), Campensis (ll. 258–62, 276–80), a combination of Campensis and Zwingli (ll. 248–9, and perhaps 263–7) and the Vulgate (ll. 254–5 and perhaps 272, 289, 291–2). Elsewhere he could be drawing on any one or several of his sources. In amplifying the psalm, he even more radically compresses Aretino than he did in the first psalm. Though this psalm is slightly longer than the first in the scripture, Wyatt renders it in 76 lines as opposed to the 112 lines he used in the first.

217–31 Verse 1, with ll. 217–18 and 223–4 most closely related to the scriptural words. Wyatt is paraphrasing, compressing, and selecting from Aretino.

218–22 *not by their penitence ... but by the goodness/Of him:* not by an act or acts of penitence, either interior or exterior, to which the human powers contribute, as by human merit, because penitence cannot compensate for sin (although God pardons no sin without such acts of penitence), but rather by the goodness of God. Wyatt differs from Aretino in only two details: Aretino has 'not by the works of contrition or of penitence'; and Wyatt adds 'As by merit'. Aretino's 'works' and Wyatt's 'merit' make clear, I think, that Wyatt is here defining 'penitence' as an act or acts in which the human mind and will are agents, either with or without the assistance of God's grace.

He is distinguishing all such acts from the forgiving grace of God which is the only source of salvation. But, while man cannot in any way save himself, he must cooperate with the grace of God in order to apprehend God's forgiveness through faith, be sorry for his sins, and make progress towards holiness.

223 *and*] that *E*. Here 'that' might have been mistakenly construed as referring to 'heart contrite' which would, thereby, be given too much credit for the act of forgiveness.

224 *within a merciful discharge*] under the mantle of mercy *E*. Aretino has 'with the hem of mercy'.

227 *Provoked*. It is the restraint of lust, not lust, that is called forth by dread.

229 *To suffer the dolour*] exampled their error *E*.

228-9 *the charge/Of other's fault to suffer the dolour:* the burden of suffering the grief for having caused another person's fault [by bad example].

230 *was never execute*] did never it extend *E*.

232-6 Verse 2, with ll. 232-3 and 236 most closely related to the scriptural words. Wyatt is paraphrasing Aretino in all but l. 236, where he may be following any of his other sources.

233 *fault*] sin *E*.

232-3 *to whom God doth impute/No more his fault, by knowledging his sin:* to whom God no longer imputes the person's sin because the sinner has acknowledged his sin. Without a cue from any of his sources, Wyatt adds the phrases 'No more' and 'by knowledging his sin'. Together, these phrases insist that, before the sinner acknowledges his sin, God does impute the sin to him, and that acknowledgement of sin is a condition of forgiveness.

234 *cleansed*. Probably cleansèd.

235 *stripped*. Probably strippèd.

237-44 Verse 3, with ll. 237, 239, and 243-4 most closely related to the scriptural words. Wyatt is paraphrasing and compressing Aretino.

238 *Thinking by state in fault to be preferred:* (?) thinking, because I was king, I should be given a special right to sin [in secret]. Aretino has: 'since it seemed to me (I being King) that it was almost my right to be allowed not only to sin but that, in my worst deeds, the world should direct its eyes at the appearance attaching to my rank, and not to the consequences . . . of this sensuality.'

244 *roaring in excess*] that I by force express *E1*; that I did still express *E2*.

245-9 Verse 4. Wyatt seems to be paraphrasing Campensis, Zwingli, and probably their translators.

245 *increast*: increased; made even heavier.

247 *pricking*] restless *E*.

250-7 Verse 5. In this verse Wyatt follows Campensis, except for ll. 254-5 where he is translating the Vulgate.

258-62 Verse 6, with ll. 258 and 260-1 most closely related to the scriptural words. Phrases like '*Wherefore . . . tasted thy goodness/At me shall take example . . . time of grace . . . floods of harm*' make it clear that Wyatt is closely following Campensis throughout this verse, not the Vulgate as *M & T* state.

259 *as of this:* as a result of this experience [I am relating in my song].

262 *him to reach . . . the space:* the extent great enough to reach him.

263-7 Verse 7. Wyatt may be compressing Aretino, or he may be conflating Zwingli and Campensis.

264 *the place:* (?) in the place where I am.

265 *ward:* prison; imprisonment.

266 *loosed.* Probably loosèd.

267 *my joy.* If this is an address to God, it is Wyatt's addition.

268-75 Verse 8, with ll. 272-5 most closely related to the scriptural words. In ll. 268-71, Wyatt, perhaps taking hints for phrases from Aretino, creates a link between verses 7 and 8 that is not in any of his sources. Zwingli may give a cue for ll. 272-3, Aretino and possibly the 1539 Bible for l. 275.

268 *That:* so that.

269 *perceived.* Probably perceivèd.

274 *For thy address, to keep thee from wand'ring.* Wyatt's addition, though the need of direction ('address') is implied by Aretino's David in his description of the ease with which one loses one's self in the labyrinthine wood of the world.

275 *guide.* The 1539 Bible has: 'I will guide thee with mine eye.' No other sources make God's eye the 'guide'. This fact is the only piece of evidence in favour of *M & T*'s contention that the 1539 Bible was one of Wyatt's sources.

276-80 Verse 9, with ll. 277 and 280 most closely related to the scriptural words. Wyatt invents l. 276 and is paraphrasing Campensis thereafter.

276 *I]* Be *E.* Wyatt probably skipped to 'Be' in l. 277, saw the mistake, lined it out, and started with 'I ask'. If so, he was working here from a rough draft – a hypothesis that fits the unusually clean copy from l. 258 to l. 292.

I ask . . . this thing. Wyatt's addition indicates that God continues to speak. Aretino's God stops his message after the equivalent of Wyatt's l. 272. It is not clear in Wyatt or his other sources where God's speech ends. I have concluded it at l. 280 because thereafter God is referred to in the third person. But the speech could continue to the end of the psalm.

277 *that man doth ride.* Wyatt's addition.

277-80 *horse or mule . . ./That not alone doth not his master know/But, for the good thou dost him, must be tied . . . lest his guide he bite:* horse or mule that not only does not not know his master but also, in return for the good you do him, must be tied lest he bite the master that guides him.

280 See the note to l. 276 for the problem of where God's speech should conclude.

281-8 Verse 10, with ll. 281 and 287-8 most closely related to the scriptural words. Wyatt is probably paraphrasing and compressing Aretino throughout, though ll. 287-8 could derive from any of his sources.

285 *that*] but *E*. In my punctuation 'that' refers to 'fretting'. If one punctuated with a dash after 'sin' (l. 281) and after 'within' (l. 283), 'That' in l. 284 and 'that' in l. 285 would both refer to 'chastisings' (l. 281).

283-5 *in fretting still within/That never suffer rest unto the mind/Filled with offence*: in fretting always within the mind, a fretting that never allow[s] rest unto the mind which is filled with sin.

286 *heart*] mind *E*.

289-92 Verse 11, with ll. 289 and 292 most closely related to the scriptural words. Apart from l. 290, which Wyatt takes from Aretino, he is probably paraphrasing the Vulgate in this verse.

291 *your glory alway set you must*] I say set all your glory you must *E*.

293-324 Wyatt translates Aretino's narrative link closely, departing in theologically significant details only in ll. 297-300, 303, 304, and possibly 322.

293 *This song ended, David did stint his voice*] This ended, our David held his peace *E*.

294-5 *about he with his eye/Did seek the cave*] *A*; about he with his eye/ Did seek the dark cave *W*; did seek with his eye/ The dark cave *E*. In revising, Wyatt failed to delete 'dark'.

295-7 *the cave with which, withouten noise,/His silence seemed to argue and reply/Upon this peace*: the cave with which his silence seemed to converse about this peace, without noise being made by either the cave or his silence (*O*).

297 *peace, this peace that*] mercy, whereon he *E*.

297-8 *rejoice/The soul with mercy, that mercy so did cry*: with mercy make joyful the soul that did cry so [for] mercy.

299 *plentiful*] merciful *E*.

300 *withstand*: withstood; refused by the person on whom God would have mercy.

297-300 *Upon this peace ... withstand*. Wyatt's four lines, expanding Aretino's 'about the peace which he had made with God', emphasize God's mercy rather than David's peace.

301 *As ... that, in*] And as ... in *E*.

302 *Finding*] Findeth *E*.

303 *Considering his ... goodness and his grace*: considering the master's goodness and grace. Wyatt's addition places emphasis on the goodness of the master (God).

304 *distils*: lets fall in drops.

as gladsome recompense: as reparation made gladly to the master. In Aretino, David's joyful tears are a reward for his repentance.

305 *seemed*. Possibly seemèd.

306 *A marble image*] *CP*, *N*; And image made *E1*; An image made *E2*; An marble image *W*.

307 *on high*] lift up.

308 *Made.* In the text, as in Aretino, 'Made' refers to the 'marble image of singular reverence' (l. 306), not to 'eyes and hands' (l. 307).

    Made as] Seeming *E.*

    to plain, to sob, to sigh] to sight, to sob, to supp *E.*

309 *that bright sun forth sends*] down from that sun descends *E.*

309, 10 *sun :* God.

309-11 *a beam that bright sun forth sends . . .|Pierceth the cave :* a beam which the bright sun sends forth pierces the cave.

312 *chords :* strings of a musical instrument.

    Whose glancing light the chords did overglide] And with the lustre on the chords it glide *E1*; Whose small *E2.*

314 *clean tried.* Wyatt's addition. Compare CCLXV, 2.

315 *turn :* reflection.

    start : leap; come quickly.

316 *Surprised.* Wyatt's addition. It probably refers to 'David' understood rather than to 'his eyes'. The sudden flash of the light on the harp is the occasion for joy which, he realizes, is in fact the result of his repentance.

    by : as a result of.

317 *affect*] desire *E.*

318 *Barsabe.* Probably Barsabè.

319 *His left foot did on the earth erect :* he set his left foot on the earth in such a way that his left leg, to the knee, was straight. David kneels on his right knee, his weight being placed on his left leg.

321-2 *To his left side his weight he doth direct –|Sure hope of health – and harp again tak'th he.* The phrase 'Sure hope of health', which is Wyatt's addition, is obscure to me. Previous editors either punctuate ambiguously or place a stop after 'direct' and construe 'Sure hope of health' as the object of 'he tak'th'. The use of 'takes' to govern 'hope' and 'harp' seems highly improbable. My punctuation suggests that Wyatt construes placing weight on the left side as a sign of health: since the left side was traditionally regarded as the weaker side, David's willingness to place weight on it while singing to God is a sign of his increased spiritual strength. See LXXIII, 8-9, for the use of the left foot as a symbol of the appetite which moves the soul in the realm of earthly love or of an important if a weak part of the human person.

323 *His hand his tune :* his hand (sought for) his tune.

    sought his lay : sought for the words to be sung.

325-94 The third Penitential Psalm. *Psalm 38 (37* in the Vulgate). *Domine ne in furore tuo arguas me* (O Lord, do not rebuke me in your anger). When paraphrasing the scriptural words of this psalm, Wyatt at times gives a version that is independent of his sources, at times is eclectic in his use of his sources. He abandons Aretino completely from l. 364 to the end, for reasons I suggest in the notes to ll. 364-94. Probably for the same reasons he sharply curtails his amplification of the psalm at l. 364; before that line, his amplification involves a radical compression of Aretino.

325-30   Verse 1, with ll. 329-30 most closely related to the scriptural words. In ll. 325-8 Wyatt is paraphrasing, compressing, subtly altering, and selecting from Aretino. In ll. 329-30 his main source seems to be the Vulgate.

325-9   *I . . . pray|(Although in thee be no alteration|But that we men like as ourselves we say,|Measuring this justice by our mutation)|Chastise me not:*   I pray that you do not chastise me, although [in fact such prayers do not make sense because] in you there is no [possibility of] change [to be effected by prayer]; but we men speak as human beings, measuring your unchanging justice by our human notions of being able to change, [for example, a magistrate's judgement by pleading with him]. The doctrine of predestination by an unchanging God is implicit in both Aretino's and Wyatt's versions, but Wyatt's David is less certain than Aretino's about his being among the elect.

331-7   Verse 2, with ll. 331-3 and 'Such is thy hand on me' (l. 335) most closely related to the scriptural words. Wyatt is paraphrasing and compressing Aretino in this verse.

332   *of famine and fire*]   of dearth and of death *E*.

331-3   *For that . . . deep in me.*   Wyatt has a full stop after 'me' in l. 333; but his and Aretino's syntax force one to take 'For that . . . deep in me' as a subordinate clause explaining why David is plunged up from error.

334   *plunged.*   Possibly plungèd.

338-40   Verse 3.   In l. 336 Wyatt anticipates the allusion to 'flesh' in this verse, as does Aretino in his paraphrase. Wyatt, unlike any of his sources, connects the two verses syntactically with 'Nor'. The emphasis on stability and the acknowledgement of wickedness suggests that Wyatt is virtually independent of his sources in this verse, all of which speak of their bones' lacking peace or rest.

341-4   Verse 4, with ll. 341-2 most closely related to the scriptural words. Wyatt is paraphrasing and compressing Aretino in this verse.

341   *For why*]   By cause *E*.
above my head are bound]   are clome (?) above my head *E1*; are . . . crown *E2*.

343   *to ground*]   a down *E*.

343∧4]   By force whereof the evil cured scars *E*, *lined out*.

344   *willow plant*]   doth a bow *E*. Wyatt first intends to use Aretino's image of the bow bent by violence, then changes to his own simile of the willow.
haled: pulled; molested; pulled asunder.

345-8   Verse 5, with ll. 345-6 most closely related to the scriptural words. Wyatt compresses Aretino in this verse, but unlike Aretino he does not attribute the festering at least partly to new sins. Wyatt is satisfied with Aretino's other explanation: repentance for former sins has not been perfect.

345   *And*]   That *E*.

345, 348   *cured.*   Probably curèd.

346   *That festered is*]   Is festered *E*.

347   *under skin*]   still with sin *E1*; still within *E2*.

349-52   Verse 6. Wyatt is choosing details from several sources. The causal connection between 'Perceiving' and 'I live' might come from Zwingli.

351 *grudging*] gnawing E.

worm: conscience.

353–5 Verse 7. Apart from l. 354, which is Wyatt's addition, he is paraphrasing Campensis in this verse.

353 *fervent*: hot.

356–7 Verse 8. Wyatt seems to be conflating Campensis and Zwingli.

357 *That it hath forced my heart to cry and roar*] That forced hath my heart for to roar E.

358–61 Verse 9, with lines 358–9 most closely related to the scriptural words. Wyatt follows the first part of the corresponding passage in Aretino.

358–9 *thou know'st the inward contemplation/Of my desire*: (?) you know what my heart contemplates in the inmost part of its being.

361 *heart's inward restraints*: that which the heart keeps deeply inside itself.

362–3 Verse 10. Wyatt is following Campensis, Zwingli, or both.

363 *look*: the act of seeing.

364–94 From here to the end of the psalm Wyatt virtually abandons Aretino for Campensis, Zwingli, the Vulgate, and his independent paraphrase. He does not follow Aretino in verses 11–15 because in those verses Aretino's David speaks with the spirit of prophecy in the person of Christ. Wyatt reserves his David's awareness that God speaks through him for the crucial moment in which David becomes nearly certain that God forgives him (ll. 509–40). Wyatt also introduces David's sense of prophesying at ll. 640–7 as a confirmation of his faith.

From verse 16 to the end, Aretino's David returns to speaking in his own voice, but he does so with a confidence in God's favour that Wyatt probably finds alien to this part of his work.

364–8 Verse 11. Wyatt works independently of all his sources in making his friends and relatives into personifications of his virtues, reason, and wit. It is not clear whether or not his enemies are also personifications (see the note to ll. 369–71).

365–6 *My friends most sure wherein I set most trust –/Mine own virtues*] Mine own virtues wherein I set my trust/As friends most sure E.

367 *Reason and wit unjust.* Wyatt's addition.

368 *As kin unkind*] As natural kin E.

farthest gone at need: gone as far away as possible when I needed them.

369–71 Verse 12. Wyatt does not seem to be following any particular source in this verse. The problem here and in all remaining verses that refer to David's enemies is the identity of those enemies. Are they his own senses and appetites personified, as the previous verse implies by identifying his friends as virtues and his relatives as reason and wit? Or are they real people with real 'tongues' and 'wits' (l. 371)? If the latter is the case, Wyatt does not shape his material consistently, since there is no doubt that reason and wit (l. 367) are personifications of his own faculties.

369 *place*: scope; opportunity.

371 *reproach*] deceit E.

Their tongues reproach, their wits did fraud apply: their tongues devoted their energy to reproaches of me; their wits devoted their energy to deceitful practices against me.

372 Verse 13. Wyatt's independent paraphrase.

372 *yede:* went.

373-4 (to 'again'). Verse 14. Wyatt's independent paraphrase.

374-6 (from 'Knowing'). Verse 15. Wyatt's independent paraphrase.

374-5 *Knowing that from thy hand/These things proceed, thou, Lord, shalt supply*] for that to thee, O Lord,/I me direct. Thou shalt my hope supply *E1*; knowing . . . proceed but thou, Lord *E2*; knowing . . . proceed and thou, O Lord . . . *E3, with* and *and* O *in l.* 375 *in different ink from E2.*

377-9 Verse 16. Wyatt may have got 'dread' and 'fear' from Campensis's *metuebam* and 'fall' from Zwingli's *lapsu*; but otherwise he is paraphrasing independently.

380-3 (to 'cheer'). Verse 17. Wyatt seems to be taking cues from Campensis here, especially in 'everywhere/I bear my fault'.

383-4 (from 'for I'). Verse 18. Line 383 translates the Vulgate. Wyatt's phrasing in l. 384 may be influenced by Campensis or Zwingli.

383 *I my fault confess*] I confess my fault E.

384 *my desert:* my lack of desert or worthiness.

385-7 Verse 19. Wyatt may have got 'safe' and 'increase' from Joye; or he may have been freely paraphrasing the Vulgate.

386 *provokers*] evil willers E.

388-9 Verse 20. Wyatt's independent paraphrase.

388 *be bent*] shall assent E.

In evil for good against me they be bent: they are inclined towards doing evil against me in return for my goodness to them.

389 *hinder shall my good pursuit of grace.* Wyatt here departs from all his sources who say that David's enemies seek his undoing because he is doing or trying to do what is good. Wyatt's phrasing implies that David might not yet be pursuing God's grace.

390-2 Verse 21, with l. 392 most closely related to the scriptural words. In ll. 390-1 Wyatt seems mainly to be paraphrasing Campensis. The phrasing of l. 392 may come from Joye.

392 *Be not far from me gone*] nor be not from me far E.

393-4 Verse 22. Wyatt could be following any of his sources here.

393 *apace:* swiftly.

395-426 Wyatt translates this narrative link slightly more freely than the previous ones, omitting, changing, and reordering some of Aretino's details. But only a few changes have theological or psychological significance (for example, ll. 396, 399, 400, 424).

396 *Fainting for heat.* Wyatt's addition.

provoked. Probably provokèd: invited.

wind] shade E.

397 *shade*] wind *E*.

   lieth down at mids of day] resteth at mid day *E1*; rests at the mids of day *E2*.

399 *Take breath of sighs:* recovered some of his breath by sighing. The phrase 'of sighs' is Wyatt's addition.

400 *as sorrow hath assigned.* Wyatt's addition.

401-2 *t'one ... t'other:* the pilgrim ... David.

402 *pretend:* stretch forward; go forward.

403 *On sonour chords his fingers he extends*] His fingers strike upon the sonour chords *E*.

   sonour chords: sonorous strings; that is, strings of an instrument capable of giving out a sound.

406 *that trickle.* Probably 'that' refers to 'tears'. But 'that trickle' (what trickles) could just possibly be the object of 'feeling'.

408 *Th'altered senses*] His senses sparplid *E*.

407-8 *As he that bleeds in bain ... intends/Th'altered senses to that that they are bound:* as a person bleeding in a bath unconsciously focuses his senses, which have in fact been altered because he is in warm water, on the warm water to which his senses are fixed rather than on the bleeding (*O*). David, whose mind is fixed on God, is no more conscious of his weeping than a man bleeding in a warm bath is conscious of his bleeding.

409-10 *But sigh and weep he can none other thing/And look up still:* he can do nothing except sigh and weep and look up always.

410 *And look up ... unto the heaven's king.* Wyatt's addition, explaining why David is unaware even of his own weeping.

411 *cave's.* Probably disyllabic.

412 *strain:* utter.

   tears and sighs that he did strain] sighs and tears that he poured out *E*.

414 *smoky rain.* A phrase used in Chaucer's *Troilus* III, 628, to describe a very heavy rain. Perhaps the point is that the rain is so heavy and blown by the wind it looks like smoke.

415 *close:* shut up from observation; hidden; secluded.

   uncouth: unknown.

416 *record:* witness.

415-16 *But that ... pain.* Wyatt's addition.

417 *in all*] into all *E*.

419 *supped.* Probably suppèd.

   up supped had] had supped *E*.

   Of which some part when he up supped had: when he had drunk up – that is, swallowed – some of his tears.

420 *affrays:* frightens.

421-3 *Him seemeth that the shade/Of his offence again his force essays/By violence despair on him to lade:* it seems to him that the shadow cast by his sin again tries its power to load despair on him by violence. Wyatt uses 'to load despair on him' to translate Aretino's 'to seize him'.

424 *Starting ... dismays.* Wyatt's addition.
425 *strains.* See note to l. 216.

427–508 The fourth Penitential Psalm. *Psalm 51* (50 in the Vulgate). *Miserere mei Domine* (Have mercy on me, O Lord). When paraphrasing the scriptural words of this psalm, Wyatt is thoroughly eclectic in his use of his sources and at times gives a version that is independent of them. His amplification from Aretino and Campensis diminishes steadily as he progresses. From verse 16 to the end, he amplifies with independence to clarify and emphasize his theological position.

427–35 Verse 1, with ll. 427–8 and 434–5 most closely related to the scriptural words. Wyatt seems to be paraphrasing and selecting from Aretino, except in ll. 427–8 and the opening of 435 where he is following one of his other sources.

427–8 *Rue ... for thy goodness ... bountiful.* Wyatt may be taking a cue from Zwingli, Joye, or the 1535 Bible for his emphasis on goodness rather than mercy in rendering the first part of the verse.

429 *brace:* embrace; surround.

430 *Repugnant natures:* 1) the four elements which, without God's ordering force, would be repugnant to each other and produce chaos; 2) perhaps the natures of fallen men which are repugnant to God but which he nonetheless embraces and makes quiet with his forgiveness.

434 *those mercies much more than man can sin:* those mercies [which are] much greater than man's sin.

435 *that so thy grace offend.* Wyatt's addition, emphasizing God's grace.

436–41 Verse 2, with ll. 436–8 most closely related to the scriptural words. Except in l. 437, which seems to compress Aretino, Wyatt, having absorbed the sense of the verse from his sources, gives his own rendering and emphases.

436 *Again*] Oft-times *E*: (?) once more. Wyatt's sources emphasize repeated washings or better washings. As his first version in *E* suggests, Wyatt is probably compressing these notions in 'Again' rather than simply 'asking again'.

wash ... within. Wyatt's addition, possibly to exclude any inference that he is referring to baptism.

438 *as ay thy wont hath been:* [with sinners, not necessarily David]. Wyatt's addition. It seems unlikely that David is referring to his own experience of being made clean because, in the structure Wyatt is imposing on the narrative and the psalms, David has never before been genuinely aware of his sins and genuinely contrite.

439–41 *unto thee no number can be laid/For to prescribe remissions of offence/In hearts returned:* (?) no number can be imposed on you to limit the number of times you will forgive sins [or the number of sins you will forgive?] in hearts that have returned to you. Wyatt's addition. The emphasis on the number of sins and mercies in verse 1 suggests that Wyatt is here referring to the number of sins that God will forgive, despite the syntactical primacy of 'remissions' over 'offence'.

439–41 *For unto thee . . . hath said.* Wyatt's addition.

442–4 Verse 3, with ll. 442–3 most closely related to the scriptural words. Wyatt is translating the Vulgate in l. 442 and probably following the anonymous translator in l. 443. Otherwise he is paraphrasing independently.

442 *beknow:* recognize.
my negligence. Wyatt's addition.

443 *fixed.* Probably fixèd.
is fixed fast] shall still remain *E*.

444 *Thereof . . . penitence.* Wyatt's addition. Wyatt does not seem to be borrowing anything from Aretino here (contrary to the view of *M & T*) or anywhere in this verse.

445–55 Verse 4, with ll. 445, 447–8, and 452–3 most closely related to the scriptural words. Wyatt seems to be freely adapting Campensis in this verse.

446 *For none can measure my fault but thou alone.* Wyatt's addition, involving the curious logic that the only one offended is the one who can measure and presumably feel the offence fully. This logic is convenient for David because Uriah is no longer alive to forgive his murderer. But the argument also emphasizes the magnitude of the offence, because it is a sin against God, and it prepares for the conclusion that the achievement of justice rests in God alone.

447 *aghast:* afraid.

448 *judging thy sight as none:* judging your vision of my sin as unimportant.

451 *This know I and repent.* Wyatt's addition, with a possible cue from Joye's 'it repenteth me'.

452 *keep still thy word stable*] hold firm and fast thy word still k[eep] *E*: always be faithful to thy promise [to forgive the repentant].

453 *pure*] stable *E*.

454 *then forthwith justly able:* (?) then immediately made suitable [for being regarded as just] by an act of divine justice.

452–5 *keep . . ./Thy justice pure . . . because that when/I pardoned am, then . . ./Just I am judged by justice of thy grace.* Wyatt, though taking words and phrases from Campensis, puts his original stamp on this part of the verse. His David emphasizes the paradox of Reformed Christianity that divine justice is accomplished by merciful forgiveness because forgiveness entails God's imputation of justice to the sinner.

456–60 Verse 5, with ll. 457–8 most closely related to the scriptural words. Wyatt paraphrases ll. 456–8 independently and translates a portion of Aretino in ll. 459–60.

456 *lo, thing most unstable.* Wyatt's addition.

458 *from my nativity*] by corrupt nature *E*.

458⁀9 Yet lo, thou loves so the heart's trut[h.?] in inward place *E lined out.* Wyatt starts on the next verse and then decides to write ll. 459–60 as a transition.

459–60 *Be not this said for my excuse . . .|But of thy help to show necessity:*
I am not speaking of my inheritance of sin to excuse my sin but to show the
necessity of thy help [in escaping sin so deeply engrained]. Wyatt here trans-
lates Aretino's opening of his paraphrase of this verse to serve as a transition
to verse 6.

461–8 Verse 6, with ll. 461 and 467 most closely related to the scriptural
words. Wyatt is freely paraphrasing Campensis throughout this verse.

463 *overthwart:* perverted.

464 *led me not the way*] *A, CP, R*; hath not led me a way *E1*; led me no the
way *W*.

466 ` *as thou hast done alway.* As in the case of l. 438, it is not clear if David
is referring to his own past experience or to the experience of others. I think
the latter is more in keeping with the pattern of a single, major conversion
that Wyatt seems to be imposing on his material.

469–72 Verse 7, with ll. 470–2 (to 'white') most closely related to the scrip-
tural words. Wyatt is apparently paraphrasing and adding to the Vulgate
in this verse.

469 *And as . . . sore.* Wyatt's addition.

470 *hyssop:* a small bushy aromatic herb used for sprinkling in Jewish
ceremonial purifications.

472 *how:* however.

473–6 Verse 8, with ll. 473 and 475–6 (from 'Then shall') most closely
related to the scriptural words. The future tense in both parts of the verse
suggests that Wyatt is freely paraphrasing and adding to the Vulgate.

473 *health:* spiritual well-being, though the reference to 'bones' in
Wyatt, as in his sources, suggests that some sense of physical well-being will
accompany salvation.

gladsome tidings: good news, perhaps that of the Gospels which tell
of the birth, life, and death of Christ.

474–5 *When from above remission . . .|Descend on earth:* when forgiveness
of sin shall be seen to descend from heaven to earth. Wyatt's addition, pos-
sibly alluding to the coming of Christ, especially if 'gladsome tidings' refers
to the 'glad tidings' or 'good news' of the Gospels.

476 *consumed to dust.* Wyatt's sources have 'broken'.

477–8 Verse 9. Wyatt may be freely translating the Vulgate or Zwingli.

479–80 Verse 10. Wyatt independently paraphrases his sources other than
Aretino, giving his own sense of the verse's meaning.

480 *With sprite upright.* All of Wyatt's sources speak of a renewal of a
formerly upright spirit. Wyatt's David does not claim ever to have had an
upright spirit.

voided from . . . lust: cleared, purged of lust. Wyatt's addition.

481–2 Verse 11. Wyatt is apparently translating and adding to Zwingli's
version.

481 *cure:* care, attention, concern; with a possible pun on successful
medical treatment.

in unrest: into unrest. Wyatt's addition.

482 *thy sprite of holiness :* thy holy spirit. As in Aretino, this phrase probably refers to a newly awakened, sensitive conscience and the ability to confess one's sins. It probably does not imply a claim on David's part that he has achieved or is even approaching holiness.

483–4 Verse 12. Wyatt paraphrases l. 483 independently and takes a hint from Aretino in l. 484.

483 *Render to*] Return *E*.

Render to me joy. Wyatt departs from all his sources which use or imply some form of 'restore', and he does so deliberately, having first considered 'Return'. Wyatt's David has not experienced genuine joy before.

and rest. Wyatt's addition.

485–7 Verse 13, with ll. 486–7 most closely related to the scriptural words. Wyatt seems to be taking cues for key words and phrases from Aretino, the Vulgate, Zwingli, and Campensis.

488–92 Verse 14, with ll. 488 and 490–1 most closely related to the scriptural words. Wyatt having derived the sense of the verse from his sources, renders it freely, inverting its two parts and making independent additions.

488 *justification :* God's imputation of justice to the believing sinner. Joye's 'righteousmaking' is the equivalent of Wyatt's concept. The *justitiam* of the Latin sources probably refers to God's justice or righteousness. Here Wyatt makes explicit his emphasis on the theology of Reformed Christianity.

490–2 *of thyself, O God, this operation/It must proceed by purging me from blood,/Among the just that I may have relation :* this work of making me just must proceed from you, O God, by your purging me of the guilt of taking the blood of Uriah so that I may be accounted as one of the just. Line 492 is Wyatt's addition.

493–4 Verse 15. Wyatt is paraphrasing one of his Latin sources.

493 *let out the flood.* Wyatt's metaphor.

495–9 Verse 16. As *M & T* point out, Wyatt is following the sentence structure of Aretino: 'if thou hadst ... I would have done it.' But Wyatt departs from all his sources in generalizing from the issue of ceremonial sacrifices to include a denunciation of all 'outward' or external deeds in isolation from interior repentance.

495 *esteemed.* Probably esteemèd.

pleasant good : pleasingly good.

496 *disclose :* hatch, as in 'hatching mischief'.

497 *sacrifice :* 1) the sacrifice of living objects, usually involving the burning of animals in the old law; 2) probably an allusion to the sacrifice of the Mass, in which bread and wine, believed by Roman Catholics to be changed into Christ's body and blood, are sacrificed to the Father as a reenactment of Christ's sacrifice on the cross.

498 *gloze :* pretence.

499 *as men dream and devise.* Wyatt's addition, to prepare for the affirmation of outward deeds (l. 506) that God 'devises' for those who have repented.

500–2 Verse 17. Wyatt is mainly paraphrasing his sources other than Aretino, but in l. 502 he adds a phrase from Aretino.

502 *host:* 1) a victim for sacrifice; 2) the bread offered in the Roman Catholic Mass.

for pleasant host: as a pleasing sacrifice. Wyatt takes this phrase from Aretino.

503–5 Verse 18. Wyatt's interpretation of Zion and Jerusalem as metaphors for the spirit and heart probably owes something to Aretino's interpretation of the walls of Jerusalem as the peace and union of the worshippers of God which will be achieved in the church of the spirit that Christ establishes. But Wyatt is independent of all his sources in his interpretation of this verse as a prayer on behalf of the individual's spiritual strength.

503 *Make Zion:* secure the success, advancement, strength of Zion, the hill on which David built the city of Jerusalem.

504 *Inward Zion . . . of the ghost:* the interior Zion of the human spirit.

505 *Of heart's Jerusalem strength the walls still:* always strengthen the walls of the city of the heart.

506–8 Verse 19. Wyatt is writing independently of all his sources here in asserting that, after God forgives and imputes justice to the sinner, the outward deeds of the redeemed person, which proceed only from God, will please God.

509–40 In this narrative link Wyatt departs radically in substance from Aretino. Wyatt's David reflects on the truths emphasized by the Reformed Church, all of which are mysteries revealed to him in his own psalm. His response is awe and, ultimately, hope. David approaches the climax of his redemption, for now he has a nearly certain faith that God forgives him.

512 *astone:* stun; astonish; overwhelm one's presence of mind; with possible echoes of the Latin etymon meaning being struck with a thunderbolt.

509–12 *Of deep secrets . . ./The greatness did . . . astone himself:* the greatness of the deep secrets stunned him.

513 *As who might say:* as if he were a person who might say. In fact, as we learn in ll. 518–19 he does say these things, but in his heart and not aloud.

515–16 *That God's goodness would within my song entreat/Let me again consider:* let me go over in my mind again [those subjects] ('That') God's goodness would treat within and through my song. Since Wyatt places the question mark after 'alas' in l. 514, the last two lines must constitute a syntactic unit. God has been using David's song as a means of revealing truths of which David is unaware.

518 *poiseth:* ponders.

519 *forth afford:* yield.

520 *points:* makes the proper pauses in what he speaks.

522 *complisheth:* fulfils, accomplishes.

523 *worthiless desert:* one who deserves nothing because he is without worth.

524 *gratis:* out of kindness.

depart: impart.

526 *Measureless mercies to]* These measureless mercies and *E.*

528 *default:* fail; be wanting; be lacking.

530 *'gain:* against.

531–2 *by whom . . .,/Of heaven gates remission is the key:* by reason of mercy ('by whom') God's remission or forgiveness of sin is the key of heaven's gates.

530–2 *Mercy shall reign . . . key.* Wyatt is alluding to Matthew xvi, 18–19, the statement of Jesus to Peter on which the Roman Catholic Church bases its claim for the authority of the pope. Wyatt, in keeping with the position of the Reformed Church, defines God's mercy as the rock on which rests individual redemption and the congregation of true believers, and says that God's merciful forgiveness of sin is the key to the gates of heaven. *M* (185–6) suggests passages from William Tyndale's *Obedience of a Christian Man* (*WT* 355, 357) as illuminating parallels.

535 *dark of sin did hide*] sin had made him miss *E*.

537 *He dare importune*] Importun'th he *E*.

538 *ascribed*] ascrived *E*. Wyatt apparently had second thoughts about so radically misspelling a word to gain an eye-rhyme.

538–9 *to mercy is ascribed/Respectless labour :* to God's mercy is attributed a willingness to labour for human beings without respect to their worth, [and David therefore dares to importune God].

541–631 The fifth Penitential Psalm. *Psalm 102* (101 in the Vulgate). *Domine exaudi orationem meam* (Lord, hear my prayer). When paraphrasing the scriptural words of this psalm, Wyatt is eclectic in his use of his sources. Apart from ll. 553–8 and 581–9, where Aretino is his major source, he relies much more on his other sources, and he paraphrases them so freely that it is usually impossible to identify the most important of them. His amplification of this psalm is quite limited and diminishes as he progresses, probably because the psalm is itself so long. When he does amplify, as in ll. 543–9, he usually invents his matter instead of taking it from Aretino.

541–2 Verse 1.

542 *without impediment*] withouten stop or let *E*. Probably derived from Aretino's catalogue of threatening impediments: distance, the wind, or an obstruction between his voice and God's ears.

543–50 Verse 2, with ll. 543 and 545–7 most closely related to the scriptural words. Though Wyatt's David says in l. 550 that his case requires haste, Wyatt has noticeably tempered the sense of urgency present in Aretino and Campensis. His David has passed the spiritual crisis of near despair and now has genuine hope (ll. 533–7).

544 *Unto . . . government.* Wyatt's addition.

546 *and thine intent :* and thine attention. Wyatt's addition.

547 *And when I call, help my necessity*] And when so I call for help unto thee *E*.

548–50 *Readily grant . . . require.* Wyatt's addition.

551–2 Verse 3.

552 Only Campensis compares the dried bones to a fireplace or furnace.

553–5 (to 'bread of life'). Verse 4. Wyatt is following Aretino's beginning of this verse. He omits Aretino's and the scripture's 'struck or cut down' and gives his own definition of the bread of life as 'the word of truth'.

553   *my mind.* Wyatt's addition.

554, 555   *bread*]   food *E*.

556–9   Verse 5, with ll. 556–8 (to 'flesh') most closely related to the scriptural words. Wyatt is compressing and reordering Aretino. By simplifying Aretino's somewhat tangled chain of psychological causation and by adding the phrase 'my dread', he has clearly made fear the cause of David's nearly despairing. He has also changed Aretino's and all the other sources' past perfect and present tenses of the verbs to the simple past. That change in tense shows that the fear and despair being described are in the past; Wyatt's David now has a hope that precludes a present despair.

556   *and my dread.*   Wyatt's addition.

558   *Cleaved.*   Possibly from Joye's 'cleave', not necessarily from the Great Bible of 1539 as *M & T* suggest.

559   *As desperate*]   *CP, R*; I as desperate *W, A*; In deep despair *E*.

556–9   *for ... my dread,/My bones ... strength ... mind/Cleaved to the flesh and from thy sprite were fled/As desperate thy mercy for to find:*   because of my fear of damnation, my whole being was possessed with the perspective of a frightened sinner and fled from thy divine spirit; I was acting like a person who despaired of finding thy mercy.

560–3   Verse 6, with ll. 560–2 (to 'day') most closely related to the scriptural words. As in the previous verse, he changes his sources' present perfect or present tense to the past tense in order to place David's profound gloom in the past.

560   *So made I me:*   so I turned myself into.

    solein: solitary; averse to society.

562   *herself beta'en:*   betaken herself; handed herself over; committed herself.

561–2   *fleeth by proper kind/Light of the day:*   flees, according to the owl's own nature, the light of the day. Wyatt's addition. A man behaves according to his fallen or sinful nature in fleeing the light.

563   *To ruin life*]   To life alone *E*: Wyatt's addition, deliberately chosen over his first and more obvious 'to life alone'. Wyatt ascribes the deliberate self-ruin of despair and loneliness to the owl in order, obliquely, to ascribe them to the human sinner.

564–6   Verse 7. Wyatt is most probably paraphrasing Campensis, whose sparrow also sits below the roof. As in verses 5 and 6, Wyatt changes the present perfect or present of his sources to the past tense in order to place in the past David's isolation of himself from God.

564   *that ... began.*   Wyatt's addition, probably to reinforce the connection between the psalm and the narrative framework.

    waker: wakeful.

565   *was I*]   I am *E*. Wyatt was about to slip into the tense of his sources and then revised to fit his own time-scheme.

567-8 Verse 8. The Vulgate says that those who conspire against David praise him to his face; Campensis, Zwingli, and the 1535 Bible say they laugh at him. Wyatt omits both the hypocritical praise and the scornful laughter. That omission suggests, I think, that here, as in ll. 152-84, 364-8, and 385-9, Wyatt is presenting David's enemies as personifications of his depraved senses, appetites, desires, and acts.

568 *provoke*] assault *E.*

the harm of my disease: (?) [overt] harm that was [latent] in my disease as a sinner.

569-72 Verse 9, with ll. 569 and 571-2 (to 'tears') closest to the scriptural words.

570 *Of thy just word the taste might not me please*] In truth I found no taste that might me please *E*. Wyatt's addition, defining the bread of l. 569 as the word of God. Compare l. 555.

572 *from mine eyes do rain*] hail down from my eyes *E*.

do rain] did rain *R, CP.* Wyatt switches now to the present tense. The change bothered *R* and *CP*, but I think it is theologically intelligible. Once David begins to weep, even out of fear of God's wrath, the process of his repentance and forgiveness begins. Because David sees that process as continuing while he sings this psalm, Wyatt changes to the present tense to describe David's perceptions and his continuing weeping.

573-7 Verse 10, with ll. 573 and 575 most closely related to the scriptural words. Wyatt's main source appears to be Zwingli, whose syntax is closest to that of the English. Wyatt seems also to be using language and making additions suggested by the Vulgate and Aretino.

574 *Provoked by right ... disdain.* Wyatt's addition.

573-4 *wrath ... had of my pride disdain*: wrath regarded my pride with disdain.

577 *know*] *E*; corrected to knew *but in a hand that may not be Wyatt's.*

576-7 *To teach me ... helpless ... drown.* Wyatt's addition, probably to add a note of optimism to David's perceptions: David does know himself better now, he is in fact not without God's help, and he will not drown.

578 Verse 11. Wyatt apparently translates the Vulgate, changing the verb into the present tense and omitting 'like hay' after 'dry'.

579-80 Verse 12. Wyatt seems to be very freely paraphrasing the Vulgate which is the only one of his sources, other than Aretino, to use 'eternity'.

581-8 Verse 13, with ll. 582-3 and 585 most closely related to the scriptural words. Wyatt is very freely paraphrasing Aretino.

581 *frailty*] misery *E.*

all mankind] every man *E.*

581-2 *this frailty ... this misery*: original sin.

583 *that, as I find*] that is assigned *E.*

584 *Is*] For *E.*

583-4 *Zion ... /Is the people that live under thy law.* Aretino's David says that he represents Zion on behalf of the human race. In ll. 503-4 Wyatt's

David defined Zion as the spirit of the individual. Now, as he becomes more confident of his individual salvation, he prays for the Zion of the people, the Jewish people chosen by God to live under his law and the type of the Christian people who will experience the day of Christ's redeeming (l. 588). Compare John Fisher: 'In the first part of this psalm every man prayed for himself. After that now in this second part we be taught every man to pray for his neighbour and for the whole church of Christian people' (*JF* 170).

586 *long:* (?) long [awaited].

588 *Day of redeeming Zion:* Christ's redemption of mankind.

589–90 Verse 14. Wyatt omits the first part of the verse in which the people are said to love or desire to see the stones of Zion.

590 *In*] Of *E*.

    stones] *A, R, CP*; stines *W*.

    lower] lie *E*.

589–90 *to see in such decay,/In dust . . . Zion lower:* to see Zion sink into such decay, into dust.

591–2 Verse 15.

592 *thy glory shall honour*] shall honour thy glory *E*.

593–4 Verse 16. Wyatt is mainly paraphrasing either the Vulgate or Zwingli who, alone among his sources, make the connection between verses 15 and 16. Zwingli's temporal connection is closest to Wyatt's 'Then when', as is his use of 'power'.

593 *redeemeth*] saved *E1*; redeemed *E2*.

594 *mighty*] *A, R, CP*; might *W*.

595–6 Verse 17. Wyatt alone makes the causal connection between the Lord's esteem and his turning. Campensis and Zwingli, unlike the Vulgate, use the present tense.

595 *The Lord his servants' wishes so esteemeth*] The Lord hath his servants' cries esteemed *E1*; He hath his servants' wishes so esteemed *E2*.

596 *he him turn'th:* the Lord turns himself.

595–6 *servants' . . . poors'*. These nouns might be possessive singular, referring to David. But the use of the plural in succeeding lines, especially in ll. 602–3, argues for the plural possessive here.

597–600 Verse 18. Wyatt probably takes cues from Campensis's and Aretino's emphasis on the 'Lord the saviour' (Christ) and the response of future Christians to God's mercy. But Wyatt is offering an independent interpretation of the verse.

597 *To our descent this to be written seemeth*] To all mankind this published me seemeth *E1*; To all mankind this to be published seemeth *E2*.

598 *Of all . . . best.* Wyatt's addition.

597–8 *To our descent this to be written seemeth,/Of all comforts, as consolation best:* this truth which is to be written down [will] seem, of all comforts, the greatest consolation to our descendants.

599 *And*] whereb *E*.

600 *both most and least:* both those of high and low estate. Wyatt's addition, referring to 'they' (l. 599).

601–2 Verse 19.

602 *in:* on.

us] us men *E*.

603–5 Verse 20.

603 *algate:* altogether; in every way.

604 *discuss:* set free.

605 *sons of death:* those condemned to die.

606–8 Verse 21. Wyatt's use of 'occasion' and 'lauds' suggests that he is mainly paraphrasing and expanding on Campensis.

606 *gracious.* Wyatt's addition.

occasion gracious: a reason resulting from God's grace.

608 *lauds:* praises.

lasting ay. Wyatt's addition.

609–11 Verse 22. Wyatt's reference to 'one church' may derive from Aretino, whose David foresees the unity of people and kings taking place in the Christian church.

611 *so just and merciful.* Wyatt's addition.

612–17 (to 'the Lord'). Verse 23, with ll. 612–14 most closely related to the scriptural words. Wyatt presents a reading of the verse which appears to be largely independent.

612–13 *But to this sembly . . . at the full:* but in running to this assembly, my strength does not enable me to reach it completely.

616–17 *Although . . . the Lord.* Wyatt's addition, providing a transition to verse 24.

617–19 (from 'Take me'). Verse 24.

618 *though.* Wyatt's concessive conjunction has no precedent in his sources. It seems to imply that David is aware of the unimportance of his continuing to live beyond the middle of his life: 'even though you last forever, and that is all that matters, let me not die young.'

thine ever sure: thy years, always certain or secure.

620 Verse 25.

621–4 Verse 26.

623–4 *change them like apparel,/Turn*] them like apparel/Turn *E*.

625–6 Verse 27.

626 *thy years extend*] withouten end *E*.

shalt thy years extend. Wyatt alone gives a positive phrasing. His sources say that God's years will not have an end.

627–31 Verse 28, with ll. 629–31 most closely related to the scriptural words.

628 *pretend:* aspire to.

627–8 *Then since . . . pretend.* Wyatt's addition, suggesting that his David is reconciled, though with difficulty, to the possibility that he will die in the middle of his years (l. 618).

630 *in thy word are got:* are begotten in the merciful word of God, with a pun on the 'Word' or second person of the Trinity who became man in Jesus Christ.

631 *stablished*] *A, R, CP*; stabished *W*: set permanently; strengthened, rendered stable.

all in fere: all in companionship; all together.

632-63 In this narrative link Wyatt departs completely in substance from Aretino, whose David does not interpret prophecy as a sign of God's favour and does not experience and then resist the temptation to attribute value to his acts of repentance.

632-7 *When David . . . filed.* Wyatt converts Aretino's musical allusion to a theological point about the divine origin of the truths David sings.

632, 638 *perceived.* Probably perceivèd.

634 *he hath alone expressed*] of him were not expressed *E1*: he only expressed.

635 *greater sprite*: God.

that greater sprite] by greater thing *E*.

compiled: composed.

637 *forged.* Probably forgèd.

636-7 *As shawm . . . lets out the sound impressed,/By music's art forged tofore and filed*: as a shawm (a medieval musical instrument resembling an oboe) merely emits the sound that is communicated to it by the pressure of the player's breath, a sound created and perfected by the art of music before [it comes out of the instrument].

639 *revived.* Possibly revivèd.

640-1 *thereupon he maketh argument/Of reconciling unto the Lord's grace*: from the fact that God has chosen his song as an instrument for expressing truths that a mere human could not invent he argues that he is being reconciled to the Lord's grace or favour.

642-3 *Although some time to prophesy have lent/Both brute beasts and wicked hearts a place*: although some ages have given both brute beasts and wicked hearts a place to prophesy. David acknowledges, in order to deny, the argument that prophesying – speaking divine truths – does not necessarily prove one is in the favour of God.

644 *intent*: mind; understanding.

644-6 *David judgeth . . ./Himself by penance clean out of this case,/Whereby he hath remission*: David judges himself to be completely out of the category of beasts and wicked hearts by reason of the repentance whereby he has forgiveness.

647 *ginneth to allow his pain and penitence*: he begins to think highly of his suffering and external acts of repentance. David is on the verge of attributing his redemption to his own acts – a sin of spiritual pride.

648-9 *But when he weigh'th the fault and recompense,/He damn'th his deed*: but when he compares his sin with his suffering and external acts of repentance, he sees that his sin ('deed') is damnable beyond any recompense he could make for it. Wyatt's David does not lose confidence in God's forgiveness but in the value of his own external acts of repentance.

651 *all outward deed:* all external acts of repentance.
    all outward deed in] all recompense as *E*.
653 *returned again:* [to God].
654 *that doth his fault bemoan:* (the heart) that bemoans its fault.
655 *outward deed the sign or fruit alone:* an outward act of repentance –
for example, some penitential act – is at best the result and the sign of genuine
interior repentance. This doctrine may have come to Wyatt, *M* suggests (189),
through William Tyndale's *A Prologue Upon the Epistle of St Paul to
the Romans*, which translates and paraphrases and adds to Luther's preface
to the epistle: 'even so are all other good works outward signs and outward
fruits of faith and of the Spirit; which justify not a man but shew that a man
is justified already before God, inwardly in the heart, through faith, and
through the Spirit purchased by Christ's blood' (*WT* 133).
651–5 *Whereby he takes . . . fruit alone.* Wyatt's substitution for the con-
tinued uncertainty and contrition of Aretino's David.
658 *glory*] merit *E*.
659 *God*] *A, R, CP*; good *W, but word may have been tampered with.*
656–60 *With this he doth defend the sly assault/Of vain allowance of his void
desert,/And all the glory of his forgiven fault/To God alone he doth it whole
convert./His own merit he findeth in default:* with this realization of the
inadequacy of his acts of repentance, he wards off the subtle temptation to
allow his worthlessness some value, and he attributes to God alone the
glory of his sin's having been forgiven. He recognizes that his own 'merit' is
without value.

665–94 The sixth Penitential Psalm. *Psalm 130* (129 in the Vulgate).
De profundis clamavi (From the depths I have called). When paraphrasing
the scriptural words, Wyatt at times gives a version that is independent of his
sources, at times is eclectic in his use of his sources, and on occasion para-
phrases them so freely that it is impossible to identify the most important of
them. For his limited amplification of the psalm, especially in ll. 664–9 and
675–80, he takes hints from Aretino.
664–7 Verse 1, with ll. 664 and 667 most closely related to the scriptural
words. Wyatt's rendering of the verse's core most resembles that of the
Vulgate. His amplified definition of the 'depths' takes some hints from
Aretino's, but it is much more concise and therefore more striking in its
parallelism (*M & T*).
664 *deep despair.* Wyatt's addition.
    From depth of sin and from a deep despair] From depth of sin, from
deep despair *E*.
665 *depth of death:* the spiritual death of the soul.
666 *darkness' deep repair:* the 'deep haunt or resort of darkness' (*M & T*
386). Wyatt's addition. The darkness is both the literal absence of light and
the spiritual darkness of David when he repaired to the cave.
    of darkness' deep repair] where darkness doth repair *E*. Wyatt's revi-
sion is designed to maintain the 'of' parallels.

667 *Thee have I called, O Lord*] To thee, O Lord, have I called *E*.
   borrow: bail; ransom; deliverer from prison.
668-74 Verse 2, with ll. 668, 671, and 674 most closely related to the scriptural words. Wyatt compresses Aretino in ll. 672-4, but otherwise his rendering of the verse is largely independent of his sources. In ll. 668-70, instead of asking God simply to hear his voice, David lists the notes that God should hear in his voice, notes which partly echo the 'depths' in verse 1. In ll. 670-1, the addition of 'by grant' emphasizes the importance of God's grace as the cause of his hearing.
670 *by grant*: by the gift of grace. Wyatt's addition.
671 *intend*: pay heed, hearken.
672 *that to thee is not near*] but to thee is near *E1*; but to thee it is near *E2*.
674 *ear*] self *E*.
674 *Hear then my woeful plaint*. Wyatt rephrases and repeats the second part of the biblical verse already rendered in l. 671.
675-80 (to 'reign large'). Verse 3, with ll. 675 and 678 most closely related to the scriptural words. Wyatt is paraphrasing and compressing the first part of Aretino's version.
675 *what men offend*: which men commit offences. Wyatt's sources all make the offences rather than the offenders the object of God's observation.
676 *And put thy native mercy*] thy native mercy to put *E*.
677 *If just exaction demand recompense*: if the just requirement that the offender pay for his offence should lead you to demand payment.
678 *faint*: collapse into despair.
675-8 *if thou ...|If just ...|Who may endure ... Who shall not faint*. The doubling of conditional clauses and questions is original to Wyatt.
679 *At such account*: at such an accounting for one's conduct.
   Dread and not reverence: fear of punishment and not awe in the face of goodness.
680 *large*: completely; fully; at large.
679-80 *Dread and not reverence|... large*. Wyatt's addition.
680-2 (from 'But thou'). Verse 4. Wyatt may be taking cues from Campensis's statement that mercifully forgiving sins is natural to God and that the sinner's response to being forgiven is 'right worshipping' of God. But Wyatt is largely independent of his sources in rendering this verse: he alone says that God seeks love and that it is the hope of God's mercy which moves us to love him.
683-7 Verse 5. In ll. 683-4 Wyatt may be freely paraphrasing Zwingli, Campensis, or the 1535 Bible, each of which combines references to the speaker's hope and the hope of his soul. In ll. 685-7 Wyatt may owe something to Aretino in David's statement that his 'pretence' or claim to worth rests in God's word and promise of mercy.
683 *have set my confidence*] have ever set my trust *E*.
684 *My soul such trust doth evermore approve*: my soul always finds this confidence proved good by its experience.

685 *of eterne excellence*] of excellence *E*.

686 *promise . . . just:* 1) a promise regular in operation and hence to be counted on; 2) a promise full and complete.

mercy's promise that is alway just] just promise that is infallible *E*.

687 *my . . . pretence:* my [only] claim to worth.

688–90 Verse 6. Wyatt is paraphrasing and compressing Campensis.

688 *desirous trust:* trust that the soul will be one with God, a trust permeated by the desire to be one with God.

690 *thrust:* thirst.

691–3 Verse 7.

692 *arn:* are.

his property: his natural quality. Campensis has 'he is most merciful by nature'.

693 *Plenteous ransom shall come*] Plentiful ransom is *E1*; Plentiful ransom com'th *E2*.

694 Verse 8. Wyatt omits his sources' reference to Israel.

695–726 In this narrative link Wyatt departs substantially from Aretino. Aretino's David feels assured that God has heard his prayers and forgiven him because of an inexplicable joy that he feels. He goes on to have a vision of Christ's incarnation, birth, life, death, harrowing of hell, resurrection, and ascension. Wyatt's ll. 695–710 freely imitate the vision of Aretino's David, but ll. 711–26 are completely independent of Aretino. Wyatt presents God's favour as producing not only forgiveness but temporal benefits.

696 *David*] David into a deep *E*.

it seemeth unto me] as it seemeth to me *E*.

699 *the Word:* the second person of the Holy Trinity that became man in Jesus Christ.

confound] resound *E*.

700 *humble ear:* (?) the humble ear of the Virgin Mary who, in listening to the word of God spoken by the angel Gabriel, became the mother of the Word (*M & T*).

701 *mortal habit:* the flesh or body.

702 *shade:* to hide partially, as by a shadow.

704 *Do way*] Shake off *E*.

703–5 *that Word . . ./Do way that veil by fervent affection,/Torn off with death (for death should have her doom):* that Word of God in Christ [will] dispense with that veil of the flesh out of his fervent affection for us, a veil torn off with Christ's death in the crucifixion (for death should have her power of judgement over his mortal body).

706 *lighter:* more brightly.

707 *Than*] *M* conjectures; The *W*.

glint] *W*(?); glutt *A, R, possibly E*. The word is unclear in *E*. If 'glint' meaning 'gleam' or 'a shining' is the correct reading, it is the first occurrence of the word as a noun before the nineteenth century. Wyatt may have formed the word from the verb 'glint' or 'glent', meaning 'to shine'. The 'glint of light' is presumably something like the first ray of the sun.

lome: leam; shine.

708 *Man*] Sin *E*.

death hath her destruction: 1) the death of the body is not final in that the human body will be raised and joined with the soul at the last day; 2) the second and more frightful 'death' of the soul in sin, as a result of which the soul suffers eternally in hell, will not be experienced by those whom God forgives.

709 *That mortal veil*: 1) Christ's body, which rises from the tomb on Easter; 2) the human body, which will rise from the grave at the last day.

710 *David assurance of his iniquity*: David has certainty that his sin is forgiven.

712 *forbear*: keep back; spare.

712-13 *his son/From death for me*] the deth/Of his dear son *E*.

714 *My*] Our *E*.

715 *depart*: impart; apportion out.

717 *grace*] bounty *E*.

719 *most do crave*] ask him most *E*.

720 *suit without respect*] forceable request *E*: request pressed on God without any hesitation inspired by respect for God.

721 *to the grave*] with his host *E*.

my son: Absalom, who tried to replace his father, but was ultimately defeated and slain. See 2 Samuel xv–xviii.

724 *reject*: thrown back.

725 *sured*. Probably surèd: assured.

726 *suit of his pretence*: the request of what he is claiming from the God who delights in requests.

727-75 The seventh Penitential Psalm. *Psalm 143* (142 in the Vulgate). *Domine exaudi orationem meam* (Lord, hear my prayer). When paraphrasing the scriptural words, Wyatt frequently gives a version that is independent of his sources, at times is eclectic in his use of his sources, and on occasion paraphrases them so freely that it is impossible to identify the most important of them. He makes less use of Aretino than in any of the preceding psalms. His limited amplification, especially in ll. 727–43, is generally his own invention.

727-32 Verse 1. Unlike Aretino's David, Wyatt's David knows he has been pardoned.

727, 728, 732 *Hear ... hear ... /Complish ... answer ... /Perform*. Wyatt uses five imperatives; his sources use two or three.

728 *Complish my boon*: accomplish my request.

729 *Not by desert but for thine own behest*: not because of my deserving but because of your own promise. Wyatt's addition, probably inspired by Aretino.

730-1 *thou promised mine empire/To stand stable*. Wyatt's addition, connecting the psalm with the preceding narrative in which David asks that his temporal rule be saved from the attacks of his son Absalom (l. 721). The promise to which David refers is given in 2 Samuel vii, 8–17.

731 *after thy justice*] for thine own justice *E*: according to your own justice [which is mingled with mercy and which is imputed to the repentant sinner].

732 *require:* 1) request; 2) need.

733–6 Verse 2. Wyatt, having arrived at the sense of the verse from all his sources, gives a paraphrase which takes some details from several of them.

733 *of law after the form and*] according to just right in the *E1*; of justice after such form and *E2*.

    not of law after the form: not according to the form of the law.

734 *To enter judgement:* to enter into a judicial cause or trial.

    thrall bondslave] bond *E*.

735 *his*] thy *E1*; my *E2*.

    To plead his right: [who would have] to plead the righteousness of his acts and hence his right to that which he requests.

736 *Before thy sight no man his right shall save:* before thy sight human righteousness shall save no man.

737–43 Verse 3, with ll. 740–3 most closely related to the scriptural words. Wyatt paraphrases this verse with virtually complete independence of his sources.

738 *pricking spurs*] sufferance that *E*.

737–39 *For of myself ... my righteousness ... I have/Scant risen up:* for with my own power, with my own righteousness, I have scarcely risen up [from beastliness].

740–52 See the general note to ll. 750–2 for the problem created by the tenses throughout this passage.

740 *my en'my:* my son, Absalom.

741 *lustiness:* vigour.

742 *herns:* corners, nooks, hiding places.

    rife: great.

    to flee his rage so rife] as man in mortal strife *E1*; to flee his furious stri *E2*.

743 *me forced as dead*] constrained me for *E*.

744–5 Verse 4. Wyatt paraphrases this verse with virtually complete independence of his sources. He alone makes it, in parallel with 'For that my en'my' (l. 740) and 'For that in herns' (l. 742), a subordinate clause in a periodic sentence, the main clause of which begins in verse 5 ('I had recourse').

745 *heart ... sprite ... force:* spiritual and physical strengths. David's interior struggle had caused him to lose all strength.

746–50 (to 'mercies were'). Verse 5, with ll. 746–8 most closely related to the scriptural words.

746 *to times that have been past*] unto the times that have been *E*.

747 *in all my dread.* Wyatt's independent addition. See the note to ll. 750–2 for the problem of when this dread was felt.

750 *were*] are *E*.

748–50 *that ever last ... mercies were.* Wyatt's independent addition.

749–50 *above those wonders all/Thy mercies were :* thy mercies were superior to all those wonders.

750–2 (from 'Then lift'). Verse 6. Wyatt appears to be combining phrases from several sources and adding his own. Wyatt's sources do not agree on the tense of the verse. Campensis uses the past; Zwingli, Joye, and the 1535 Bible use the present; Aretino shifts from past to present. Wyatt originally concludes verse 5 in the present and uses the present throughout verse 6; see the textual variants for ll. 750 and 751. Then he changes them all to the past, possibly influenced by Campensis. He thereby links this verse with verses 3, 4, and 5 as an account of the past action of David's enemy and his own past request for God's grace or help in response to his enemy's attacks. Logically, these events had to precede David's entry into the cave. But psychologically and spiritually, the deeds which God performed while David was in 'dread' (l. 747), David's awareness of God's mercies, and his appeal to God for grace have occurred in the cave. Wyatt, I suspect, is not in command of his material here. An adjustment of the passage's tenses – 'have fled' (l. 745), 'have recourse' (l. 746), 'do remember' (l. 747) 'do peruse' (l. 748), 'know' (l. 749), 'are' and 'lift' (l. 750), and 'does call' (l. 751) – would bring chronology and psychology into accord.

750 *lift :* lifted.

in haste. Wyatt's addition.

751 *did*] doth *E*.

752 *grace :* (?) God's loving kindness which forgives David's sins; *or* God's material aid against Absalom. Although the problem of chronology makes certainty impossible, I think Wyatt intends the former. David is probably recalling his prayers for grace or spiritual help within the cave.

753–7 (to 'pit'). Verse 7.

753 *afore I fall.* Wyatt's addition.

754 *apace :* swiftly; immediately.

755 *that I be laid*] to make me seem *E*.

756 *count :* the sum total, the number reckoned up.

headling : with head forward, headlong.

756–7 *pass/Into the pit :* (?) die; *or* go to hell. In so far as David is praying for help against Absalom, the first construction seems most probable. The David whom Wyatt has presented in the psalms – finally repentant and confident of redemption – should not be fearing hell at this point.

757–61 (from 'Show me'). Verse 8.

757 *betimes :* early in the morning; speedily.

758 *I wholly do*] wholly do I *E*.

depend. Possibly from Campensis's *pendeo* (hang).

757–8 *aid ... grace :* aid against Absalom ... kindness. The context suggests that these terms refer to God's temporal and material assistance and his kindness towards David in the affairs of the kingdom.

759 *And in thy hand*] Do me to know *E*.

staid: set.

And in . . . staid: Wyatt's addition.

760 *what way:* in what direction.

wolt I bend: wilt that I turn my steps.

761 *For unto thee I have raised up my mind.* Probably a translation of the Vulgate's *quia ad te levavi animam meam.*

762–4 Verse 9. In ll. 763–4 ('for I . . . secret protection'), Wyatt is translating Campensis.

762 *that that do intend.* Wyatt's addition.

762–3 *that that do intend/My foes to me:* that action which my foes intend to perform against me.

763 *me assigned*] been assigned *E.*

765–8 Verse 10. Wyatt's David, like Aretino's, introduces a concern for the process of becoming holy, that is, acting in accord with God's will. But he does not abandon the concern for his external foes. Rather, from here to the end of the psalm, he perceives an almost causal connection between becoming holy and being helped by God in his struggle with Absalom.

765–6 *that I by thee may find/The way to work the same in affection:* that I, with your help, may find the way to do your will with my will.

767 *upright sprite*] sprite shall guide *E;* sprite upright *R, CP.*

768 *In:* into.

769–71 Verse 11.

769 *name, Lord*] name *E.*

for thy name: for the sake of thy name; for the honour that will be brought to thy name.

769–70 *revive my sprite/Within the right that I receive by thee:* 1) revivify my soul [which has been slain by sin] with the righteousness that you impute to it and then gradually effect in it; 2) revive my will to struggle against my external foes with the righteousness that you impute and effect in my soul. The soul's righteousness is virtually a cause of the human vigour needed to combat external enemies.

772–5 Verse 12. Wyatt's sources differ in the tenses and moods of their first two main verbs. Campensis, his anonymous translator, the Vulgate, and Aretino use the future indicative; Zwingli, Joye, and the 1535 Bible use the imperative. In his first version Wyatt uses the future indicative (see the textual variant to ll. 772–5). In his final version, Wyatt distinguishes between the present perfect ('hast fordone') and the future indicative ('shalt confound'). The revision, I think, differentiates between the iniquity of David's own interior attitudes and desires, which God has already put an end to, and his external foes, whom God shall in the future overthrow.

772 *fordone:* put an end to.

772–5] There, whilst thou shalt of thy benignity
   Confound my foes and them destroy that seek
   To hunt my life by their iniquity,
   Since [Thus *E2*] I thy servant humbly thee beseek. *E1.*

OTHER POEMS

CLIII. *E.*

In Wyatt's hand.

The couplet, in poulter's measure, translates ll. 1–3 of Petrarch's *Rime* 129 (*M & T* 345), a *canzone*. It is not possible to determine if Wyatt originally intended to translate the whole *canzone* or regarded this couplet as a complete poem.

CLIV. *E, A, T.*

In Wyatt's hand in *E*, with many revisions by Wyatt, at least six of which (ll. 19, 29, 35, 41, 51, 61) involve rhymes which show that Wyatt was composing in *E*; in Wyatt sections of *A* and *T*.

The only source so far identified is Johannes de Sacrobosco's *Tractus de Sphaera*, the most used elementary textbook on astronomy and cosmography from the thirteenth to the seventeenth century (*The Sphere of Sacrobosco and Its Commentators*, edited and translated by Lynn Thorndike, 1949). David Scott ('Wyatt's Worst Poem', *TLS* 13 September 1963, p. 696) identified the source and proved that Wyatt used mainly two pages in a version with a commentary by J. Faber Stapulensis in one of three editions – 1527, 1534 or 1538. Wyatt picked out ideas, phrases, words, and the periods of revolution of the spheres, but he arranged this and his other material to suit his own purpose – which is itself unclear since he left the poem unfinished.

The poem's unfinished state and its position in *E* – after the Psalms and the last work by Wyatt in the manuscript – may be evidence that its composition was interrupted by Wyatt's death in 1542. Scott argues that the fragment was written in October 1539 on the supposition that it was intended to help celebrate the completion of the great clock at St James's Palace (now at Hampton Court) in a ceremony included in the welcome of Anne of Cleves, Henry VIII's new Queen; he attributes its fragmentary state to Wyatt's abrupt departure for the court of Charles V in mid-November on an embassy which caused his absence during the celebrations and the passing of the poem's occasion. One additional fact with possible bearing on the date is Wyatt's statement, in his first version of l. 51, that Mars 'moveth all this war' – a phrase immediately deleted, probably for the sake of rhyme. In May 1538 Charles V, Francis I, and Pope Paul IV agreed to a ten-year truce in the conflict with which Wyatt's diplomatic missions involved him. In the summer of 1542 war broke out again between Charles V and Francis I. The reference in l. 51 could suggest that the fragment was composed before May 1538 or between the summer of 1542 and Wyatt's death in October that year.

T entitles the poem: 'The song of Iopas unfinished.'

1 *When Dido feasted first the wand'ring Trojan knight.* See Virgil, *Aeneid* I, 723–47, for Dido's feasting of Aeneas and for Iopas's song, during the feast, about the moon, sun, origin of men and beasts, weather, constellations, and seasons.

2 *Juno's wrath.* See *Aeneid* I, 4.

4 *crisped.* Probably crispèd.

3–4 *That ... Atlas did teach ... Iopas sang in his song:* Iopas sang what Atlas had taught him. See *Aeneid* I, 740–1. Virgil's Iopas has long hair ('*crinitus*') and a golden harp.

6 *heaven:* the expanse in which planets and stars are seen. Wyatt moves immediately from this imprecise and general term to a technical description of the 'heavenly pow'rs' or 'heavens' as nesting spheres.

frame: structure.

7 *heavenly pow'rs, by more pow'r kept in one:* (?) eight heavenly spheres, maintained in a unified system by the greater ('more') power of the ninth sphere, the 'first moving heaven' (l. 11); *or* nine heavenly spheres, maintained in a unified system by the greater power of God. The first reading makes sense of 'this heaven' in l. 10 – as if it had already been mentioned – and might refer to the ninth sphere's causing the motion and the 'even continual course' of the other spheres (l. 16). In favour of the second reading is Sacrobosco's reference to the power of the 'glorious and sublime God'; but he refers to God as the disposer of the four elements, not the spheres. In either case the spheres are powers because of the influence which they – and the stars and planets fixed in eight of them – have on each other and on the earth and its inhabitants.

8 *Repugnant kinds, in mids of whom the earth hath place alone:* the four elements, contrary or even contradictory to each other in their natures, in the middle of which earth alone has a fixed place. Earth is in the middle of the four elements in the sense that it lies beneath water, air, and pure fire; it alone does not move.

7–8 *Or thus: of heavenly pow'rs ... /Repugnant kinds:* or let us define the world in this [more precise] way: [it is the frame or structure] of heavenly powers [and] repugnant kinds.

10 *Without the which:* around the earth (*O*).

in equal weight. Sacrobosco says that the earth, by its weight, avoids the great motion of the extreme spheres equally in every direction. Wyatt may be adapting this idea and language to his description of the first moving heaven, ascribing to it a weight that balances the weight of the earth and keeps it at all points equally distant from the earth.

15 *his restless source*] restless recourse *E*.

source: rising motion. Compare 'recourse' (*E*): movement towards and running back.

With ... swift sway the first and with ... source: the first moving heaven, with swift revolution and rising motion.

16 *even.* Probably monosyllabic (e'en).

17 *world ... within that ... case:* the eight spheres within the container or shell of the first moving heaven.

19–20 *object/Against:* directly opposite.

20 *dividing just the round by line direct:* dividing the spheres in exactly equal parts by a straight line from pole to pole.

21 *by'imagination*. Wyatt's apostrophe may have been intended to create the appearance of the metrically correct number of syllables (12). Compare LXXVI, 14 and note.

23 *described by stars not bright*] described by stars bright *E2*; as axle is the line *E1*.

described by stars: descried, observed, perceived as a result of stars.

24 *hight*: called, named.

25 *devise*: draw in our imagination. Compare l. 21.

27 *Which of water nor earth . . . have kind*: which have the nature of neither water nor earth, of neither air nor fire.

29 *simple and pure, unmixed*] unmixed, simple and pure *E*.

uncorrupt, simple and pure, unmixed: made of a single substance, not mixed or compounded of the four elements, and hence incorruptible. The substance, called 'ether', was material but 'simple' and hence not inclined by nature to 'corrupt' into parts.

31 *those erring seven*: those wandering seven planets.

23–31 *. . . these been called the poles . . . |Arctic . . . Antarctic . . . |The line . . . |As axle . . . nor fire . . . |Therefore the substance . . . pure, unmixed ; . . . fixed ; . . . they stray*]

As axle is upon the which the whole [th'heaven *E1*] about doth go;
Which of water nor earth, of air nor fire hath kind;
Therefore the substance of the same were hard for man to find.
For it is uncorrupt . . .,
And so we say been those stars that in the same been fixed;
And eke those erring seven in circles as they stray *E2*.

In *E1* the axle is that of the eighth sphere, or firmament, only. Wyatt revised it to include all eight spheres within the first moving heaven. In both versions he failed to make Sacrobosco's distinction between the axis of the first mover (and implicitly of the earth), whose poles are properly called the Arctic and Antarctic, and the axis of the other eight spheres distant from the former by 23 degrees and 51 minutes and with different poles. Wyatt was apparently trying to correct this error in the last lines of the fragment; instead he introduced a new confusion by omitting mention of the eighth sphere (see ll. 75–7 and note).

Wyatt's revisions of ll. 26–31 created a further problem. Including all eight spheres led him to use 'stars' for both the fixed stars and planets – a usage he continues throughout the poem. But in revising l. 30's 'the same' to 'those same' he dealt with the planets' material nature and thereby eliminated the need of l. 31's reference to it. He probably kept l. 31 because he wanted to explain the planets' 'erring' ways.

31–3 *those erring seven in circles as they stray –|So called because against that first they have repugnant way|And smaller byways too*: the wandering seven planets 'stray in circles' because, during their general movement eastward, they move backwards or retrogress at certain intervals and then resume an eastward direction. They are called 'erring' or 'wandering' ('planet' is derived from the Greek meaning 'wanderer') because of their two movements: 1) their eastward movement, in union with their spheres, on a path ('way') contrary to ('repugnant') the westward movement of 'that first' moving heaven; and 2) those 'smaller byways' or 'circles' in which they 'stray' from that primary movement. To explain these 'byways' Ptolemy postulated epicycles: movements by the planets in small circles whose centres rest on the circumferences of the large circles (deferents) described by the planets in moving with their spheres around the earth. Wyatt repeats this description of two movements in ll. 66-8.

35   *the widest*:   the sphere largest in diameter.

36   *space*:   time.

38   *even*.   Probably monosyllabic (e'en).

40, 42   *sly*:   stealthy.

40   *slack*:   slow in movement; lacking energy.

39-40   *another between those heavens two/Whose moving is so sly*:   another sphere between the first moving heaven and the firmament. Wyatt follows Faber in introducing a second moving heaven, bringing the total number of spheres to ten. Elsewhere he adheres to Sacrobosco's nine-sphere hypothesis. Faber says this second mover makes a rotation in 49,000 years.

41   *next to the starry sky*]   under the firmament *E2*; that moveth under that *E1*.

42   *aged*.   Probably agèd.

45   *bowt*:   orbit, circuit.

41-5   *The seventh heaven . . ./All those degrees that gather'th up with aged pace . . ./And doth perform the same . . ./Doth carry . . . Saturn*:   the seventh heaven, which gathers up all those degrees with aged pace and performs the same, carries Saturn.

51   *in three hundred days*]   moveth all this war *E*.

54   *In the same the day his eye, the Sun, therein he sticks*:   the Sun, which is the day's eye, sticks there in the fourth sphere.

55-6   *The third, that governed is by that that govern'th me/And love for love and for no love provokes as oft we see*:   the third sphere, which is governed by the planet Venus that governs me and that often excites love in our hearts for people who do not love us as well as for people who do love us.

57   *space*:   time.

60   *calcars*:   calculators of horoscopes at birth; astrologers.

61   *sky*:   one of the heavenly spheres.

     That sky, is last and first next us, those ways hath gone: the Moon, [which] is the last sphere if we reckon from the outermost sphere inward but the first and nearest ('next') sphere if we reckon from the earth outward, has travelled those paths.

63   *sway*:   the motion of a rotating or revolving body.

64   *brown*:   dusky, dim.

     now bent]   *A*; no bent *E*.

67   *himselves*:   themselves.

69-70   *the Sun doth stray least . . ./The starry sky hath but one course, that*

we have called the eight : the Sun has the smallest epicycle, [and of course]
the sphere of the fixed stars, which we have called the eighth sphere, has only
one movement of its own (the epicycles of ll. 67–8 being confined to planets).
76 *about*] ed.; bout E2; ap E1.

75–7 ... *these movings of these seven/Be not about that axletree of the first
moving heaven;/For they have their two poles directly t'one to t'other* ...
The spheres of the seven planets revolve on an axis which, according to
Sacrobosco, is at an angle to and 23 degrees and 51 minutes away from the
axis of the first moving heaven; the planets' axis has its own poles opposite
each other. Wyatt is apparently trying to correct the mistake in ll. 25–31 by
introducing the separate axis and movement of the eight spheres inferior to
the first moving heaven. But in specifying 'seven' he omits the eighth sphere
of the fixed stars, or 'firmament'. Perhaps he was uncertain whether the
eighth sphere revolved on the axis of the first mover or that of the planets.

Poems Attributed to Sir Thomas Wyatt
After the Sixteenth Century

RONDEAU

See head-note to Rondeaux on p. 337.

CLV. E, D.

5 *given me leave:* told me to go.

7 *so*] D; too E. It was possible for a scribe to misread 'so' as 'to'. I think that 'so' makes better sense after 'For': 'I did not rejoice at being rejected because I loved her so surely.' It also prepares better for the antithetical 'But' of l. 8; loving 'too' surely *was* reason for ceasing to love.

12 *my first address:* my stance with respect to the lady before I loved her – presumably one of detached courtesy.

13 *press:* crowd (of rivals?); condition of being hard pressed.

SONNETS

See head-note to Sonnets on p. 341.

CLVI. D.

3 *lin:* cease.

4 *pease:* quiet, pacify.

8 *grow:* flourish.

12 *me feed:* minister to my desire.

14 *often:* frequent.

That often change doth please a woman's mind. Compare Petrarch's *Rime* 183, ll. 12–14 (*M & T* 424): 'Woman is by nature a changeable thing; whence I know well that a loving condition in the heart of woman lasts a very short time.' Perhaps ll. 13–14 echo a proverb, 'Woman's mind and winter wind change oft' (*Tilley* W673 and *ODEP* 74); and l. 14, 'A woman's mind is always mutable' (*Tilley* W674) (*M & T*).

CLVII. D.

2 *And after the old proverb:* and [I do so] in keeping with the old proverb. Chaucer puts 'the old proverb': 'He hasteth wel that wisely kan abyde' (*CT* VII, 1053). Compare the proverbs 'Everything comes to him who waits' (*ODEP* 179) and 'He that can stay, obtains' (*Tilley* S835 and *ODEP* 619) (*M & T*).

3 *my lady.* F says that the lady is Fortune, an interpretation that makes

good sense of 'provide' (l. 4). But the speaker's beloved seems more likely to be his 'lady'.

4 *provide*: make provision for, or satisfy [your needs].

5 *tarry the tide*: (?) wait for the promised time of prosperity; abide my time. See ll. 1–2 and note.

6. *ye*: (?) the lady (*M & T* 427); *or* one, a person. If the latter, the tone is ironic.

10 *as who saith*: as they say; as the saying goes.

13 *plain*: plain-spoken in rejecting me.

14 *yet shall not obtain*: yet [I] shall not obtain [my desire].

CLVIII. *B.*

Line 5, with an 'ard' rhyme, is apparently missing. It would perfect the sonnet form and, it is to be hoped, the defective sense of the first quatrain.

4 *Seeing*] *ed.*; Seith *B.*

Seeing from the foot in midway I was forward: seeing that I had advanced half-way up the rock from the base.

6 *No heart so hardy nor courage*: (?) there being no heart or courage so hardy.

7 *shroud*: (?) a rope or set of ropes leading from a ship's mast to a deck; hence, a high thing to climb.

10 *the rock of love and perfect joy*. Presumably this is a rock climbed earlier in the allegorical journey. Having known love, joy, and then despair (l. 11), he is now trying to climb back to the heights of love.

11 *Bained*: bathed.

CLIX. *B.*

M & T, who introduced this poem into the Wyatt canon, doubt that it is by him.

1 *bolstered words*: (?) padded or bombastic language.

2 *As who saith, bidden I should obey*: as by one who says that I, having been told to obey, should obey.

4 *underband*: (?) fasten [me] under [you] with a band or shackle.

6 *bewray*: betray; reveal.

8 *wean my will*: (?) detach my will [from its freedom].

9 *The free ye think to force*] *ed.*; The free ye force *B.*

14 *fears*] *ed.*; force *B.*

13–14 *For like acquaintance of like scathe/Is my 'no fears' of your 'no faith'*: (?) for an acquaintance like [to your threatening words] and of like potential for harm is my lack of fear of your lack of fidelity [and your consequent attempt at tyranny].

CLX. *B.*

M & T, who introduced this poem into the Wyatt canon, apparently doubt that it is by him because of its unusual amount of alliteration.

1 *Driving*] *changed to* Driven: rushing, hastening.

2 *Between two stools my tail goeth to the ground.* Proverbial; see *Tilley* S900 and *ODEP* 43 (*M & T*).

5 *Doth dread that it dare and hide that would appear:* fears its inclination to dare show its love and hides that love which would show itself.

6 *at liberty I go bound.* Compare XXVI, 8; LXXXV, 11; CLXXXVII, 32.

7 *For pressing:* with respect to hastening forward boldly, to venturing. *proffer:* offer my heart or love.

8 '*Back off thy boldness. Thy courage passeth care*': 'Do not behave boldly. Your courage surpasses your worry or fear, [so behave boldly].' The sounds he hears are contradictory, the first inspired by his fear, the second by his desire.

11 *cause causeth for dread of my decay:* it (the doubt) creates cause for fear that I shall fall into ruin.

12 *thought*] words *original B and changed immediately*. *In thought all one:* single-minded in my love.

14 *inward perfect:* inwardly perfect or single in my love of you.

EPIGRAMS

See head-note to Epigrams p. 364.

CLXI. *D.*

In *D* follows a poem attributed to 'Wyat' in margin of *E* and in Wyatt section of *T*. But otherwise the section of 6 poems in *D* which it begins does not appear to be a group of Wyatt's poems.

Compare LXXIV, LXXV, LXXVIII, and CLXXV. See the head-note to LXXIV for the suggestion that these poems constitute a group and have Serafino's *Canzona de la Patientia* as inspiration.

5 *fit:* 1) a painful experience; 2) a part of a song (continuing the meta-phor of l. 3).

6 *Hereafter comes not yet:* the future, which has not yet arrived, may bring a better response from the one who has wronged me, and, if not, a less patient response from me. Proverbial, with the suggestion that the future will be disagreeable; see *Tilley* H439, *ODEP* 293, and CCLX, 7 (*M & T*).

CLXII. *B.*

The poem freely imitates Serafino's *strambotto*, *Ahime tu dormi*, with some details from another *strambotto* by Serafino, *Tu dormi*, a companion piece to the first (*M & T* 412–13). For discussion of the handling of these sources, see A. M. Endicott (*FR*). Wyatt's fondness for Serafino's *strambotti* makes his authorship more probable than usual among the poems of doubtful authorship taken from *B*.

8 *my life to waste.* Compare LXXVIII, 8 (*Muir*).

CLXIII. *H, NA.*

In *H* follows a poem by Wyatt; in what might be a Wyatt section of that manuscript and, in the view of *Harrier* (22), a probable Wyatt section on folios missing from *A* and printed in *NA*.

The poem's first three lines translate three lines from Petrarch's *Rime* 84 (*M & T* 432), and the rest is a very free imitation of Petrarch's poem. The latter takes the form of a dialogue between the lover and his eyes in which the eyes defend themselves from the lover's accusations. The English poem does not use the dialogue form and thereby excludes the eye's defence.

1 *Plain.* Petrarch has 'weep'.
3 *him:* the heart.
9 *brand:* burning; a piece of burning wood.
10 *With such desire to strain that past your might :* (?) with a desire of such intensity that it afflicts ('strains') the heart beyond the power of the eyes alone to afflict the heart; *or* with a desire of such power that it raises the fire in the heart to an intensity beyond that which the eyes alone could produce.
12 *flamed.* Probably flamèd.

CLXIV. *H78* (1–7), *A, T.*

T places the poem among 'Uncertain Authors' with the title 'Of the lover's unquiet state'.

I print the poem from *H78*, where it is a self-contained riddle in the form of a single question. It is followed by an 'Answer', given below, which is probably by a different author. The unintelligible third line of the answer seems to be aiming at the idea that the lady is slow to grant sexual favours to the friends she 'loves':

> Love thou hast which thou dost lack,
> With goodwill granted of her truly.
> But yet to grant her friends be slack,
> So ye be doing and yet chastely.
> For sloth and fear you cannot win,
> So you are ready now to begin.

In *A* and *T* the poem is followed by the next poem, another riddle in a different manner and probably by a different author but incorporated by *A* and *T* as a conclusion to this poem.

3 *full fair :* quite directly, quite completely.
5 *applied :* devoted my energy to; handled vigorously.
6 *Whereby I see I lose*] *ed.*; Whereby I lose *H78*; Thus may I say I lose *A*; Still thus to seek and lose *T*. *A*'s 'say' may be an alternate spelling for 'see'.
7 *new*] *A*; now *H78*; newest *T*.

CLXV. *A, T.*

T prints the poem among 'Uncertain Authors'. In *A* and *T* this riddle is presented as the concluding part of the preceding poem. The speaker in both poems seems to be 'loved' by his mistress but denied her sexual favours.

1 *wilful riches:* riches that proceed from the will, which is the faculty of loving.

4 *scarceness:* poverty.

CLXVI. *D.*

F claims the poem is a madrigal on the grounds that its rhyme scheme is the same, except for its relation to syntactic breaks, as Petrarch's *Rime* 121, a madrigal (the ultimate source of I).

1 *th'eternal fire:* the fire of hell.

1-4 *My love . . . may not attain.* The speaker identifies the fire of hell with the frustrated desire of the damned to see God and defines his love as like that frustrated desire.

6 *by . . . extremity:* (?) probably by the lady's extreme severity or rigour. It is not clear if the speaker, like the souls in hell, has offended his 'goddess'.

6-7 *restrained by great extremity/The sight of her:* kept back from the sight of her by very extreme circumstances.

8 *avail:* efficacy.

O puissant love and power of great avail: O mighty love which has the power of being greatly effectual in accomplishing its ends, [in this case, the suffering of the lover].

9 *By whom . . . may . . . death assail:* as a result of his love, death may take the lover's life.

CLXVII. *D.*

Precedes in *D* a poem which, in *E*, is in Wyatt's hand; but the poem by Wyatt is in the midst of a group of poems in *D* for which there is no evidence of Wyatt's authorship.

2 *rejoice:* rejoice at.

3-4 *remain/To:* remain in the condition of.

5 *cursed.* Probably cursèd.

6-7 *procured a careless mind/For me:* produced a mind [in the lady] which is without care for me.

7 *unfeigned.* Probably unfeignèd.

11 *speedless proof:* profitless experience.

12 *lust:* 1) wish; *and* probably as a pun 2) have strong sexual desire.

CLXVIII. *D.*

6 *ill:* badly.

CLXIX. D.

The speaker is a woman who says that 'it is a small loss to lose a suitor who is put off by a single refusal' (*M & T* 424) and who lacks good sense.

3–4 *And wit they lack that would make moan/Though all such pique were wiped away*: and those shrinking lovers, who would moan even if all such vexation were gone, lack wit.

CLXX. D, B, Stark, Folger (in a longer version).

In *Folger* precedes a poem by Wyatt.

M (92–3) suggests that this version in *D* and *B* is a reduction of CCL. He argues that the second and fourth lines of each quatrain in the longer version are 'too good to have been tacked on to another poem'. I assume that the shorter version is the original, but for a similar reason – the second and fourth lines in the longer poem are too good to have been dropped in revision.

The text I print derives from the premise that *D*, *B*, and *Stark/Folger* are three independent witnesses to the original.

1 *for I care not*] *D, B*; *changed in B to* I care not; *and* spare not *Stark, Folger.*
3 *dread*] *D, Stark, Folger*; fear *B*.
4 *Think*] *D, Stark, Folger*; Make *changed to* Say *B*.
   fear] *D, Stark, Folger*; dread *B*.
5 *For*] *D, B*; But *Stark, Folger*.
6 *recketh*] *B, Stark, Folger*; recks *D*.
10 *and spare not*] *B, Stark, Folger*; for I care not *D*.

CLXXI. B.

4 *Iarbas.* Dido purchased a piece of land on the coast of Africa from a local chieftain, Iarbas, and on that land built Carthage. Iarbas sought Dido's hand in marriage, threatening her with war if she refused. To escape him, she built a funeral pyre on which she stabbed and burned herself before the people.
5 *see Fortune*: take a clear and critical look at Fortune.
8 *lies*: the lies told by Virgil, that I committed suicide because of frustrated love of Aeneas.

CLXXII. B.

This epigram may be remotely indebted to Sannazaro's *strambotto* '*De Venere, et Priapo*' (*M* 177).

2 *Did on*: did put on.
   mighty Mars the red. Compare Chaucer, *CT* I (A), 1969 (*Da*).
3 *his targe she might not steer*: his shield she might not manage.
6 *Priapus*: 1) the god of procreation, characterized by a large phallus; 2) a phallus.
   gan] *M & T*; can *B*.

CLXXIII. H, NA.

At the end of what might be a Wyatt section of H and, in the view of Harrier (22), in a probable Wyatt section on folios missing from A and printed in NA.

CANZONI

See head-note to Canzoni on p. 383.

CLXXIV. B, D.

The poem freely imitates a *canzonetta* in Book I of *Gli Asolani* by Pietro Bembo (1470-1547) (*M & T* 391-2). The English poem departs mainly from the Italian by presenting a cruel mistress, not a personified Love, as the cause of the lover's plight. The argument of the poem depends on the mistress's cruelty having two contrary aspects: her beauty, which excites in him the flame or pain of desire; and her rejection of him, which causes in him the tearful pain of near-despair. Each pain competes with but does not eradicate the other, as water, threatening to extinguish a fire, can in part be evaporated by the fire. One of two deaths is possible for the lover, but the 'double death' (l. 36) from desire and despair is not. If the mistress would 'withdraw' (l. 31) her beauty from his presence, he would die of despair. If she would cease overtly rejecting him and remain in his presence, he would die of frustrated desire because she would never, on the premise that she wants him to die, gratify his desire. She could, on the other hand, 'withdraw' her 'cruelty' (l. 1) in the other sense of giving herself to him, in which case he would not die at all. The notion that her ceasing overtly to reject him would end his tears and thereby let him burn to death is a central and implausible connection between psychology and metaphor in the poem.

Bembo's *canzonetta* consists of four seven-line stanzas rhymed ababbbb, cdcdddd, etc. The stanzas interweave three-beat and five-beat lines. In rhyme scheme and the use of lines of different length, the English poet makes an attempt to imitate the Italian.

4 *Devised.* Probably devisèd.
  Devised for the nonce: plotted by the mistress for the occasion. The phrase suggests that her cruelty is deliberate and arbitrary.
9 *And cannot die for pain:* but cannot die because the two potentially mortal pains which she makes him sustain conflict with each other.
17 *that do redress*] D; doth then redress B, *changed later to* that doth oppress.
19 *these:* these tears.
25 *then:* therefore, so. I take ll. 24-7 to refer, by way of summary, to both the pain of desire and the pain of rejection. If that assumption is correct, 'then' does not express temporal sequence and 'pains' does not refer only to the pain of desire.
29 *would no nother:* would will no other [fate for me].

31 *the one or other:* your presence or your overt rejection of me.
32 *cruelness*] B, D; cruelty *later correction in B.*
33 *doubtless*] B; doubles D; perdie *later correction in B.*
32–3 *your cruelness/Doth let itself, doubtless:* (?) your cruelty doubtless
hinders or works against itself [because it has two competing aspects].
34 *that*] ed.; it B, D.
35 *nor I.* Implying that he is not alive, though not dead.

CLXXV. D.

Compare LXXIV, LXXV, LXXVIII, and CLXI. See the head-note to
LXXIV for the suggestion that these poems constitute a group and have
Serafino's *Canzona de la Patientia* as inspiration. Lines 1–2 of this poem
translate ll. 1–2 of Serafino's.

1 *of:* with *or* in. Compare LXXIV, 19.
7, 9 *have:* suffer.
7 *nay:* denial.
11–12 *Patience without desert/Is grounder of my smart:* patience with
undeserved wrong treatment is itself a reason why my pain continues.
24 *But suffer:* but to suffer.
26 *chanced.* Probably chancèd.

CLXXVI. D.

The poem is a free imitation of the first two stanzas of Petrarch, *Rime* 135
(*M & T* 428). Petrarch goes on to compare the lover with other wonders of
nature.

1 *wonders*] N; wondrous D.
7 *compared.* Probably comparèd.
5–7 *unto that that men may see/Most monstrous thing of kind,/Myself may
best compared be:* I may best be compared to that which men consider the
most monstrous thing of nature. The speaker goes on to compare himself to
two 'monsters' of nature.
9–12 *There is . . . ship unsure.* The rock is a 'magnetic stone supposed to
be in the Gulf of Bengal (mentioned by various ancient authorities, e.g.
Ptolemy, *Geography* vii, 2)' (*M & T* 429).
18 *Of her this thing ensueth:* concerning her the following thing happens.
17–20 *A bird . . . she reneweth.* The phoenix, a unique bird that burns
itself and regenerates itself from its own ashes.
22 *alone:* unique.

BALLADES

See the head-note to Ballades on p. 396.

CLXXVII. D.

Some critics have suggested that the poem's source is Petrarch's *Rime* 1
(*M & T* 422), but the resemblances are too general to be good evidence. If

the poem is by Wyatt, he was apparently intending to send 'abroad' a 'book' of his poems for which this poem would have been both a preface and an envoy in the medieval tradition of farewells to books.

11   *scuse:* excuse.

12, 24   *indite:* put into words.

12   *to indite*] ed.; t'indite D.

14   *her puissant might:* the powerful might of the law [that governs the life of the lover].

31   *noting*] M (80); moving D; musing M & T.

CLXXVIII. *E* (two versions, first deleted).

Follows two poems attributed to 'Tho.' in *E*.

7, 14, 21, 28   *the eye is traitor of the heart:* 1) the eye reveals the inclination of the heart (see 'betray' in l. 35); 2) the eye gives up the heart to the enemy (a rival lover). Alludes to the proverb 'The eye is window of the heart'; see *Tilley* E231 (*Da*).

8   *To frame all well:* to ensure that this disagreement will end happily.

10-12   *who will assent/To do but well, do nothing why/That men should deem the contrary:* a person who intends to do nothing but what is good does nothing to lead others to suspect the contrary.

15-16   *that look all sole/That I do claim ... to have:* that look which I claim all for myself alone.

17   *go seek the school:* should not try to learn.

19-20   *than heart vouchsafe/By look to give in friendly part:* (?) than that a heart should show a gracious willingness by a look, to give itself in a friendly way.

22   *suspect:* suspicion.

24   *deemed*] N; denied E.

25   *of*] E1; not in E2.

25-6   *Then is it not of jealousy,/But subtle look of reckless eye/Did range too far to make me smart:* then it is not a matter of my jealousy; but the subtle look of your reckless eye ranged so far that it made me feel pain.

32   *Whether the stroke did stick or glance:* whether the chance blow of your eye, [as if it were a weapon], did stick in the other man's eye or glance off it.

33-4   *But scuse who can, let him advance/Dissembled looks:* (?) but let the person who can excuse such behaviour use, in a pushy way, looks that do not reveal the heart; *or* but let that person who can excuse insincere looks come forward and defend them.

35   *betray:* reveal.

38   *he*] ed.; not in E1, E2.

29-42   *But I ... show the heart*] not in E1.

CLXXIX. *D, B.*

There is an unusual change of rhythm in this poem, from a four-beat line in the first stanza to a predominantly three-beat line in the second.

3 *mine eye might blear :* might dim my awareness [that you are having an affair with 'other friends'?].

7 *gloze:* veil with specious comments; explain away.

9 *Prate:* chatter; talk long to no purpose.

paint: 1) colour highly in order to deceive; 2) deceive with specious words.

10 *wreck*] *B*; work *D*.

11 *care*] *ed.*; cansse (?) *D*; can so *N*, *F*.

15 *this*] the *B*.

16–17 *If I have ... the loss*] *Written as one line in D and B to preserve a couplet-ending parallel to that of the first stanza.*

CLXXX. *D, Ash, B, T.*

Among 'Uncertain Authors' in *T*. *M & T*, who introduced the poem into Wyatt's canon, say that it is 'presumably not' by him. The first letters of the stanzas constitute an anagram of Wyatt's name (T-A-W-I-T). But see *Rollins* (II, 277) for the evidence that such an anagram is more probably a tribute to Wyatt by another poet than an indication of Wyatt's authorship.

Ash has the following additional stanza:

> He is in wealth that feeleth no woe;
> But I may sing and thus report,
> Farewell my joy and pleasure too.
> Thus may I sing without comfort,
> For sorrow hath caught me in her snare.
> Alas, why could I not beware,
>   So often warned?

Ash orders the stanzas 2, 4, 6, 3, 5, 1. *B* orders them 1, 2, 4, 3, 5. I have adopted *D* as copy-text on the assumptions that *D* is the poet's revision of a version of *Ash* and that *B* conflates the two versions. If this assumption is correct, *Ash*'s extra stanza was omitted because it was judged weak.

3 *worketh*] *Ash, B, T*; workes (*possibly two syllables*) *D*.

worketh ... her kind: behaves according to her nature.

6 *want:* the lack of insight.

9 *chanced.* Probably chancèd.

10–11 *in despair to have redress/I find my ... remedy:* I find my remedy is to take relief in despair.

20 *Even.* Probably monosyllabic (e'en).

chiefest. Probably monosyllabic (chief'st).

25 *to my pain my wealth is happed:* in my experience of well-being I have found my pain.

34 *bare:* barren; taken away.

CLXXXI. *D.*

4 *abused:* deceived; ill used.

13–14 *to fet/Such fruit ... as of love ensueth:* to fetch such consequences as result from love.

15 *to get:* to be got.

16 *And of the loss the less the ruth:* and, [now that I am detached from love], the less is the sorrow that results from losing a beloved.

20 *withsave:* save, preserve.

22 *grounded grace:* the privilege [of rational detachment from love] established in him. The attribution of the grace to Fortune (l. 23) seems to rule out 'divine grace' as a meaning. See also note to l. 36.

23 *Thanked.* Probably thankèd.

32 *love's.* Probably disyllabic.

34 *passed:* endured.

36 *that*] *N* conjectures; of *D.* 'yt' in *D*'s source might have been misread as 'of'.

The power that love so late outcast: the power [of rational detachment] that so recently cast out love. *F* and *M & T* defend the original reading of the line on the grounds that the speaker is distinguishing between the philandering of his youth and the 'grounded grace' (l. 22) of a permanent love in his maturity. But the 'power' of permanent love was not cast out recently ('late'); indeed, it did not exist until recently. And it makes no sense to say that philandering love, which has been cast out recently, 'shall never cease within my breast' (l. 35).

CLXXXII. *D.*

2, 8 *That:* that which, what.

3 *no more*] *N*; more *D.*

7 *Hap evil or good:* (?) whether evil or good happen; *or* let evil or good happen.

8 *as well in worth:* (?) in good part (*M & T*).

15 *To put in proof this doubt to know:* to make trial of, to challenge this fear [of mine] to know [the truth].

19–20 *such fruit/As with my heart my words be meant:* such evidence of worth as will show that my words are spoken with all my heart.

21 *proof of this consent:* test of this [possible] sympathy for me [on her part].

CLXXXIII. *D.*

F, who introduced the poem into the Wyatt canon, does not think it is by him. As she points out, Wyatt generally avoids classical allusions.

F thinks this poem is an imitation of a Spanish form called *Glosa* or 'commentary' in which the initial couplet or verse proposes the subject that is commented on by the rest of the poem. It is just possible that the couplet is the 'burden' of a poem in carol form and should be repeated after each stanza. Compare CCXII and CCXVIII for poems that are more clearly examples of the carol, though in a modified form.

2, 46 *again:* in return.

5 *Whereas I love:* where I love; in my love of this person.

5–6 *no redress/To no manner of pastime:* no restoration of my life to any kind of pleasure or amusement.

8 *wearish*] *M & T*; werilye *D*: sickly, feeble; lean, shrivelled.

11 *there as is disdain:* where there is disdain [in return for love].

14 *train:* (?) course of actions; *or* trickery.

24 *Record of:* testimony of; *or* that which is recorded by.

Terence. Publius Terentius Afer (185?–159 B.C.) was a Roman writer of comedies that typically involve competition, between an old man and a young man aided by a servant, for the love of a young woman.

28 *mort:* dead.

cold as any stone. Proverbial; see *Tilley* S876 (*M & T*).

29–30 *This causeth unkindness of such as cannot skill/Of true love:* the unkindness of those who do not know how to offer true love causes this [set of miseries described by Terence].

31 *our lord*] her lord *F, M & T*. Although the emendation makes better historical sense than the reference to Jesus Christ in 'our lord', 'the suicide of Lucrece was much debated by theologians and it is possible that the author of this poem either did not realize that she lived before the Christian era, or else regarded her as a kind of forerunner of Christian martyrs' (*M & T* 422).

35 *her nigh friends:* friends near her.

36 *guerdon:* reward.

31–6 *Lucrece . . . was betrayed.* Lucrece, or Lucretia, the wife of Lucius Tarquinius Collatinus, was raped by Sextus Tarquinius, the son of the tyrannical king, Tarquinius Superbus. She informed her husband, her father, and their friends of the deed, exacted an oath of vengeance from them, and then stabbed herself. Lucius Junius Brutus, one of the friends of her family, led the people in a revolt against the Tarquins, drove them out of Rome, and established a republic in (according to tradition) 509 B.C. The story was told by Livy and Ovid but would have been most easily available in Chaucer's *Legend of Good Women* 1680–1885.

37 *Whereas:* where.

42 *give sentence:* render, as in a court of law, the authoritative judgement that will be executed in practice.

44 *But true heart for true love:* but that a true and loving heart should be the reward for true love.

49 *the cordial vein:* the vein that carries the blood to the heart from the extremities.

50 *revulsed by no manner of art:* drawn out by any kind of medical art.

51 *Unto:* until.

CLXXXIV. D.

The third line of each stanza is repeated as the stanza's version of the refrain.

3 *that once I had:* that I once possessed her and her love. Compare CCXXXIII, 5.

5-6 *Let them frown on that least doth gain;/Who did rejoice must needs be glad:* let those lovers who have gained very little from their love continue to frown; those who did find joy in their love must not frown but be glad [even though the love has ended].

7 *ween'st]* ed.; weenest D.

thou ween'st to reign: you expect to prevail [? over my contentment].

9 *overthwart:* wrongly; crossly.

10 *coyly:* having a coy appearance.

30 *Their kind it is.* Proverbial; see *Tilley* W674 (*Da*).

31 *Yet I protest she hath no name:* now, as before (ll. 25-6), I insist I will not reveal her name.

CLXXXV. D.

This epistle may be addressed to the body and soul of human beings generally (ll. 1-2, 8-10, 35) or to two people who do not know the writer and to whose body and soul he particularly addresses his warnings, largely proverbial, about false friends. I think the former more likely. The writer may be a ghost (l. 35).

2-3 *(and this my intent/As I do here):* (?) and this is my intention as I act in this life. I suspect the text here is corrupt.

2-4 *I send ... my intent ... you to advertise/Lest that ... your deeds you do repent:* I send this letter to warn you lest you perform deeds which you end up repenting.

5 *shent:* reproached, scolded.

6 *says as he thinks.* Proverbial; see *Tilley* S725.

9 *wills]* ed.; will D.

8-11 *The body and the soul to hold together ... the one to love the other/It increaseth your bruit:* for the body and soul to care for and love each other increases the reputation of both.

13 *yourselves: either* body and soul, *or* two people addressed. The context created by ll. 8-11 strongly suggests that the body and soul are being addressed here and urged to maintain a stoic self-containment.

13 *Trust ... no moe.* Alludes to the proverb 'Wherever you see your friend, trust yourself'; see *Tilley* F724 (*Da*).

14 *may fortune be:* may by chance turn out to be.

such as ye think ... foe. Proverbial (*S* 64).

15 *Beware hardily ere ye have any need:* be boldly on your guard before you have any obvious need to be.

22 *Fair words make fools fain:* the fair words of other people make only fools glad. Proverbial; see *Tilley* W794 and *ODEP* 188 (*M & T*).

23 *bearing in hand*: being deluded or abused through another's false pretences.

bearing . . . woe. Proverbial; see *Tilley* H94 (*Da*).

24 *time trieth troth*: time alone will put to the test and thereby determine who is loyal. Proverbial; see *Tilley* T338 and *ODEP* 660.

24–5 *refrain/And from such as be ready to do*: keep yourself from people, and especially from those who appear to act as friends.

27 *cause causeth much*: (?) a false friend who causes trouble causes much trouble.

29 '*To wise folks few words*': a few words are sufficient for wise people. Proverbial; see *Tilley* W781 and *ODEP* 728.

37 *chaff*: livelihood (*M & T*).

38 *wanting that he has*: lacking that which he in fact possesses.

40 *at adventure*: recklessly.

36–41 *Written lifeless at the manor place . . . the twenty day of March.* Letters of the period conventionally ended with this kind of phrase, stating where and when the letter was written. Here the writer apparently has a manor house or place but wanders about instead of living in it – a fact that, along with his being 'lifeless', suggests he is a ghost. *Da* reads 'manner place' (kind of place).

42 *And hath him recommended to the cat and mouse*: (?) and has written something to recommend himself to all tastes (*M & T*).

CLXXXVI. D.

The hope alluded to in this poem, disappointed by someone who appeared faithful but proved untrue (l. 22), could be of various kinds – political, for example, as well as amatory.

3 *The great abuse that did me blind*: the great deception that blinded me into thinking I was secure in my hope.

5 *Yet of my grief I feign me glad*: yet I make myself appear happy with that situation or person that caused my grief.

6 *am*] *M & T*; on *D*.

7 *slipper hold*: slippery grip. Compare XLIX, 1–2, and CCXV, 8.

8 *I thought it well, that I had wrought*: I thought the situation or relationship I had created was sound.

9 *ensue*: seek after [the fruition of that situation or relationship I had wrought].

12 *For least I recked that most I rue*: for I paid least attention to that which now I most regret [that is, the possibility that what seemed certain should prove unstable, or that the person who seemed loyal should prove untrue].

14 *want of all my cure*: (?) the reason I lack all cure.

22 *feigned.* Probably feignèd.

24–5 *That sure I think there can none be/Too much assured without mistrust*: so that surely I think there can be no one who receives excessive assurance without mistrusting that assurance.

34-5 *for the doubt of this distress/...redress:* (?) reparation for the fearful apprehension of this distress [continuing?].

CLXXXVII. *D.*

Because the reason for the speaker's despair is not specified, it could be disappointment in an area of experience other than love – in politics, for example.

6-7 *That helpeth most, I know certain,/May not withstand:* that which helps a person most in desperate situations, I know for certain, may not resist despair.

8-9 *May not withstand that is elect/By Fortune's most extremity:* may not resist what is determined – that is, despair and death – by the greatest extreme of ill fortune.

10-12 *all in worth to be, except/Withouten law or liberty –/What vaileth then unto my thought:* to be entirely in a state of worthiness, but to be without the law [of her love for me?] or the liberty [of not being in love?] – what in these circumstances can remedy my thought of despair and death.

15 *is*] *ed.*; in *D.*

19-21 *So great disdain doth me provoke/That dread of death cannot defend/This deadly stroke:* such great disdain of me [by her?] provokes me to suicide so that the fear of death cannot prevent this act of killing myself.

25-28 *play his part/To do this cure against his kind –/For change of life from long desert/To place assigned:* play its part in achieving this cure which is against its own nature – for the sake of changing my life from a position of long deserving to the [hellish] place assigned me [by her refusal to give love?] and by God for suicides.

31-32 *To loose the bond of my restore/Wherein is bound my liberty:* to untie the bond of expecting my restoration to favour, the bond in which my freedom [from being in love with her?] is restrained.

CLXXXVIII. *D, GG* (1-24).

Precedes in *D* a poem, *CCXXI*, frequently ascribed to Wyatt but without external evidence.

2 *or think*] *N*; and think *D, GG.*
   not] *N conjectures*; that *D, GG.*
   or ... or: either ... or.

3-4 *But what or why myself best knows/Whereby I think and fear not:* but I myself best know what or why it is that I think and what or why it is I do not fear.

5 *think*] like *GG*; link *Rollins conjectures.*

5-6 *But thereunto I may well think/The doubtful sentence of this clause:* but with respect to that subject of thinking and fearing, I may well think the thought in this following passage that shows how full of doubt and fear I really am.

13 *At that I see I cannot wink:* I cannot wink at what I see. The speaker is apparently implying that the unfaithful behaviour of the person addressed should be kept as secret as possible.

19 *none doubt*] *N*; no doubt *D*, *GG*.

19–20 *Perchance none doubt the dread I see ;/I shrink at that I bear not :* perhaps no other people fear the kind of conduct I see as frightening; I, unlike them, shrink in fear from what I cannot bear.

22 *Unto :* until.

25–6 *If it be not, show no cause why/I should so think :* if it is not true that you are unfaithful, do not act in a way that causes me to think you are unfaithful.

CLXXXIX. *B*.

Resembles LXXIX in mood and in the pastoral setting of ll. 22–38, but the stanza form is not used by Wyatt elsewhere.

6–7 *For cause itself doth neither mar nor make/But even as the patient doth it take :* but the external cause of grief itself neither mars nor makes good a person's claim to be the greatest sufferer; what matters is how the person who bears that cause responds to it subjectively.

11 *of relief*] *ed.*; in relief *B*.

19 *worms :* glow-worms.

30 *groans*] *J. C. Maxwell conjectures*; grievance *B*.

35 *stunned :* struck dumb.

CXC. *B*.

This stanza form is used in XCIII, probably by Wyatt, and in CLXXXVII, for which there is no external evidence of Wyatt's authorship. The last words in ll. 7 and 14, missing because the manuscript is torn, are easily inferred in this form from the words beginning the following stanza.

5 *shewed that word to hear :* (?) appeared to hear that word.

16 *thou smast :* (?) you did smite.

18 *though thou revert :* (?) even though you return to your former attitude towards me.

31 *yet to live*] *ed.*; yt doth live *B changed to* yt do live.

CXCI. *B*.

11 *they :* (?) deadly pains.
   increased] *ed.*; increase *B*.

21 *'pity' for 'patience' and 'conscience' for 'wrong' :* (in the song) her 'pity' would be substituted for my 'patience' and her 'conscience' for my 'wrong'.

CXCII. *B*.

This poem is apparently addressed to a woman trying to hide a love affair in which she is involved.

1 *prat :* (?) prater, one who talks to little purpose; *or* tricky, cunning person (metaphorical use of 'prat', meaning 'trick'). I think, given 'wily',

the second meaning is more likely. A prater is closely associated with a gossip and is therefore not likely to be accused of trying to hide the truth.

4 *peer out*: peep out so as just to be seen.

if often ye it use: if you often use the device of dissembling words.

6-7 *For heartly love unspied long to last,/If ye assay*: (?) if you try for [to make] a heartfelt love to continue unspied for long.

8-9 *from a fire ... smoke shall ... out*. Proverbial; see *Tilley* F282 (*Da*).

10 *for*] *ed.*; a for *B*.

10-11 *for a cripple to halt and counterfeit/And be not spied*. Proverbial; see *Tilley* H60 and *ODEP* 272. Compare Chaucer, *Troilus* IV, 1457-8: 'It is ful hard to halten unespied/Byfore a crepel, for he kan the craft' (*M & T*).

14 *to blear our eyes*. Compare Chaucer, *CT* I (A), 3865: 'blerying of a proud milleres ye' (*M & T*).

17 *wreak*: harmed.

18 *And ready*: (?) and [you will be] ready.

19-20 *apply/To your own faults*: (?) apply [yourself] to [remedying] your faults.

21 *make men to ... muse*. Compare CXXXV, 7 (*M & T*).

27 *Leave off, therefore*. Compare XI, 7 (*M & T*).

CXCIII. B.

This poem was run together with LXIV by the scribe of *B*. LXIV is in the Wyatt section of *T*.

4 *The question is 'yours?' or else 'mine own?'*: the question is [whether I am going to be] yours, or [I am going to be] my own person. See l. 24.

5 *To be upholden*: (?) to be held up or kept in hand without a commitment from you. See l. 10. The *OED* does not record this meaning, but the context seems to demand it.

still to fawn: for me always to fawn on you

6 *no*] *ed.*; non *B*.

such obedience: such obedience to you on my part.

7-8 *To have such corn as seed was sown,/That is the worst*: (?) to have our relationship turn out the way it has begun – that is, without commitment on your part and with fawning on my part – is the worst possible result. Proverbial; see *Tilley* S209, 210, and *ODEP* 608.

10 *To uphold*. See l. 5.

11 *Sith*] *ed.*; Seith *B*.

16 *naught*] *changed later to* aught.

Where naught is got, there is no loss: since I have got nothing from you to this point, I lose nothing if you say 'nay'.

18-19 *so sore/But that I may forbear to dote*: so violent that it would keep me from stopping my doting on you.

24 *I mine own, that yours may not*: I, who may not be yours, will be my own person. See l. 4.

22-4 *If that ... may not*. Compare XCVI, 10, 12.

CXCIV. *B.*

1 *Had I wist that now I wot.* Line 1 echoes the proverb 'Beware of "had I wist" ' (*Tilley* H8 and *ODEP* 270).

1–2 *Had I wist that now I wot/For to have found that now I find:* had I known what now I know so that I should have found what now I find.

4 *feigned.* Probably feignèd.

5 *fixed:* it was fixed.

8 *It is not the thing that I pass on:* the deed itself is not the thing that I judge, [but rather the spirit behind the deed]. Compare VI, 6.

12 *maintenance:* deportment, behaviour.

14 *Rooted:* what is rooted. The original spelling, 'roted', can also be construed as 'rotted', but the emphasis on continuance favours 'rooted'.

CXCV. *B.*

3 *droppy:* given to dropping. *OED*'s first recorded instance is 1625.

8 *O man misfortunate.* The speaker of the poem is addressing the murdered man.

12 *shalt receive:* shall [you] receive.

14 *Moe]* ed.; So *B.*

20 *haft:* handle.

22 *Come off:* come along; hurry up.

25 *raught:* reached.

CXCVI. *B.*

1 *heavy]* hearty *original B.*

3 *wander . . . without a guide.* Compare CCLXI, 62–3 (*M & T*).

5 *so]* ed.; see *B.*

12 *sickerness:* certainty.

18 *contrary:* contrarily; in a contrary way.

24 *that steering it doth]* that my death *original B changed to* that it doth *and then changed to reading in text.*

CXCVII. *B.*

The men addressed in this poem were executed on 17 May 1536 for alleged sexual involvement with Anne Boleyn. Lord Rochford, Anne's brother, was charged with incest. Sir Henry Norris, Sir Francis Weston, Sir William Brereton, and Mark Smeaton were charged with adultery. Smeaton, a court musician, confessed under torture, or the threat of it, and may have implicated the others. (*L* 26–36)

3 *to:* ought to.

6 *affects:* affections; feelings.

9 *What though to death desert be now their call:* what does it matter if deserving to die be what now calls them to death.

12 *wealthily]* *Maxwell*; wealthy *B.*

those so wealthily did reign: those who so prosperously held power.

15 *set this offence apart:* setting this offence aside; except for this offence.
16 *some be be gone:* some who are gone.
20 *Even.* Probably monosyllabic (e'en).
17–20 *all I do not thus lament/But as ... reason doth me bind./But as the most doth all their deaths repent,/Even so do I by force of mourning mind:* (?) I do not thus bewail the deaths of all the execu.ed; rather reason determines the intensity of my lament. But as most people at least regret the deaths of all of them, so do I, as a result of my mind's inclination to mourn the fallen.
21, 53 *hadst*] *ed.*; haddest *B.*
23 *Since as it is so:* since what the latter say is true.
28 *That is:* (thou) who art.
31 *far overseen:* very much betrayed into a blunder.
35 *accept*] *ed.*; except *B.*
   All words accept: all people accept the words.
35, 36 *didst*] *ed.*; diddest *B.*
37–8 *we .../Most part:* most of us.
39 *hear so rife:* 1) hear so frequently; *or* 2) hear to have been so many in number.
45 *thee lament*] *M & T*; lament ye ?*B.*
48 *giv'st*] *ed.*; givest *B.*
50 *deserved.* Probably deservèd.
51 *forced.* Probably forcèd.
53 *above thy poor degree.* Compare CXIX, 28 (*M & T*).
55 *A rotten twig.* The phrase echoes the proverb 'Who trusts to rotten boughs may fall' (*Tilley* B557). Compare XXXI, 14, and CCIII, 33 (*M & T*).
56 *slipped thy hold:* escaped your grasp.
57 *in hearty wise:* in a heartfelt, sincere manner.
61 *help*] *ed.*; hepe *B.*

CXCVIII. *B.*

5, 27 *in your lot:* in your decision or choice made by the casting of lots.
12 *If*] *ed.*; Of *B.*
good] gyd *spelling in B for rhyme with 'tried'.*
   my wealth and health is the good: my well-being resides in goodness.
13 *knit the knot.* Compare LXVII, 8; CXXIV, 9; CLXXXI, 37; CCVI, 11; and CCXXXIII, 16 (*Muir*).
17 *that:* him whom.
18 *shot:* reckoning; the bill kept in a tavern.
24 *My fault's for thinking naught at all:* (?) my fault is thinking nothing [of myself].

CXCIX. *B.*

This obscure poem apparently turns on a 'debate' (l. 20) about why the lover failed to win the lady's love. The expert judges in causes of love say he came too late (l· 16). The lady says he came too soon (l. 17). There may be a pun on 'come': 'to experience sexual orgasm'. That meaning was certainly established by the end of the sixteenth century; see Eric Partridge, *Shakespeare's Bawdy* (1969), p. 81.

1 *should most :*   should most perceive.

2 *The ... sufferance :*   my suffering.

4 *they of such life which be expert :*   the experts in love.

5 *burn uncertain :*   (?) burn with an uncertain flame; hesitant out of fear and therefore 'too late' (l. 7).

9 *entreated :*   treated.

10 *among the other :*   among the others [who love her].

11 *though unvised which was too busy :*   (?) though what was too eager was ill-advised; *or* though ill-advised about what was too eager.

13 *But thither I came not ; yet came I :*   (?) but I did not reach her – that is, her love; yet I came to her.

16 *judged :*   judged [by the experts in love].

17 *too hastily :*   too soon [in the lady's view].

20 *let see :*   come on (an imperative that intensifies the imperative 'judge').

CC. B.

3 *excused :*   excused [if I try to withdraw my heart (ll. 9, 22) and mind (l. 22) from my love of this man].

5 *For]*   ed.; But B.

8 *be but false]*   *M & T*; be false *original B changed to* be for false.

8, 16, 24 *new-fangledness.*   Compare LXXX, 19, and CCXXVIII, 27.

6–8 *For want of truth ... /Of him ... /It would not be but false new-fangledness :*   because of his lack of truth, his response to me would only be his unfaithful pursuit of new mistresses.

12 *thought gold :*   thought to find gold.
brittle glass.   Compare XXII, 12.

13–14 *Now it is this ye know ; something it was/Not so promised :*   (?) now you know this is the truth; it was not something of this sort that you promised.

20 *thus]*   ed.; this B.

21 *I can no more :*   I can no longer [bear to love him].

CCI. B.

3 *false mistrust :*   unfounded mistrust [of me?].
noy :   annoy; cause harm.

9 *thou content :*   (?) you [are] content [with me]; *or* you gratify [my desire for you].

10, 13 *What :*   for what reason; why.

12 *To make ... be led]*   My joy and all from me to hide *original B.*

15 *pass full light :*   disregard with complete contempt.

17 *of any part :*   on any side; in any quarter.

20 *But I, alas, ... such thing.*   The 'alas' seems odd since the 'mistrust' (l. 18) would be of the speaker who would suffer the 'smart' of guilt without

complaint (l. 19). Perhaps 'alas' expresses dismay at the fact that the lady does not grant his suit despite the fact that there is no cause to mistrust him.
21–2 *by mishap and cruel lot,|... forsake me not:* do not forsake me as a result of some mischance and cruel misfortune.

CCII. B.

5 *if I buy their fault too dear:* if I am being made to pay too high a price for their insincerity.

8–9 *Though frailty fail not to appear|In them that wail as well as I:* though infidelity appears in those who feign their complaints in a way that makes them sound as convincing as my genuine complaints.

15 *their]* ed.; *thy B.* The poem's rhetorical structure dictates that the first part of each stanza refer to the false and unstable lovers, with whom the speaker contrasts himself in the second part of the stanza. It is also more logical that the speaker would describe the false lovers' wills and loves as governed by chance rather than by the lady's love or absence of love for them. This emendation also has the virtue of saving the charge against the lady for the climax of the poem (l. 27). An editorializing scribe might well have read that change back into l. 15; or the scribe might have confused 'their' spelled with a 'y' ('theyr') for 'thy'.

18–19 *I by choice myself have tried|And not by chance;:* I have subjected myself to this severe test of my patience by choice and not as the result of chance. If the semi-colon were placed after 'tried' (*M & T*), the phrase 'not by chance' would refer to 'Then have I wrong' (l. 21).

25 *diversely:* (?) in a way that is not good; perversely; *or* in their various ways.

27 *for thine:* for your fault of changeableness.

SONGS (I)

See head-note to Songs on pp. 408–9.

CCIII. D.

This poem is probably indebted to Serafino's *Fui serrato nel dolore* (*M & T* 424–6) for its laughing refrain and the sense of entanglement in the first and last stanzas.

1, 22 *love's.* Possibly disyllabic.

2 *torment:* tormented.

8 *weary]* *M & T*; very *D.*

14 *proveth.* Probably monosyllabic (prov'th).

13–14 *Everything that fair doth show|When proof is made it proveth not so:* everything that appears fair does not prove to be so when it is tested by experience.

21 *ruled.* Probably rulèd.

25 *feigned.* Probably feignèd.

words ... wind. Proverbial; see *Tilley* W833 (*Da*).

31 *lime:* bird-lime, a glutinous substance spread on twigs, by which birds may be caught.

31-2 *Was never bird tangled in lime/That brake away in better time.* The lines echo the proverb 'The more the bird caught in lime strives, the faster he sticks' (*Tilley* B380) (*M & T*).

34 *scaped.* Probably scapèd.

33-4 *I that rotten boughs did climb/And had no hurt, but scaped free.* The lines echo the proverb 'Who trusts to rotten boughs may fall' (*Tilley* B557). Compare XXXI, 14 (*M & T*).

CCIV. *E, B, D* (ll. 13–30).

Lines 13–30 occur in *D* between two poems by Wyatt.

1-2 *smart ... shirt*] spelled smert ... shert in *E*.

2 *The ... chance shapen afore my shirt:* the fate shaped or determined before my first shirt was made, that is, before my birth. Proverbial; compare Chaucer, *CT* I (A), 1566, 'That shapen was my deeth erst than my shert.'

4 *soaked:* drawn.

5 *over*] *later correction E;* our *E, B.*

8 *enlarded*] *B;* enlarged *E:* filled ('with pain') as with lard or fat.

9 *assented:* come to a resolution or conviction [of love].

10 *sithens*] since *B.*

13 *undeserved.* Probably undeservèd.

causer of undeserved change: the lady causes the change in her attitude towards the lover who does not deserve that changed attitude.

14 *By:* as a result of.

17 *proof too much:* proof too great (compare l. 11).

18 *coloured:* disguised; fair-seeming.

24 *price hath privilege truth to prevent:* money (of a wealthy suitor) has the prerogative to act or walk before a true and faithful love; 'prevent' can also mean 'frustrate' or 'defeat'; but 'privilege', in its technical meaning as a prerogative attaching to rank, points to a metaphor drawn from court ceremony in which the higher ranking person precedes the lower ranking – with rank in this case determined by money instead of worth.

29-30 *I quit th'enterprise of that that I have lost/To whomsoever lust for to proffer most:* the act of taking in hand what I have lost I relinquish to whoever wishes to offer the most [money to her]. The charge that the lady sells herself, first made in 'price' of l. 24, is here reinforced by the impersonal tone of a business transaction: the speaker gives up his attempt to recover a piece of lost property ('that') and concedes to the highest bidder the option of trying to take possession.

CCV. *E.*

In *E* between a poem of doubtful authorship and one attributed to 'Wyat' in the margin.

A leaf, with the earlier stanzas of this poem, is missing from *E.*

1 *it:* (?) the heart of the speaker.
5 *will . . . will:* desire it; will it.
8 *say yourself:* say to yourself.
express: definite, explicit, unmistakable in import.

CCVI. *H78*; *T* and *H* in revised versions.

H78 entitles the poem: 'T. Wyatt of Love.' But *T* attributes his version to Surrey. An examination of the variants suggests that *H78* is a copy of the earliest version; that *T* printed from a revision of the earliest version in which the first stanza was rewritten, three stanzas were dropped, and two new stanzas were added; that *H* conflated a copy of the earliest version and *T*, relocated the sixth stanza after the second, dropped one of *T*'s additions, and added a new stanza. If this hypothesis is correct, *T* and *H*, while introducing errors (for example, 'appease' for 'augment' in l. 8), are also independent witnesses to the earliest version by which *H78* can be corrected. The following is the version in *H*:

As oft as I behold and see
The sovereign beauty that me bound,
The nearer my comfort is to me,
Alas, the fresher is my wound.

As flame doth quench by rage of fire
And running streams consumes by rain,
So doth the sight that I desire
Appease my grief and deadly pain.

Like as the fly that seeth the flame
And thinks to play her in the fire,
That found her woe, and sought her game,
Whose grief did grow by her desire.

When first I saw these crystal streams
[First when I saw those crystal streams *T*]
Whose beauty made this [my *T*] mortal wound,
I little thought within these [her *T*] beams
So sweet a venom to have found.

Wherein is hid the cruel bit
Whose sharp repulse none can resist,
And eke the spur that straineth each wit
To run the race against his list.

But wilful will did prick me forth.
Blind Cupid did me whip and guide.
[And blind Cupid did whip and guide *T*]
Force made me take my grief in worth.
My fruitless hope my harm did hide.

> I fall and see mine own decay,
> As he [one *T*] that bears flame in his breast
> Forgets, for pain, [in pain *T*] to cast away [put away *T*].
> The thing that breedeth his [mine *T*] unrest.
>
> And as the spider draws her line,
> 30   With labour lost I frame my suit.
> The fault is hers, the loss is mine:
> Of ill-sown seed such is the fruit.

T does not have stanzas 3, 5, and 7 of the *H* version, and has the following stanza after stanza 6:

> As cruel waves full oft be found
> Against the rocks to roar and cry,
> So doth my heart full oft rebound
> Against my breast full bitterly.

Given *T*'s passion for regularity, he would surely have chosen *H*'s version of l. 22 if that version had been prior to his and available. *H* seems to be sophisticating the pronouns in ll. 26 and 28 of *T*.

While it is not possible to determine with certainty the author of any version, it seems probable – given *T*'s attribution of the shortest version to Surrey – that Wyatt is responsible for the earliest version reflected in *H78*, that Surrey is responsible for the version reflected in *T* and, perhaps, in *H*. Unlike the author of *T*, the author(s) of *H78* and *H* focus on the Petrarchan contraries of love's attractiveness and danger.

T entitles the poem: 'The lover describes his restless state.'

3, 7 *Even.* Possibly monosyllabic (e'en).
5 *As flame*] *T*, *H*; For as the flame *H78*.
5-8 *As flame by force doth quench the fire/And ... streams consume the rain,/... so do I ... desire/To augment my grief and deadly pain:* as the flame burns up the material of fire and hence puts out the fire, and as streams swallow up the rain, so I desire to feel even greater grief and pain ('flame' and 'streams') so that grief and pain ('fire' and 'rain') will come to an end in death.
11 *So shall I knit an endless knot:* so shall I, as is natural for a lover, experience the seemingly endless contraries of love, [indeed the very mixture of hot and cold that never occurs in nature outside the lover].
13 *When I first saw*] *ed.*; When I foresaw *H78*; First when I saw *T*; When first I saw *H*.
    crystal streams: eyes shining like streams made of crystal.
17 *mine*] *T*, *H*; my *H78*.
19 *Forgets, for thought*] *ed.*; Forgets *H78*(1); Forgetful thought *H78*(2); Forgets in pain *T*; Forgets, for pain, *H*.
19-20 *Forgets, for thought, to put away/The thing:* forgets, because of contemplating the flame, to cast it away.
20 *mine*] *T*; my *H78*; his *H*.

21 *Like as the fly doth seek:* I am like the fly that seeks.

22 *playeth.* Probably monosyllabic (play'th).

23 *Who findeth her woe and seeketh her game:* who, in seeking her amusement, finds her pain. Alludes to the proverb 'The fly that plays too long in the candle singes its wings at last'; see *Tilley* F394 (*Da*).

26 *With*] *H*; As *H78*.

25–6 *draw her line/With labour lost:* spins her web only to have it torn and hence lose the fruit of her labour.

27 *The gain is hers:* the gain [presumably in flattery to her pride] belongs to the lady I love. *H* simplifies the line with 'fault', though elsewhere in the poem the lover and Cupid, not the lady, are blamed for the lover's predicament.

28 *ill*] *H*; evil *H78*.

Of ill-sown seed such is the fruit. Alludes to the proverb 'Of evil grain no good seed can come'; see *Tilley* G405 (*Da*).

CCVII. *A, D.*

Preceded in *A* by two poems ascribed to Wyatt by *T*; followed in *D* by a poem which, in *E*, is written and corrected in Wyatt's hand.

D has the unvarying refrain:

> Wherefore all joy I do refuse
> And cruel will thereof accuse.

2 *Is*] *D*; If *A*.

forced. Probably forcèd.

4 *to it I must consent:* I must give in to despair.

6, 7, 12, 18 *cruel will.* The speaker refers to the lady's will, but the reader may see that the speaker's will is at fault for giving its 'consent' (l. 4) to despair and refusing all joy.

13 *might see:* might have seen.

CCVIII. *D, Stark, Folger.*

Occurs before CIX in *Stark* and *Folger*.

John Hall composed a moralizing parody of this poem and provided a musical setting which he recommended also for his parody of CIX; see Hall's *The Court of Virtue* (1565), ed. Fraser, 191–3. Compare XCIV and CIX and head-notes.

3, 28 *hath in hold my heart:* has my heart in its grip.

9 *That*] *Stark, Folger*; For *D*.

where I trust I am deceived. Proverbial; see *S* 64 (*Da*).

11 *had'st*] *Folger*; haddest *Stark, D.*

12 *which way my hope to crave:* (?) in whatever way [was appropriate] to beg for [the satisfaction of] my hope; *or* in whatever way my hope [was inclined] to beg for [its satisfaction].

14 *we ... lose that other save:* we lose what others save. Alludes to the proverb 'No man loses but another wins'; see *Tilley* M337 (*Da*). The speaker presumably is referring to successful rivals.

16 *And use to work*] *Folger*, *M*; to work *Stark*; In worth to use *D*.
18 *once my loss*] else my life *Stark*, *Folger*.
   once: once and for all.
29 *brought my mind to pass*: accomplished my intention.

CCIX. *D*.

4, 8, 12, 16, 20, 24 *well*] *ed*.; will *D*.
4 *our will*: what we desire.
5 *yea*: the assent to love, probably the partner's, which proves worse than refusal as a source of pain.
7 *In love*] *N*; I love *D*.
9 *hearts*] *ed*.; heart *D*.
11 *ill*] *ed*.; evil *D*.
15 *Alas*] *N*; Alas alas *D*.
19–20 *Since of mishap ours is alone/To love*: since of all possible misfortunes only ours is to love.
20 *yet*] *N*; it *D*.
23 *know*] *N*; trow *D*.

CCX. *D*, *B*.

The initial letters of each stanza form the name 'Shelton'; Mary Shelton's name is written at the foot of the page.

3 *True of belief in whom is all my trust*: faithfully believing in the person in whom I have placed all my trust.
5, 10, 15, 20, 25, 27, 30, 35 *still*: (?) always; *or* now as formerly.
6 *hold*: place of refuge; stronghold.
7 *I drive*]: I defer [speaking].
   do] *B*; doth *D*.
8 *How long to live*: how long I am to live.
9 *break*: utter; divulge.
11 *Encrease*: increase. The acrostic demands the initial 'E'.
13 *discussed*: declared; made known.
14 *refrain*: refrain from loving.
18 *Record that knoweth, and if this be not just*: let the person who knows better testify, if what I am about to say is not just.
19 *whereas*: where.
   way] nay *B*.
20 *ever still he*] still alway I *B*.
19–20 *no way/But serve . . . he must*: no other way but that he must serve.
23 *requit*] quited *B*; be quit *M*: to be repaid.
25 *for to . . . he*] to . . . I *B*.
26 *Ontruth*] *ed*.; Untruth *B*; Untrue *D*. The acrostic demands the initial 'O'.

by] B; be D.

Ontruth by trust : (?) the lack of truth in another person together with my trust in that person.

29 *like reward :* a reward like the usual unjust reward Fortune bestows on me.

32 *not*] *ed.*; nor D.

33 *True of belief hath always been my trust :* (?) I have always placed my trust in faithful belief [in the person I love].

31–5 *Never to cease nor yet like . . . still I must*] Not in B.

CCXI. D.

Occurs in D before CXXVIII which is attributed to 'Tho.' in E.

6 *good :* good one (a term of address).

11 *abject :* cast off, rejected.

13 *travail :* 1) labour; 2) travelling.

16 *humbly*] *ed.*; humbly D.

18 *Even.* Probably monosyllabic (e'en).

CCXII. D, BM.

Follows in D two poems attributed to 'Tho.' in E.

N suggests that the poem is an imitation of a Spanish form called *Glosa* or 'commentary' in which the initial couplet proposes the subject that is commented on by the rest of the poem, with expressions from the couplet being woven into the stanzas. *F* argues that the poem is in a tradition of Middle English poems in which an introductory couplet or short verse serves as 'the text' for the following poem. I think it is possible that the tradition to which *F* refers is in fact that of the carol in which the opening couplet or verse is the 'burden' repeated after each stanza. If this poem stems from the carol tradition, it might best be described as in the form of a modified carol, in which a part of the burden is repeated after each stanza. Many examples of the modified carol occur in the early Tudor song-books (*Stevens* 351–425). Compare CLXXXIII and CCXVIII.

2 *even.* Probably monosyllabic (e'en).

6 *reward :* regard, consider, look upon.

   meant : purposed; set as an objective.

7, 12, 17, 22, 27, 32, 37. *Even.* Possibly monosyllabic (e'en).

8–9 *To feign . . . is not my mind*/*Nor to refuse such as I find :* it is not my intention merely to pretend [that I am making this commitment now], nor to refuse [to accept whatever I find is your wish for me in the future].

21 *trace :* track or path made by the passage of the beloved's feet.

26 *words do obtain :* [your] words prevail.

29 *love in deed I will ensue :* I will pursue as my goal loving you in action.

35 *as true as gospel.* Proverbial; see *Tilley* G378 and *ODEP* 672 (*M & T*).

36 *expel :* 1) drive out; 2) reject from consideration.

CCXIII. *D.*

8 *mischieved:* injured; brought to ruin.
5–8 *Alack . . . one mischieved.* Probably the poet is rhyming pronounced but unstressed 'ed' syllables at the ends of these lines.
12 *bestad:* 1) situated, circumstanced; 2) hard pressed.
15–16 *spare/Into your presence:* (?) refrain [from going] into your presence.

CCXIV. *D.*

Follows in *D* a group of ten poems, eight of which are almost certainly by Wyatt; but it is not in the same hand as those ten poems.

5 *acquit:* repay.
11 *have more:* (?) have more faith.
15 *a':* have.
23 *deservest.* Probably disyllabic (deserv'st).

CCXV. *D.*

6, 12, 18, 24, 30. Note pun on 'the/thee' in refrain. The word 'thee' (l. 9) is spelled 'the' in MS.
7–8 *the change of wearied mind/And slipper hold:* the change of your mind, grown weary of me, and my grasp of you, grown slippery.
10 *a burning faith in changing fire:* (?) a fidelity that is burning up (disappearing) in a fire that changes the thing it burns.
11 *my part:* (?) for my part; as far as I am concerned in the affair.
13 *change of chance in love:* change in love caused by chance.
27 *my surety so doth glance:* (?) my certainty about you in this way moves rapidly away.
28–9 *Repentance now shall quit thy pain,/Never to trust the like again:* my repentance shall repay the pain you have taken on my behalf (ironic), my repentance taking the form of never trusting another person in the same way again.

CCXVI. *D.*

The punctuation of the first three stanzas is arbitrary. The full stop could come after the second line of each, giving the refrain an object. But the linking of the first three lines of each stanza by rhyme and the example of the last two stanzas argue for a stop after the third line, if anywhere.

1–2 *intent/Of such a truth as I have meant:* intending (willing) of such a loyalty to you as I have intended.
6 *life ye know since when:* life you have been aware of since when it began.
7 *tell:* 1) reckon up; estimate; 2) give an account of.
11 *denays:* denials.
15 *mind:* way of thinking and feeling; intention; purpose.
19 *moved:* altered, budged.

CCXVII. D.

2 *love's.* Perhaps disyllabic.
   hath ... forgot] doth ... forget *M & T.*
16 *eyes*] *M & T*; ears *D.*
19 *What vaileth truth or steadfastness.* Compare IV, 1-2.
31 *hate*] *M & T*; cruelty *D.*
33 *void :* avoid.
   mate] *M & T*; mote *D :* (?) checkmate in chess.
34 *slip the knot.* See LXVII, 8 and the note.

CCXVIII. D.

This poem is probably a modified carol. The opening couplet is the 'burden' repeated in full after every other stanza and in part, as a refrain, after each stanza. Many examples of the modified carol occur in the early Tudor song-books (*Stevens* 351-425). Compare CLXXXIII and CCXII.

F points out that the speaker is a woman (see ll. 10, 16-17, 20-1, 28-9). *M & T* suggest that the poem may be by a woman. The mysterious 'it' of the couplet and refrain probably refers to her marriage to a person other than the man who is her friend (l. 10), sweetheart (l. 15), and master (l. 27).

1-2 and throughout   *this is my lot ;/No thing to want, if it were not :*   this is my fate [and I accept it]. There would be no thing that I would lack if that one circumstance were not in existence.
3 *even.* Probably monosyllabic (e'en).
8 *scarce*] *ed.*; scace *D.*
10 *giveth.* Possibly monosyllabic (giv'th).
11 *happiest :*   the happiest person.
15 *heart :* sweetheart.
27 *A master.* This master is probably her lover rather than her husband.
28 *whom*] *M & T*; hom *D.*
29-30 *for that intent/That :*   for the end or purpose that; with the intention that.
32-3 *It doth suffice/To speak few words among the wise.* Proverbial; see *Tilley* W781 and *ODEP* 728.

CCXIX. D, B.

2 *To set so light :*   to regard as so unimportant.
13 *knowest.* Probably monosyllabic (know'st).
14 *Love's.* Probably disyllabic.
15 *mate :*   1) checkmate in chess; 2) one of a pair.
18 *won :*   conquered [by my enemy].

CCXX. D.

In *D* precedes a poem attributed to 'Wyat' in margin of *E* and in Wyatt section of *T*. But otherwise the section of *D* in which it appears does not appear to be a group of Wyatt's poems.

The last words of a stanza are repeated as the first words of the next stanza. The rhythm seems to be four heavy stresses to the line separated by at least one and usually two relatively unstressed syllables. The rhyme scheme is abab, etc. To preserve these formal characteristics throughout the poem I have emended ll. 16, 20, 21, 23–4.

3 *most privy:* 1) (?) most privily; with complete secrecy; *or* 2) into a place totally withdrawn from her and all human company.

7 *sprites:* spirits.

8, 9 *kit:* cut.

12 *turned.* Probably turnèd.

16 *all worldly*] *ed.*; and worldly *D*.

17 *private:* deprived of.

20 *Alas, what remedy*] *N* conjectures; What remedy *D*.

22 *suspiring:* sighing.

23–4 *Farewell, all pleasure. Welcome, pain and smart.*/*Now welcome, death. I am ready to die.*] *N* conjectures; Now welcome. I am ready to depart./ Farewell all pleasure. Welcome pain and smart. *D*.

CCXXI. *D, B* (9–40), *Bannatyne.*

In *D* this poem precedes two poems in Wyatt sections of *T* and *A*.

A shorter and probably earlier version in carol form exists in MS Latin 35 in the University of Pennsylvania Library. The 'burden' of the carol, to be repeated after each of the stanzas, is the first couplet of this poem. The author of this poem apparently turned the burden into the first stanza and added stanzas 3, 5, 6, 8, 9, and 10. See R. L. Greene (*FR*).

5 *indifferently:* with indifference to matters outside my control and in the control of Fortune, including the opinion of others.

11 *the mean:* the middle ground between extremes of feeling and action; here, for example, the mean between mirth and sadness would be a kind of sobriety which indicates that he has not given his heart away to 'folks' who might 'feign' affection for him. The notion is a popularized version of Aristotle's concept that virtue lies between extremes of vice.

14 *Some of pleasure and some of woe:* some judging me a man of pleasure and some a man of woe.

16 *But I am*] *B*; But am *D*.

17 *But since that*] *B, Bannatyne*; But since *D*.
    do thus decay] take that way *B*; do take that way *Bannatyne*.
    do . . . decay: (?) fall off [from the truth]; fail [in their judgements].

22 *evil.* Probably slurred into one syllable.

31 *weed:* garment distinctive of a person's way of life.

40 *be*] die *B*.

CCXXII. *B, BM* (preceded by first two stanzas of CCXXXI).

7 *Nor never shall ye other prove:* and you shall never prove me to be other than honest.

12 *even.* Probably monosyllabic (e'en).

CCXXIII. *B.*

The manuscript is torn, so the words concluding ll. 4, 7, 8, 12, 16 are supplied by speculation.

3 *unworthy:* unworthy [of your hostility].
4 *wilt not]* *M & T*; will not *B.*
5 *Fainest when I would obtain:* when I would be most glad to obtain [my desire].

CCXXIV. *B.*

2, 5 *Thus]* *ed.*; This *B.*
4 *whose meekness:* the heart's inability to resist loving.
14 *pass:* care [for the person who loves me].
15 *would fainest:* would willingly, gladly love.

CCXXV. *B, Folger.*

This poem shares the refrain with CXII and is probably a later imitation of that poem. The version in *B* also appears later than that in *Folger*; see especially ll. 10, 20, and 22 (*M* 133).

1 *Duress]* During *Folger.*
4, 8, 12, 16 *sighest.* Probably monosyllabic (sigh'st).
4 *will]* *Folger*; wilt *B.*
6 *The tears . . . do leak]* *ed.*; The tears void that from thy eyes do leak *B*; The tears that from thine eyes doth leak *Folger.*
10 *Thou strives . . . all too weak]* Thou pullest the strings that be too weak *Folger.*
11 *told]* *Folger*; toll *B.*
14 *regards]* *M & T*; regard *B*; regarded *Folger.*
15 *saith]* seeing *Folger.*
19 *alive]* to live *Folger.*
20 *Ever to sigh . . . never break]* Why sigh'st thou, heart, and will not break *Folger.*
21 *Wherefore, . . . show redress]* *M & T*; Wherefore pity now should redress *B*; I pray thee, Pity, show redress *Folger.*
22 *come]* *Folger*; comes *B.*
   thy vengeance wreak] thyself awreak *Folger.*

CCXXVI. *B.*

5 *in press:* in the thick of the fight.
13 *strive against the tide.* The phrase echoes the proverb 'It is hard to strive against the stream' (*Tilley* S927 and *ODEP* 627). Compare CII, 27, and CVII, 5–6 (*M & T*).
14 *I . . . who doth abide:* I, who wait.
15 *sufferance to heart's desire is guide:* passive acceptance [of one's present position] is the guide to achieving the desires of one's heart.

CCXXVII. *B*.

M & T, who introduced this poem into the Wyatt canon, doubt that it is by him.

1 *Defamed guiltiness by silence unkept:* my guilt spread abroad, not kept [secret] by silence.
2 *detect:* detected.
4 *Shall I:* if I shall.
5 *Betrayed by trust.* Proverbial; see *S* 64 (*Maxwell*).
5-6 *Betrayed by trust . . ./By promise unjust my name defiled:* (?) I have been betrayed by someone I trusted [to keep secret the name of you, my mistress], and therefore my name has been defiled by his unjust promise [to keep your name secret if I revealed it to him] (*M & T*).
8 *Will I:* if I will.
10 *spare not to refuse me your presence:* do not spare me the punishment of refusing me your presence. This request for punishment is surprising in a poem asking forgiveness.
11-12 *Unless ye perceive ye do refrain/From doing amiss, will I live again:* (?) unless you see that your own behaviour is perfect, I will live again. These lines, virtually unintelligible in their context, may be a last-minute suggestion that only the morally perfect have a right to refuse forgiveness and hence a new life to the sinner, and that the lady is not herself morally perfect.

CCXXVIII. *B*.

This poem is not an answer to the preceding poem in *B*. It is not clear to what poem in the canon, if any, it is an answer. But compare CXXVII and see the head-note to that poem for the complex meanings of 'fantasy' and 'fancy'.

The mention of 'proffered service' in l. 5 indicates that the speaker of this poem is a woman.

3 *new nor old:* new nor old lovers.
4 *It:* your expectation that I will retain you as a lover.
5, 8 *nothing:* in no way; not at all.
6 *fain it properly:* (?) rejoice in it thoroughly.
16 *feigned.* Probably feignèd.
foolish feigned: (?) foolishly fashioned.
21-2, 25-8 The male lover, like the woman, has been promiscuous.
27 *new-fangled wit:* mental inclination to promiscuity. Compare LXXX, 19.
28 *proved:* approved, commended.
31 *The smartless:* the person suffering no pain – that is, the woman speaking.

CCXXIX. *B.*

M & T, who introduced this poem into the Wyatt canon, doubt that it is by him.

In ll. 16 and 24 the object of 'have not' is presumably the money or social position required for marriage to the lady. In all the other refrains, the object of 'have not' can be 'you' ('each other' in l. 28) as well as 'money or position'. The same appears true of 'more' in l. 10.

17 *sure:* assure.
25-6 *this resisteth all my trust . . ./That ye again will love me steadfastly:* all my trust that you will love me steadfastly in return resists this [attempt to delay our union].
27 *pass . . . hardily:* pass between us with strength.

CCXXX. *B.*

1 *at mine own will.* Compare XCVII, 1 (*M & T*).
4 *fervent fire.* Compare CXXXII, 33 and CXLVII, 17 (*M & T*).
10 *mourning*] *M & T*; mournings *B*.
    wreak: (?) avenge. Though the *OED* does not give 'wreak' as a spelling of 'wreck', the latter, meaning 'destroy', would make better sense in the context.
22 *my woeful*] *ed.*; this careful *B*.
23 *this careful*] *ed.*; my woeful *B*; *changed in B to* the woeful. The phrase 'careful pain' in the penultimate line of each stanza seems a principle of construction in this poem. I suspect the scribe mistakenly exchanged 'this careful' and 'my woeful' and then sophisticated the redundant 'my' to 'the'.
27 *my wearied breast.* Compare XCI, 17.
28 *his:* its.

CCXXXI. *B, BM* (1–8), *Ramsden.*

In *BM*, the two stanzas precede the five stanzas of CCXXII. This poem is set to music as a three-part song in *Ramsden. Stevens* (445) conjectures that the song was composed around 1530.

1 *sore*] so *M conjectures* (*139*).
2 *That:* so that.
5 *all of one sort:* (?) all in the same manner.
9 *but now of late:* (?) only recently [that you have stopped loving me].
9–10 *but now of late./Not long ago*] not now of late/But long ago *M conjectures* (*139*).
10 *knew my pain:* (?) understood and pitied my pain.
16 *and cannot:* and be a person who cannot.

CCXXXII. *B.*

1 *undeserved.* Probably undeservèd.
9 *The place of sleep.* Compare LXXXI, 6 (*M & T*).

10 *unquiet enemy.* Compare LXXXI, 4 (*M & T*).

14 *That lust liketh, desire doth it deny:* my desire [not to offend?] denies me what my lust likes.

CCXXXIII. *B.*

11 *times.* Probably disyllabic.

16 *knit the knot.* See CXCVIII, 13 and the note.

19 *new-fangled.* Compare LXXX, 19.

22 *Welcome, my joy.* Compare XCII, 25-6.

23-4 *apaid/Of me ... to claim ye quit:* content to claim that you are rid of me.

31 *rehearst:* described; mentioned.

CCXXXIV. *B.*

9 *are out of thought:* (?) grow out of deliberation [rather than genuine feeling]; *or* are gone from your remembrance.

15 *feigned.* Probably feignèd.

21, 50 *falsed.* Probably falsèd.

21 *falsed faith.* Compare XCIV, 23, and XCVII, 22.

23 *slip the knot.* See LXVII, 8 and the note.

29 *Each*] *M & T*; Eke *B.*

35 *tokens*] letters *original B.*

39-40 *what dread .../Thou hadst once spied thy bills to write:* (?) what fear [and hence emotional involvement] you once discovered [in yourself] as you wrote your letters [to me].

43 *forged.* Probably forgèd.

45 *thereto:* appropriate for this purpose.

48 *Without offence to forge my woe:* to make me unhappy without my having offended you.

CCXXXV. *B.*

Harrier (74) thinks the small 'w' in margin may be an ascription.

1, etc. *Quondam:* once; formerly.

3 *trod the trace:* walked the path of hard experience.

8 *Promise made not to dissever:* we having made a promise not to separate.

9 *laughed ... did but smile:* (?) laughed [with joy] ... did but smile [with a sly intent].

10 *Then quondam was I:* (?) then already I was destined to be a former lover.

14 *among the moe:* among the large number no longer in her favour.

CCXXXVI. *B.*

1 *they*] *M & T*; yt *B.*

1-2 *Spite of their spite which they .../Do stick to force my fantasy:* in spite of the malicious action, or the feeling of malice, which they thrust [on me] to do violence to my love for you.

4   *To be thine own assuredly.* Compare CCXI, 22 (*M & T*).

5   *thereat by spite to spurn:* to kick with spite at my devotion.

6, 12, 18, 24, 30 *fancy:* love. See the head-note to CXXVII for the complex set of related meanings of 'fancy' and 'fantasy' (l. 2).

9–10 *flit/As doth the water to and fro.* The phrase echoes the proverb 'false as water'; see *Tilley* W86 (*M & T*).

11 *Spite . . . their spite:* regard with contempt their spite; with a possible double pun: spit [on] their spit; pierce with a sharp weapon their sharp weapon.

15 *May grease:* [they] may grease.

15–16 *lie/Of busy brains:* tell lies with the inventions of their busy brains.

17 *the prick they spurn:* they kick against the prick; like oxen, they ;utilely resist the goad; they act futilely. Proverbial; see *Tilley* F433 and *ODEP* 333 (*M & T*).

20 *Whose]* ed.; Whom *B*.
    naught: not.

23 *spite:* feel spite; with a pun on 'spit'.

25 *thereat to list or lour:* to look with pleasure or to frown at my love.

28 *seek:* drive out by attack (*Da*).

29 *spite:* feel spite; with a pun on 'spit'.

CCXXXVII. *Douce.*

Echoes lines in LXIV, which is in Wyatt section of *T*.

2   *degree:* social position.

3   *Chosen . . . by election:* chosen by divine election, as in Protestant doctrine. Here and throughout the first three stanzas the speaker attributes responsibility for his love to a force greater than himself.

5   *not like to speed:* not likely to succeed [in gaining the object of my love].

9, 18 *fancy, fantasy.* See the head-note to CXXVII for the complex meanings of these words. The appetites of fallen men can influence the workings of fancy, distorting the image of what has been perceived into an image of what one wants to perceive. Hence the speaker in this poem is deluded by his fancy into regarding the unattainable as attainable and into being so obsessed by the object of his amorous inclination that he is blind to remedy; in both ways fancy makes his mind foolish.

9   *blind]* ed.; bind *Douce*.

13 *hoped.* Probably hopèd.

18 *fantasy]* *M & T*; fancy *Douce*.

CCXXXVIII. *Stark, Folger, BM.*

In *Folger* follows a poem by Wyatt.

I assume that an early version (*BM*) was revised – that the second stanza was deleted, a new final stanza added, and some other substantive changes made (as in l. 15) – but that later scribal redactions introduced erroneous departures from correct readings still preserved in *BM* (as in ll. 3–4). But, as *M* warns (132), the poem has apparently been 'passed round in such a fluid state that an editor is almost in the position of the ballad collector faced with so many variants that it is hard to determine whether he is dealing with one poem or many'.

3 *here she*] *ed.*; here ye *BM* (*?possibly a misreading of* here she); her joy *Folger*; her love *Stark*.

bind] *BM, Folger*; blind *Stark*.

4 *Except :* without.

near] *BM*; now *Stark, Folger*.

4⌃5] She hath mine heart all other before.
So hath she my body, she may be sure.
Nothing on earth may glad me more
Than to spend them both to do her pleasure. *BM*.

9 *flatter*] *Folger, BM*; *not in Stark*.

10 *do*] dare *Folger*.

11 *do write*] *Folger, BM*; to write *Stark*.

15 *to kiss*] *ed.*; kiss *Stark*.

I would . . . to kiss] But yet, rather than she shall miss *BM*.

16 *suffer*] *ed.*; to suffer *BM*; to bind *Stark*.

15–20 *I would . . . her loving gentleness*] *Not in Folger*.

17–20 *I am abashed . . . her loving gentleness*] *Not in BM*.

CCXXXIX. *Folger*.

Between two poems by Wyatt.

6 *therefore*] *ed.*; for *Folger*.

7 *My words . . . express*] *ed.*; *line omitted in Folger*.

15 *fainest :* most gladly.

18 *caused.* Probably causèd.

21–2 *here an end . . ./In purpose for to serve her still :* here is an end to my complaint, accompanied by the intention to serve her always.

23 *I think*] *M & T*; think *Folger*.

for to part I think none ill : (?) I think no ill of her because of our having to separate.

SONGS (2)

CCXL. *A, B* (5 stanzas only and in different order: 1, 4, 3, 6, and 7).

The order of the stanzas in *A* is superior to that in *B*, and *A* has two additional stanzas. But *B*'s readings are superior to *A*'s in the stanzas they have in common. I print the stanzas of *A* in *A*'s order, but I print *B*'s readings for the shared stanzas. In so doing, I assume that, after *B* was copied, the poet added two stanzas to *B*'s source and rearranged their order, and that the text of *A*, with its additional stanzas in the improved order, was corrupted in details in the course of transmission.

1 *trow*] prove *A*.

10 *mickle*: great prize.

12 *tickle*: unreliable; changeable.

14 *flitted you fro*: departed from you.

15 *ware*: merchandise.

    brickle: brittle; liable to break.

9–16 *Your fair words ... have thought so*] Not in *B*.

18 *Full oft-times*] Oft-times *A*.

23 *lade*] led *A*: burdened.

28–30 *To stay that by kind/Could never yet find/In change to say 'whoa'*: to restrain that which, because of changeable nature, could never yet find the way to say to itself 'whoa' [as to a horse] in the course of changing.

31 *This mean I by your mind*: I mean this description with respect to your mind.

33 *wax nor writing*: neither the wax used in applying a seal to a contract nor the writing therein.

34 *certain assure ye*: certainly make sure of you as a partner.

42 *mistrust*: mistakenly trust.

43 *I care not a fly*. Proverbial; see *Tilley* F396 and *ODEP* 211 (*M & T*).

53 *betake*: commit; commend.

55 *break*: tame, like a horse. Compare l. 30.

CCXLI. *D, B*.

Ascribed to Thomas, Lord Vaux, in *B*.

CCXLII. *D*.

2 *set*: fixed [in its love for me].

3 *such wrong me wrought*: done to me such wrong.

9 *can know*] *ed*.; know *D*.

14 *draught*: 1) a move in chess; 2) a harness on an animal that pulls something; 3) load. Line 16's 'mate' makes it clear that a move in chess is the primary meaning, but a pun might be intended.

    drawn awry: moved amiss; moved at an angle.

16 *have the mate*: checkmate the opponent in the game of chess. Is the lover saying that endurance now of the false move of the beloved in the game of love will make possible a future victory over this love and its pain?

17–18 *But note I will this text/To draw better the next*: (?) but I will give special heed to this text (the poem?) to remind myself to select a better lover the next time.

CCXLIII. *D2, D1* (incomplete version).

D1 is between a poem classified by *T* as doubtful and a poem not by Wyatt. *D2* is in a group of poems of which there is no evidence of Wyatt's authorship.

The poem is of a genre derived from the medieval French *chanson à personnages* or dramatic song in which the poet overhears the complaint of a young woman or, later, of a male lover (*F*).

3, 61 *semblant:* appearance, demeanour.
6 *chanced.* Probably chancèd.
23–8 *Love did assign ... will be true*] *D1*; *not in D2.*
30 *her*] *D1*; *his D2.*
46 *Am left*] *N*; Armless *D.*
50 *feigned.* Probably feignèd.
53 *even.* Possibly monosyllabic (e'en).

CCXLIV. *D.*

The term 'love' throughout can refer to the lover's appetite and the self-deception it leads him into; it can also refer to the deception practised on the lover by the person with whom he falls in love.

5 *abused.* Probably abusèd.
   love's abused band: (?) the bond of [seeming] love [in fact] violated by the lover's self-deception and the beloved's deceit; *or* love's deceived company or troop.
7 *Th'abuse:* the condition of being deceived; the condition of being ill used.
8–9 *a kind/Which kindleth by abuse:* a type that begins to burn as a result of deception.
11 *fancy.* See the head-note to **CXXVII** and the poem itself for the complex meanings of this word.
13 *fond:* foolish.
14 *vain:* empty; meaningless.
17 *bewray:* reveal; expose.
18 *frame:* fabricate; contrive.
19 *grame*] *M & T conjecture*; game *D*: anger; vexation.
21 *can:* can frame, contrive.
25 *served.* Probably servèd.
   served with: 1) supplied with; 2) gratified by.
26–8 *some can this concile/To give the simple leave/Themselves for to deceive:* some of those loved by simple-minded lovers can reconcile themselves to allowing those simple-minded lovers to go on deceiving themselves.

CCXLV. *D.*

9 *You promised*] *ed.*; And you promised *D.*
14 *part:* share in the relationship; with a possible pun on French *perte*, meaning 'loss' (*M & T*).
15 *Thought*] *N*; Though *D.*
15–17 *Thought for to take/It is not my mind,/But to forsake:* it is not my intention to take time to reflect, but immediately to forsake.
18 *One so unkind*] *N*; *line omitted in D.*

23 *But that you*] *N*; But you *D*.
22–3 *Can ye say nay*/*But that you said :* can you deny that you said.

CCXLVI. D.

3 *down*] *M & T*; done *D*.

CCXLVII. B.

'Passed', throughout the poem, means 'put up with', 'endured'.

6 *As trifles to this last*] *ed.*; Are trifle to the last *B*: as if they were trifles compared to this last experience.
8 *sue and serve*] serve and sue *original B*.
19 *By length of time ere now :* on previous occasions, after a certain length of time.
20 *attained.* Probably attainèd.
22 *Another had my place.* Compare CCXV, 21 (*M & T*).
27 *Evil.* Probably slurred to one syllable.
28 *meed :* reward.
31, 44 *loved.* Probably lovèd.
32 *liked*] *M & T*; lacked *B*. Probably likèd.
34 *fruit*] *M & T*; fault *B*.
39–40 *them . . . their :* the persons told.
56 *too long delays.* Compare XXXV, 14, and CCIII, 26.
63 *pained.* Probably painèd.
68 *now*] *ed.*; enow *B*.
69 *For :* because.

CCXLVIII. B.

2 *detract :* delay.
7 *When time :* at which time.
17 *feigned.* Probably feignèd.
19 *wrest :* strain; twist.

CCXLIX. B.

2 *friends*] *ed.*; friend *B*.
2–6 *My friends why should I blame*/*That from the fault advise me*/*That conquered my good name . . .*/*That laughed :* why should I blame my friends who advise me to depart from the fault that conquered my good name . . . (my friends that laughed).
7–9 *bound my heart . . .*/*To think this pain a play,*/*That would and never may :* insisted that my heart, which would possess her and never may, consider this pain of loving a trifling matter.
13 *is*] *ed.*; his *B*.
12–13 *For proof hath taught his property*/*That . . . pain is hell :* for experience has taught [me] what is the characteristic quality of experience, namely, that pain is hell.
15 *cold and hot :* chill and fever of loving.

16 *fancies:* loves born of mere fancy. See the head-note to CXXVII for the complex set of related meanings of 'fancy'.

18 *to make:* to create [such fancies].

19 *Grudge one:* let the person grumble.

feels] ed.; feel *B.*

21–3 *life . . ./As fast and wake abed:* life as led by those who fast and wake up in bed. Compare CXXI, 9.

26 *well-fed.* A rhyme with 'heart' and 'smart' is demanded by the rhyme-scheme.

28 *Slipped the knot.* See LXVII, 8 and the note.

30 *lucky lot:* fortunate condition of life that has fallen to me [as a result of a lucky cast of the lot].

39 *a bird in hand.* The phrase may echo the proverb 'A bird in hand is better than two in the bush' *Tilley* B363 and *ODEP* 44). But here the perspective is the bird's, and it does not like being in someone's hand.

42 *do't] ed.;* dott *B.* A possible alternative is 'dote'.

43 *To slip . . . the cage.* A line ending in a rhyme with 'cage' and 'rage' is required here or later to complete the triplet.

45 *wilful rage:* freely and perversely chosen madness.

CCL. *Stark, Folger; D* and *B* in shorter version.

In *Folger* precedes a poem by Wyatt.

See head-note to CLXX for the relationship of the two versions. I assume that the writer of this version felt free to change the line-order of CLXX, pronouns, and details of diction necessary to accommodate the added lines. *M* (92–3) assumes that the right line-order is reflected in CLXX.

1, 19 *spare:* show mercy or forbearance.

3 *for I care not] D, B; changed in B to* I care not; and spare not *Stark, Folger.*

4 *For I am] Folger;* For even I am *Stark.*

6 *fancy] ed.;* fantasy *Stark, Folger.* For the complex meanings of this word, see the head-note to CXXVII.

9 *But]* For *D, B.*

11 *recketh] B, Stark, Folger;* recks *D.* Probably monosyllabic (reck'th).

14 *Though you think I am caught] ed.;* But as one that recketh not *Stark, Folger;* It is too dearly bought *M.*

15 *you] Stark, Folger;* ye *D, B.*

18 *But that I] Stark, Folger;* That I *M.*

19 *So love] ed.;* To love *Stark, Folger;* But love *D, B.* A capital 'S' might be misconstrued as a capital 'T'.

CCLI. *Folger.*

Precedes in *Folger* a poem in Wyatt section of *A.*

The text is so hopelessly corrupt that I have felt free to make several conjectural emendations for the sake of producing mere sense, especially in the first stanza. I have also construed the 'etc.' after l. 20 in *Folger* as an indication that ll. 9-12 should be repeated there and after each stanza as a 'burden' or 'chorus'. The fact that the rhythmic pattern of those four lines differs from the rest supports that construction.

1 *might*] *ed.*; may *Folger*.

1-2 *surmise/My fantasy to resist:* devise a way to resist my inclination to love. For the complex meanings of 'fantasy' pertinent here, see the head-note to CXXVII.

4 *love her I did list*] *ed.*; call on had I wist *Folger*.

5 *though it must suffice*] *ed.*; thought it to suffice *Folger*.

11, 23, 35, 47 *whatever*. Probably disyllabic (whate'er).

29 *ask for*] *ed.*; ask *Folger*.

31 *though I that nave sworn*] *ed.*; yet though I have sworn *Folger*.

38 *my true desire:* my genuine desire, which is for you to love me.

40 *Creep out of the fire:* fall out of love gradually.

41 *And know that you intend not*] *ed.*; line omitted in *Folger*.

42 *To give*] *ed.*; Give *Folger*.

44 *Let me to have mine own:* let me have my own heart and love back – that is, let me fall out of love – immediately and once and for all.

CCLII. *Folger.*

The text is so hopelessly corrupt that I have felt free to make several conjectural emendations for the sake of producing mere sense, especially in the second and last stanzas.

9-11 *Unknowingly fell my heart/Into my foe's cruel hand;/And ere I could astart*] *ed.*; Unknown again my heart/Into my foe's hand,/And ever I could astart *Folger*.

14 *scarce:* not quite.

16 *not so:* not full of care or concern for me, with a pun on the preceding line's 'careful'.

17 *nights*] *M & T*; night *Folger*.

30, 38 *fro:* from.

32 *feigned.* Probably feignèd.

33 *fever quartan:* a fever characterized by the occurrence of a paroxysm every fourth day.

37 *Not*] *ed.*; No *Folger*.

45 *for the nonce*] *ed.*; by once *Folger*. Often 'for the nonce' is used as a mere 'filler' in Middle English verse. I cannot make sense of 'by once'.

47 *revoke his love*] *ed.*; revoke *Folger*.

SONGS (3)

CCLIII. *D.*

2 *My shoe is trod awry:* I have gone astray; I have fallen from virtue. Proverbial; see *Tilley* S373 (*M & T*). Wyatt's is the first instance recorded.

3 *cark:* fret, be anxious.

4 *To sing lullay by by.* N suggests that this allusion to singing lullabies implies that the lady speaking the poem has been left with a child by her unfaithful lover.

6 *shift :* expedient.

8 *To love for love again :* to love in return for love; to reciprocate love.

9 *pretence :* 1) expressed intention or purpose; and perhaps, with unconscious irony; 2) pretext.

21 *grieved.* Probably grievèd.

22 *laid his faith to borrow.* Compare Chaucer, *CT* I (A), 1622.

21–2 *But most grieved my heart/He laid his faith to borrow :* but what most grieved my heart was that he committed his faith in a pledge [and was lying].

23 *falsed*] N; falsehood D. Probably falsèd.

28 *of your speed :* from being hasty.

29 *seely :* 1) innocent; 2) deserving of pity; 3) foolish, simple.
seely woman] N; woman D.

33–4 *they whom you trust ... deceive you shall.* Proverbial; see S 64 (*Da*).

CCLIV. *D.*

Follows in *D* a poem which, in *E*, is in Wyatt's hand; but the poem by Wyatt is in the midst of a group of poems in *D* for which there is no evidence of Wyatt's authorship.

2 *my will :* 1) what I desire; 2) what I desire carnally.

3 *I repent where I was pressed :* 1) I view with regret the situation in which I was urged [by my will]; *or* 2) I view with regret the woman [by whose beauty] I was urged. The lover's use of the passive voice ('was pressed') and the vague 'where' may suggest a reluctance to acknowledge responsibility for falling in love. But 'will' and 'fancy' expose him as the primary cause of his own love.

4 *My fancy to fulfil :* 1) to satisfy my amorous inclinations; 2) to make my dream, or delusive imagining, come true. The lover's will, or carnal desire, can generate sexual fantasies and move him to fall in love with someone who seems to answer to those fantasies and whom he thinks might satisfy his lust. Compare XCIII, 20–3, CXXVII, and CCXLIV, 8–14. See the head-note to CXXVII for further discussion of 'fancy'.

7 *put in ure :* put into use [in my way of looking at the world]; become accustomed to.

18 *fondly :* foolishly.

22 *withsave :* save.

CCLV. *D.*

2 *refuse :* refusal.

28 *By yielding :* as a result of giving in to the source of woe.

29 *told :* said.

31 The rhyme scheme suggests that a line is missing here.

36 *trade :* way of life.

37 *Have*] F; Hawe D.

CCLVI. *D, A* (1–12, 25–36, 43–8).

Above the poem in *D* is written 'learn but to sing it'. In *A* the poem is inscribed 'To Smith of Camden', probably the name of an Elizabethan broadside ballad to the tune of which this lyric might be sung (*Hughey* II, 10). The ballad may have been about the suicide of a Henry Smith, son of a Thomas Smith of Camden (see W. Maynard in *FR*).

4 *strange:* unfriendly; cold.

6 *to*] *A*; to to *D*.

10 *That:* I that.

15 *feigned.* Probably feignèd.

13–15 *I am not he/By false assays ... can bear in hand:* (?) I am not the kind of person [who] can deceive [another] by false love proposals.

16 *must*] *ed.*; most *D*.

18 *understand* (understood): believed.

22 *pursueth:* torments.

24 *pass upon:* care about.

30 *withdraw this enterprise:* retire from this dangerous undertaking.

34–6 *I shall refrain/By painful power/The thing that most hath been my grief:* 'I will by the painful power, or exercise of reason, refrain from beholding her who is the real cause of my misery' (*N* 586).

39 *which*] *ed.*; with *D*; that *A*.

42 *the right*] *ed.*; right *D*.

37–42 *I shall not miss/To exercise/The help thereof which doth me teach/That .../To keep the right within my reach:* I shall not fail to use the helpful wisdom gained from this experience which teaches me that [I ought] to keep the rational course of behaviour within my reach.

47–8 *Shall be my lot/To quit the craft:* it shall be my good fortune to repay the cunning.

CCLVII. *B.*

Wyatt uses a comparable form in CXL, but there the stressed syllables in the short lines are never juxtaposed, and the long lines have only three clear stresses. *M & T*, who introduced this poem into the Wyatt canon, suspect it is not his.

12 *setteth my heart right naught:* treats my heart as absolutely nothing.

CCLVIII. *B.*

Wyatt uses this stanza form in CXXVIII. The rhyme words in ll. 3, 4, and 8 probably are stressed on the last syllable.

12 *Eased.* Probably easèd.

15 *revert:* go back to a condition of not loving.

CCLIX. *B.*

2 *Look, lo, where*] *ed.*; Look low. See where *B.* Probably a scribe read 'low' back from l. 8, and then he, or another, thought another verb, like 'See', necessary for the sense. The result is an extra-metrical line in *B.*

4 *at hand*] *ed.*; a hand *B.*

7, 12 *methought*] *ed.*; my thought *B.*

8 *looked.* Probably lookèd.

13 *may heal:* who may heal.

24 *In hope*] *M & T*; In so hope *B.*

release: release from woe.

CCLX. *B.*

4 *Error:* an error, [with respect to your own future happiness, to have left me]; a moral error to have left me.

6 *May hap:* it may chance.

7 *hereafter comes not yet.* Proverbial; see *Tilley* H439 and *ODEP* 293. Compare CLXI, 6 (*M & T*).

12 *Which:* who.

16 *fashion*] *M & T*; festn *B.*

fashion to spell: (?) special method to read or make out [my mind towards you].

17 *word:* speech.

19–20 *What though new broom sweep very clean,/Yet cast not the old away.* 'A new broom sweeps clean' is proverbial; see *Tilley* B682, B683, and *ODEP* 450 (*M & T*).

21 *That serves not sometime:* what serves not on some occasions.

23–4 *store of household is well had/To keep the best:* the supplying of a household is well achieved and maintained by keeping the best.

CCLXI. *B.*

Two rough versions of stanzas 1, 2, 4, and 5 exist in Huntington MS, EL 1160. One of them is printed in Russell Hope Robbins, ed., *Secular Lyrics of the XIVth and XVth Centuries* (1952), pp. 14–15. In the latter, the refrains are 'and all for one' (stanzas 1 and 3), 'and all for fear of one' (stanza 2), and 'and all for love of one' (stanza 4). In the other version the refrain in stanzas 1 and 3 is the same as that in *B.* The shorter versions are more probably corruptions than sources of the longer version.

6 *banished from my bliss.* Compare LXXXIX, 5 (*M & T*).

9 *certain:* certainty.

16 *greenwood tree:* a tree in the woods when the trees are in leaf.

17 *brakes:* ferns, bracken.

27 *Makes me think on a roe:* (?) it makes me think of you as a roe.

31 *coast:* place, region.

32 *turtles:* turtledoves, often presented as types of conjugal affection and constancy.

44   *ways:*   (?) ways [of speaking or singing].

46   *please me*]   *M & T*; please *B*.

51   *my thought:*   the object of my thought.

62   *wander*]   ed.; wandered *B*.

66   *The winter nights that are so cold.*   Compare CIX, 27 (*M & T*).

67   *storms*]   ed.; conjectured *M & T*; a gap in *B*.

71–2   *A woeful man such desert life/Becometh:*   such a desolate life suits a woeful man.

74   *causers of this strife.*   Compare XVII, 14 (*M & T*).

74–5   *the causers of this strife/And all for your love:*   those who cause my pain and our separation do so because they love you. The speaker has apparently been banished by, or on behalf of, a rival.

CCLXII. *B, D.*

6   *misliked.*   Probably mislikèd.

5–6   *certain/Of all misliked most:*   certainly, of all her lovers, the one most disliked.

8   *so me hold*]   *D*; me behold *B*.

22   *wight:*   (the lady).

28–9   *forth trace/A patient pace:*   tread forward at a patient rate of stepping.

45   *sweat*]   *D*; swear *B*.

46–8   *For all my hire … give her heart a heat:*   as wages [for my sweating] set fire to her heart.

60   *my*]   *D*; me *B*.

CCLXIII. *B, D* (1–4).

'The rhyme to the third line of each stanza is in the middle of the fourth, and there is a concealed internal rhyme in the second and third lines of each stanza' (for example, would/should, be/see, then/men). 'In the first respect, but not in the second, it resembles [CCLXV], which also has a similar refrain' (*M & T* 405).

Throughout the poem, 'causeless' means both 'without reason' or 'without offence on my part' and 'without a disease' – the ordinary source of 'smart' or pain. Again, compare CCLXV.

1   *belay:*   enclose.

2   *would*]   mean *D*.

3   *those eyes:*   those eyes of yours.

4   *grudge:*   murmur; scruple, misgiving.

     grudge of heart]   groans (?) *D*. The poem breaks off after this word in *D*.

5, 10, 15, 20, 25   *Causeless because that I have suffered smart:*   because I have suffered pain for no reason.

6   *unclose:*   cause to open.

9   *As hell:*   as in a hell; like a hell.

11   *not*]   *M & T*; no *B*.

17 *Once cause it, then return unto my health:* (?) cause my pain only this one time, and then revert to [causing] my well-being. Presumably she caused his well-being before she made it clear she would not return his love.

23 *worthy blame:* worthy of blame.

24 *knoweth.* Probably monosyllabic (know'th).

that knoweth not thought of heart: (?) who does not have a thought in his mind; who cannot think.

CCLXIV. *B* (1-20), *Folger.*

8 *homely]* *Maxwell;* whumly *B;* womanly *Folger.*

12 *needs must]* *Folger;* needs I must *B.*

24 *Is hers all only and no moe:* is entirely hers alone and no one else's.

26 *terrestrial:* terrestrial [sphere]; earth.

30 *heartily:* in a kind-hearted way.

21-30 *Wheresoever ... my whole desire]* not in *B.*

CCLXV. *B.*

The last syllable of the third line rhymes with the fourth syllable of the fourth line (recure/insure, blame/game, etc.).

Throughout the poem 'cause', in 'without cause' and 'causeless', means both 'reason' or 'offence on my part' and 'disease'. There is therefore no redundancy in the phrase 'without cause causeless' because the speaker's heart is suffering pain without having given offence to the lady and without there being a disease in his heart – the ordinary cause of pain. Compare CCLXIII for the rhyme scheme and a similar use of 'cause' in the refrain.

4 *I you insure]* *M;* I insure *B.* See head-note for the pattern of rhyme that necessitates this emendation.

5 *thus]* ed.; that *B.* Compare l. 30.

4-5, 29-30 *heart/That without cause causeless thus suffer'th smart:* heart that thus suffers pain without offence on my part and without a disease in my heart.

17-18 *And yet, alas, among all my mischief,/Nothing at all that ye regard:* and still, alas, in the midst of all my distress, you do not regard my distress at all.

25 *by cause:* by your agency.

28 *for all my hire:* as my total payment [for serving you].

29 *fire swelting my ... heart:* the fire of passion that is scorching my heart.

PSALM 37

CCLXVI. *Psalm 37* (36 in the Vulgate). *Noli emulare in maligna* (Do not envy the wicked). *E* (1-36), *A.*

Follows Wyatt's paraphrase of the seven Penitential Psalms in *A;* in *E* precedes a poem in Wyatt's hand; written, like Wyatt's paraphrase of the Penitential Psalms, in *terza rima.* Harrier (202) argues that Wyatt has written in his own hand the words 'their felicity' in l. 4. I think he is probably right. If he is, this filling of a gap comes so close to authorial revision that the poem, according to my criteria of attribution, should be placed in the first section of poems attributed to Wyatt in the sixteenth century, preferably before the Paraphrase of the Penitential Psalms.

This poem is a fairly close translation of a Latin paraphrase of Psalm 37 (36 in the Vulgate) by Joannis Campensis. A few words and phrases in the poem suggest that the English poet might have consulted an anonymous English translation of Campensis, *A Paraphrasis . . .*: see 'like grass' (l. 5), 'Patiently abide' (ll. 19, 28), 'thy mind' (l. 24), 'scorn the threat'nings' (l. 38), and 'shall be sure' (l. 86). But these could be coincidental similarities, and the Latin text is clearly the poet's major source. Additions to the original occur mainly at the ends of lines and are probably for the sake of rhymes.

For a discussion of Campensis, of the editions in which his paraphrase was available, of the *Paraphrasis*, and of Wyatt's paraphrase of the Penitential Psalms, see the head-note to the latter on pp. 452–6. Wyatt used both Campensis and Zwingli in that paraphrase, but there is no certain evidence of Zwingli's influence on this translation.

The verses of the Latin Vulgate are interspersed in the commentary of *M & T* (328–32).

1–4 *Although . . . by their felicity.* Verse 1.
1 *th'outrageous:* the person guilty of violent or gross wrongs.
3 *seemeth*] *A*; senith *E*.
3–4 *The wealth of wretches . . . |Move not thy heart:* let not the wealth of wretches (persons of reprehensible character) move your heart.
4 *by their felicity.* An addition.
5–6 *They shall . . . wither suddenly.* Verse 2.
7–9 *Stablish . . . day to day.* Verse 3.
10–11 *And if . . . can lust.* Verse 4.
10 *time thy . . . song:* sing your song in [good] time or rhythm. The musical metaphor replaces the original's 'takest thy pleasure'.
11 *whatso:* whatsoever, whatever.
12–14 *Cast upon . . . thy cares all.* Verse 5.
12 *that right thy wrong:* (?) (God) who shall put right your sin. An addition.
13 *upright and just.* An addition.
14 *cares.* Probably disyllabic.
15–18 *And he . . . the noon call.* Verse 6.
15 *discussed:* made known, declared, manifested.
16 *Bright as the sun*] *N*; Upright all the sun *E*; Upright as the sun *A*.
17 *curseds' wealth:* the well-being of those who are cursed for their evil.
19–23 *Patiently . . . wicked folk . . .* Verse 7.
19 *assured.* Probably assurèd.
assured grace. An addition.
20 *sends*] *A*; send *E*.

21   *purchase:*   that which is acquired; gains, acquisitions.

23   *To wicked folk.*   There is a gap in both *E* and *A* after these words. *Mason* (*TLS*) argues that the Latin original suggests the poet ran out of material.

24–6   *Restrain . . . to commit.*   Verse 8.

25–6   *eschew/By their like deed such deeds for to commit:*   avoid committing evil deeds as a result of the example of their evil deeds.

27–9   *For wicked . . . to heir.*   Verse 9.

28   *abide:*   wait for the Lord (*O*).

29   *possede:*   possess.

30–3   *The wicked . . . blast of air.*   Verse 10.

32   *staring:*   ostentatious.

    and his staring array]   and eke his strange array *A*.

33   *as blast of air.*   An addition.

34–5   *The sober . . . so plentiful.*   Verse 11.

34   *sober:*   moderate, temperate. The original has 'modest' or 'meek'.

    wield: 1) possess; 2) govern.

36–7   *Him to . . . girning ireful.*   Verse 12.

37   *girning:*   showing the teeth in rage; snarling.

    ireful: full of ire; angry.

37–112   *And gnash . . . their trust forever*]   *A*; *not in E*.

38–40   *The Lord . . . him seech.*   Verse 13.

39   *tide:*   1) time; 2) the tide of the sea. Apparently a pun on the original's 'time', with the second meaning becoming the basis for the drowning metaphor in l. 40, which is an addition to the original.

40   *seech:*   seek.

41–4   *They have . . . to devour.*   Verse 14.

41   *unsheathed.*   Probably unsheathèd.

    brands: swords.

43   *To overthrow the.*   The line is incomplete in *A*. *F* conjectures: 'To overthrow the just; stretched forth their hands.'

45–6   *The sword . . . most endeavour.*   Verse 15.

45   *fonds:*   (?) tries; *or* plays the fool in this way. An addition.

47–9   *A little . . . gathered wickedly.*   Verse 16.

48   *and eke the high power.*   An addition.

50–1   *Perish shall . . . just assuredly.*   Verse 17.

51   *stablish:*   establish; protect; preserve.

52–3   *The just . . . for evermore.*   Verse 18.

52   *men's*]   *Da*; man's *A*.

54–6   *And of . . . for food.*   Verse 19.

55   *dismal days:*   the evil or unlucky days of the medieval calendar; perhaps generally, evil or unlucky days.

    wrap: enwrap, enfold.

57–60   *Therewhilst . . . smoky cloud.*   Verse 20.

57   *Therewhilst:*   in the meantime; in the time during which the just survive and prosper.

58 *To God's enemies*] N; The God's enemies A.

61-3 *Borrow'th ... doth require.* Verse 21.

64-5 *Who will'th ... rooted away.* Verse 22.

64 *Who will'th him well for right:* he who wills the just, generous man well in the interest of righteousness.

65 *banneth*] Mason (*TLS*); banish A.

Who banneth him: he who curses the just, generous man.

66-7 *His steps ... lust assay.* Verse 23.

67 *please him shall what life him lust assay:* the way or condition of life that the just man chooses to attempt shall prove pleasing to him.

68-9 *And though ... him stay.* Verse 24.

69 *Catching his hand, for God:* for God, catching his hand.

straight him stay: immediately steady him, support him, make him stand upright.

70-2 *... for to be.* Verse 25.

70-1] *omitted from A.* The anonymous translator's version gives the sense: 'I was young and after a long life am become an old man; yet have I not seen a righteous man desolate ...'

73-5 *The just ... fresh and green.* Verse 26.

76 *Flee ill, do good, that ... last alway.* Verse 27.

77-80 *For God ... to naught.* Verse 28.

77 *the right*] M (84); th'upright A. Campensis has 'what is right'.

81-2 *The just ... have wrought.* Verse 29.

81 *wield:* 1) possess; 2) govern.

82 *as they have wrought:* (?) because of what they have achieved. An addition.

83-4 *With wisdom ... as it ought.* Verse 30.

83 *With wisdom shall the wise man's mouth him able:* (?) a wise man's mouth shall empower him to speak with wisdom; *or* a wise man's mouth shall strengthen him with the wisdom that it speaks. The original has: 'The wise man's mouth shall touch on, or speak, wisdom.'

85-6 *With God's ... be sure.* Verse 31.

87-8 *The wicked ... his busy care.* Verse 32.

87 *watcheth the just for to disable:* is watchful in order to disable the just man.

88 *slay*] N; see A.

doth his busy cure: takes care in a busy way.

89-91 *But God ... without fail.* Verse 33.

90 *By tyranny:* as a result of tyranny; at the hands of a tyrant.

90-1 *nor yet by fault unpure/To be condemned in judgement without fail:* nor yet, as a result of his impure act, certainly to be condemned [by God] at the time of judgement (O).

92-6 *Await therefore ... it record.* Verse 34.

93 *in patience to prevail:* in the patient confidence that you will prevail [over the wicked].

94 *of thine own accord:* (?) as a result of your own motion or behaviour.

This phrase seems to contradict the idea that God, not man, does the raising. It is an addition which may be a virtually meaningless filler for the sake of a rhyme with 'Lord'.

95   *in surety:*   in or from a position of security.

96   *that thou may it record.*   An addition.

97–8   *I have . . . lasting ay.*   Verse 35.

97   *sheen:*   to shine; to glisten.
    like gold.   An addition.

99–102   *But even . . . fresh array.*   Verse 36.

99   *even anon and scant:*   just shortly thereafter.
    his seat was cold.   An addition.

103–5   *Let uprightness . . . to abound.*   Verse 37.

106–7   *All wicked . . . wicked's end.*   Verse 38.

106   *reversed:*   having experienced a reversal of fortune.
    shall be untwined] ed.; shall untwined *A*: shall be undone, destroyed.

108–9   *Health . . . should offend.*   Verse 39.

109   *strength:*   strengthen.

110–12   *The Lord . . . trust forever.*   Verse 40.

111   *cursed*] curseds' *M* (85).

OTHER POEMS

CCLXVII. *A.*

The poem appears at the end of a Wyatt section of *A* and before a gap of eight folios in the manuscript. *N* suggests that it is both a proem to and 'argument' of CCLXVI, which it follows in *A*, and that the Earl addressed in l. 6 is the Earl of Surrey (lxxxvi–lxxxvii, n. 2). But it could be the proem to the paraphrase of another psalm by Wyatt on the pages now missing from the manuscript (*Hughey* II, 245); or it could be the proem to the paraphrase of a psalm by another poet.

1   *assured truth:*   assured conviction that I knew the truth.

2   *Contemned:*   viewed with contempt.

3   *go'th*] ed.; goeth *A*.

4–5   *In deeming hearts, which none but God there can,/And his dooms hid, whereby man's malice grow'th:*   in judging the hearts of men, which no one but God is able to do, and his judgements hidden, as a result of which man's wickedness grows in his treatment of others whom he wrongly judges.

CCLXVIII. *B.*

M & T, who introduced this poem into the Wyatt canon, apparently doubt that it is by him. To make some sense of this otherwise unintelligible poem, I have presented it as a dialogue, with the woman as the first speaker because of the reference to 'drabs' in l. 6.

1   *Double . . . strange:*   I have been double . . . strange in my relation to my first love.

4 *The deed is done and I not denied:* my deed of infidelity is done, and I have not been denied by my first love to whom I have been unfaithful.

5 *My troth mistaken and I untried:* (?) my loyalty was misapprehended by my first love [because I have been disloyal], and yet I am not placed on trial by him.

6–7 *If double drabs were so defied,/As worthy is their wandering wit:* (?) if double strumpets were rejected by their first lovers the way I am – that is, not at all – their promiscuity would be as worthy of admiration as mine.

9 *unquit:* (?) unrequited by a comparable fault (l. 10) on my part.

11–12 *Forborne for fear. Nay, love is it/Whereby is bound the body so:* (?) [a comparable fault on my part] is not performed because I fear losing you. No, [I take that back]. It is love which so binds my body to you.

15–16 *Pain or pleasure, woe or wealth,/Wounded by words, and lacks advance:* (?) in pain or pleasure, in woe or well-being, [I am] wounded by words, and [I am a person who] lacks advance.

CCLXIX. *B.*

Compare LXXXVI, LXXXVII, and CXXVI for play on the word 'hap'. In this poem, as a noun, it can mean a change in fortune (ll. 1, 11); what happens by fortune or chance (l. 8); bad fortune or luck (l. 16, 'mishap' ll. 6, 12); or Fortune personified (ll. 23, 24, 25, 28). As a verb it means 'happens' or 'occurs'.

1, 11, 22, 33 *unlooked.* Probably unlookèd.

6 *mishap*] *ed.*; mis hap *B.*

7 *abject:* thrown off.

13 *prefate:* prefated, predestined.

14 *had sworn:* (?) had sworn that they would have bad luck.

16 *at his own lust:* as Fortune pleases.

21 *whole:* healthy.

24 *thrown* ('throwen' in the original). Probably disyllabic.

27 *rede:* advise.

30 *trade:* track; trail.

CCLXX. *H78.*

The only identified 'Sir Thomas Gravener' was knighted after Wyatt's death (*M & T* 439).

3 *prest:* ready, eager, prompt.

10 *at:* in.

19 *Vivit post funera Virtus:* Virtue lives on after burials.

Glossary

ABBREVIATIONS

a. : adjective.
adv. : adverb.
impers. : impersonal.
infin. : infinitive.
intr. : intransitive.
pa. pple : past participle.
pa. t. : past tense.

pers. : person(al).
ppl a. : participial adjective.
pple : participle.
refl. : reflexive.
sb. : substantive, noun.
tr. : transitive.
vb : verb.

again : against.
an; an(d) if : if; even if.
anon : at once; soon.
assay : *vb*, attempt, try; *sb.*, attempt, effort, endeavour.
astart : escape.
ay : continually; forever.
ban : curse; chide with angry language.
band : bond; fetter; state of bondage.
boot : advantage; use; relief; remedy; reward.
bourd : game; jest; bantering.
careful : full of care.
case : condition, plight.
charge : *vb*, fill; burden; *sb.*, burden.
cheer : face, facial expression; disposition shown by facial expression; cheerfulness.
consume : rot; waste away.
crisped : tightly curled.
cure : care; heed; remedy.
diverse : different, varying; differing from what is right, good or profitable, and hence perverse; several, many.
do (a)way : do away with; annihilate; erase; cancel; put an end to.
doubt : fear; suspect.
dure : endure (*intr.*); last.
eke : also.
error : wandering; mistake.
erst : earlier; formerly.
fain : gladly; with pleasure; willingly.

fast: a., adv., firm(ly).

Fortune: the personification, usually as a goddess, of chance as the cause of events and consequences which, paradoxically, assume a pattern – the alternation between prosperity and ruin, and usually a fall from prosperity to ruin.

fret: tr., gnaw; consume or wear away by gnawing; intr., waste away.

froward: having a tendency to act in a way contrary to the dictates of reason; perverse; of evil disposition.

game: fun; amusement; joke.

gladsome: pleasant, cheering.

grave: engrave; impress deeply.

grudge: tr., trouble, vex; intr., complain; be discontented; feel envy.

guise: manner; usual way of behaving; course of life; style of dress.

hap: vb, happen; sb., chance occurrence; condition resulting from chance or fortune; change in fortune; good luck; bad luck, ill fortune; Fortune (personified).

health: well-being.

hire: reward; payment; wages.

iwis: certainly.

kind: sb., nature.

leech: physician.

leese: lose; destroy.

let: vb, hinder; prevent; sb., hindrance.

list, pa. t. and pa. pple list: 1) impers., pleases; hence, *me list:* it pleases me, I like, I desire; 2) pers., often with infin., like, desire, choose; hence, *I list:* I like.

lust, 3rd pers. impers. lusteth: 1) impers., pleases; hence *me lusteth:* it pleases me, I like, I desire; 2) pers., desire.

methink(s), pa. t. methought: it seems to me.

mischief: harm done by another; condition of distress.

moe: more.

most: greatest.

muse: wonder; ponder.

ne: not; nor.

not: ne wot; know not. See *wot.*

other: others.

perdie: by God (an oath).

plain: complain.

plaint: complaint; grieving.

press: vb, oppress, often implying the physical act of pressing down; urge; apply pressure to; sb., crowd; the thick of the crowd; crowding or pressure by persons; the condition of being crushed, squeezed.

proof: experience; the test of experience; trial or attempt to prove valid; evidence.

prove: put to the test of experience; discover or demonstrate by experience.

provoke: call forth; invite; excite; bring about; exacerbate.

quit, pa. t. and *pa. pple quit :* repay, requite; set free; get rid of; deprive.
readily : promptly, quickly.
reck : care; heed; acknowledge.
recure : cure; remedy; help.
redress : vb, restore, compensate for; *sb.,* help; relief, remedy; compensation, reparation.
refrain : tr. and *refl.,* restrain, check; give up; shun; *intr.,* cease; give up.
rue : pity, have pity.
sith(ens) : since.
slake : assuage; diminish; reduce in intensity; render less vigorous.
smart : physical or mental pain; suffering; sorrow.
sore : a., adv., painful(ly); severe(ly); harsh(ly); deep(ly); *sb.,* sickness; mental suffering; sorrow; anxiety.
speed : vb tr., cause one to succeed; *intr.,* succeed; prosper; *sb.,* success.
spill : tr., ruin; destroy; kill; *intr.,* degenerate; perish.
stay : sustain; support.
sterve : starve; die in lingering death.
still : always; unceasingly; now as formerly.
stint : tr., cut short; stop; *intr.,* cease.
sure : a., adv., certain(ly); secure(ly).
thorough : through.
train : vb, draw; persuade; convert; lead astray; deceive; *sb.,* deceit, guile; lure, bait, something dragged along or laid on the ground – such as a piece of meat – to lure an animal into a trap; treachery; artifice; a series of actions; a way of life; baggage and equipment following an army.
trow : believe.
truth : troth; fidelity; true love; truthful and plain speech; pledge; consistent and upright behaviour..
try : tr., refine or separate metal from dross; distinguish; separate; refine; *tr.* and *intr.,* test or examine and thereby determine (something to be true or genuine); ascertain (the truth).
use : vb, become or be accustomed; *sb.,* usage; custom; habit.
vaileth : avails; profits; accomplishes.
want : vb tr., lack; *intr.,* fail; *sb.,* lack, absence.
ware : vb, take care; *a.,* wary; prudent.
weal(th) : well-being, spiritual or (rarely) material or both; happiness.
ween : expect; think.
while : period of time.
wight : person.
wist, pa. t. and *pa. pple* of *wit :* know.
wont, pa. t. wonted : to be accustomed.
wonted : ppl a., accustomed.
wot, pres. pple wotting : know.
wreak : vb, give vent to, gratify (a feeling); *refl.,* avenge; *sb.,* harm.
wreck : see *wreak.*

Index of First Lines